Communications
in Computer and Information Science 259

W0227340

Tai-hoon Kim   Hojjat Adeli   Wai-chi Fang
Javier García Villalba   Kirk P. Arnett
Muhammad Khurram Khan (Eds.)

Security Technology

International Conference SecTech 2011
Held as Part of the Future Generation
Information Technology Conference, FGIT 2011
in Conjunction with GDC 2011
Jeju Island, Korea, December 8-10, 2011
Proceedings

 Springer

Volume Editors

Tai-hoon Kim
Hannam University, Daejeon, Korea
E-mail: taihoonn@hannam.ac.kr

Hojjat Adeli
The Ohio State University, Columbus, OH, USA
E-mail: adeli.1@osu.edu

Wai-chi Fang
National Chiao Tung University, Hsinchu, Taiwan, R.O.C.
E-mail: wfang@mail.nctu.edu.tw

Javier García Villalba
Universidad Complutense de Madrid, Spain
E-mail: javiergv@fdi.ucm.es

Kirk P. Arnett
Mississippi State University, Oktibbeha, MS, USA
E-mail: kpa1@msstate.edu

Muhammad Khurram Khan
King Saud University, Riyadh, Saudi Arabia
E-mail: mkhurram@ksu.edu.sa

ISSN 1865-0929   e-ISSN 1865-0937
ISBN 978-3-642-27188-5   e-ISBN 978-3-642-27189-2
DOI 10.1007/978-3-642-27189-2
Springer Heidelberg Dordrecht London New York

Library of Congress Control Number: 2011943020

CR Subject Classification (1998): C.2, K.6.5, D.4.6, E.3, J.1, H.4

Typesetting: Camera-ready by author, data conversion by Scientific Publishing Services, Chennai, India

Printed on acid-free paper

Springer is part of Springer Science+Business Media (www.springer.com)

Foreword

Security technology is an area that attracts many professionals from academia and industry for research and development. The goal of the SecTech conference is to bring together researchers from academia and industry as well as practitioners to share ideas, problems and solutions relating to the multifaceted aspects of security technology.

We would like to express our gratitude to all of the authors of submitted papers and to all attendees for their contributions and participation.

We acknowledge the great effort of all the Chairs and the members of Advisory Boards and Program Committees of the above-listed event. Special thanks go to SERSC (Science and Engineering Research Support Society) for supporting this conference.

We are grateful in particular to the speakers who kindly accepted our invitation and, in this way, helped to meet the objectives of the conference.

December 2011   Chairs of SecTech 2011

Preface

We would like to welcome you to the proceedings of the 2011 International Conference on Security Technology (SecTech 2011) – the partnering event of the Third International Mega-Conference on Future-Generation Information Technology (FGIT 2011) held during December 8–10, 2011, at Jeju Grand Hotel, Jeju Island, Korea

SecTech 2011 focused on various aspects of advances in security technology. It provided a chance for academic and industry professionals to discuss recent progress in the related areas. We expect that the conference and its publications will be a trigger for further related research and technology improvements in this important subject.

We would like to acknowledge the great effort of the SecTech 2011Chairs, Committees, International Advisory Board, Special Session Organizers, as well as all the organizations and individuals who supported the idea of publishing this volume of proceedings, including the SERSC and Springer.

We are grateful to the following keynote, plenary and tutorial speakers who kindly accepted our invitation: Hsiao-Hwa Chen (National Cheng Kung University, Taiwan), Hamid R. Arabnia (University of Georgia, USA), Sabah Mohammed (Lakehead University, Canada), Ruay-Shiung Chang (National Dong Hwa University, Taiwan), Lei Li (Hosei University, Japan), Tadashi Dohi (Hiroshima University, Japan), Carlos Ramos (Polytechnic of Porto, Portugal), Marcin Szczuka (The University of Warsaw, Poland), Gerald Schaefer (Loughborough University, UK), Jinan Fiaidhi (Lakehead University, Canada) and Peter L. Stanchev (Kettering University, USA), Shusaku Tsumoto (Shimane University, Japan), Jemal H. Abawajy (Deakin University, Australia).

We would like to express our gratitude to all of the authors and reviewers of submitted papers and to all attendees, for their contributions and participation, and for believing in the need to continue this undertaking in the future.

Last but not the least, we give special thanks to Ronnie D. Caytiles and Yvette E. Gelogo of the graduate school of Hannam University, who contributed to the editing process of this volume with great passion.

This work was supported by the Korean Federation of Science and Technology Societies Grant funded by the Korean Government.

December 2011

Tai-hoon Kim
Hojjat Adeli
Wai Chi Fang
Javier Garcia Villalba
Kirk P. Arnett
Muhammad Khurram Khan

Organization

General Co-chair

Wai Chi Fang   NASA JPL, USA

Program Co-chairs

Javier Garcia Villalba   Complutense University of Madrid, Spain
Kirk P. Arnett   Mississippi State University, USA
Muhammad Khurram Khan   King Saud University, Saudi Arabia
Tai-hoon Kim   GVSA and University of Tasmania, Australia

Publicity Co-chairs

Antonio Coronato   ICAR-CNR, Italy
Damien Sauveron   Université de Limoges/CNRS, France
Hua Liu   Xerox Corporation, USA
Kevin Raymond Boyce Butler   Pennsylvania State University, USA
Guojun Wang   Central South University, China
Tao Jiang   Huazhong University of Science and
                                          Technology, China
Gang Wu   UESTC, China
Yoshiaki Hori   Kyushu University, Japan
Aboul Ella Hassanien   Cairo University, Egypt

Publication Chair

Yong-ik Yoon   Sookmyung Women's University, Korea

International Advisory Board

Dominik Slezak   Inforbright, Poland
Edwin H-M. Sha   University of Texas at Dallas, USA
Justin Zhan   CMU, USA
Kouich Sakurai   Kyushu University, Japan
Laurence T. Yang   St. Francis Xavier University, Canada
Byeong-Ho Kang   University of Tasmania, Australia
Aboul Ella Hassanien   Cairo University, Egypt

Program Committee

Abdelouahed Gherbi	Hsiang-Cheh Huang	Raphael C.-W. Phan
Abdelwahab Hamou-Lhadj	Hyun-Sung Kim	Reinhard Schwarz
Ahmet Koltuksuz	J.H. Abbawajy	Rhee Kyung-Hyune
Albert Levi	Jan de Meer	Robert Seacord
Ana Lucila S. Orozco	Javier Garcia Villalba	Rodrigo Mello
ByungRae Cha	Jongmoon Baik	Rolf Oppliger
Chamseddine Talhi	Jordi Forne	Rui Zhang
Chantana Chantrapornchai	Jungsook Kim	SangUk Shin
Chin-Feng Lai	Justin Zhan	S.K. Barai
Christos Kalloniatis	Kouichi Sakurai	Serge Chaumette
Chun-Ying Huang	Larbi Esmahi	Sheng-Wei Chen
Costas Lambrinoudakis	Lejla Batina	Silvia Abrahao
Despina Polemi	Luigi Buglione	Stan Kurkovsky
Dieter Gollmann	Martin Drahansky	Stefanos Gritzalis
Dimitris Geneiatakis	Martin Drahansky	Sungwoon Lee
E. Konstantinou	Masahiro Mambo	Swee-Huay Heng
Eduardo B. Fernandez	Michael VanHilst	Tony Shan
Fangguo Zhang	Michele Risi	Wen-Shenq Juang
Feng-Cheng Chang	N. Jaisankar	Willy Susilo
Filip Orsag	Nobukazu Yoshioka	Yannis Stamatiou
Georgios Kambourakis	Panagiotis Nastou	Yi Mu
Gerald Schaefer	MalRey Lee	Yijun Yu
Han-Chieh Chao	Man Ho Au	Yingjiu Li
Hiroaki Kikuchi	Mario Marques Freire	Yong Man Ro
Hironori Washizaki	Paolo D'Arco	Yoshiaki Hori
Hongji Yang	Paolo Falcarin	Young Ik Eom
Howon Kim	Petr Hanacek	Yueh-Hong Chen
	Pierre-François Bonnefoi	Yun-Sheng Yen
	Qi Shi	

Special Session Organizers

Namje Park
Hee Joon Cho

Table of Contents

On Fast Private Scalar Product Protocols

Ju-Sung Kang[1] and Dowon Hong[2]

[1] Department of Mathematics, Kookmin University
Jeongreung3-Dong, Seongbuk-Gu, Seoul, 136-702, Korea
jskang@kookmin.ac.kr
[2] Information Security Research Division, ETRI
161 Gajeong-Dong, Yuseong-Gu, Daejeon, 305-350, Korea
dwhong@etri.re.kr

Abstract. The objective of the private scalar product protocol is that the participants obtain the scalar product of the private vectors of all parties without disclosure of all the private vectors. Private scalar product protocol is an important fundamental protocol in secure multi-party computation, and it is widely used in privacy-preserving scientific computation, statistical analysis and data mining. Up to now several private scalar protocols have been proposed in order to meet the need for more efficient and more practical solutions. However it seems that these efforts are unsuccessful from the security point of view. In this paper we show that two fast private scalar product protocols, which were recently proposed as very efficient secure protocols, are insecure.

Keywords: Private scalar product protocol, Secure multi-party computation, Privacy-preserving data mining, Cryptography.

1 Introduction

The secure multi-party computation problem deals with the situation that two or more parties want to process a computation based on their private inputs, but neither party is willing to disclose its own input to anybody else. The general secure multi-party computation problem is solvable by using the circuit evaluation protocols, but the solutions derived by the general result for some special cases still can be impractical. In fact Goldreich [10] pointed out that special solutions should be developed for special cases for efficiency reasons. The private scalar product computation protocols are solutions for special cases of the general secure multi-party computation problem. A private scalar product computation protocol forms the basis of various applications ranging from privacy-preserving cooperative scientific computations to privacy-preserving data mining. The objective of the protocol is that one of the participants obtains the scalar product of the private vectors of all parties. Several private scalar product protocols have been proposed until now [6,7,17,12,9]. Basically, there are two kinds of methods to perform the private scalar product. One is taken by using only linear algebraic techniques to obtain the computational efficiency, the other is with

T.-h. Kim et al. (Eds.): SecTech 2011, CCIS 259, pp. 1–10, 2011.

cryptographic primitives such as oblivious transfer protocols and homomorphic public-key encryption schemes for the high security.

Du and Atallah [6,2] proposed two private scalar product computation protocols which are based on the 1-out-of-n oblivious transfer protocol and the homomorphic public-key encryption scheme, respectively. However Goethals et al. [9] showed that the protocols of [6,2] based on the oblivious transfer are insecure, and they described a provably private scalar product protocol based on the homomorphic encryption and improved its efficiency so that it can also be used on massive datasets. In [7] Du and Atallah proposed an efficient private scalar product protocol using an untrusted third party Ursula, but Laur and Lipmaa [13] proved that this protocol has serious weakness. Vaidya and Clifton [17] pointed out the scalability problem of the protocols in [6,2], and proposed a linear algebraic solution for the private computation of scalar product that hides true values by placing them in equations masked with random values. The private scalar product protocol in [17] was broken by Goethals et al. [9]. Another linear algebraic method for a private scalar product protocol was proposed by Ioannidis et al. [12], but Huang et al. [11] showed that this protocol is also insecure.

On the other hand, although there are several solutions for the private computation of scalar product, the need for more efficient and more practical solutions still remains. Recently, two fast private scalar product protocols have been proposed to meet the need of efficiency. Trincă and Rajasekaran [16] proposed two protocols for privately computing boolean scalar products which applicable to privately mining association rules in vertically partitioned data. Amirbekyan and Estivill-Castro [1] presented a very efficient and very practical secure scalar product protocol based on the variant of permutation protocol (Add Vectors Protocol) of [6] without using the homomorphic public-key encryption. In this paper, we show that the private scalar product computation protocols of [16] and [1] are absolutely insecure.

2   Private Scalar Product Protocols

Let $X \cdot Y = \sum_{i=1}^{n} x_i y_i$ denote the scalar product of two vectors $X = (x_1, \ldots, x_n)$ and $Y = (y_1, \ldots, y_n)$. The security model of the private scalar product protocol (PSPP) is based on the theory developed under the name of secure multiparty computation (SMC) [10]. Assume that Alice holds one input vector $X = (x_1, \ldots, x_n)$ and Bob holds the other input vector $Y = (y_1, \ldots, y_n)$. They want to compute the scalar product $X \cdot Y$ without each learning anything about the other's input except what can be inferred from the result $X \cdot Y$. We consider here that each party is semi-honest. The semi-honest party is the one who follows the protocol correctly, but at the same time keeps information received during communication and final output for further attempt to disclose private information from the other party. A semi-honest party is sometimes called an honest but curious one. Goldreich has provided a formal definition of privacy with respect to semi-honest behavior, refer to [10] for the details.

2.1   PSPPs with Cryptographic Primitives

In PSPPs based on conventional cryptographic techniques, the 1-out-of-n oblivious transfer protocols and the homomorphic public-key encryption schemes are mainly used as its sub-protocol. An 1-out-of-n oblivious transfer protocol [3,14] refers to a protocol that one party, called the sender, has n inputs $x_1, \ldots, x_n$ at the beginning of the protocol and the other party, called the chooser, learns one of the inputs x_i for some $1 \leq i \leq n$ of its choice at the end of the protocol without learning anything about the other inputs and without allowing the sender to learn anything about i.

A public-key encryption scheme is called homomorphic when $E_{pk}(x) \cdot E_{pk}(y) = E_{pk}(x+y)$, where E_{pk} denotes an encryption function with a public-key pk. One of the most efficient currently known secure homomorphic public-key encryption scheme was proposed by Paillier [15] and then improved by Damgård and Jurik [5]. A useful property of homomorphic encryption schemes is that an addition operation can be conducted based on the encrypted data without decrypting them. Meanwhile, in 2009, Gentry [8] discovered the first fully homomorphic encryption scheme using lattice-based cryptography. A cryptosystem which supports both addition and multiplication, thereby preserving the ring structure of the plaintexts, is known as fully homomorphic encryption. However Gentry's scheme and all another fully homomorphic encryption schemes published up to now are impractical. Although it is a theoretical breakthrough in cryptography, we do not mention any more about the fully homomorphic encryption scheme, since in this paper we concentrate on the PSPPs without cryptographic primitives.

Du and Atallah [6,2] proposed two PPSPs which are based on the 1-out-of-n oblivious transfer protocol and the homomorphic public-key encryption scheme, respectively. However Goethals et al. [9] showed that the protocol of [6,2] based on the oblivious transfer is insecure, and they described a provably private scalar product protocol based on the homomorphic encryption and improved its efficiency so that it can also be used on massive datasets. It seems that some previously proposed PSPPs with the homomorphic public-key encryption schemes are secure, but they still suffer from a large computational overhead.

2.2   PSPPs with Linear Algebraic Techniques

PSPPs taken by using only linear algebraic techniques are practical solutions to securely solve scalar product between two parties. Vaidya and Clifton [17] proposed an linear algebraic solution for the private computation of scalar product that hides true values by placing them in equations masked with random values. A simplified version of Vaidya-Clifton's protocol was proposed by [4]. However PSPPs of [17] and [4] are analyzed their insecurity by Goethals et al. [9] and Huang et al. [11]. Another linear algebraic method for a private scalar product protocol was proposed by Ioannidis et al. [12], but Huang et al. [11] showed that one party of this protocol is absolutely insecure.

Recently, two fast PSPPs based on linear algebraic techniques have been proposed. Trincă and Rajasekaran [16] proposed two PSPPs for computing boolean scalar products which applicable to privately mining association rules in vertically partitioned data. Amirbekyan and Estivill-Castro [1] presented a very efficient and very practical PSPP based on the variant of permutation protocol in [6] without using the homomorphic public-key encryption scheme. In this paper, we scrutinize the PSPPs in [1] and [16], and analyze their insecurity.

3   Insecurity of Protocol by Trincă and Rajasekaran

Trincă and Rajasekaran [16] proposed two fast multi-party protocols for privately computing boolean scalar products with applications to privacy-preserving association rule mining in vertically partitioned data. They insisted that their protocols are secure and much faster than the previous protocols. However, in this section, we show that their protocols are absolutely not private.

Assume that there exist k parties $\mathcal{P}^{(1)}, \mathcal{P}^{(2)}, \ldots, \mathcal{P}^{(k)}$ and for each $1 \leq i \leq k$, $\mathbf{X}^{(i)} = \left(X_1^{(i)}, \ldots, X_n^{(i)} \right)^T$ is the boolean column vector with n entries corresponding to party $\mathcal{P}^{(i)}$, where $\mathbf{A}^T$ denotes the transposed matrix of $\mathbf{A}$. The parties want to collaboratively compute the scalar product $\mathbf{X}^{(1)} \cdot \mathbf{X}^{(2)} \cdots \mathbf{X}^{(k)}$ without any party revealing its own vector to the other parties.

Protocol 1. *(SECProtocol-I of Trincă and Rajasekaran [16])*

- Inputs: For each $1 \leq i \leq k$, $\mathcal{P}^{(i)}$ has a secret vector $\mathbf{X}^{(i)} = \left(X_1^{(i)}, \ldots, X_n^{(i)} \right)^T$.
- Outputs: All parties obtain the scalar product $\mathbf{X}^{(1)} \cdot \mathbf{X}^{(2)} \cdots \mathbf{X}^{(k)}$.

1. $\mathcal{P}^{(k)}$ randomly selects $1 \leq t \leq 2^n$, and forms an $n \times 2^n$ matrix $M^{(k)} = \left(M_{i,j}^{(k)} \right)_{n \times 2^n}$, where the t-th column of $M^{(k)}$ is $\mathbf{X}^{(i)}$ and the rest of the entries are randomly generated in such a way that $M^{(k)}$ contains all possible boolean column vectors of size n within its columns. $\mathcal{P}^{(k)}$ sends $M^{(k)}$ to $\mathcal{P}^{(k-1)}$.

2. Upon receiving $M^{(k)}$ from $\mathcal{P}^{(k)}$, $\mathcal{P}^{(k-1)}$ performs the following process:
   (a) $\mathcal{P}^{(k-1)}$ forms an $n \times 2^n$ matrix $M^{(k-1)}$ from $M^{(k)}$, where the (i, j) entry of $M^{(k-1)}$ is $M_{i,j}^{(k-1)} = X_i^{(k-1)} M_{i,j}^{(k)}$ for all $1 \leq i \leq n$ and $1 \leq j \leq 2^n$.
   (b) $\mathcal{P}^{(k-1)}$ splits the the set of column indices $C = \{1, 2, \ldots, 2^n\}$ into equivalent classes in such a way that j_1 and j_2 are in the same equivalence class if j_1-th and j_2-th columns are the same.
   (c) For each equivalence class $C_i = \{i_1, i_2, \ldots, i_l\}$ that has at least two indices ($l \geq 2$), $\mathcal{P}^{(k-1)}$ randomly select $l - 1$ indices from C_i, and for those $l - 1$ indices, it replaces the corresponding columns with vectors that are not already present in the matrix. After this replacement, the new matrix is $M_{full}^{(k-1)}$ which contains all possible column vectors of size n within its columns. The correspondence between $M^{(k-1)}$ and $M_{full}^{(k-1)}$ given by the tuple $full^{(k-1)} = (f_1, f_2, \ldots, f_{2^n})$, where $\mathcal{P}^{(k-1)}$ knows that the j-th column in $M^{(k-1)}$ moved on the position f_j in $M_{full}^{(k-1)}$.

(d) The matrix $M_{full}^{(k-1)}$ is transformed into $M_{perm}^{(k-1)}$ by applying a random permutation $perm^{(k-1)}$ of $\{1, 2, \ldots, 2^n\}$ to column vectors of $M_{full}^{(k-1)}$.

(e) $\mathcal{P}^{(k-1)}$ sends $M_{perm}^{(k-1)}$ and $prod^{(k-1)}$ to $\mathcal{P}^{(k-2)}$, where $prod^{(k-1)}$ is the product between $full^{(k-1)}$ and $perm^{(k-1)}$ such that j-th element in $prod^{(k-1)}$ is l, if j-th element in $full^{(k-1)}$ is i and i-th element in $perm^{(k-1)}$ is l.

3. Upon receiving $M_{perm}^{(k-1)}$ and $prod^{(k-1)}$, $\mathcal{P}^{(k-2)}$ performs similar process as the previous sub-steps of $\mathcal{P}^{(k-1)}$, and generates $M_{perm}^{(k-2)}$ and $prod^{(k-2)}$. Then $\mathcal{P}^{(k-2)}$ defines $pprod^{(k-2)}$ as the product between $prod^{(k-1)}$ and $prod^{(k-2)}$, and sends $pprod^{(k-2)}$ and $M_{perm}^{(k-2)}$ to the next party $\mathcal{P}^{(k-3)}$.

4. For each $j = k-3, k-4, \ldots, 2$, $\mathcal{P}^{(j)}$ performs similar process as the previous sub-steps of $\mathcal{P}^{(k-2)}$, and generates $M_{perm}^{(j)}$ and $prod^{(j)}$. Then $\mathcal{P}^{(j)}$ defines $pprod^{(j)}$ as the product between $pprod^{(j+1)}$ and $prod^{(j)}$, and sends $pprod^{(j)}$ and $M_{perm}^{(j)}$ to the next party $\mathcal{P}^{(j-1)}$.

5. $\mathcal{P}^{(1)}$ also generates $M_{perm}^{(1)}$ and $pprod^{(1)}$ upon receiving $M_{perm}^{(2)}$ and $pprod^{(2)}$ from $\mathcal{P}^{(2)}$, computes the tuple $SP = (s_1, s_2, \ldots, s_{2^n})$ such that each $s_j = z$ if j-th element of $pprod^{(1)}$ is i and the number of 1's in the i-th column of $M_{perm}^{(1)}$ is z. $\mathcal{P}^{(1)}$ sends $SP = (s_1, s_2, \ldots, s_{2^n})$ to $\mathcal{P}^{(k)}$.

6. $\mathcal{P}^{(k)}$ obtains the scalar product $s_t = \mathbf{X}^{(1)} \cdot \mathbf{X}^{(2)} \cdots \mathbf{X}^{(k)}$ from SP, and sends s_t to all the others as a result of the scalar product.

Trincă and Rajasekaran [16] also proposed SECProtocol-II, an improved version of Protocol 1 (SECProtocol-I), that will reduce its complexity significantly. In SECProtocol-II, for each component of private vectors, SECProtocol-I is used iteratively. Thus insecurity of SECProtocol-I implies that of SECProtocol-II. That is, it is sufficient to show that SECProtol-I is insecure. We can obtain the following fact that Protocol 1 (SECProtocol-I) is absolutely insecure.

Fact 1. In Protocol 1, the private vector $\mathbf{X}^{(k-1)}$ of $\mathcal{P}^{(k-1)}$ is absolutely disclosed to $\mathcal{P}^{(k-2)}$, and for each $2 \leq j \leq k-2$, all positions of which their component values of $\mathbf{X}^{(k-1)}, \ldots, \mathbf{X}^{(j)}$ are commonly 1 are disclosed to $\mathcal{P}^{(j-1)}$. $\mathcal{P}^{(k)}$ also can expose the all component positions which their values are commonly 1 within the private vectors $\mathbf{X}^{(k-1)}, \ldots, \mathbf{X}^{(1)}$.

Proof. We show that there are disharmony among the security levels of different parties in Protocol 1. At first, $prod^{(k-1)}$ and $M_{perm}^{(k-1)}$ reveal all column vectors of $M^{(k-1)}$, since $\mathcal{P}^{(k-1)}$ receives only $M^{(k)}$ from $\mathcal{P}^{(k)}$. Then $\mathcal{P}^{(k-2)}$ can determine all component values of $\mathbf{X}^{(k-1)}$ from $M^{(k-1)}$ as follows: for each $i = 1, 2, \ldots, n$, $X_i^{(k-1)} = 0$ if the i-th row vector of $M^{(k-1)}$ is zero vector, and $X_i^{(k-1)} = 1$ if the i-th row vector of $M^{(k-1)}$ is nonzero vector. That is, $\mathcal{P}^{(k-2)}$ absolutely exposes the private vector $\mathbf{X}^{(k-1)}$ of $\mathcal{P}^{(k-1)}$.

Secondly, we show that for each $2 \leq j \leq k-2$, $\mathcal{P}^{(j-1)}$ can expose an information about all positions of which their component values of $\mathbf{X}^{(k-1)}, \ldots, \mathbf{X}^{(j)}$ are commonly 1. Let the number of components having value 1 in $\mathbf{X}^{(j)}$ be h, then there exist 2^h equivalent classes of columns in the matrix $M^{(j)}$. Since $prod^{(j)}$

is the product between $full^{(j)}$ and $perm^{(j)}$, it contains all information about the 2^h columns and their position changes. Meanwhile, $\mathcal{P}^{(j-1)}$ receives $M_{perm}^{(j)}$ and $pprod^{(j)}$, where $pprod^{(j)}$ is the product between $pprod^{(j+1)}$ and $prod^{(j)}$. Thus $\mathcal{P}^{(j-1)}$ can learn component positions which their values are commonly 1 of $\mathbf{X}^{(k-1)}, \ldots, \mathbf{X}^{(j)}$, since $pprod^{(j+1)}$ contains information of cumulative components having value 1 from $\mathbf{X}^{(k-1)}$ to $\mathbf{X}^{(j+1)}$.

On the other hand, $\mathcal{P}^{(k)}$ receives only the vector $SP = (s_1, s_2, \ldots, s_{2^n})$ from $\mathcal{P}^{(1)}$. However $\mathcal{P}^{(k)}$ can learn component positions which their values are commonly 1 of $\mathbf{X}^{(k-1)}, \ldots, \mathbf{X}^{(1)}$ from SP and $M^{(k)}$. In fact, each $s_i (1 \leq i \leq 2^n)$ is the value of scalar product $\mathbf{X}^{(k-1)} \cdots \mathbf{X}^{(1)} \cdot M_i^{(k)}$, where $M_i^{(k)}$ denotes the i-th column vector of $M^{(k)}$. Hence $\mathcal{P}^{(k)}$ can know the all component positions which their values are commonly 1 of private vectors $\mathbf{X}^{(k-1)}, \ldots, \mathbf{X}^{(1)}$, since $M^{(k)}$ contains all possible boolean column vectors of size n.

Note that the private vector $\mathbf{X}^{(k)}$ of initiator $\mathcal{P}^{(k)}$ is concealed in out of 2^n column vectors within $M^{(k)}$. Thus the privacy of $\mathcal{P}^{(k)}$ is preserved with complexity $O(2^n)$.   □

Trincă and Rajasekaran [16] described their protocols by considering a running example involving three parties. We also here present an extended example involving four parties in order to understand easily our attack of Fact 1.

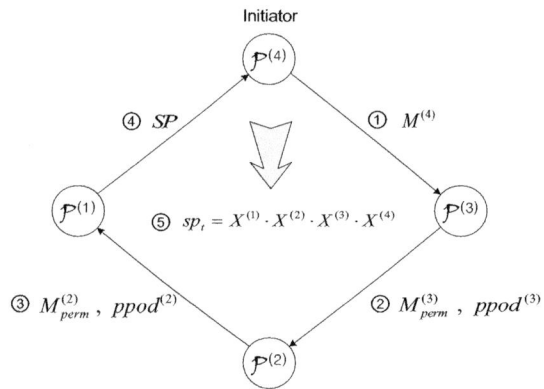

Fig. 1. Overall process of Protocol 2 with four parties

Example 1. Let $\mathcal{P}^{(1)}, \mathcal{P}^{(2)}, \mathcal{P}^{(3)}, \mathcal{P}^{(4)}$ be four parties that want to collaboratively compute the scalar product $\mathbf{X}^{(1)} \cdot \mathbf{X}^{(2)} \cdot \mathbf{X}^{(3)} \cdot \mathbf{X}^{(4)}$ by performing Protocol 1, where

$$\mathbf{X}^{(1)} = \begin{pmatrix} 1 \\ 1 \\ 1 \end{pmatrix}, \quad \mathbf{X}^{(2)} = \begin{pmatrix} 1 \\ 1 \\ 0 \end{pmatrix}, \quad \mathbf{X}^{(3)} = \begin{pmatrix} 0 \\ 1 \\ 1 \end{pmatrix}, \quad \mathbf{X}^{(4)} = \begin{pmatrix} 0 \\ 1 \\ 0 \end{pmatrix}$$

are the vectors of size $n = 3$ corresponding to $\mathcal{P}^{(1)}, \mathcal{P}^{(2)}, \mathcal{P}^{(3)}, \mathcal{P}^{(4)}$, respectively. Let $\mathcal{P}^{(4)}$ be the initiator of Protocol 1. Figure 1 shows the overall process of performing Protocol 1.

Attacks of some parties against private vectors $\mathbf{X}^{(1)}$, $\mathbf{X}^{(2)}$, and $\mathbf{X}^{(3)}$ are described in Figure 2. $\mathcal{P}^{(2)}$ can expose all component values of $M^{(3)}$ from $M_{perm}^{(3)}$ and $pprod^{(3)}$. Since the first row of $M^{(3)}$ is zero vector, we learn that the first component value of $\mathbf{X}^{(3)}$ should be zero. Similarly the second and third component values of $\mathbf{X}^{(3)}$ are one, since the corresponding rows of $M^{(3)}$ are non-zero vectors. That is, $\mathbf{X}^{(3)} = (0,1,1)^T$ is absolutely disclosed to $\mathcal{P}^{(2)}$.

From $M_{perm}^{(2)}$ and $pprod^{(2)}$, $\mathcal{P}^{(1)}$ of Figure 2 can recover the matrix which contains a cumulative information of $\mathbf{X}^{(3)}$ and $\mathbf{X}^{(2)}$. Thus $\mathcal{P}^{(1)}$ learns that the second component values of the private vectors $\mathbf{X}^{(3)}$ and $\mathbf{X}^{(2)}$ are commonly one, since the second row of recovered matrix is a non-zero vector. That is, $\mathcal{P}^{(1)}$ exposes that $\mathbf{X}^{(3)} = (*,1,*)^T$ and $\mathbf{X}^{(2)} = (*,1,*)^T$, where "$*$" denotes unknown value. The initiator $\mathcal{P}^{(4)}$ of Figure 2 receives the vector $SP = (sp_1,\ldots,sp_8)$, and for each $i = 1,\ldots,8$, $sp_i = \mathbf{X}^{(1)} \cdot \mathbf{X}^{(2)} \cdot \mathbf{X}^{(3)} \cdot M_i^{(4)}$, where $M_i^{(4)}$ is the i-th column vector of $M^{(4)}$. Then $\mathcal{P}^{(4)}$ can expose that $\mathbf{X}^{(3)} = (*,1,*)^T$, $\mathbf{X}^{(2)} = (*,1,*)^T$, and $\mathbf{X}^{(1)} = (*,1,*)^T$.

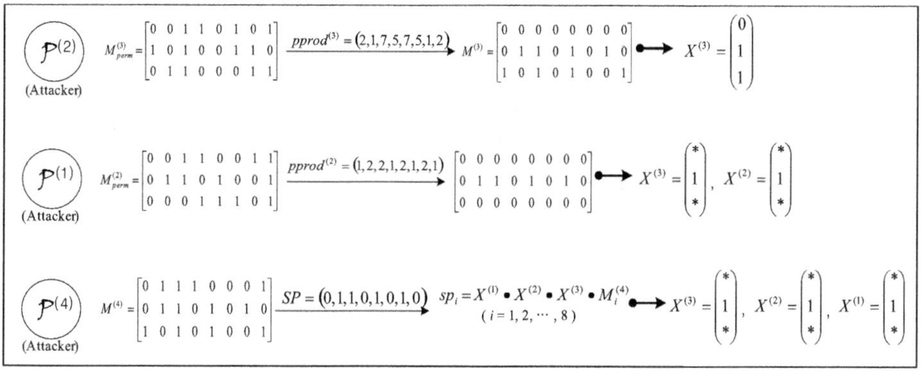

Fig. 2. Attacks of some parties against private vectors

On the other hand, we are able to consider an observation attack against Protocol 1. In Fact 1, all attackers are one of the participants within the protocol. At this point we regard an observer as a passive attacker which it can collect all public information and be eager to disclose private information of participants within the protocol. An observer in Example 1 can collect all information of $M^{(4)}$, $M_{perm}^{(3)}$, $M_{perm}^{(2)}$, $pprod^{(3)}$, $pprod^{(2)}$, and SP. Figure 3 shows that $\mathbf{X}^{(1)} = (*,1,*)^T$, $\mathbf{X}^{(2)} = (*,1,0)^T$, and $\mathbf{X}^{(3)} = (0,1,1)^T$ are disclosed to an observer.

4 Insecurity of Protocol by Amirbekyan and Estivill-Castro

Amirbekyan and Estivill-Castro [1] proposed a new simple private scalar product protocol which is based on the Add Vectors Protocol. The Add Vectors Protocol

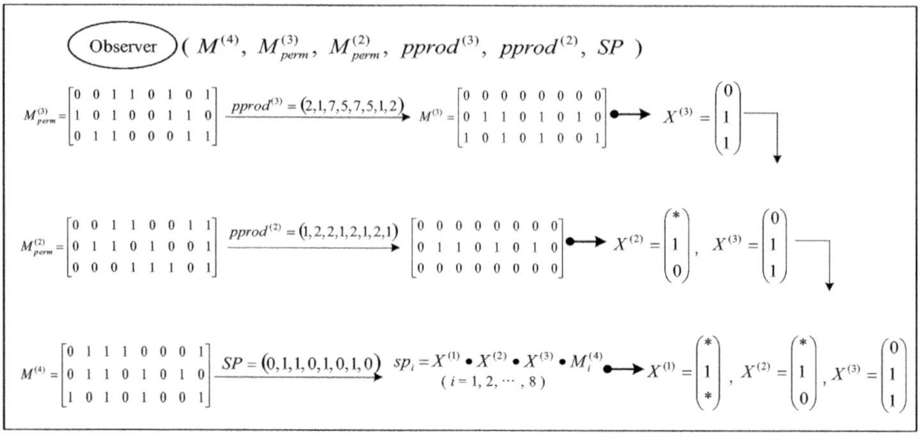

Fig. 3. Observation attack against private vectors

was introduced by Du and Atallah [6] as the "permutation protocol". In the Add Vectors Protocol, Alice has a vector X while Bob has vector Y and a permutation π. The goal of the Add Vectors Protocol is for Alice to obtain $\pi(X + Y) = \pi(x_1 + y_1, \ldots, x_n + y_n)$. Since the entries are randomly permuted, Alice cannot find Y and Bob also cannot know X. Du and Atallah [6] proposed an Add Vectors Protocol by using the homomorphic public-key encryption scheme, while in the Add Vectors Protocol, Amirbekyan and Estivill-Castro [1] used the simple method of adding a random vector consisting of the same random number. Moreover they used the relation

$$2\sum_{i=1}^{n} x_i y_i = \sum_{i=1}^{n} x_i^2 + \sum_{i=1}^{n} y_i^2 - \sum_{i=1}^{n} (x_i - y_i)^2$$

to obtain the following private scalar product protocol.

Protocol 2. *(Amirbekyan and Estivill-Castro [1])*

 – Inputs: Alice has a secret vector X, Bob has a secret vector Y.
 – Outputs: Alice and Bob get $X \cdot Y$.

1. Alice generates a secret random number c, and sends $X' = (x_1 + c, x_2 + c, \ldots, x_n + c)$ to Bob.
2. Bob computes $X' - Y$ and permutes it by generating a random permutation π of $\{1, 2, \ldots, n\}$. Bob sends $\sum_{i=1}^{n} y_i^2$ and $\pi(X' - Y) = (x_{\pi(1)} + c - y_{\pi(1)}, x_{\pi(2)} + c - y_{\pi(2)}, \ldots, x_{\pi(n)} + c - y_{\pi(n)})$ to Alice.
3. Alice gets $\pi(X - Y) = (x_{\pi(1)} - y_{\pi(1)}, x_{\pi(2)} - y_{\pi(2)}, \ldots, x_{\pi(n)} - y_{\pi(n)})$ by subtracting c from the all components of $\pi(X' - Y)$, and obtains the scalar product

$$X \cdot Y = \frac{1}{2} \left(\sum_{i=1}^{n} x_i^2 + \sum_{i=1}^{n} y_i^2 - \sum_{i=1}^{n} (x_{\pi(i)} - y_{\pi(i)})^2 \right).$$

Alice sends $X \cdot Y$ to Bob.

In [1], the authors mentioned about that there are some information leaks in the Add Vectors Protocol of Protocol 2 for some special cases such as the component values in Alice's vector are equal. For these special cases, they proposed a revised version such that at the first step Alice generates a random vector R ensure that $X + R$ will be always a vector with non-equal component values. Alice and Bob perform twice Protocol 2 for the inputs $(X + R, Y)$ and (R, Y), respectively, then Alice can obtain $X \cdot Y = (X + R) \cdot Y - R \cdot Y$. Hence this revised version is also insecure, if Protocol 2 is not secure. We can show that Alice is absolutely insecure in Protocol 2.

Fact 2. In the process of performing Protocol 2, the private vector X of Alice is absolutely disclosed to Bob. On the contrary, the privacy of Bob's vector Y is preserved to Alice as the computational complexity that Alice guesses the value of Y is $O(n!)$.

Proof. Note that

$$X' \cdot Y = (X + C) \cdot Y = X \cdot Y + C \cdot Y = X \cdot Y + c \sum_{i=1}^{n} y_i \, ,$$

where $C = (c, c, \dots, c)$. Bob knows the values of $X' \cdot Y$ and $X \cdot Y$ by performing Protocol 2, then he obtains the secret number c of Alice by computing $c = (X' \cdot Y - X \cdot Y) / \sum_{i=1}^{n} y_i$. That is, Bob can expose the private vector $X = X' - C$ of Alice.

On the other hand, Alice knows $\pi(X - Y)$ and $\sum_{i=1}^{n} y_i^2$. By guessing a permutation π out of $n!$ permutations, Alice can estimate the corresponding Y and determine its correctness by computing the value of $\sum_{i=1}^{n} y_i^2$. Thus Alice can obtain the correct value of Y with computational complexity about $n!$. □

5   Conclusion

In this paper, we have studied on the security of private scalar product computation protocols. Two kinds of methods are used in the previous PSPPs. One method is based on the cryptographic primitives such as homomorphic public-key encryption schemes, and the other is based on the only linear algebraic techniques. It seems that some proposed PSPPs based on the homomorphic public-key encryption schemes are secure, but they still cause a computational overload. On the contrary some previous PSPPs based on the only linear algebraic techniques are relatively efficient and more practical, but it is still doubtable whether these protocols would be secure. We have analyzed insecurity of the two recently proposed PSPPs based on the linear algebraic techniques, and shown that the protocols of Trincă and Rajasekaran [16] and Amirbekyan and Estivill-Castro [1] are absolutely insecure.

Acknowledgements. This research was partially supported by research program 2011 of Kookmin Uninersity in Korea and Next-Generation Information Computing Development Program through the National Research Foundation of Korea(NRF) funded by the Ministry of Education, Science and Technology (Grant No. 2011-0029925).

References

1. Amirbekyan, A., Estivill-Castro, V.: A new efficient privacy-preserving scalar product protocol. In: The 6th Australian Data Mining Conference (AusDM 2007), pp. 205–210 (2007)
2. Atallah, M.J., Du, W.: Secure Multi-Party Computational Geometry. In: Dehne, F., Sack, J.-R., Tamassia, R. (eds.) WADS 2001. LNCS, vol. 2125, pp. 165–179. Springer, Heidelberg (2001)
3. Brassard, G., Crépeau, C., Robert, J.M.: All-or-Nothing Disclosure of Secrets. In: Odlyzko, A.M. (ed.) CRYPTO 1986. LNCS, vol. 263, pp. 234–238. Springer, Heidelberg (1987)
4. Clifton, C., Kantarcioglu, M., Lin, X., Vaida, J., Zhu, M.: Tools for privacy preserving distributed data mining. SIGKDD Explorations 4(2), 28–34 (2003)
5. Damgård, I., Jurik, M.: A Generalisation, a Simplification and some Applications of Paillier's Probabilistic Public-Key System. In: Kim, K.-C. (ed.) PKC 2001. LNCS, vol. 1992, pp. 119–136. Springer, Heidelberg (2001)
6. Du, W., Atallah, M.: Privacy-preserving statistical analysis. In: Proceedings of the 17th Annual Computer Security Applications Conference, pp. 102–110 (2001)
7. Du, W., Atallah, M.: Protocols for secure remote database access with approximate matching, CERIAS Tech Report 2001-02, Department of Computer Sciences, Purdue University (2001)
8. Gentry, C.: Fully Homomorphic Encryption Using Ideal Lattices. In: The 41st ACM Symposium on Theory of Computing, STOC (2009)
9. Goethals, B., Laur, S., Lipmaa, H., Mielikäinen, T.: On Private Scalar Product Computation for Privacy-Preserving Data Mining. In: Park, C.-S., Chee, S. (eds.) ICISC 2004. LNCS, vol. 3506, pp. 104–120. Springer, Heidelberg (2005)
10. Goldreich, O.: Secure Multi-Party Computation, Final Draft Version 1.4 (2002), http://www.wisdom.weizmann.ac.il/
11. Huang, Y., Lu, Z., Hu, H.: Privacy preserving association rule mining with scalar product. In: Proceedings of NLP-KE 2005, pp. 750–755. IEEE (2005)
12. Ioannidis, I., Grama, A., Atallah, M.: A secure protocol for computing dot-products in clustered and distributed environments. In: Proceedings of the International Conference on Parallel Processing, ICPP 2002 (2002)
13. Laur, S., Lipma, H.: On private similarity search protocols. In: Proceedings of 9th Nordic Workshop on Secure IT Systems (NordSec 2004), pp. 73–77 (2004)
14. Naor, M., Pinkas, B.: Oblivious transfer and polynomial evaluation. In: Proceedings of the 31st ACM Symposium on Theory of Computing, pp. 245–254 (1999)
15. Paillier, P.: Public-Key Cryptosystems Based on Composite Degree Residuosity Classes. In: Stern, J. (ed.) EUROCRYPT 1999. LNCS, vol. 1592, pp. 223–238. Springer, Heidelberg (1999)
16. Trincă, D., Rajasekaran, S.: Fast Cryptographic Multi-Party Protocols for Computing Boolean Scalar Products with Applications to Privacy-Preserving Association Rule Mining in Vertically Partitioned Data. In: Song, I.-Y., Eder, J., Nguyen, T.M. (eds.) DaWaK 2007. LNCS, vol. 4654, pp. 418–427. Springer, Heidelberg (2007)
17. Vaidya, J., Clifton, C.: Privacy preserving association rule mining in vertically partioned data. In: Proceedings of the 8th ACM SIGKDD International Conference on Knowledge Discovery and Data Mining, pp. 639–634 (2002)

A Survey on Access Control Deployment

Vivy Suhendra

Institute for Infocomm Research, A*STAR, Singapore
vsuhendra@i2r.a-star.edu.sg

Abstract. Access control is a security aspect whose requirements evolve with technology advances and, at the same time, contemporary social contexts. Multitudes of access control models grow out of their respective application domains such as healthcare and collaborative enterprises; and even then, further administering means, human factor considerations, and infringement management are required to effectively deploy the model in the particular usage environment. This paper presents a survey of access control mechanisms along with their deployment issues and solutions available today. We aim to give a comprehensive big picture as well as pragmatic deployment details to guide in understanding, setting up and enforcing access control in its real world application.

Keywords: access control, deployment, socio-technical system.

1 Introduction

Access control is indispensable in organizations whose operation requires sharing of digital resources with various degrees of sensitivity. Innovations in business models such as cloud computing, matrix-structuring and inter-enterprise collaborations further necessitate sophisticated access management to enforce customized security policies beyond conventional office boundaries.

An effective access control system should fulfill the security requirements of *confidentiality* (no unauthorized disclosure of resources), *integrity* (no improper modifications of resources), and *availability* (ensuring accessibility of resources to legitimate users) [27]. A complete access control infrastructure covers the following three functions:

1. **Authentication:** identifying a legitimate user. The proof of identity can be what the user *knows* (password or PIN), what the user *has* (smart card), what the user *is* (biometrics), or a combination of the above (multi-factor authentication). For each of these identification methods, there exist choices of authentication schemes and protocols. A comprehensive survey of authentication technologies is available from IETF [24]; we leave this function outside the scope of this paper.

2. **Authorization:** granting or denying permission to an authenticated user to perform certain operations on a resource based on security policies. Authorization is the core of access control where most of the complexity lies, and is

T.-h. Kim et al. (Eds.): SecTech 2011, CCIS 259, pp. 11–20, 2011.

the focus of this article. The process involves defining *access control policies* as rules to regulate access, choosing an *access control model* to encapsulate the policies, and implementing *access control mechanisms* to administer the model and enforce the defined controls.

3. **Accountability:** tracing or logging of actions performed by a user within the system for later auditing. This function mainly involves technical solutions (log management and security, limited automation of auditing process) and corporate management (manual inspection, crisis response), and shall not be discussed in depth here.

Technologies for these functions can be supplied by separate vendors. Existing enterprise resource management systems typically provide an authorization framework coupled with logging features, with interfaces to popular choices of authentication mechanisms (e.g., Kerberos) assumed to be already in place.

There have been comprehensive conceptual treatments of access control [27,29,26,11] as well as ongoing research on the various security aspects. Despite this, effective access control remains a challenge in real world application, as it heavily involves unpredictable human factor and response to social environments that cannot be thoroughly accounted for with one-stop solutions [30]. This article therefore examines access control as a *socio-technical* system from the perspective of deployment, focusing on pragmatic issues in setting up and enforcing access control policies with flexibility to suit the social application contexts.

2   Access Control Policies and Models

Regulation of access is expressed as *policies*, which are high-level rules defined for the particular organization or project. A common policy, for example, is "separation of duties", which prohibits granting a single person access to multiple resources that together hold high damage potential when abused. Laying down the policies requires taking into account the work nature, objectives, criticality of resources handled, and so on. The policies are also dynamic as they adapt to the change in these influencing factors.

Diverse as they are, access control policies can be categorized into two based on the underlying objective. *Discretionary* access control essentially leaves access permissions to the discretion of the resource owner. These policies can be highly flexible, but weak in security. They are commonly implemented using direct, explicit identity-based mechanisms such as Access Control List (ACL), which maps individual users to individual resource permissions. On the other hand, *non-discretionary* access control regulates access through administrative action (rule-based). Examples are Mandatory Access Control (MAC) where regulations are imposed by a central authority, and policies that impose constraints on the nature of access (time, history, user roles, etc.) [11].

Such access rules are configured into control mechanisms using a *policy language*. A prevailing standard for this purpose is XACML (eXtensible Access

Control Markup Language) [21], an XML-based language that supports fine-grained access control. Proposals for new access control languages to handle particular needs continue to emerge as well [19].

Configuring access control policies is a non-trivial and highly critical process, and it should be subjected to periodic review and verification to ensure that security policies are correctly expressed and implemented. Proposed verification methods include formally testable policy specification [2], detection of anomalies or conflicting rules via segmentation technique [10], and analysis tools that enable policy administrators to evaluate policy interpretations [13].

Bridging the policies and the actual mechanisms to enforce them are *access control models*. Each model has emerged with specific concepts catering to the different needs of the different fields, but as they evolve to more extensive usage, their application domain boundaries have also blurred. The remainder of this section examines major access control models that are representative of the concepts in their category: role-based, attribute-based, and risk-based.

2.1   Role-Based Access Control (RBAC)

The RBAC [28,7] model fits static organizational hierarchy where members have defined roles or tasks (e.g. HR Manager, Network Admin), and the roles determine the resources they need to access (e.g. payroll database, server configurations). RBAC essentially maps users to roles and roles to permissions, as many-to-many relationships (Figure 1(a)). It can be considered a higher-level form of Access Control List (ACL), which is built into all modern operating systems, and thus can be implemented on top of ACL without much difficulty. Enterprise management systems that cater to general industries typically employ some form of customized Role-Based access control, often in conjunction with their proprietary Information Rights Management technology; as seen in Microsoft SharePoint and Oracle PeopleSoft.

Aside from the basic (*core*) RBAC model, there are three extended RBAC models [11]: *hierarchical RBAC*, supporting role hierarchy and rights inheritance; *statically constrained RBAC*, supporting static constraints (e.g., on role assignment); and *dynamic constrained RBAC*, supporting time-dependent constraints (e.g., activation of roles). Many variants further refine these models for specific requirements [6,22]. There have also been efforts to adapt RBAC for distributed environments, where multiple policy decision points need to reconcile dynamic changes in job functions as well as diverse sets of users who may not be known throughout the system [1,31].

Administration. Roles are identified and assigned permissions through the *role engineering* process, either via the *top-down* approach which takes a job function and associates needed permissions to it, or the *bottom-up* approach which takes existing user permissions and aggregates them into roles [32]. The bottom-up approach has been more popular because much of the process can be automated, giving rise to research efforts in *role mining* [8,17].

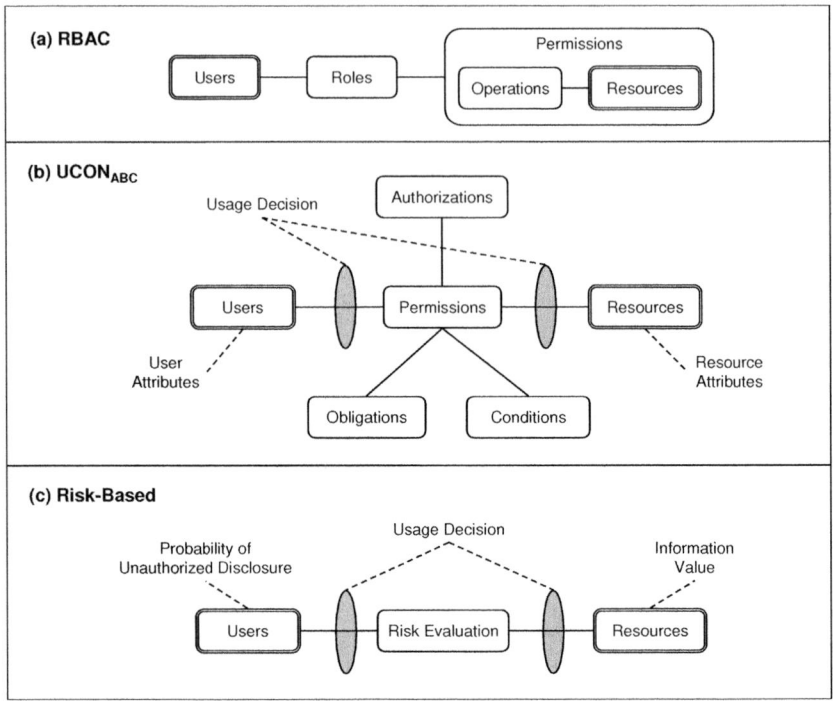

Fig. 1. Illustrated principles of access control models: (a) RBAC; (b) UCON_{ABC}; (c) Risk-Based

Limitation. The notion of roles, while intuitive to administer, may limit the granularity of control over resources, as users of the same role inevitably share the same permissions assigned to that role. This may be mitigated via advanced role administration, e.g., by making use of inheritance in a role hierarchy, or refining static roles into workflow-centric tasks [9]. However, the principle remains that permissions are tied to roles, which have to be defined beforehand.

2.2   Usage Control (UCON_{ABC})

The UCON_{ABC} model [23] provides a means for fine-grained control over access permissions. It is so named because it is described in terms of **A**uthorizations, o**B**ligations, and **C**onditions. Fundamental to UCON_{ABC} is the concept of *attributes* attached to both users and resources (Figure 1(b)). Attributes can be any information deemed relevant for granting access, such as the user's location or how many times the resource has been accessed. Permissions for a particular resource are specified in terms of conditions on attribute values: users with attribute values that meet the conditions are allowed access. Thus access rights to a resource can be assigned without needing to predict the full set of potential users. Further, attributes are mutable—they can be updated after an access (e.g., access count), and users can perform actions to fulfill the obligations necessary to access the resource (e.g., agreeing to terms and conditions). As such, authorization may take place before or during access (on-going). An example of on-going authorization is a system where users can stay logged in by periodically clicking on an advertisement banner.

Administration. Delegation of rights in UCON$_{ABC}$ is largely concerned with the question of which *authority* can set and verify attribute values that will grant access to a user. In open environments, a distributed authority is usually preferred over a central authority, where several users can assert attributes of other users and resources, with an administrator or the resource owner acting as authority root in case of conflicting assertions [25].

Limitation. The expressive power of UCON$_{ABC}$ comes at the cost of complexity. Unlike for RBAC, operating system support is not readily available, thus UCON is often implemented at the application layer. It may also need database support if attributes are complex or tied to personal information. This complexity may lead to error-prone deployment in heterogeneous environments.

2.3   Risk-Based Access Control

The Risk-Based Access Control [5,20] is motivated by highly dynamic environments where it is often difficult to predict beforehand what resources a user will need to access. In such environments, rigid access control that prevents users from accessing information in a timely manner may result in loss of profit or bad crisis response. The Risk-Based model makes real-time decisions to grant or deny a user access to the requested resource, by weighing the risk of granting the access against the perceived benefit (Figure 1(c)). In the Quantified Risk–Adaptive Access Control (QRAAC) variant [5], this risk is computed as $risk = V \times P$, where V is the information value, reflecting the sensitivity level of the resource, and P is the probability of unauthorized disclosure, reflecting the trustworthiness of the user. The security policy is then specified in terms of risk tolerance levels, which will determine the permissions given at the points of decision.

Administration. The *risk assessment* process measures information value of resources, estimates probability of abuse, and sets risk tolerance levels. It is largely dependent on the organization's security objectives. Information value may be measured as costs from loss of availability (if gained access turns into a Denial of Service attack), loss of confidentiality (in case of unauthorized disclosure after access), and loss of integrity (if the resource is modified to a worse state) [18]. Probability of access abuse can be estimated by considering various scenarios enabled by existing policies [14].

Limitation. Risk assessment is a subjective process that requires expertise and careful analysis. This makes Risk-Based model difficult to deploy.

3   Enforcing Access Control with Flexibility

Once the access control model and policies are set up, the underlying access control mechanisms will ensure that they are enforced in normal operation. However, this is often not enough to guarantee the desired level of security, simply because it is hardly possible to anticipate all usage scenarios when laying down the policies. Even in models that enable access decisions to be made real-time (e.g., risk-based models), there is a lack of ability to distinguish between malicious break-in and well-intentioned infringements, such as those necessary in emergencies (e.g., a nurse taking charge of a patient while the doctor is unavailable) or those done in the best interest of the organization (e.g., an IT support staff tracing content of email attachments to resolve a crash). Access control deployment that apply over-restrictions in favor of strong security can be prone to circumvention attempts by its users wanting only "to get the job done" [30] and ironically exposed to higher risk. This problem is recognized to arise from the fact that access control is a socio-technical system for which current technical solutions are yet to satisfactorily anticipate conflicting social contexts in which they will be applied [16]. To mitigate the problem, additional mechanisms can be applied on top of the underlying access control models, to allow fine-tuned enforcement and achieve flexibility without sacrificing security.

3.1   Overriding Permissions

If it is commonly observed that truly legitimate users need to circumvent access control via offline means in order to access the resource, it may be worthwhile to set up standalone, overriding permissions that apply to these users. This may be done by tweaking the access control mechanism or adding special policies, for example, in the spirit of discretionary access control where the resource owner explicitly specifies who are allowed access [12].

This approach can achieve flexibility at relatively low risk, assuming that the overriding permissions are set by an authority with full rights over the resource (e.g., the owner). The effect is localized to information owned by the user who exercises the override option. In principle, it introduces no additional risk that is not already there (due to circumvention attempts) while providing a way for the access control exception to be properly captured in audits.

3.2   Break-Glass Mechanism

Studies of access control in the real world have shown that there often arise emergency situations that require violation of policies so that an ordinary user can gain access to critically needed resource and solve the crisis [30]. While Risk-Based Access Control model enables ad-hoc upgrade of privileges, the deployment as-is does not guarantee proper crisis response; that is, risk assessment may fail to override the decision to deny access, or the incident may not be recognized as an emergency that requires special handling. In organizations with static access control such as RBAC, the existing solution is to employ a *break-glass* strategy that will override access control decisions. The term is derived

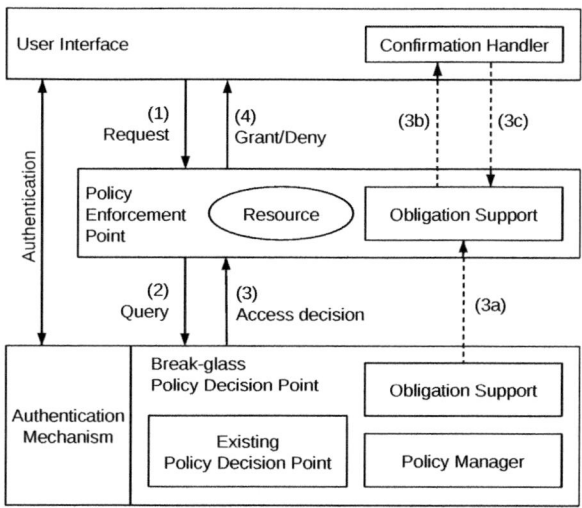

Fig. 2. The break-glass architecture and message flow [3]. Upon access request from user (1), the Policy Enforcement Point consults the Policy Decision Point (2). In normal operation, regular access decision based on existing policy is made (3) and access is either granted or denied (4). In break-glass operation, the special policy is invoked (3a) and access is granted after prompting the user to fulfill the required obligation (3b) and receiving confirmation (3c).

from the simple but insecure way to achieve this, which is to create a special temporary account with the highest privileges, stored in a place that a user can break into in emergencies. This practice is extremely vulnerable to misuse if the account falls into malicious hands.

A proper break-glass policy can be integrated into access control models without affecting normal operation [3], by carefully specifying how to recognize an emergency situation and allow selective access to necessary resources (Figure 2). The Rumpole model [15] uses the notions of *competence* to encode information on the user's capability to access the resource without causing harm, and *empowerment* to encode whether contextual constraints are met (e.g., whether the access will break critical policies such as separation of duties). Each can reflect one of the four values "true", "false", "conflict", or "unknown", to further provide evidence to support the access control decision.

In all cases, break-glass should be invoked along with a strict accountability function (logging and auditing), which should be made transparent to users in order to discourage abusing the permission beyond the emergency requirement.

3.3 Violation Management

Isolated situations that do not constitute an emergency may also call for violation of normal access restrictions in order to achieve a higher operational goal

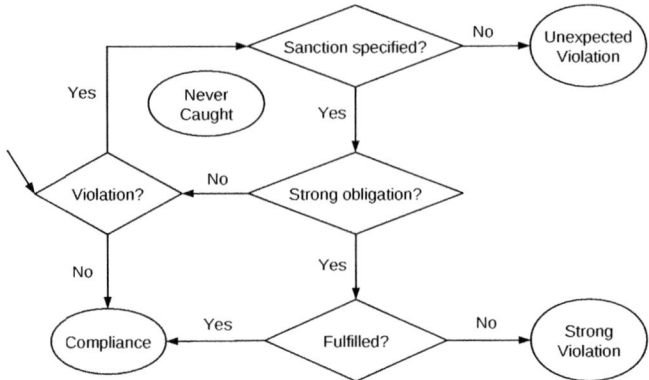

Fig. 3. Logical flow of violation management (simplified from [4]). "Compliance" captures the situation where no violation occurs, or all resulting sanctions are fulfilled. Violation occurs when a non-permitted event happens, or a violable obligation is not fulfilled. If no sanction is specified for a violation, it is concluded as "Unexpected Violation". If the sanction is a strong obligation (i.e., not violable), it must be fulfilled to achieve compliance, else it is a "Strong Violation". If the violation leads to infinite sequence of unfulfilled weak (violable) obligations, it is concluded as "Never Caught".

[16]. Suppose an IT support staff needs to troubleshoot a crash in the email application, but does not have the permission to look at the client's email exchanges. Following the legitimate procedure of escalating the problem to higher authority might delay resolution more than simply asking the client for that permission. For security interests, such acceptable workaround should be properly accounted and audited as an "allowed" violation.

One proposed approach to manage violation in access control is to define *sanctions*, which are obligations that users must perform to justify policy violations [4]. Compliant behaviour is considered achieved as long as corresponding sanctions are applied whenever violations occur. The system can then distinguish between malicious attempts and justifiable infringements by checking whether or not sanction-obligations are fulfilled. The implementation requires the mechanism to check (1) the occurence of violation, (2) the existence of sanction corresponding to the violation, and (3) the enforcement of sanction (Figure 3).

Another violation management approach is to enhance the access control model with on-demand escalation and audit [33]. The principle is to carefully couple information access, audit, violation penalties and rewards, so that self-interested employees may obtain more information than strictly needed in order to seize more business opportunities while managing security risks responsibly.

4   Conclusion

Deployment of access control begins with defining the security policies, which may require knowledge of the concerned resources (access method, criticality, etc.), the potential users, and the nature of security breaches to prevent. Any special requirement in the handling of specific situations, such as priority rules to apply during emergencies, should also be identified. Based on this, a suitable access control model can be selected and configured with the defined policies. Mechanisms required to support the workings of the model, including all necessary augmentations, are then installed. Each of these implementation steps should be verified to ensure that all policies are correctly put in place.

In practice, an organization may find it more hassle-free to purchase enterprise resource management systems that come bundled with access control. Factors such as migration cost and user-friendliness will then affect the choice, and it may instead adjust policies to fit the available means. Even then, the organization should ensure that its security objectives are met via careful configuration, and consider adopting additional means of security enforcement to fill any perceived gap.

We can be certain that access control, along with the challenges in enforcing it, will continue to evolve as information systems keep up with both technological advances and interaction trends. In face of this, it would seem prudent to never fully rely on any single solution, but to assume that breaches may and will happen, and to have both preventive and curative measures ready for them.

References

1. Barker, S.: Action-status access control. In: SACMAT, pp. 195–204 (2007)
2. Brucker, A.D., Brügger, L., Kearney, P., Wolff, B.: An approach to modular and testable security models of real-world health-care applications. In: SACMAT, pp. 133–142 (2011)
3. Brucker, A.D., Petritsch, H.: Extending access control models with break-glass. In: SACMAT, pp. 197–206 (2009)
4. Brunel, J., Cuppens, F., Cuppens, N., Sans, T., Bodeveix, J.P.: Security policy compliance with violation management. In: FMSE, pp. 31–40 (2007)
5. Cheng, P.C., Rohatgi, P., Keser, C., Karger, P.A., Wagner, G.M., Reninger, A.S.: Fuzzy multi-level security: An experiment on quantified risk-adaptive access control. In: 2007 IEEE Symp. on Security and Privacy, pp. 222–230 (2007)
6. Damiani, M.L., Bertino, E., Catania, B., Perlasca, P.: GEO-RBAC: A spatially aware RBAC. ACM Trans. Inf. Syst. Secur. 10 (2007)
7. Ferraiolo, D.F., Sandhu, R.S., Gavrila, S., Kuhn, D.R., Chandramouli, R.: Proposed NIST standard for role-based access control. ACM Trans. Inf. Syst. Secur. 4, 224–274 (2001)
8. Frank, M., Buhmann, J.M., Basin, D.: On the definition of role mining. In: SACMAT, pp. 35–44 (2010)
9. Fu, C., Li, A., Xu, L.: Hierarchical and dynamic security access control for collaborative design in virtual enterprise. In: IEEE ICIME, pp. 723–726 (2010)
10. Hu, H., Ahn, G.J., Kulkarni, K.: Anomaly discovery and resolution in web access control policies. In: SACMAT, pp. 165–174 (2011)
11. Hu, V.C., Ferraiolo, D.F., Kuhn, D.R.: Assessment of access control systems. Tech. Rep. NIST Interagency Report 7316, NIST (September 2006)
12. Johnson, M.L., Bellovin, S.M., Reeder, R.W., Schechter, S.E.: Laissez-faire file sharing: access control designed for individuals at the endpoints. In: NSPW, pp. 1–10 (2009)

13. Ledru, Y., Qamar, N., Idani, A., Richier, J.L., Labiadh, M.A.: Validation of security policies by the animation of Z specifications. In: SACMAT, pp. 155–164 (2011)
14. Ma, J., Logrippo, L., Adi, K., Mankovski, S.: Risk analysis in access control systems based on trust theories. In: Proc. 2010 IEEE/WIC/ACM Int'l Conf. on Web Intelligence and Intelligent Agent Technology, vol. 3, pp. 415–418 (2010)
15. Marinovic, S., Craven, R., Ma, J., Dulay, N.: Rumpole: a flexible break-glass access control model. In: SACMAT, pp. 73–82 (2011)
16. Massacci, F.: Infringo ergo sum: when will software engineering support infringements? In: FoSER, pp. 233–238 (2010)
17. Molloy, I., Li, N., Li, T., Mao, Z., Wang, Q., Lobo, J.: Evaluating role mining algorithms. In: SACMAT, pp. 95–104 (2009)
18. Nguyen, N.D., Le, X.H., Zhung, Y., Lee, S., Lee, Y.K., Lee, H.: Enforcing access control using risk assessment. In: Proc. 4th European Conf. on Universal Multiservice Networks, pp. 419–424 (2007)
19. Ni, Q., Bertino, E.: xfACL: an extensible functional language for access control. In: SACMAT, pp. 61–72 (2011)
20. Ni, Q., Bertino, E., Lobo, J.: Risk-based access control systems built on fuzzy inferences. In: ASIACCS, pp. 250–260 (2010)
21. OASIS: eXtensible Access Control Markup Language (XACML) Version 3.0. Committee specification 01, OASIS (August 2010),
    http://docs.oasis-open.org/xacml/3.0/xacml-3.0-core-spec-cs-01-en.pdf
22. Ouyang, K., Joshi, J.B.D.: CT-RBAC: A temporal RBAC model with conditional periodic time. In: IPCCC, pp. 467–474 (2007)
23. Park, J., Sandhu, R.S.: The $UCON_{ABC}$ usage control model. ACM Trans. Inf. Syst. Secur. 7, 128–174 (2004)
24. Rescorla, E., Lebovitz, G.: A survey of authentication mechanisms version 7. Internet-draft, Internet Engineering Task Force (February 2010),
    http://tools.ietf.org/search/draft-iab-auth-mech-07
25. Salim, F., Reid, J., Dawson, E.: An administrative model for $UCON_{ABC}$. In: Proc. 8th Australasian Conf. on Information Security, vol. 105, pp. 32–38. Australian Computer Society, Inc., Darlinghurst (2010)
26. Salim, F., Reid, J., Dawson, E.: Authorization models for secure information sharing: A survey and research agenda. ISeCure, The ISC Int'l Journal of Information Security 2(2), 69–87 (2010)
27. Samarati, P., di Vimercati, S.d.C.: Access control: Policies, models, and mechanisms. In: Focardi, R., Gorrieri, R. (eds.) FOSAD 2000. LNCS, vol. 2171, pp. 137–196. Springer, Heidelberg (2001)
28. Sandhu, R.S., Coyne, E.J., Feinstein, H.L., Youman, C.E.: Role-based access control models. Computer 29(2), 38–47 (1996)
29. Sandhu, R.S., Samarati, P.: Access control: Principles and practice. IEEE Communications Magazine 32, 40–48 (1994)
30. Sinclair, S., Smith, S.W.: What's wrong with access control in the real world? Security & Privacy 8(4), 74–77 (2010)
31. Tripunitara, M.V., Carbunar, B.: Efficient access enforcement in distributed role-based access control (RBAC) deployments. In: SACMAT, pp. 155–164 (2009)
32. Vaidya, J., Atluri, V., Warner, J., Guo, Q.: Role engineering via prioritized subset enumeration. IEEE Trans. Dependable and Secure Computing 7(3), 300–314 (2010)
33. Zhao, X., Johnson, M.E.: Access governance: Flexibility with escalation and audit. In: Proc. 43rd Hawaii Int'l Conf. on System Sciences, pp. 1–13 (2010)

Data Anonymity in Multi-Party Service Model

Shinsaku Kiyomoto, Kazuhide Fukushima, and Yutaka Miyake

KDDI R & D Laboratories Inc.
2-1-15 Ohara, Fujimino-shi, Saitama, 356-8502, Japan
kiyomoto@kddilabs.jp

Abstract. Existing approaches for protecting privacy in public database consider a service model where a service provider publishes public datasets that consist of data gathered from clients. We extend the service model to the multi-service providers setting. In the new model, a service provider obtains anonymized datasets from other service providers who gather data from clients and then publishes or uses the anonymized datasets generated from the obtained anonymized datasets. We considered a new service model that involves more than two data holders and a data user, and proposed a new privacy requirement. Furthermore, we discussed feasible approaches searching a table that satisfies the privacy requirement and showed a concrete algorithm to find the table.

Keywords: k-Anonymity, Privacy, Public DB, Multi-Party.

1 Introduction

Privacy is an increasingly important aspect of data publishing. Sensitive data, such as medical records in public databases, are recognized as a valuable source of information for the allocation of public funds, medical research and statistical trend analysis [1]. Furthermore, secondary-use of personal data has been considered a new market for personalized services. A service provider makes an anonymized dataset from original data, such as records of service use, and distributes the anonymized datasets to other service providers. The service providers can improve their services of using anonymized datasets.

However, if personal private information is leaked from the database, the service will be regarded as unacceptable by the original owners of the data[11]. Thus, anonymization methods have been considered a possible solution for protecting personal information[8]. One class of models, called *global-recoding*, maps the values of attributes to other values [38] in order to generate an anonymized dataset. Generalization methods modify the original data to avoid identification of the records. These methods generate a common value for some records and replace identifying information in the records with the common value.

Existing approaches consider a service model where a service provider publishes datasets that consist of data gathered from clients. We extend the service model to the multi-service providers setting. That is, a service provider obtains anonymized datasets from other service providers who gather data from clients

T.-h. Kim et al. (Eds.): SecTech 2011, CCIS 259, pp. 21–30, 2011.

and then publishes or uses the anonymized datasets generated from the obtained anonymized datasets.

In this paper, we considered a new service model that involves more than two data holders and a data user, and proposed a new privacy requirement. Furthermore, we discussed feasible approaches searching a table that satisfies the privacy requirement and showed a concrete algorithm to find the table.

The rest of the paper is organized as follows; section 2 provides related articles. Privacy definitions are summarized in section 3. We presented a new service model in section 4, and then an new adversary model and privacy protection schemes are proposed in section 5. We conclude this paper in section 6.

2   Related Work

Samarati and Sweeney [32,31,35] proposed a primary definition of privacy that is applicable to generalization methods. A data set is said to have *k-anonymity* if each record is indistinguishable from at least $k - 1$ other records with respect to certain identifying attributes called *quasi-identifiers* [10]. Minimizing this information loss thus presents a challenging problem in the design of generalization algorithms. The optimization problem is referred to as the k-anonymity problem. Meyerson reported that optimal generalization in this regard is an NP-hard problem[29]. Aggarwal *et al.* proved that finding an optimal table including more than three attributes is NP-hard [2]. Nonetheless, k-anonymity has been widely studied because of its conceptual simplicity [4,26,27,39,37,33]. Machanavajjhala *et al.* proposed another important definition of privacy in a public database [26]. The definition, called *l-diversity* assumes a strong adversary having certain background knowledge that allows the adversary to identify the object persons in the public database.

There are several methods of generating k-anonymization tables. Samarati proposed a simple binary search algorithm for finding a k-anonymous table[31]. A drawback of Samarati's algorithm is that for arbitrary definitions of minimality, it is not always guaranteed that this binary search algorithm can find the minimal k-anonymity table. Sun *et. al.* presented a hash-based algorithm that improves the search algorithm[33]. Aggarwal *et al.* proposed an $O(k)$-approximation algorithm [3] for the k-anonymity problem. A greedy approximation algorithm [23] proposed by LeFevre *et al.* searches optimal multi-dimensional anonymization. A genetic algorithm framework [19] was proposed because of its flexible formulation and its ability to allow more efficient anonymization. Utility-based anonymization [40] makes k-anonymous tables using a heuristic local recoding anonymization. Moreover, the k-anonymization problem is viewed as a clustering problem. Clustering-based approaches [5,36,25,41] search a cluster with k-records.

Differential Privacy [12,13] is a notion of privacy for perturbative methods based on the statistical distance between two database tables differing by at most one element. The basic idea is that, regardless of background knowledge, an adversary with access to the data set draws the same conclusions, whether a person's data are included in the data set. That is, a person's data has an insignificant effect on the processing of a query. Differential privacy is mainly studied in relation to perturbation methods[14,15,16] in an interactive setting. Attempts to apply differential privacy to search queries were discussed in [20]. Li et al. proposed a matrix mechanism [24] applicable to predicate counting queries under a differential privacy setting. Computational relaxations of differential privacy had been discussed in [30,28,17].

Another approach for quantifying privacy leakage is an information-theoretic definition proposed by Clarkson and Schneider [9]. They modeled an anonymizer as a program that receives two inputs: a user's query and a database response to the query. The program acted as a noisy communication channel and produced an anonymized response as output. Hsu et al. provides a generalized notion [18] in decision theory for making a model of the value of personal information. An alternative model for quantification of personal information is proposed in [6]. In the model, the value of personal information is estimated by the expected cost that the user has to pay for obtaining perfect knowledge from given privacy information. Furthermore, the sensitivity of different attribute values are taken into account in the average benefit and cost models proposed by Chiang et al.[7]. Krause and Horvitz presented utility-privacy tradeoffs in online services [21,22].

The main objective of this paper is to extend k-anonymity definition for a multi-party service model. We propose a new adversary model and a solution to obtain an anonymization table satisfying a new privacy definition.

3 Privacy Notion

In this section, two major notions of privacy are introduced and a privacy requirement for general cases is defined.

3.1 k-Anonymity

A database table T in which the attributes of each clients are denoted in one record is in the public domain and an attacker obtains the table and tries to distinguish the record of an individual. Suppose that a database table T has m records and n attributes $\{A_1, \ldots, A_n\}$. Each record $\mathbf{a^i} = (a_1^i, \ldots, a_n^i)$ can thus be considered an n-tuple of attribute values, where a_j^i is the value of attribute A_j in record $\mathbf{a^i}$. The database table T itself can thus be regarded as the set of records $T = \{\mathbf{a^i} : 1 \leq i \leq m\}$. The definition of k-anonymity is as follows;

Definition 1. (k-Anonymity)[31] A table T is said to have k-anonymity if and only if each n-tuple of attribute values $\mathbf{a} \in T$ appears at least k times in T.

3.2 l-Diversity

The definition of k-anonymity does not on its own encompass the concept of an adversary who has background knowledge that can help them distinguish records [26]. As a result, several extensions to the basic idea have been proposed, including *l-diversity* and recursive (c, l)-*diversity*, as well as other suggestions in [27,34,39]. Some extended variants of *l*-diversity have been proposed; for simplicity of discussions in the paper, we only consider the basic notion *l-diversity*. The definition, *l-diversity* evaluates sensitive attributes in a table T. The definitions are described as follows:

Definition 2. (*l-Diversity*) [26] A database table is said to have *l-diversity* if all groups of data that have the same quasi-identifiers contain at least l values for each sensitive attribute.

3.3   Privacy Requirement

We use a privacy parameter k' for defining a privacy requirement. The objective of the privacy protection method in this paper is that we achieve k'-level privacy for privacy protection of data owners. The k'-level privacy is that an adversary cannot distinguish a person from a group of k' members. If we assume an adversary who only has knowledge about the quasi-identifiers of a victim, the k'-level privacy is equal to k-*anonymity* under the condition $k' = k$. However, where we assume adversaries that have several types of background knowledge, k-*anonymity* is not enough for k'-level privacy. Thus, we require both k'-*anonymity* and k'-*diversity* for k'-level privacy.

4   Service Model

In this section, we explain a service model as an extension for more than three service providers.

4.1   Anonymization Table

A quasi-identifier is an attribute that can be joined with external information to re-identify individual records with sufficiently high probability [10]. Generally, a anonymization table $T = (T^q|T^s)$ consists of two types of information: a subtable of quasi-identifiers T^q and a subtable of sensitive attributes T^s. Since the sensitive attributes represent the essential information with regard to database queries, a generalization method is used to modify (anonymize) T^q in order to prevent the identification of the owners of the sensitive attributes, while retaining the full information in T^s.

4.2   Multi-Party Service Model

We assume a service model as Figure 1. Data owners use two different services A and B. Two data holders, A and B, gather information from data owners and

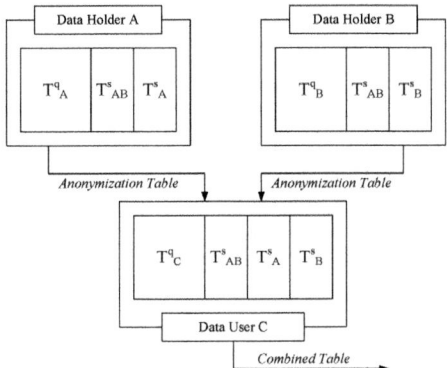

Fig. 1. Service Model

make an anonymization table to identify data owners that use both services. The data owners agree that the anonymized data of them are distributed to other service providers (data users). Communication channels between data holders and data users are securely protected and all data holders and data users are assumed to be honest. The data holders produce anonymization tables $T_A = (T_A^q|T_{AB,A}^s) = (T_A^q|T_{AB}^s|T_A^s)$, and $T_B = (T_B^q|T_{AB,B}^s) = (T_B^q|T_{AB}^s|T_B^s)$ to a data user, respectively. The table T_{AB}^s consists of common sensitive attributes in both T_A and T_B. We accept the case that the table T_{AB}^s is empty, where $T_A^q = T_B^q$. The holders produce the anonymization tables for data user C. Data user C merges two anoymization tables into an anonymization table T_C that includes all values of sensitive attributes T_{AB}^s, T_A^s, and T_B^s. The merged anonymization table is named as a combined table. Data user C uses the combined table for the service. An example service is an analysis service; a data user collects some anonymization tables from several service providers and finds some properties in the combined table.

Quasi-identifiers T_A^q and T_B^q are merged into a new quasi-identifier T_C^q. T_C^q is generated as follows. We define q_A^i is a small block of T_A^q that has the same attributes and s_A^i is columns of sensitive attributes corresponding to q_A^i. The symbol s_{AB}^i is a common sensitive attribute value in T_{AB}^s. The records are merged as $|q_C^g|s_{AB}^h|s_A^i|s_B^j|$ where the condition $s_{AB}^h = s_{AB}^i = s_{AB}^j$ is satisfied. Where $q_A^i \in T_A^q$, $q_B^j \in T_B^q$, and $q_A^i \in q_B^j$, q_B^j is selected as $q_C^g = q_B^j$. If $q_A^i \notin T_B^q$, the merged records are $|q_C^g(= q_A^i)|s_{AB}^h|s_A^i| * |$, where the symbol $*$ is an empty value. Similarly, records is merged as $|q_C^g(= q_B^i)|s_{AB}^h| * |s_B^j|$ where $q_B^i \notin T_A^q$. Example tables are shown in Figure 2. An adversary obtains the combined table and tries to find the record of a victim from the table. For example, if the adversary knows quasi-identifiers, as "1985, Male, 0124*, and Europe", and two sensitive attributes, as "Weight = Slim" and "Commute = Walk", for a victim, then the adversary can find that the second record is for the victim and the disease is "Chest Pain".

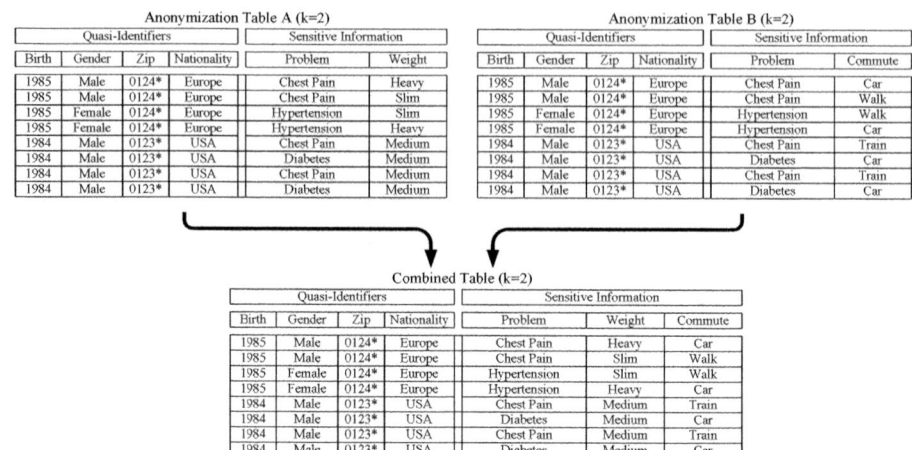

Fig. 2. Example Table

5   Proposal

In this section, we present a new adversary model for multi-service providers setting and anonymization methods for protecting the data holder's privacy.

5.1   Adversary Model

If we consider the existing adversary model and that the anonymization tables produced by the service providers satisfy k'-level privacy, the combined table also satisfies k'-level privacy. However, we have to consider another type of adversary in our new service model. In our service model, the combined table includes many sensitive attributes; thus, the adversary may distinguish a data owner using background knowledge about combinations of sensitive attribute values of the data owner. If the adversary finds a combination of known sensitive attributes only on one record, the adversary can obtain information; the record is a data owner that the adversary knows, and the remaining sensitive attributes of the data owner. We model the above type of a new adversary as follows;

π-*knowledge Adversary Model.* An Adversary knows certain π sensitive attributes $\{s_1^i, ..., s_j^i, ..., s_\pi^i\}$ of a victim i. Thus, the adversary can distinguish the victim from an anonymization table where only one record has any combinations (maximum π-tuple) of attributes $\{s_1^i, ..., s_j^i, ..., s_\pi^i\}$.

Our goal is that the combined table satisfies k'-level privacy against the π-*knowledge adversary.*

5.2   Approach

In this section, we consider effective approaches to achieve k'-level privacy against the π-*knowledge adversary.* The table includes three sensitive attributes, where two data holders produce an anonymization table and each anonymization table has two sensitive attributes where one of the attributes is common to another anonymization table. We assume that the generalization of values in sensitive attributes is not accepted. There are two strategies for modifying the combined table: modification of quasi-identifiers and modification of sensitive attributes.

Modification of Quasi-identifiers. The first attempt is to modify quasi-identifiers of the combined table. The data user generates the merged table from two anonymization tables as follows. First, the data user simply merges the records in two tables as $|q_C^g|s_{AB}^h|s_A^i|s_B^j|$. Then, the data user modifies q_C^q to satisfy the following condition, where θ is the total number of sensitive attributes in the merged table.

CONDITION FOR k'-LEVEL PRIVACY. For any tuple of p attribute values in any record ($1 \le p \le \pi$), at least k' records that have the same tuple of the attribute values exist in a table, and at least k' different records exist in a block that has the same values of quasi-identifiers.

For example, in Figure 2, 2-level privacy is achieved against an adversary who knows the sensitive attributes *weight* and *commute*, where the quasi-identifier *gender* is generalized to "*". However, the modification is not effective against an adversary that knows the quasi-identifiers "1985, Male, 0124*, and Europe", and two sensitive attributes, as "Problem = Chest Pain" and "Weight = Slim", for a victim. At least two records for any pair where two attribute values are the same and the remaining attribute is different is needed for 2-level privacy against any 2-knowledge adversary in this example. Thus, it is difficult for this approach to apply to a small combined table.

Modification of Sensitive Attributes. The second approach is to modify sensitive attributes in the combined table for the condition. If a sub-table $|s_{AB}^h|s_A^i|s_B^j|$ that consists of sensitive attributes is required to satisfy k'-anonymity for k'-level privacy. Some sensitive attribute values are removed from the table and changed to * to satisfy k'-level privacy. Note that we do not accept that all sensitive attributes are * due to avoiding no information record.

We can combine both approaches for more efficient anonymization of the table. Figure 3 is an example of 2-level privacy tables using two approaches. Any 2-knowledge adversary can distinguish one record from the table.

5.3   Algorithm for Modification

An algorithm that find k'-level privacy is executed as follows;

1. The algorithm generalize quasi-identifiers to satisfy the condition that each group of the same quasi-identifiers has at least $\pi \times k'$ records.
2. The algorithm generates all tuples of π sensitive attributes in the table.
3. For a tuple, the algorithm finds all records that have the same sensitive attributes as the tuple or has * for sensitive attributes and make them a group. We define the number of the sensitive attributes in the group is θ. The algorithm generates a partial table that consists of $\theta - \pi$ sensitive attributes and checks whether the partial table has at least k' different combinations of sensitive attributes.

Quasi-Identifiers				Sensitive Information		
Birth	Gender	Zip	Nationality	Problem	Weight	Commute
1985	*	0124*	Europe	Chest Pain	Heavy	Car
1985	*	0124*	Europe	*	*	Walk
1985	*	0124*	Europe	Hypertension	Slim	Walk
1985	*	0124*	Europe	*	*	Car
1984	Male	0123*	USA	*	*	Train
1984	Male	0123*	USA	Diabates	*	Car
1984	Male	0123*	USA	Chest Pain	Medium	*
1984	Male	0123*	USA	Diabetes	Medium	Car

Fig. 3. Example of k'-Level Privacy Table

4. If the partial table does not satisfy the above condition, the algorithm picks a record from other groups that have different tuples of π sensitive attributes, and changes the π sensitive attributes to $*$. The algorithm executes this step until the partial table has up to π different combinations of sensitive attributes.
5. The algorithm executes step 3 and step 4 for all tuples of π sensitive attributes in the table.

6   Concluding Remarks

In this paper, we considered a new service model that involves more than two data holders and a data user, and proposed a new privacy requirement for k'-level privacy based on π-*knowledge adversary*. Furthermore, we discussed feasible approaches to finding a table that satisfies the privacy requirement and showed a concrete algorithm to find the table. We can extend the scheme to a situation where more than two tables are merged and have the same quasi-identifiers and one sensitive attribute. Other privacy notions, such as extensions of l-*diversity*, will be applicable to the scheme. Another remaining issue is to improve the efficiency of the modification algorithm, even though it is a NP-hard problem to find the optimal table. We will consider these remaining issues in future research.

References

1. Adam, N.R., Wortmann, J.C.: Security-control methods for statistical database: a comparative study. ACM Comp. Surv. 21(4), 515–556 (1989)
2. Aggarwal, G., Feder, T., Kenthapadi, K., Motwani, R., Panigrahy, R., Thomas, D., Zhu, A.: Anonymizing Tables. In: Eiter, T., Libkin, L. (eds.) ICDT 2005. LNCS, vol. 3363, pp. 246–258. Springer, Heidelberg (2005)
3. Aggarwal, G., Feder, T., Kenthapadi, K., Motwani, R., Panigrahy, R., Thomas, D., Zhu, A.: Approximation algorithms for k-anonymity. Journal of Privacy Technology (2005)
4. Al-Fedaghi, S.S.: Balanced k-anonymity. In: Proc. of WASET, vol. 6, pp. 179–182 (2005)
5. Byun, J.-W., Kamra, A., Bertino, E., Li, N.: Efficient k-anonymity using clustering technique. In: Proc. of the International Conference on Database Systems for Advanced Applications, pp. 188–200 (2007)

6. Chiang, Y.C., Hsu, T.-S., Kuo, S., Wang, D.-W.: Preserving confidentially when sharing medical data. In: Proc. of Asia Pacific Medical Information Conference (2000)
7. Chiang, Y.-T., Chiang, Y.-C., Hsu, T.-S., Liau, C.-J., Wang, D.-W.: How Much Privacy? – A System to Safe Guard Personal Privacy While Releasing Databases. In: Alpigini, J.J., Peters, J.F., Skowron, A., Zhong, N. (eds.) RSCTC 2002. LNCS (LNAI), vol. 2475, pp. 226–233. Springer, Heidelberg (2002)
8. Ciriani, V., De Capitani di Vimercati, S., Foresti, S., Samarati, P.: k-anonymous data mining: A survey. In: Privacy-Preserving Data Mining: Models and Algorithms. Springer, Heidelberg (2008)
9. Clarkson, M.R., Schneider, F.B.: Quantification of integrity. In: Proc. of 23rd IEEE Computer Security Foundations Symposium, pp. 28–43. IEEE (2010)
10. Dalenius, T.: Finding a needle in a haystack —or identifying anonymous census record. Journal of Official Statistics 2(3), 329–336 (1986)
11. Duncan, G., Lambert, D.: The risk of disclosure for microdata. J. Buisiness & Economic Statistics 7, 207–217 (1989)
12. Dwork, C.: Differential Privacy. In: Bugliesi, M., Preneel, B., Sassone, V., Wegener, I. (eds.) ICALP 2006, Part II. LNCS, vol. 4052, pp. 1–12. Springer, Heidelberg (2006)
13. Dwork, C.: Differential Privacy: A Survey of Results. In: Agrawal, M., Du, D.-Z., Duan, Z., Li, A. (eds.) TAMC 2008. LNCS, vol. 4978, pp. 1–19. Springer, Heidelberg (2008)
14. Dwork, C., Kenthapadi, K., McSherry, F., Mironov, I., Naor, M.: Our data, Ourselves: Privacy via Distributed Noise Generation. In: Vaudenay, S. (ed.) EUROCRYPT 2006. LNCS, vol. 4004, pp. 486–503. Springer, Heidelberg (2006)
15. Dwork, C., McSherry, F., Nissim, K., Smith, A.: Calibrating Noise to Sensitivity in Private Data Analysis. In: Halevi, S., Rabin, T. (eds.) TCC 2006. LNCS, vol. 3876, pp. 265–284. Springer, Heidelberg (2006)
16. Dwork, C., Rothblum, G.N., Vadhan, S.: Boosting and differential privacy. In: Proc. of IEEE FOCS 2010, pp. 51–60 (2010)
17. Groce, A., Katz, J., Yerukhimovich, A.: Limits of Computational Differential Privacy in the Client/Server Setting. In: Ishai, Y. (ed.) TCC 2011. LNCS, vol. 6597, pp. 417–431. Springer, Heidelberg (2011)
18. Hsu, T.-S., Liau, C.-J., Wang, D.-W., Chen, J.K.-P.: Quantifying Privacy Leakage Through Answering Database Queries. In: Chan, A.H., Gligor, V.D. (eds.) ISC 2002. LNCS, vol. 2433, pp. 162–176. Springer, Heidelberg (2002)
19. Iyengar, V.S.: Transforming data to satisfy privacy constraints. In: Proc. of ACM SIGKDD 2002, pp. 279–288. ACM (2002)
20. Kodeswaran, P., Viegas, E.: Applying differential privacy to search queries in a policy based interactive framework. In: Proc. of PAVLAD 2009, pp. 25–32. ACM (2009)
21. Krause, A., Horvitz, E.: A utility-theoretic approach to privacy and personalization. In: Proc. of AAAI 2008, vol. 2, pp. 1181–1188 (2008)
22. Krause, A., Horvitz, E.: A utility-theoretic approach to privacy in online services. Journal of Artificial Intelligence Research 39, 633–662 (2010)
23. LeFevre, K., DeWitt, D.J., Ramakrishnan, R.: Mondrian multidimensional k-anonymity. In: Proc. of the 22nd International Conference on Data Engineering (ICDE 2006), pp. 25–35. IEEE (2006)
24. Li, C., Hay, M., Rastogi, V., Miklau, G., McGregor, A.: Optimizing linear counting queries under differential privacy. In: Proc. of PODS 2010, pp. 123–134. ACM (2010)

25. Lin, J.-L., Wei, M.-C.: An efficient clustering method for k-anonymization. In: Proc. of the 2008 International Workshop on Privacy and Anonymity in Information Society (PAIS 2008), pp. 46–50. ACM (2008)

26. Machanavajjhala, A., Gehrke, J., Kifer, D.: l-diversity: Privacy beyond k-anonymity. In: Proc. of ICDE 2006, pp. 24–35 (2006)

27. Machanavajjhala, A., Gehrke, J., Kifer, D.: t-closeness: Privacy beyond k-anonymity and l-diversity. In: Proc. of ICDE 2007, pp. 106–115 (2007)

28. McGregor, A., Mironov, I., Pitassi, T., Reingold, O., Talwar, K., Vadhan, S.: The limits of two-party differential privacy. In: Proc. of IEEE FOCS 2010, pp. 81–90 (2010)

29. Meyerson, A., Williams, R.: On the complexity of optimal k-anonymity. In: Proc. of PODS 2004, pp. 223–228 (2004)

30. Mironov, I., Pandey, O., Reingold, O., Vadhan, S.: Computational Differential Privacy. In: Halevi, S. (ed.) CRYPTO 2009. LNCS, vol. 5677, pp. 126–142. Springer, Heidelberg (2009)

31. Samarati, P.: Protecting respondents' identities in microdata release. IEEE Trans. on Knowledge and Data Engineering 13(6), 1010–1027 (2001)

32. Samarati, P., Sweeney, L.: Generalizing data to provide anonymity when disclosing information. In: Proc. of the 17th ACM SIGACT-SIGMOD-SIGART Symposium on Principles of Database Systems (PODS 1998), p. 188 (1998)

33. Sun, X., Li, M., Wang, H., Plank, A.: An efficient hash-based algorithm for minimal k-anonymity. In: ACSC 2008: Proceedings of the Thirty-First Australasian Conference on Computer Science, pp. 101–107 (2008)

34. Sun, X., Wang, H., Li, J., Truta, T.M., Li, P.: (p^+, α)-sensitive k-anonymity: a new enhanced privacy protection model. In: Proc. of CIT 2008, pp. 59–64 (2008)

35. Sweeney, L.: Achieving k-anonymity privacy protection using generalization and suppression. J. Uncertainty, Fuzziness, and Knowledge-Base Systems 10(5), 571–588 (2002)

36. Truta, T.M., Campan, A.: K-anonymization incremental maintenance and optimization techniques. In: Proceedings of the 2007 ACM Symposium on Applied Computing (SAC 2007), pp. 380–387. ACM (2007)

37. Truta, T.M., Vinay, B.: Privacy protection: p-sensitive k-anonymity property. In: Proc. of ICDE 2006, pp. 94–103 (2006)

38. Willenborg, L., de Waal, T.: Elements of Statistical Disclosure Control. LNS, vol. 155. Springer, Heidelberg (2001)

39. Wong, R.C.-W., Li, J., Fu, A.W.-C., Wang, K.: (α, k)-anonymity: an enhanced k-anonymity model for privacy preserving data publishing. In: Proc. of ACM SIGKDD 2006, pp. 754–759 (2006)

40. Xu, J., Wang, W., Pei, J., Wang, X., Shi, B., Fu, A.W.-C.: Utility-based anonymization using local recoding. In: Proc. of ACM SIGKDD 2006, pp. 785–790. ACM (2006)

41. Zhu, H., Ye, X.: Achieving k-Anonymity via a Density-Based Clustering Method. In: Dong, G., Lin, X., Wang, W., Yang, Y., Yu, J.X. (eds.) APWeb/WAIM 2007. LNCS, vol. 4505, pp. 745–752. Springer, Heidelberg (2007)

A Noise-Tolerant Enhanced Classification Method for Logo Detection and Brand Classification

Yu Chen and Vrizlynn L.L. Thing[*]

Institute for Infocomm Research
1 Fusionopolis Way, 138632, Singapore
{ychen,vriz}@i2r.a-star.edu.sg

Abstract. This paper introduces a Noise-Tolerant Enhanced Classification (N-TEC) approach to monitor and prevent the increasing online counterfeit product trading attempts and frauds. The proposed approach is able to perform an automatic logo image classification at a fast speed on realistic and noisy product pictures. The novel contribution is three-fold: (i) design of a self adjustable cascade classifier training approach to achieve strong noise tolerance in training, (ii) design of a Stage Selection Optimization (SSO) method which is compatible with the training approach to improve the classification speed and the detection accuracy, (iii) development of an automatic classification system which achieves promising logo detection and brand classification results.

Keywords: boosting, cascade classifiers, noise tolerant, logo detection, brand classification.

1 Introduction

With the booming e-commerce market, the increasing online product fraud cases is drawing significant attentions [1][2]. Examples of online product frauds include trading counterfeits of luxury or well-recognized products with misleading advertisements. Currently, text based searching methods are used to detect those illegal online trading activities. However, those methods may fail due to the avoidance of using brand-related words in the product descriptions. To protect the producers' interests, the brands' reputations and to prevent illegal trading of counterfeit products, an automatic logo detection system is essential. Such a system is expected to identify if a seller is trying to sell products which belong to a brand of interest, even if the seller does not mention any brand related descriptions in the corresponding web pages.

Although the Adaptive Boosting (Adaboost) [3][4] based Viola-Jones approach [5][6] [7][8] is designed as a general purpose pattern detection approach [9], it suffers from the low tolerance to noise effects in the training datasets, which is a very likely problem in the applications of logo image detection or

---

[*] Corresponding author.

T.-h. Kim et al. (Eds.): SecTech 2011, CCIS 259, pp. 31–42, 2011.
© Springer-Verlag Berlin Heidelberg 2011

brand classification [10][11]. Our proposed logo classification system enhances the Viola-Jones training approach with the extended feature pool [13] to reduce or eliminate the negative impact of the noise in the training datasets, while generating fast and accurate clusters for the applications of the logo detection and brand classification.

The rest of the paper is organized as follows. In Section 2, we provide a review of the Viola-Jones approach and an introduction to the logo detection and brand classification problems. The system design is introduced in Section 3. The experiments and results are presented in Section 4. The conclusion and future work are presented in Section 5 and 6, respectively.

2   Research Background

To address the research background and significance of this paper, a review of the Viola-Jones approach and an introduction to logo detection and brand classification are presented in this section.

2.1   Introduction to Logo Detection and Brand Classification

The differences between the logo detection and the other popular detection applications such as face are addressed here to illustrate the necessity and significance of this research. The logo detection here is defined as the application of the pattern detection on the arbitrary images for obtaining the information on the existences and the locations of the product logo in interest. The desired logo detection approach should be able to train and detect any brand logo, e.g. Louis Vuitton, Chanel, and Gucci with affordable computation costs and acceptable detection accuracy. The expected detectable product logo should have relatively fixed appearances in shape, curvature and intensity contrast.

The brand classification targeted in this research is based on the logo image detection. The image could be classified into a certain brand if one or more associated logo regions are detected. For fraud prevention in E-Commerce, the target/input images could be any arbitrary image. The brand classification can be considered as a rare event detection and has a high demand of low false positive rates.

Although, the Viola-Jones approach can perform a fast and accurate detection in terms of False Positive (FP) [12], its performance degrades significantly on training with the noisy datasets [14]. For most brand logos, the training logo image dataset has larger intra-class variations than the training datasets for other popular objects such as face.

Logos can be produced with a wide range of materials such as fabrics, leathers and metal. Therefore, the intra-class variations on the textures, intensities and logo design details can be significantly large.

As claimed in [14], the cascade of classifiers is trained using a set of predefined training constraints for each of the stage classifier. Such a cascade training scheme is efficient for most of the training tasks such as training with conventional face datasets. When processing with datasets with considerably large intra-class variations or class noise (mis-labeled), such a cascade training method often falls into an extreme stage classifier training situation which accumulates many weak classifiers without improvement on the results. Such a situation may prevent the training completion or lead to over-fitting.

In this research, the expected logo detection system should work for a wide range of the logo images in training and detection. The training approach is expected to support the noisy datasets and generate results with satisfactory performances in detection. Meanwhile, the training performance on the less noisy or noise-free datasets should not be affected. Thus, we propose a Noise-Tolerant Enhanced Classification (N-TEC) system which is robust to the noisy training datasets and can train the less-noisy or noise-free datasets with similar performance as the classic Viola-Jones approach.

3   The Design of the N-TEC Training Approach

The design of the N-TEC system is motivated by the observation that the training results of Viola-Jones approach on the noisy datasets can be improved significantly by adjusting the pre-set fixed constraints for training some of the stage classifiers. When processing noisy training data with the Viola-Jones approach, with fixed and pre-set stage training constraints, the stage training process is very likely to encounter severe difficulty in finding a combination of weak classifiers to fulfil training conditions. When the system falls into such an extreme stage training situation, the training algorithm may keep adding features to improve the stage performance with minimal effect, while loading extreme heavy computation burden on the detection/operation phase.

The proposed training approach has the capability to detect the extreme training situation and adjust the training constraints adaptively in order to trim the noisy training data and thus, continue the training with the trimmed and less noisy data. The implemented N-TEC training approach is able to perform the automatic training, and the system is able to deal with training dataset with more severe noise effects. Next, we present our design of the N-TEC cascade training approach.

3.1   N-TEC Cascade Training System

In N-TEC, the system firstly retrieves the user defined initial training constraints as the required stage performances in terms of TP and FP rates. These base training constraints can be adjusted adaptively during the training process. If previous trained out stage classifiers exist, the system loads the classifiers and calculates the performance indicated by the TP and FP rates corresponding to the previous stages; otherwise, the training starts from the initial stage.

If the cascade performances reach the pre-defined performance requirements, the system would generate the final cascade classifier. Otherwise, it starts the training process for a new stage classifier generation.

3.2 Stage Training Approach

Algorithm 1 shows the stage training algorithm/pseudo code for the N-TEC stage training approach. Table 1 is the glossary table for Algorithm 1.

Table 1. Glossary table for Algorithm 1

Term	Definition
P	Positive training dataset
N	Negative training dataset
R	Stage training constraints, e.g. minimum Tp and iteration amount
C_i	Stage/strong classifier with a index as i
c_{ij}	Weak classifier of stage classifier C_i with a index as j
R_{adp}	Updated traiing constraints which is adaptively adjusted from R

Algorithm 1. The N-TEC stage classifier training algorithm
1: Provide positive training data P, negative training data N, and stage performance requirement set R.
2: The output is a strong classifier Ci which ensembles a set of weak classifiers c_{i1}, c_{i2}, c_{if}.
3: For j = 1; performances of current strong classifier c_{i1}, c_{i2}, c_{ij} does not meet R; j++.
 3.1: Training cij with Adaboost weak classifier training algorithm;
 3.2: Assemble c_{ij} to C_i;
 3.3: Monitor the training progress with the training adjustment unit (TAU).
 3.4: If TAU triggers the adjusted training process
  3.4.1. Update R with the adaptive adjustment training constraints R_{adp} which is generated by TAU, exit the for loop and restart the training with P, N, Radp.
4: Generate the stage classifier

The original Viola-Jones stage training approach is modified to combine with our training adjustment unit (Section 3.3). The initial stage performance requirements set, R, consists of predefined parameters as the stage training constraints. The weak classifier training (step 3.1) is performed with the feature selection, classifier design and weight updates schemes from Adaboost. For each iteration the weak classifier training, the progress is monitored by the training adjustment unit. The number of the iterations and the performance of the current assembled classifier are evaluated to determine if the system faces an extreme training condition. If so, the adjustment unit would generate the adjusted training requirements R_{adp}, based on the current training progress. If the adjustment unit activates the adjusted training, the system replaces R with R_{adp} and restarts the stage training. Otherwise the stage training will continue until the stage classifier is generated.

3.3 Training Adjustment Unit

The proposed training adjustment unit (TAU) is to monitor the progress of the stage training and generate the adjusted training constraints. Table 2 and Algorithm 2 show the glossary table and design algorithm for TAU, respectively.

Table 2. Glossary table for Algrithm 2

Term	Definition
TPs	Set of TP rates as tp_1, $tp_2...tp_i$ for current stage classifier C_i as c_1, $c_2...c_i$
FPs	Set of FP rates as fp_1, $fp_2...fp_i$ for current stage classifier C_i as c_1, $c_2...c_i$
S	Defined as {TPs, FPs}
TP_{min}	The minimum TP as stage training requirement
FP_{max_adap} and TP_{min_adap}	The adaptively adjusted training constraints for maximum FP and minimum TP, respectively
dif_{tp-fp_i}	The difference between TP and FP rates for the ith feature of the stage classifier
dif_{max}	The biggest difference between TP and FP rates
fp_{max_dif}	The false positive rate which is corresponding to the weak classifier that gives dif_{max}
L1 and L2	The rigid and the relaxed thresholds for the amount of iterations, repetitively
T1 and T2	The thresholds of the differences on TP and FP rates of weak classifiers, respectively
N_{gap}	The amount of iterations used to trace back for the weak classifier trained previously
T_{fp}	The threshold to determine if the FP_{max_adap} will be too lenient
$Incr_{factor\_fp}$	The factor to increase the fp_{max_dif} in order to obtain FP_{max_adap}
$Decr_{factor\_tp}$	The factor to decrease the TP_{min} in order to obtain TP_{min_adap}

```
Algorithm 2. Training Adjustment Unit
1: Provide the training progress parameters set S, the current
training requirement TP_min
2: Outputs: FP_max_adap, TP_min_adap will be generated,
if the extreme training condition is detected
3: For n = 1;  n <= i ; n++ //n is the index of the current/latest
   dif_tp-fp_n=tp_n-fp_n;
4: Calculate  dif_max , as dif_max = Max( DIF_tp-fp_n );
where DIF_tp-fp_n is set of dif_tp-fp_1, dif_tp-fp_2...dif_tp-fp_n
and update fp_max_dif
5:if ( ( (fp_n  fp_n-N_gap<=T2)  && (tp_n  tp_n-N_gap  <= T1 && n >= L2)
|| n >=L1 )
//detect the extreme training conditions by evaluate the current
TP and FP rates and the number of iterations
```

```
//generate the adaptive training constraints adjustments
5.1:If the adjusted false positive training constraints is not
too lenient  fp_max_dif  <= T_fp
    Adjusted TP rate remain the same with current training setup
    as TP_min_adap = TP_min;
    Increase the training constraints for the FP rate:
    FP_max_adap  = fp_max_dif  * Incr_factor_fp;
5.2: Otherwise // the adjusted FP constraint is set too lenient,
the adjustment is focused on releasing constraint on TP rate
    TP_min_adap = TP_min * Decr_factor_tp;
    FP_max_adap = fp_max_dif;
5.3:trigger the adjusted training
```

The TAU starts by searching for the iteration which yields the best performance, by calculating the differences between the TP and FP rates for each weak classifier (iteration). The weak classifier that gives the biggest difference between the TP and FP rates can be considered as the one yielding the best performance. The fp_{max_dif} is the false positive rate associated with that iteration. The extreme training situation is detected by evaluating the training performance of the current stage and the number of processed iteration. The evaluation is conducted by calculating the differences/progresses in terms of the TP and FP rates between current iteration with the iteration which is N_{gap} times before.

Through observation, for most of the successful stage training with moderate stage training constraints in TP and FP rates, such as minimum stage TP = 0.995 and the maximum stage FP = 0.5, the number of iterations should not be too large. Otherwise, it is very likely that the iteration number may keep increasing without making meaningful progress in the TP or FP performance, or the large number of the gathered weak classifiers lead to over fitting, especially when trained with noisy datasets. Thus, one sufficient condition to indicate that the system has fallen into the extreme training situation is that the iteration count exceeded a predefined threshold L1. The other condition is to evaluate the training progress in terms of the TP and FP rates when the number of iterations is greater than a lower threshold L2. The current iteration is compared with the iteration N_{gap} times ahead, if the performance associated with the current iteration is not meaningfully improved, this means that the differences in TP and FP are less than the predefined thresholds T1, and T2, respectively. The stage training can then be considered as having entered the extreme training situation.

Once the extreme training situation is detected, a set of adjusted training constraints for re-training the current stage classifier will be generated. The purpose of generating the adjusted training constraints is to identify the iteration with the best performance and exclude the subsequent less efficient ones. Recall that the more the iterations/features are included in the stage classifier, the heavier the computation burden the operation side will incur. Due to the decrease in each iteration's TP and FP rates at different speeds, it is possible that the

TP rate may drop faster than the drop in the FP rate when processing the noisy datasets. Either the TP or the FP rate can be a sufficient factor to search for the iteration with the best performance. Thus, the TAU obtains the iteration of interest by searching for the biggest difference between TP and FP rates at all iterations. The adjusted training requirements are then generated based on this identified iteration's TP and FP rates.

When starting the training with the adaptively adjusted requirements, the entire set of positive training data will be evaluated by the existing stage classifiers. Those positive samples that fail to pass through the existing classifiers will be excluded from the subsequent training stages. The majority of positive training samples can be grouped as qualified training samples by passing through all the trained stages. On the other hand, a small portion of positive training samples which fail to pass the trained stages is considered to be unqualified positive training samples or noise. This systematic process of adjusted training continues until the system passes through the extreme training conditions. Through experiments, we found out that such a process can work very well as a data cleaning scheme on the noisy training data.

The adaptive training requirements are obtained by increasing the FP rate first. As mentioned above, the adjusted training may keep repeating and the adjusted FP rate may keep increasing. There are two situations that need to be considered when generating the adaptive training constraints based on the TP and FP rates from the iteration of interest. If the adjusted FP rate is not too lenient which can be determined by $fp_{max\_dif} <= T_{fp}$, the FP rate increases to $fp_{max\_dif} * Incr_{factor\_fp}$, while the minimum TP rate for re-training remain the same with current one. On the other hand, if fp_{max_dif} is greater than T_{fp}, this means that the TP rate should be decreased to trim more positive data. In this situation, the adjusted TP is obtained by increasing the current minimum TP rate to $TP_{min\_adap} = TP_{min} * Decr_{factor\_tp}$; and the adjusted FP is obtained through $FP_{max\_adap} = fp_{max\_dif}$.

3.4 Stage Selection Optimization

Like the Viola-Jones training approach, the N-TEC training approach also trains each stage classifier independently. Thus, we propose a Stage Selection Optimization (SSO) method to further improve the detection speed and the accuracy of the trained out cascade classifiers.

Some of the trained out stage classifiers yield a lower TP rate with higher FP rates. Those stage classifiers are trained to trim the noisy training data. In the detection phase, these classifiers would increase the computation complexity significantly. Thus, a stage selection optimization method is needed. After the cascade classifier reaches a desired training requirement, the stages which give undesired performances would be deleted. An undesired stage performance is defined as $FP\_stage > maxfalsealarm * 1.618$ && $TP\_stage < TP_{min}/1.618$, where the FP_stage and Tp_stage refers to the stage FP and TP rate, respectively. maxfalsealarm and TP_{min} refer to the predefined stage training constraints on the maximum FP rate and minimum TP rate, respectively.

Since the cascade TP and FP rates would both be increased after the removal of the stages, the remaining stage classifiers would be trained again with the same positive and negative training data. After the stage removal, there would be some remaining noise data in the training dataset. However, the undiscarded stage classifiers can give a good detection performance on the target object. Thus, much of the noise data from the positive training dataset would be filtered out by these remaining stage classifiers. The training constraints are set to be adaptive based on these remaining stage classifiers. If the filtered out positive training data is greater than 15% percent of the total data, one can assume that the positive training dataset has a large portion of noisy data. Otherwise, one can assume that the positive training data is less noisy. We set rigid training constraints if the training data is less noisy. Otherwise, less rigid training constraints are applied.

To accelerate the detection speed of the trained out N-TEC classifiers, the sequence of the stages are re-arranged so that the stages with fewer features are set to be ahead of the stages with more features. The insight of the scheme is that, most of the sub-images on the subject image would be processed with first few stages. The deeper the stage is, the less sub-images it could face. Thus, the first stages with fewer features can reject most of the sub-windows with lighter computation burden. Because each of the stages is trained independently, there is little difference in the performances of TP and FP rate between the re-arranged classifiers with the original ones. The processing speed is significantly improved by such a scheme.

4   Experiments of Logo Detection and Brand Classification

We conducted experiments by applying our N-TEC method to two logo image detection and brand classification problems, so as to evaluate the performance based on the detection results. We also carried out comparisons between the N-TEC and the modified Viola-Jones approach. In order to perform the training on the noisy logo image dataset, the Viola-Jones approach [13] is modified to use a fixed amount of iterations for training each of the stage classifiers instead of using the fixed predefined training constraints on the expected stage TP and FP rates.

The targeted brands are Louis Vuitton(LV) and Chanel. Table 3 gives the amount of training and testing samples used in our experiments. The positive training images are randomly collected on-line from the images of products including bags, shoes, shirts, etc. The negative images are those that do not have the target logo.

The testing dataset were collected from the Ebay website. To make the test data collection non-subjective and more realistic, we used the Ebay search engine to search for the name of each brand and obtain the first 200 images which contain the target logo in each search.

Among the positive images for the two brands, the positive data for LV has large intra-class variations. The Chanel positive training images were shown to

Table 3. The training and testing datasets used in the logo detection

Brand	Positive training samples	Negative training samples	Testing samples
Louis Vuitton	2848	5229	200
Chanel	1552	5228	200

be less noisy, as most of the Chanel products have one or more large logos built on the metal or leathers which enable relatively rigid logo appearances.

For training LV model under the N-TEC approach, good performances are given by training using a minimum TP rate of 99.5% and maximum FP rate of 0.5. For training both brand models using the modified Viola-Jones approach, good performances are given by the minimum TP rate of 99.5% and iterations count of 10. As the training data for Chanel can be considered as less noisy, good performances are provided by using N-TEC with constraints of a minimum TP rate of 99.8% and maximum FP rate of 0.05 and using the modified Viola-Jones approach with constraints of a minimum TP rate of 99.8% and iterations of 20. For a fair comparison, the training of N-TEC and modified Viola-Jones were terminated when the cascade classifiers reach a FP rate of $< 1 * 10^{-6}$.

Table 4 and 5 show the performance comparisons between N-TEC and the modified Viola-Jones on the logo detection for LV and Chanel, respectively. There were a total of 1603 and 331 logo patches on the 200 testing images for LV and Chanel, respectively.

Table 4. The performances comparison between N-TEC and modified Viola-Jones on the logo detection for Louis Vuitton

Classifier	TP rate in training	FP rate in training	TP rate in testing	FP rate in testing
N-TEC	92.4860%	2.73898e-7	54.46%	0/125080796
Modified Viola-Jones	96.6643%	5.83764e-6 * 0.0000	51.22%	1047/125080796

The dimensions of the collected LV testing images vary from 222 * 166 to 800 * 800. The number of sub-windows generated from the sliding window is 125,080,796. The dimensions of the collected Chanel testing images vary from 240 * 320 to 800 * 700. The number of sub-windows generated from the sliding window is 141,285,971.

From the comparisons, it clearly shows that, N-TEC out-performs the modified Viola-Jones on the training datasets of LV which suffers from the attribute noise. The performances of both the approaches on Chanel are close. With the given training constraints, N-TEC completed the training without activating the adaptive training approach and it performed similarly as the Viola-Jones training approach in this case.

Table 5. The performances comparison between N-TEC and modified Viola-Jones on the logo detection for Chanel

Classifier	TP rate in training	FP rate in training	TP rate in testing	FP rate in testing
N-TEC	98.8402%	5.31029e-006 * 0.018122	51.66%	8/141285971
Modified Viola-Jones	98.8402%	1.15164e-005 * 0.004250	51.36%	8/141285971

In terms of the classification performance which is more important in the application of E-commerce frauds detection, those experiments show promising results as detailed in the Table 6. A brand classification result is considered as a true positive if one or more logo is correctly detected within the target image. We count every FP detection result for a false positive classification. The classification results can be further improved with larger training datasets. The illustrated low FP experimental results can be further improved by training the cascade to reach a lower FP rate in training.

Table 6. The classification results from N-TEC on LV and Chanel testing datasets

Classification rate with N-TEC	LV	Chanel
TP classification	149/200	140/200
FP classification	0/200	8/200

5   Conclusion

In this paper, we introduce a Noise-Tolerant Enhanced Classification (N-TEC) system for the logo detection and brand classification. For many brands, the intra-class variations of the logo images are considerably large. Further more, the quality of many realistic product images used in E-Commerce are very low. When trying to perform logo detection or classification on those realistic product images, the training approach should be able to deal with those very noisy training data.

The core idea of the design of N-TEC is to use a self adjustable cascade training approach to achieve strong noise tolerance. In our N-TEC system, a new Training Adjustment Unit (TAU) is proposed to automatically monitor the training progress for training each stage. The TAU is designed to monitor the training and relax the training constraints adaptively when the stage training falls into an extreme training condition. The adjusted constraints for retraining are obtained based on the TP and FP rates of the feature with the best classification performance, in order to trim off the noisy data with the highest confidence and to continue training the subsequent stages with the trimmed and less noisy data.

The SSO method was proposed to remove the stage classifiers with low performance in detection and further improve the detection performance by retraining the remaining classifiers and re-order the sequence of the re-trained cascade classifiers to achieve a faster detection speed.

The experiments and comparisons with the modified Viola-Jones approach were conducted on the logo detection and brand classification. The experimental results show that the N-TEC approach is able to carry out fast and accurate logo detection or brand classification when processing realistic and noisy product images. The brand classification experimental results show promising potential of N-TEC in E-commerce fraud detection.

6 Future Work

We discuss two potential ways to improve N-TEC as future work. First, we plan to introduce more methods as view cues to enhance the feature detection phase. As only the wavelet-like Haar features were used here, some logo images may respond poorly to these features. A fusion of other methods such as the HOG features and binary patterns may improve the performance of the system.

The second direction may be to enhance the system with online or semi-online training. The logo design may vary (from products, time, etc.) and the same appearance of the same logo target may also vary due to different lighting conditions, and skew and rotation effects during image taking. A major difference between training for the logo detection and other pattern detection is the quality of the training datasets. Some training samples are extremely similar which makes the manual data collection a challenge. With the huge image resources available online, most of the data can be collected to enlarge the positive training dataset. However, if many of them are too similar, the enlarged training dataset would not help with the training or detection performance and can add on to the computation burden. Thus, with (semi) online training, the collected positive data can be collected automatically and the collected data can be investigated/tested first to identify similarity.

References

1. International Authentication Association: Counterfeit Statistics (2010),
   http://internationalauthenticationassociation.org/content/
   counterfeit_statistics.php
2. Otim, S., Grover, V.: E-commerce: a brand name's curse. Electronic Markets 20(2), 147–160 (2010)
3. Freund, Y., Schapire, R.E.: A decision-theoretic generalization of on-line learning and an application to boosting. Journal of Computer and System Sciences 55(1), 119–139 (1997)
4. Friedman, J., Hastie, T., et al.: Additive logistic regression: A statistical view of boosting. Annals of Statistics 28(2), 337–374 (2000)
5. Zhang, C., Zhang, Z.: Boosting-Based Face Detection and Adaptation. Synthesis Lectures on Computer Vision. Morgan and Claypool (2010)

6. Zhang, C., Zhang, Z.: A Survey of Recent Advances in Face Detection. Microsoft Research Technical Report, MSR-TR-2010-66 (2010)
7. Castrillon, M., Deniz, O., et al.: A comparison of face and facial feature detectors based on the Viola-Jones general object detection framework. Machine Vision and Applications 22(3), 481–494 (2011)
8. Li, S.Z., Zhang, Z.Q.: FloatBoost learning and statistical face detection. IEEE Transactions on Pattern Analysis and Machine Intelligence 26(9), 1112–1123 (2004)
9. Viola, P., Jones, M.J., et al.: Detecting pedestrians using patterns of motion and appearance. International Journal of Computer Vision 63(2), 153–161 (2005)
10. Mita, T., Kaneko, T., Hori, O.: Joint haar-like features for face detection. In: 10th In ICCV (2005)
11. Viola, P., Platt, J., Zhang, C.: Multiple instance boosting for object detection. In: Advances in Neural Information Processing Systems (2005)
12. Viola, P., Jones, M.J.: Robust real-time face detection. International Journal of Computer Vision 57(2), 137–154 (2004)
13. Lienhart, R., Maydt, J.: An extended set of haar-like features for rapid object detection. In: Proceedings of 2002 International Conference on Image Processing, vol. I, pp. 900–903 (2002)
14. Tuzel, O., Porikli, F., et al.: Pedestrian detection via classification on Riemannian manifolds. IEEE Transactions on Pattern Analysis and Machine Intelligence 30(10), 1713–1727 (2008)
15. EBAY: Images of search results, http://www.ebay.com/
16. Rowley, H.A., Baluja, S., et al.: Neural network-based face detection. IEEE Transactions on Pattern Analysis and Machine Intelligence 20(1), 23–38 (1998)

A Family Constructions of Odd-Variable Boolean Function with Optimum Algebraic Immunity

Yindong Chen

College of Engineering, Shantou University
Shantou, Guangdong, People's Republic of China
ydchen@stu.edu.cn

Abstract. Algebraic immunity is a novel cryptographic criterion proposed to against algebraic attacks. In order to resist algebraic attacks, Boolean functions used in cryptosystem should have high algebraic immunity. This paper generalizes Dalai's and Chen's constructions, and gets a new family constructions for odd-variable Boolean function with optimum algebraic immunity. By employing different transformations of Boolean functions, there would generate different constructions.

Keywords: algebraic attacks, Boolean function, algebraic immunity, recursive construction.

1 Introduction

Algebraic attack became a hot cryptanalysis method in recent years [1, 2, 3, 4, 5, 6, 7, 8]. To implement algebraic attack, attackers firstly construct equation system between the input bits (the secret key bits) and the output bits, then recover the input bits by solving the equation system with efficient methods. By searching low degree annihilator, some LFSR-based stream ciphers such as Toyocrypt, LILI-128 [1], SFINKS [5], etc. were successfully attacked. To resist algebraic attack, a new cryptographic property of Boolean functions which is known as *algebraic immunity* (AI) has been proposed by Meier *et al.* [2]. The AI of a Boolean function expresses its ability to resist standard algebraic attack. Thus the AI of Boolean function used in cryptosystem should be sufficiently high. Courtois and Meier [1,2] showed that, for any n-variable Boolean function, its AI is upper bounded by $\lceil \frac{n}{2} \rceil$. If the bound is achieved, we say the Boolean function have optimum AI. Obviously, a Boolean function with optimum AI has strongest ability to resist standard algebraic attack. Therefore, the construction of Boolean functions with optimum AI is of great importance.

Dalai *et al.* [15, 14] presented Boolean functions with optimum AI in even variables by an recursive construction. It's a second order recursive construction. However, further study [14] showed that the functions are not all balanced. Another class of constructions [16, 17, 18] contains symmetric functions. Being symmetric, they present a risk if attacks using this peculiarity can be found in the future. Moreover, they do not have high nonlinearities either [19]. Li [21, 22, 23] proposed a method to construct all $(2k+1)$-variable Boolean functions with

T.-h. Kim et al. (Eds.): SecTech 2011, CCIS 259, pp. 43–52, 2011.

optimum AI from one such given function. The construction has theoretical sense. Carlet and Feng [24] proposed a well construction based on the Boolean functions' trace representation. Their Boolean functions have not only optimum AI but also high nonlinearity. Furthermore, they also have a good behavior against fast algebraic attacks, at least for small values of the number of variables. The drawback of the construction is the high complexity of the computation for the value of $f(x)$.

Based on Dalai's construction, Chen proposed an improved construction for odd-variables Boolean functions with optimum AI [25]. The constructed Boolean functions not only have optimum AI but also be balanced [25].

In this paper, we generalize Chen's construction and derive a family construction of odd-variable Boolean function with optimum AI. Then by using different special transformations of Boolean functions, there would produce different constructions.

The organization of the paper is as follows. In the following section we give some preliminaries about Boolean functions. In Section III, we present the family construction, and prove that the constructed Boolean functions have optimum AI. Some example construction are to show in Section IV. Section V concludes the paper.

2   Preliminaries

2.1   Boolean Function

Let $\mathbb{F}_2 = \{0, 1\}$ be the finite field with two elements. Then a *Boolean function* in n variables is defined as mapping from $\mathbb{F}_2^n$ into $\mathbb{F}_2$. Denote by B_n the set of all n-variable Boolean functions. A basic representation of a Boolean function $f(x_1, \cdots, x_n)$ is by the output column of its *truth table*, i.e., a binary string of length 2^n,

$$f = [f(0, 0, \cdots, 0), f(1, 0, \cdots, 0), \cdots, f(1, 1, \cdots, 1)].$$

For an n-variables Boolean function f, we define its *support* and *offset* as

$$\text{supp}(f) = \{x \in \mathbb{F}_2^n | f(x) = 1\},$$
$$\text{offset}(f) = \{x \in \mathbb{F}_2^n | f(x) = 0\}.$$

The *Hamming weight* $\text{wt}(f)$ of f is the size of $\text{supp}(f)$, i.e., $\text{wt}(f) = |\text{supp}(f)|$. It counts the number of 1's in the truth table of f. We say f is *balanced*, if the truth table contains an equal number of 1's and 0's, i.e., $|\text{supp}(f)| = |\text{offset}(f)|$, implying $\text{wt}(f) = 2^{n-1}$.

Any Boolean function has another unique representation as a multivariate polynomial over $\mathbb{F}_2$, called the *algebraic normal form* (ANF):

$$f(x_1, \cdots, x_n) = a_0 + \sum_{1 \leq i \leq n} a_i x_i + \sum_{1 \leq i \leq j \leq n} a_{ij} x_i x_j$$
$$+ \cdots + a_{12\cdots n} x_1 x_2 \cdots x_n,$$

where the coefficients $a_0, a_i, a_{ij}, \cdots, a_{12\cdots n} \in \mathbb{F}_2$.

The *algebraic degree* $\deg(f)$ of f is the number of variables in the highest order term with nonzero coefficient.

2.2   Algebraic Immunity of Boolean Function

Definition 1.   *[2] Given $f \in B_n$, we define*

$$\text{Ann}(f) = \{g \in B_n \,|\, f \cdot g = 0\}.$$

Any function $g \in \text{Ann}(f)$ is called an *annihilator* of f.

Definition 2.   *[2] Given $f \in B_n$, we define its algebraic immunity, denote by* $\text{AI}(f)$, *as the minimum degree of all nonzero annihilators of f and of $f + 1$, i.e.,*

$$\text{AI}(f) = \min\{\deg(g)|0 \neq g \in \text{Ann}(f) \cup \text{Ann}(f + 1)\}.$$

For $f \in B_n$, it has been proved that $\text{AI}(f) \leq \lceil \frac{n}{2} \rceil$ [2]. If $\deg(f) = \lceil \frac{n}{2} \rceil$, we say it has optimum AI.

The AI of a Boolean function expresses its ability to resist standard algebraic attack. So, Boolean functions with higher AI (even optimum AI) is preferred in cryptosystem. Note that although AI is not a property that can resist all kinds of algebraic attacks, but clearly still a necessary one.

2.3   The Concatenation Operation of Boolean Function

We can use a binary string of length 2^n to express an n-variable Boolean function, and denote by "$\|$" the concatenation of binary strings.

Proposition 1.   *For $\forall f = f_1 \| f_2$, where $f_1, f_2 \in B_n$,*

  i) $f \in B_{n+1}$, *and* $f = f_1 + x_{n+1}(f_1 + f_2)$;
  ii) *for $\forall g \in \text{Ann}(f)$, decompose it as $g = g_1 \| g_2$ where $g_1, g_2 \in B_n$, then $g_1 \in$* $\text{Ann}(f_1)$ *and* $g_2 \in \text{Ann}(f_2)$.

Proposition 2.   *For $\forall f = f_1 \| f_2 \| f_3 \| f_4$, where $f_1, f_2, f_3, f_4 \in B_n$,*

  i) $f \in B_{n+2}$, *and* $f = f_1 + x_{n+1}(f_1 + f_2) + x_{n+2}(f_1 + f_3) + x_{n+1}x_{n+2}(f_1 + f_2 + f_3 + f_4)$;
  ii) *for $\forall g \in \text{Ann}(f)$, decompose it as $g = g_1 \| g_2 \| g_3 \| g_4$, where $g_1, g_2, g_3, g_4 \in B_n$, then* $g_1 \in \text{Ann}(f_1)$, $g_2 \in \text{Ann}(f_2)$, $g_3 \in \text{Ann}(f_3)$, *and* $g_4 \in \text{Ann}(f_4)$.

2.4   The Transformation of Boolean Function

A transformation t_n for n-variable Boolean function is a mapping from B_n into B_n. and denote by T_n the set of all such t_n. Denote $\mathbf{T} = T_1 \times T_2 \times \cdots$, and $\tau = (t_1, t_2, \cdots) \in \mathbf{T}$, where $t_i \in T_i (i \geq 1)$. For $\forall f \in B_n$, we define

$$\tau(f) = t_n(f).$$

Clearly, τ is a list of transformations with different number of variables. Let $\mathbf{B} = \bigcup_{n \geq 1} B_n$. Here are two simple examples of $\mathbf{T}$:

- identity transformation (τ_{iden}): $f \to f$ $(\forall f \in \mathbf{B})$;
- complement transformation (τ_{comp}): $f \to f + 1$ $(\forall f \in \mathbf{B})$.

For conveniences sometimes, we denote $\bar{f}$ for $\tau_{\mathrm{comp}}(f)$.

Another example a little complex is

$$\tau : \begin{cases} f \to f, & f \in B_n \ (n \text{ even}); \\ f \to f + 1, & f \in B_n \ (n \text{ odd}). \end{cases}$$

Definition 3. *A transformation $\tau \in \mathbf{T}$ is said to be consistent with "$\|$", if and only if for $\forall n > 1$, $\forall f \in B_n$, there is*

$$\tau(f) = \tau(f_1) \| \tau(f_2),$$

where $f = f_1 \| f_2$, and $f_1, f_2 \in B_{n-1}$. Denote by $\mathbf{T}_{\mathrm{C}}$ the set of all transformations that are consistent with "$\|$".

Definition 4. *We say a transformation $\tau \in \mathbf{T}$ preserves AI, if and only if for $\forall n \geq 1$ and $\forall f \in B_n$, there is*

$$\mathrm{AI}\big(\tau(f)\big) = \mathrm{AI}(f).$$

Denote by $\mathbf{T}_{\mathrm{P}}$ the set of all transformations that preserve AI.

We now generalize the concept of composite operation "$\circ$" on $\mathbf{T}$: for $\forall \tau_1, \tau_2 \in \mathbf{T}$, define

$$\tau_1 \circ \tau_2 = (\mathsf{t}_{1,1} \circ \mathsf{t}_{2,1}, \ \mathsf{t}_{1,2} \circ \mathsf{t}_{2,2}, \ \cdots),$$

where $\tau_1 = (\mathsf{t}_{1,1}, \mathsf{t}_{1,2}, \cdots)$ and $\tau_2 = (\mathsf{t}_{2,1}, \mathsf{t}_{2,2}, \cdots)$.

Denote $\mathbf{T}_{\mathrm{CP}} = \mathbf{T}_{\mathrm{C}} \bigcap \mathbf{T}_{\mathrm{P}}$. One can check that $\mathbf{T}_{\mathrm{CP}}$ is closed under the composite operation "$\circ$" and $\tau_{\mathrm{iden}}, \tau_{\mathrm{comp}} \in \mathbf{T}_{\mathrm{CP}}$.

Proposition 3. *For $\forall \tau \in \mathbf{T}_{\mathrm{CP}}$ and $\forall f \in B_n$, let $f = f_1 \| f_2$, $f_1, f_2 \in B_{n-1}$, then*

i) $\tau(f) = \tau(f_1) \| \tau(f_2)$;
ii) $\mathrm{AI}\big(\tau(f)\big) = \mathrm{AI}(f)$.

3   Construction of Odd-Variable Boolean Function with Optimum Algebraic Immunity

Based on the idea of Dalai's construction, a construction for odd-variable Boolean function with optimum AI is proposed as following.

Construction 1

$$\begin{cases} \phi_{2k+1} = \bar{\phi}_{2k-1} \| \bar{\phi}_{2k-1} \| \phi_{2k-1} \| \phi_{2k-1}^1, \\ \phi_{2k+1}^i = \bar{\phi}_{2k-1}^{i-1} \| \bar{\phi}_{2k-1}^i \| \phi_{2k-1}^i \| \phi_{2k-1}^{i+1}, \end{cases}$$

with the base step $\phi_{2k+1}^0 = \phi_{2k+1}$, $\phi_1^j = x_1 + (j \bmod 2)$, $i \geq 1$, $k, j \geq 0$.

The Boolean function ϕ_{2k+1} is proved to have optimum AI and be balanced. Here, we'll generalize the upper construction and get a family constructions. Then, there would be more constructions for odd-variables Boolean function with optimum AI.

Construction 2 *Given* $\tau \in \mathbf{T}_{\mathrm{CP}}$,

$$\begin{cases} \phi_{2k+1} = \tau(\phi_{2k-1})\|\tau(\phi_{2k-1})\|\phi_{2k-1}\|\phi^1_{2k-1}, \\ \phi^i_{2k+1} = \tau(\phi^{i-1}_{2k-1})\|\tau(\phi^i_{2k-1})\|\phi^i_{2k-1}\|\phi^{i+1}_{2k-1}, \end{cases} \tag{1}$$

with the base step $\phi^0_{2k+1} = \phi_{2k+1}$, $\phi^j_1 = x_1+(j \bmod 2)$, $i{\geq}1$, $k,j{\geq}0$.

For convenience in description, we define $\phi^{-1}_{2k+1} = \phi^0_{2k+1} = \phi_{2k+1}$, then the recursion (1) can be simplified as

$$\phi^i_{2k+1} = \tau(\phi^{i-1}_{2k-1})\|\tau(\phi^i_{2k-1})\|\phi^i_{2k-1}\|\phi^{i+1}_{2k-1}. \tag{2}$$

To prove that ϕ_{2k+1} has optimum AI, we need intermediate results. For technical reasons, during our proofs, we will encounter certain situations when the degree of a function is negative. As such functions do not exist, we will replace them by function 0.

Lemma 1. *Assume that the function* $\phi_{2t+1} \in B_{2t+1}$ *has been generated by Construction 2 and* $\mathrm{AI}(\phi_{2t+1})=t+1$ *for* $1{\leq}t{\leq}k$. *If there exists* $g{\in} \mathrm{Ann}\left(\iota(\phi^i_{2k+1})\right)$, $h{\in} \mathrm{Ann}\left(\iota(\phi^{i+1}_{2k+1})\right)$, *such that* $\iota \in \mathbf{T}_{\mathrm{CP}}$, $\deg(g+h){\leq}k-i-1$ *and* $i{\geq}0$, *then* $g = h$.

Proof. We prove it by induction on k.

For the base step $k=1$, it can be easily checked. Now we prove the induction step. Assume that the induction assumption holds until k, we are to prove it for k.

Suppose there's $g{\in} \mathrm{Ann}\left(\iota(\phi^i_{2k+1})\right)$, $h{\in} \mathrm{Ann}\left(\iota(\phi^{i+1}_{2k+1})\right)$, such that $\iota \in \mathbf{T}_{\mathrm{CP}}$, $\deg(g+h){\leq}k-i-1$, $i{\geq}0$. Decompose g and h as

$$\begin{cases} g = g_1\|g_2\|g_3\|g_4, \\ h = h_1\|h_2\|h_3\|h_4, \end{cases}$$

where $g_1, g_2, g_3, g_4, h_1, h_2, h_3, h_4 \in B_{2k-1}$.

By Proposition 2,

$$\begin{aligned} g + h = {}&(g_1+h_1) \\ &+ x_{2k}(g_1+g_2+h_1+h_2) + x_{2k+1}(g_1+g_3+h_1+h_3) \\ &+ x_{2k}x_{2k+1}(g_1+g_2+g_3+g_4+h_1+h_2+h_3+h_4). \end{aligned}$$

Let $\iota' = \iota \circ \tau$. Since $\iota, \tau \in \mathbf{T}_{\mathrm{CP}}$, then $\iota' \in \mathbf{T}_{\mathrm{CP}}$, too.

By Recursion (2), we have

$$\begin{cases} \iota(\phi^{i+1}_{2k+1}) = \iota'(\phi^i_{2k-1})\| \iota'(\phi^{i+1}_{2k-1})\| \iota(\phi^{i+1}_{2k-1})\| \iota(\phi^{i+2}_{2k-1}), \\ \iota(\phi^i_{2k+1}) = \iota'(\phi^{i-1}_{2k-1})\| \iota'(\phi^i_{2k-1})\| \iota(\phi^i_{2k-1})\| \iota(\phi^{i+1}_{2k-1}), \\ \iota(\phi_{2k+1}) = \iota'(\phi_{2k-1})\| \iota'(\phi_{2k-1})\| \iota(\phi_{2k-1})\| \iota(\phi^1_{2k-1}). \end{cases}$$

a) $\deg(g_1+h_1) \le \deg(g+h) \le k-i-1 = (k-1)-(i-1)-1$.

  - If $i > 0$, then $g_1 \in \mathrm{Ann}\left(\iota'(\phi_{2k-1}^{i-1})\right)$, $h_1 \in \mathrm{Ann}\left(\iota'(\phi_{2k-1}^{i})\right)$.
    According to the induction assumption, $g_1 = h_1$.
  - If $i = 0$, then $g_1, h_1 \in \mathrm{Ann}\left(\iota'(\phi_{2k-1})\right)$. Thus $g_1+h_1 \in \mathrm{Ann}\left(\iota'(\phi_{2k-1})\right)$.
    By Proposition 2, $\mathrm{AI}\left(\iota'(\phi_{2k-1})\right) = \mathrm{AI}(\phi_{2k-1}) = k$.
    Since $\deg(g_1+h_1) \le k-1$, we have $g_1 + h_1 = 0$, i.e., $g_1 = h_1$.

b) $\deg(g_2+h_2) \le \deg(g+h)-1 \le (k-i-1)-1 = (k-1)-i-1$, $g_2 \in \mathrm{Ann}\left(\iota'(\phi_{2k-1}^{i})\right)$
   and $h_2 \in \mathrm{Ann}\left(\iota'(\phi_{2k-1}^{i+1})\right)$. Then according to the induction assumption, we
   have $g_2 = h_2$.

c) $\deg(g_3+h_3) \le \deg(g+h)-1 \le (k-i-1)-1 = (k-1)-i-1$, $g_3 \in \mathrm{Ann}\left(\iota(\phi_{2k-1}^{i})\right)$
   and $h_3 \in \mathrm{Ann}\left(\iota(\phi_{2k-1}^{i+1})\right)$. Then according to the induction assumption, we
   have $g_3 = h_3$.

d) $\deg(g_4+h_4) \le \deg(g+h)-2 \le (k-i-1)-2 = (k-1)-(i+1)-1$, $g_4 \in \mathrm{Ann}$
   $\left(\iota(\phi_{2k-1}^{i+1})\right)$ and $h_4 \in \mathrm{Ann}\left(\iota(\phi_{2k-1}^{i+2})\right)$. Then according to the induction assumption, we have $g_4 = h_4$.

Hence we get $g_1=h_1$, $g_2=h_2$, $g_3=h_3$, $g_4=h_4$, i.e., $g = h$ which finishes the proof.

$\square$

Lemma 2. *Assume that the function $\phi_{2t} \in B_{2t}$ has been generated by Construction 2 and $\mathrm{AI}(\phi_{2t+1})=t+1$ for $1 \le t \le k$. If there exists $g \in \mathrm{Ann}\left(\iota(\phi_{2k+1}^{i})\right) \cap \mathrm{Ann}\left(\iota(\phi_{2k+1}^{i+1})\right)$ such that $\iota \in \mathbf{T}_{\mathrm{CP}}$, $\deg(g) \le k+i+1$ and $i \ge 0$, then $g = 0$.*

Proof. We prove it by induction on k.

For the base step $k = 0$, it's easy to check that if $g \in \mathrm{Ann}\left(\iota(\phi_1^{i})\right) \cap \mathrm{Ann}\left(\iota(\phi_1^{i+1})\right)$, then $g = 0$. Now we prove the induction step. Assume that the induction assumption holds until k, we are to prove it for k.

Suppose there's $g \in \mathrm{Ann}\left(\iota(\phi_{2k+1}^{i})\right) \cap \mathrm{Ann}\left(\iota(\phi_{2k+1}^{i+1})\right)$ such that $\deg(g) \le k+i+1$, $i \ge 0$. Decompose g as

$$g = g_1 \| g_2 \| g_3 \| g_4,$$

where $g_1, g_2, g_3, g_4 \in B_{2k-1}$.

According to Proposition 2,

$$g = g_1 + x_{2k}(g_1+g_2) + x_{2k+1}(g_1+g_3)$$
$$+ x_{2k}x_{2k+1}(g_1+g_2+g_3+g_4).$$

And then

$$\begin{cases} \deg(g_1) \le k+i+1, \\ \deg(g_1+g_2), \deg(g_1+g_3) \le k+i, \\ \deg(g_1+g_2+g_3+g_4) \le k+i-1, \end{cases}$$

since $\deg(g) \le k+i+1$.

Let $\iota' = \iota \circ \tau$. Since $\iota, \tau \in \mathbf{T}_{\mathrm{CP}}$, then $\iota' \in \mathbf{T}_{\mathrm{CP}}$, too.

By Recursion (2), we have

$$\begin{cases} \iota(\phi_{2k+1}^{i+1}) = \iota'(\phi_{2k-1}^{i}) \| \iota'(\phi_{2k-1}^{i+1}) \| \iota(\phi_{2k-1}^{i+1}) \| \iota(\phi_{2k-1}^{i+2}), \\ \iota(\phi_{2k+1}^{i}) = \iota'(\phi_{2k-1}^{i-1}) \| \iota'(\phi_{2k-1}^{i}) \| \iota(\phi_{2k-1}^{i}) \| \iota(\phi_{2k-1}^{i+1}), \\ \iota(\phi_{2k+1}) = \iota'(\phi_{2k-1}) \| \iota'(\phi_{2k-1}) \| \iota(\phi_{2k-1}) \| \iota(\phi_{2k-1}^{1}). \end{cases}$$

a) $\deg(g_4) = \deg\big(g_1 + (g_1+g_2) + (g_1+g_3) + (g_1+g_2+g_3+g_4)\big) \le k+1+i = (k-1)+ (i+1)+1$, and $g_4 \in \mathrm{Ann}\big(\iota(\phi_{2k-1}^{i+1})\big) \bigcap \mathrm{Ann}\big(\iota(\phi_{2k-1}^{i+2})\big)$. By the induction assumption, $g_4 = 0$. Then

$$g = g_1 + x_{2k}(g_1+g_2) + x_{2k+1}(g_1+g_3) \\ + x_{2k}x_{2k+1}(g_1+g_2+g_3),$$

and $\deg(g_1+g_2+g_3) \le k+i$.

b) $\deg(g_3) = \deg\big((g_1+g_2) + (g_1+g_2+g_3)\big) \le k+i$, and $g_3 \in \mathrm{Ann}\big(\iota'(\phi_{2k-1}^{i})\big) \bigcap \mathrm{Ann}\big(\iota'(\phi_{2k-1}^{i+1})\big)$. According to the induction assumption, $g_3 = 0$.

c) Similarly, it can be proved that $g_2 = 0$. Then

$$g = (1 + x_{2k} + x_{2k+1} + x_{2k}x_{2k+1})g_1,$$

and $\deg(g_1) = \deg(g) - 2 \le k+i-1$.

d) − If $i > 0$, then $g_1 \in \mathrm{Ann}\big(\iota'(\phi_{2k-1}^{i-1})\big) \bigcap \mathrm{Ann}\big(\iota'(\phi_{2k-1}^{i})\big)$. According to the induction assumption, $g_1 = 0$.
   − If $i = 0$, then $\deg(g_1) \le k-1$.
   For $\iota' \in \mathbf{T}_{\mathrm{CP}}$, note that $\mathrm{AI}\big(\iota'(\phi_{2k-1})\big) = \mathrm{AI}(\phi_{2k-1}) = k$.
   Hence, we have $g_1 = 0$, since $g_1 \in \mathrm{Ann}\big(\iota'(\phi_{2k-1})\big)$,

Therefore, we get $g = 0$. This completes the proof. □

Theorem 1. *The function ϕ_{2k+1} $(k>0)$ obtained in Construction 2 has optimum algebraic immunity, i.e.,*

$$\mathrm{AI}(\phi_{2k+1}) = k+1.$$

Proof. We prove Theorem 1 by induction on k. For the base step $k = 1$, it can easily be checked.

Now we prove the inductive step. Assume that the induction assumption holds until k, we are to prove it for k. It just need to prove that for $\forall g \in \mathrm{Ann}(\phi_{2k+1}) \bigcup \mathrm{Ann}(\phi_{2k+1}+1)$, if $\deg(g) \le k$, there should be $g = 0$.

Decompose g as

$$g = g_1 \| g_2 \| g_3 \| g_4,$$

where $g_1, g_2, g_3, g_4 \in \mathbf{B}_{2k-1}$.

According to Proposition 2,

$$g = g_1 + x_{2k}(g_1+g_2) + x_{2k+1}(g_1+g_3) \\ + x_{2k}x_{2k+1}(g_1+g_2+g_3+g_4).$$

And then

$$\begin{cases} \deg(g_1) \leq k, \\ \deg(g_1+g_2), \deg(g_1+g_3) \leq k-1, \\ \deg(g_1+g_2+g_3+g_4) \leq k-2, \end{cases}$$

since $\deg(g) \leq k$.

1) Suppose $g \in \mathrm{Ann}(\phi_{2k+1})$.

   Note the recursion $\phi_{2k+1} = \tau(\phi_{2k-1}) \| \tau(\phi_{2k-1}) \| \phi_{2k-1} \| \phi_{2k-1}^1$. By Proposition 2, $g_1, g_2 \in \mathrm{Ann}\left(\tau(\phi_{2k-1})\right), g_3 \in \mathrm{Ann}(\phi_{2k-1})$ and $g_4 \in \mathrm{Ann}(\phi_{2k-1}^1)$. Thus $g_1+g_2 \in \mathrm{Ann}\left(\tau(\phi_{2k-1})\right)$. Note that $\mathrm{AI}\left(\tau(\phi_{2k-1})\right) = \mathrm{AI}(\phi_{2k-1}) = k$, by induction assumption. Hence $g_1+g_2 = 0$. Therefore,

   $$g = g_1 + x_{2k+1}(g_1+g_3) + x_{2k}x_{2k+1}(g_3+g_4).$$

   and $\deg(g_3+g_4) \leq k-2 = (k-1)-1-0$. By Lemma 1, there is $g_3 = g_4$. Then $g_3 \in \mathrm{Ann}(\phi_{2k-1}) \bigcap \mathrm{Ann}(\phi_{2k-1}^1)$. Since $\deg(g_1+g_3) \leq k-1$ and $\deg(g_1) \leq k$, then $\deg(g_3) \leq k = (k-1)+0+1$ According to Lemma 2, $g_3 = 0$. Therefore,

   $$g = (1+x_{2k+1})g_1.$$

   And then $\deg(g_1) = \deg(g)-1 \leq k-1$. Note that $g_1 \in \mathrm{Ann}\left(\tau(\phi_{2k-1})\right)$ and $\mathrm{AI}\left(\tau(\phi_{2k-1})\right) = k$. Thus $g_1 = 0$ and then $g = 0$.

2) Suppose $g \in \mathrm{Ann}(\phi_{2k+1}+1)$. By similar argument in 1), it also can prove that $g = 0$.

Hence, for $\forall g \in \mathrm{Ann}(\phi_{2k+1}) \bigcup \mathrm{Ann}(\phi_{2k+1}+1)$, if $\deg(g) \leq k$ then $g = 0$. According to induction principle, $\mathrm{AI}(\phi_{2k+1}) = k+1$. □

4   Examples and Further Work

Choose $\tau_{\mathrm{comp}} \in \mathbf{T}_{\mathrm{CP}}$, it's easy to see that Construction 1 is a special case of Construction 2. For another example, choose $\tau = \tau_{\mathrm{iden}} \in \mathbf{T}_{\mathrm{CP}}$. And then there would result in the following construction.

Construction 3

$$\begin{cases} \phi_{2k+1} = \phi_{2k-1} \| \phi_{2k-1} \| \phi_{2k-1} \| \phi_{2k-1}^1, \\ \phi_{2k+1}^i = \phi_{2k-1}^{i-1} \| \phi_{2k-1}^i \| \phi_{2k-1}^i \| \phi_{2k-1}^{i+1}, \end{cases}$$

with the base step $\phi_{2k+1}^0 = \phi_{2k+1}$, $\phi_1^j = x_1+(j \bmod 2)$, $i \geq 1$, $k, j \geq 0$.

According to Theorem 1, the Boolean function ϕ_{2k+1} in Construction 3 has optimum AI, too. However, it can be easy to see that ϕ_{2k+1} in Construction 3 is not balanced, while that in Construction 1 is balanced. Thus, in Construction 2, by using different transformations of $\mathbf{T}_{\mathrm{CP}}$, the constructed Boolean function ϕ_{2k+1}'s have an equal AI, but maybe different other cryptographic properties. Construction 1 and Construction 3 is an example for balance property. Therefore, our further word is to determine how to choose a suitable transformations of $\mathbf{T}_{\mathrm{CP}}$ for constructing Boolean functions with good cryptographic properties.

5   Conclusion

In this paper, we proposed a family constructions of odd-variable Boolean function with optimum algebraic immunity. By using different transformations which are consistent with concatenation operation and preserve algebraic immunity, there would correspond to different constructions of the family. How to choose a good transformation to construct good Boolean functions is a further work.

Acknowledgement. This work was supported in part by the National Natural Science Foundation of China (Grant 61103244), and in part by the STU Scientific Research Foundation for Talents (Grant NTF10018).

References

1. Courtois, N.T., Meier, W.: Algebraic Attacks on Stream Ciphers with Linear Feedback. In: Biham, E. (ed.) EUROCRYPT 2003. LNCS, vol. 2656, pp. 345–359. Springer, Heidelberg (2003)
2. Meier, W., Pasalic, E., Carlet, C.: Algebraic Attacks and Decomposition of Boolean Functions. In: Cachin, C., Camenisch, J.L. (eds.) EUROCRYPT 2004. LNCS, vol. 3027, pp. 474–491. Springer, Heidelberg (2004)
3. Armknecht, F., Krause, M.: Algebraic Attacks on Combiners with Memory. In: Boneh, D. (ed.) CRYPTO 2003. LNCS, vol. 2729, pp. 162–175. Springer, Heidelberg (2003)
4. Courtois, N.T.: Algebraic Attacks on Combiners with Memory and Several Outputs. In: Park, C.-S., Chee, S. (eds.) ICISC 2004. LNCS, vol. 3506, pp. 3–20. Springer, Heidelberg (2005)
5. Courtois, N.T.: Cryptanalysis of SFINKS. In: Won, D.H., Kim, S. (eds.) ICISC 2005. LNCS, vol. 3935, pp. 261–269. Springer, Heidelberg (2006)
6. Batten, L.M.: Algebraic Attacks Over GF(q). In: Canteaut, A., Viswanathan, K. (eds.) INDOCRYPT 2004. LNCS, vol. 3348, pp. 84–91. Springer, Heidelberg (2004)
7. Faugère, J.-C., Joux, A.: Algebraic Cryptanalysis of Hidden Field Equation (HFE) Cryptosystems Using Gröbner Bases. In: Boneh, D. (ed.) CRYPTO 2003. LNCS, vol. 2729, pp. 44–60. Springer, Heidelberg (2003)
8. Armknecht, F.: On the Existence of low-degree Equations for Algebraic Attacks, http://eprint.iacr.org/2004/185
9. Courtois, N.T., Klimov, A., Patarin, J., Shamir, A.: Efficient Algorithms for Solving Overdefined Systems of Multivariate Polynomial Equations. In: Preneel, B. (ed.) EUROCRYPT 2000. LNCS, vol. 1807, pp. 392–407. Springer, Heidelberg (2000)
10. Kipnis, A., Shamir, A.: Cryptanalysis of the HFE Public Key Cryptosystem by Relinearization. In: Wiener, M. (ed.) CRYPTO 1999. LNCS, vol. 1666, pp. 19–30. Springer, Heidelberg (1999)
11. Adams, W.W., Loustaunau, P.: An Introduction to Gröbner Bases. AMS, USA (1994)
12. Courtois, N.T.: Fast Algebraic Attacks on Stream Ciphers with Linear Feedback. In: Boneh, D. (ed.) CRYPTO 2003. LNCS, vol. 2729, pp. 176–194. Springer, Heidelberg (2003)
13. Armknecht, F.: Improving Fast Algebraic Attacks. In: Roy, B., Meier, W. (eds.) FSE 2004. LNCS, vol. 3017, pp. 65–82. Springer, Heidelberg (2004)

14. Carlet, C., Dalai, D.K., Gupta, K.C., et al.: Algebraic Immunity for Cryptographically Significant Boolean Functions: Analysis and Construction. IEEE Transactions on Information Theory 52(7), 3105–3121 (2006)
15. Dalai, D.K., Gupta, K.C., Maitra, S.: Cryptographically Significant Boolean Functions: Construction and Analysis in Terms of Algebraic Immunity. In: Gilbert, H., Handschuh, H. (eds.) FSE 2005. LNCS, vol. 3557, pp. 98–111. Springer, Heidelberg (2005)
16. Braeken, A., Preneel, B.: On the Algebraic Immunity of Symmetric Boolean Functions. In: Maitra, S., Veni Madhavan, C.E., Venkatesan, R. (eds.) INDOCRYPT 2005. LNCS, vol. 3797, pp. 35–48. Springer, Heidelberg (2005)
17. Dalai, D.K., Maitra, S., Sarkar, S.: Basic Theory in Construction of Boolean Functions with Maximum Possible Annihilator Immunity. Design, Codes and Cryptography 40(1), 41–58 (2006)
18. Carlet, C.: A method of construction of balanced functions with optimum algebraic immunity, http://eprint.iacr.org/2006/149
19. Carlet, C., Zeng, X., Li, C., et al.: Further properties of several classes of Boolean functions with optimum algebraic immunity, http://eprint.iacr.org/2007/370
20. Armknecht, F., Carlet, C., Gaborit, P., Künzli, S., Meier, W., Ruatta, O.: Efficient Computation of Algebraic Immunity for Algebraic and Fast Algebraic Attacks. In: Vaudenay, S. (ed.) EUROCRYPT 2006. LNCS, vol. 4004, pp. 147–164. Springer, Heidelberg (2006)
21. Li, N., Qi, W.-F.: Construction and Analysis of Boolean Functions of $2t+1$ Variables with Maximum Algebraic Immunity. In: Lai, X., Chen, K. (eds.) ASIACRYPT 2006. LNCS, vol. 4284, pp. 84–98. Springer, Heidelberg (2006)
22. Li, N., Qi, W.: Boolean function of an odd number of variables with maximum algebraic immunity. Science in China, Ser. F 50(3), 307–317 (2007)
23. Li, N., Qu, L., Qi, W., et al.: On the construction of Boolean functions with optimal algebraic immunity. IEEE Transactions on Information Theory 54(3), 1330–1334 (2008)
24. Carlet, C., Feng, K.: An Infinite Class of Balanced Functions with Optimal Algebraic Immunity, Good Immunity to fast Algebraic Attacks and Good Nonlinearity. In: Pieprzyk, J. (ed.) ASIACRYPT 2008. LNCS, vol. 5350, pp. 425–440. Springer, Heidelberg (2008)
25. Chen, Y.: A Construction of Balanced Odd-variable Boolean Function with Optimum Algebraic Immunity. preprint

Design of a Modular Framework
for Noisy Logo Classification in Fraud Detection

Vrizlynn L.L. Thing, Wee-Yong Lim, Junming Zeng,
Darell J.J. Tan, and Yu Chen

Institute for Infocomm Research,
1 Fusionopolis Way, 138632, Singapore
vriz@i2r.a-star.edu.sg

Abstract. In this paper, we introduce a modular framework to detect
noisy logo appearing on online merchandise images so as to support
the forensics investigation and detection of increasing online counterfeit
product trading and fraud cases. The proposed framework and system
is able to perform an automatic logo image classification on realistic
and noisy product images. The novel contributions in this work include
the design of a modular SVM-based logo classification framework, and its
internal segmentation module, two new feature extractions modules, and
the decision algorithm for noisy logo detection. We developed the system
to perform an automated multi-class product images classification, which
achieves promising results on logo classification experiments of Louis
Vuitton, Chanel and Polo Ralph Lauren.

Keywords: noise-tolerant, logo detection, brand classification, digital
forensics, fraud detection.

1 Introduction

While the popularity of selling merchandise online (e.g. by end-users to sell their
second-hand merchandises, and retailers to sell their products at a lower operating cost) is growing, the cases of online product fraud are increasing at an alarm-
ing rate [1,2], with some merchants starting to use these same platforms to sell
counterfeit products. Examples of online product fraud cases include the trading
of luxury counterfeits such as clothings, handbags and electronic products, or
selling products with misleading advertisements. Currently, the text searching
based methods can be used to identify such illegal online trading activities. However, these methods may fail due to fraudulent merchants' intentional avoidance
of the use of brand-related keywords in the product descriptions or the intentional use of multiple brands' names to confuse text-based detection systems.
To protect the producers' interests, the brands' reputation and to detect and
prevent illegal trading of counterfeit products, an automatic logo detection system is essential. Such a system is expected to identify if a seller is trying to sell
products which belong to a brand of interest, even if the seller does not mention
any brand name in the product item's title or description, or the corresponding
web pages.

T.-h. Kim et al. (Eds.): SecTech 2011, CCIS 259, pp. 53–64, 2011.

In this paper, we propose the design of a modular SVM-based framework and the internal modules to perform segmentation, feature extractions and the decision algorithm to detect and classify logos with noise-tolerant support. The main objective in this work is to produce a system to achieve the detection and classification of logos despite the presence of noise in product images. This presents a challenge because in existing work on logo detection [3,4,5,6,7,8], it is often assumed that the logo presentation on images or videos is clear for advertisement purpose, the contrast between the logo and the background is high, and the logo is sufficiently large and prominently displayed at a centralised location. However, such assumptions will not be valid in the event of low quality images used for the advertisement of counterfeits or even legitimate products on online auction sites. We take the above-mentioned constraints into considerations when designing the system. We then implemented the system to perform an automated multi-class product images classification, which achieves promising results on brand classification experiments of Louis Vuitton (LV), Chanel and Polo Ralph Lauren (PRL).

The rest of the paper is organized as follows. We define the logo detection problem in Section 2. The framework and system design are introduced in Section 3. The internal modules of the system are proposed in Section 4. The experiments and results are presented in Section 5. The conclusion and future work are addressed in Section 6.

2   Logo Detection Problem on Merchandise Images

There are significant differences between the logo detection problem and other popular detection applications such as face detection. We discuss the differences here to illustrate the necessity and significance of this research. The logo detection here is defined as the application of the distinct feature extraction and description of contours/regions on the arbitrary merchandise images for detecting the presence of the brand logo of interest. The system can be trained to detect any brand logo, e.g. LV and Chanel with affordable computational cost and acceptable detection accuracy. The expected detectable logo should have relatively fixed appearances in shape, curvature and intensity contrast. However, in realistic cases, the logos often have a larger intra-class variation. The reason is that the logo can be present on a wide range of materials such as fabrics, leathers and metal, and therefore, the intra-class variations on the textures, intensities and pattern's local details can be significantly large. Therefore, these factors increase the challenges in detecting logo on merchandise images and have to be taken into consideration in this work.

3   Framework and System Design

In most image object recognition algorithms, the steps can generally be broken down to (i) Segmentation, (ii) Feature Extraction and Description and (iii) Classification. The segmentation process involves breaking down an image into

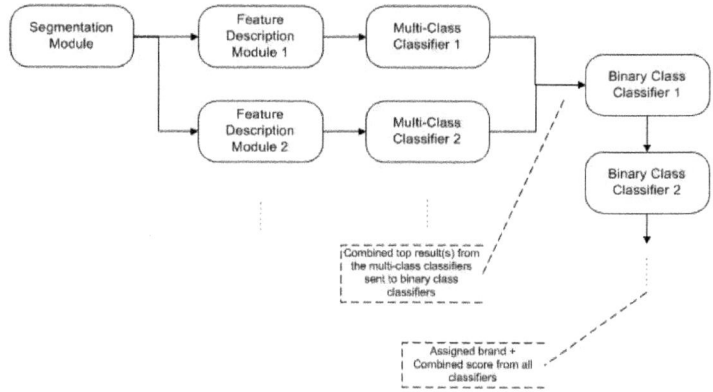

Fig. 1. Modular Framework of the Logo Classification System

several regions of which one or more of these regions may contain or represents the object-of-interest in the image. An obvious way to segment a test image will be to use a sliding window at multiple scales to crop sample regions in a given test image for testing [9] or having grids of overlapping blocks [10]. While these segmentation methods performs a comprehensive search through the image, they present misalignment problems when the sample windows or blocks do not encompass the whole object-of-interest in the image or that there is a overly large border around the object-of-interest. Moreover, this comprehensive search through the test image at multiple scales means that the feature description at each sample window will need to be generated relatively fast in order to ensure an acceptable overall processing time during testing. Thus, the use of sliding windows will always result in a compromise between the accuracy of detection rate and the computational complexity. In our system, instead of searching the whole test image with an equal emphasis on all regions, we apply an edge-based heuristic method of obtaining relevant samples in a given test image. This segmentation method not only segments regions but also capture shapes in the image.

For most practical image object recognition tasks, the majority of the samples obtained from a given test image are likely to be outliers that do not belong to any of the 'valid' class to be identified. To help reduce the wrong classification of these 'noise' samples, a multi-class classifier is trained with a prior library of outlier samples. However, given the infinite variations an outlier can take on, the trained outlier class in the multi-class classifier is unlikely to be sufficient to eliminate all outliers in a given test image. In the proposed framework, this problem is alleviated by classifying a sample using both multi-class and binary class classifiers. The corresponding binary class can then carry out further outlier filtering.

The proposed framework (Figure 1) supports the use of more than one binary and multi-class classifiers by taking the average of their classification scores. If each test image contains objects that are outliers or of a particular class, then the image is classified by taking the maximum classification scores among its samples that have been classified as one of the 'valid' classes. There are several binary and multi-class classifiers available that can be used to classify images (or more accurately, the descriptions of the images). The multi-class classifier used in our system is the Support Vector Machines (SVM) [11,12,13]. The binary classifier explored and used in our implementation is the Principal Component Analysis (PCA). The implementation of these classifiers are elaborated in Section 4.

4   Design of Internal Modules

To detect the presence of a logo, a test image will first go through the Segmentation module to generate test samples. Each sample is then sent to the feature description modules to generate a distinctive description that distinguish samples containing/representing objects-of-interest from samples that do not. The different feature descriptions for each sample are then sent to the multi-class classifiers. Next, the relevant model in the binary class classifiers is used for verifying the samples with the top result returned by the multi-class classifier module.

For example, a sample after being labelled as Class A by a multi-class classifier will then be tested against the Class A model of the binary class classifier. If there are more than one type of binary classifier available, the sample can be classified by all these binary classifiers. The combined score given by the multi-class classifier and the binary class classifier(s) will be computed. The binary class classifier(s) will not change the class label given by the multi-class classifier to another label (except 'outlier') but can only modify the score for the assigned class label given by the multi-class classifier. However, a low enough score or negative assignment(s) by the binary classifier(s) can be used to indicate a probable uncertainty in the assigned class label by the multi-class classifier and, thus, the class label can be re-assigned as an outlier. An outlier is regarded as a class of objects that do not belong to any of the valid classes. The final result consists of the class label and a score, calculated by taking the mean scores of the multi-class classifier and binary class classifier(s).

Finally, to get the final classification result of the given test image, the results for all the samples are sorted according to their assigned class and scores. The maximum score indicating the top logo result is obtained from this sorted list.

Our system is composed of a segmentation module, two feature extraction and description modules in the form of two multi-class SVM classifiers, and a set of binary class Principal Component Analysis (PCA) classifiers. The following subsections describe each of these modules in detail.

4.1   Segmentation

To recognize object(s) in a test image, the image is first 'broken down' into different smaller samples where one or more of such samples may represent or contain the object-of-interest. Existing segmentation approaches include the multi-scale sliding window [9], region detection around interest points [14], comprehensive overlapping region detection across the image [10], and the watershed region detection based on the eigenvalues of the Hessian matrix for each pixel [15].

The segmentation method proposed in our system is based on edge detection, and joining using the vectorization method [16] to form shapes represented as a vector of points. These shapes are referred to as 'contours'.

The edges in the images are detected using the classic Canny edge detection algorithm [17] which identifies edges based on the gray level intensity differences and uses a hysteresis threshold to trace and obtain a cleaner edge map of the image. However, the Canny edge detection algorithm is highly sensitive to noise. Even though noise can be reduced by blurring the image, it is often not known how much blurring needs to be applied to the image.

A simple heuristic method proposed in our system is to adaptively blur a given image iteratively till the number of contours found in the image is less than a pre-defined threshold or that the specified maximum number of blurring operations has been performed on the image. In an ideal situation, at least one of the contours generated by the Segmentation module shall be obtained from the shape around the brand logo in a given merchandise image, thus representing the logo. However, this may not be the case for all logos. In fact, it may not be suitable and useful to obtain only the shape of a logo in cases where the distinctive features are within the logo and not its outline.

Hence, in addition to generating contours found in images, our segmentation module also identifies and processes the region around each contour found in the test image. These regions are sample regions that can potentially cover a logo.

There are two advantages in obtaining the sample regions based on this method. First, this eliminates the need to search the image at different scales in order to segment the logo at the nearest matching scale. Even if the contour obtained around the logo is not a good representation of the logo shape, it is still possible to ensure a correct coverage around the logo as long as the contour is around the majority of the logo in the image. This implies a relative robustness against noise in the image. Second, by segmenting the image based on edges, this method saves unnecessary computation by not focusing on regions with homogeneous intensity level which are unlikely to contain any object of interest. Therefore, the two types of samples - contours and regions - allow the use of both shape-based and region-based feature description methods.

4.2   Feature Description — Shape-Based

Contours generated from the segmentation module may provide important information in identifying the logo present in the merchandise images. In this section, we describe our proposed shape-based feature description module.

Each contour can be stored as a vector of points (i.e. x and y coordinates) but the vector, by itself, is variant to translation, scale, rotation and skew transformations and thus, is insufficient to characterize the shape of the logo. To generate a description that is invariant to the translation, scale and skew transformations,

we sample 64 points from each contour. We then apply a curve orthogonaliza-
tion algorithm on the contour description [18]. The objective is to normalize the
contour with respect to translation, scale and skew transformations while maintaining the essential information of the original contour. The transformations
applied to the contour for normalization processing is shown in Equation 1.

$$\mathbf{n(s)} = \frac{1}{\sqrt{2}} \begin{bmatrix} \tau_x & 0 \\ 0 & \tau_y \end{bmatrix} \begin{bmatrix} 1 & -1 \\ 1 & 1 \end{bmatrix} \begin{bmatrix} \alpha_x & 0 \\ 0 & \alpha_y \end{bmatrix} \begin{bmatrix} \mathbf{x} - \mu_x \\ \mathbf{y} - \mu_y \end{bmatrix} \tag{1}$$

where,
$\boldsymbol{s}$ is the contour to be normalized
$\boldsymbol{n(s)}$ is the normalized contour given as a function of $\mathbf{s}$
$\boldsymbol{x,y}$ are the x- and y- coordinates of $\boldsymbol{s}$ respectively
μ_x, μ_y are the mean x- and y- coordinates of $\boldsymbol{s}$ respectively
α_x, α_y refer to the reciprocal of the square root of the second order moments
(cf. (2)) of the curve in the x and y directions, respectively, after translation
normalization (i.e. the rightmost matrix in the equation). The matrix containing
these two terms scale-normalizes the contour such that its x and y second order
moments equal 1.
τ_x, τ_y refer to the reciprocal of the square root of the second order moments
(cf. (2)) of the curve in the x and y directions, respectively (after translation
normalization, scale normalization and $\pi/4$ rotation; i.e. all the terms in the
equation except for the matrix containing these two terms)
The (p,q)-th moments, m , of a contour represented as a set of x and y coordinates
are defined as:

$$m_{pq} = \frac{1}{N} \sum_{i=0}^{N-1} x_i^p y_i^q \tag{2}$$

where,
m_{pq} is the (p,q)-th moments of a contour
N is the number of points in the contour
x_i, y_i are the i-th x and y coordinates of pixels in the contour respectively

Finally, we compute the shape-based description for each contour by taking the
magnitude of the Fourier transform of the distance between each point on the
contour and the centroid of the contour (i.e. central distance shape signature
[19]). Therefore, the rotation invariant shape-based description for the translation, scale and skew normalized contour is generated. After removing the DC
component of the magnitude of the Fourier transform (since this is dependent
only on the size of the contour of which was scale-normalized in the previous
step) and the repeated (and thus redundant) values due to the symmetric property in the Fourier transform of the real values, our shape-based description has
a total of 31 dimensions.

4.3   Feature Description — Region-Based

Despite the versatility provided by the translation, scale, skew and rotation invariant shape-based description of brand logo, there exist two shortcoming in using the shape-based descriptions — it can be difficult to obtain an accurate shape around the logo and the outline of the logo may not be its distinctive feature in some cases. To mitigate these shortcomings, the region-based descriptions are generated from the regions obtained from the segmentation module.

Unlike the shape-based descriptions, an image region contains more information than just the edges/contours and as such, a region-based descriptor needs to reduce the dimension of the data while generating a description that is distinctive enough to characterize logos that may not be exactly similar but share certain similar characteristics. Some prior well known descriptors utilize histograms based on intensity gradient magnitude or orientation in image regions [10,14], reduces the dimension of the image region based on the principal components of its set of training images [20] or uses a boosted trained selection of Haar-like features to describe image regions [9].

The region-based description module proposed in our system is based on describing a region by using a covariance matrix of pixel-level features within that region. Not only is this method able to describe regions of different sizes, any pixel-level features could be chosen to describe the image region.

In [21], nine pixel-level features were chosen. They consist of the x and y coordinates, RGB intensity values, as well as the first and second order derivatives of the image region in the x and y directions. However, it was observed that logos of the same brand can come in a wide variety of colours and as such, the RGB representation is not applicable in this case. In addition, it was noticed that the covariance between two features from the image region can be affected by the scale of the feature magnitudes [22]. Thus, we propose representing the relationship between two features in the form of the Pearson's correlation coefficient. The standard deviation of each feature distribution is also used to characterize the internal variation within the feature.

For d number of features, the covariance matrix of the features is a dxd square matrix given by Equation 3 [21]. Due to the symmetry in the non-diagonal values in the matrix, there will be only $(d^2-d)/2$ covariance values. Since the covariance between the x and y coordinates is similar for any image region, this value does not provide any distinctive characteristic to the description and is discarded. Standard deviation is taken as the square root of the variances obtained along the diagonal of the covariance matrix and the correlation coefficients are calculated by dividing the covariance values with the standard deviations of its respective two distributions. Therefore, our region-based description module has an optimized 20 dimensions for the 6 features.

$$C(i,j) = \frac{1}{n-1}\left[\sum_{k=1}^{n} z_k(i)z_k(j) - \frac{1}{n}\sum_{k=1}^{n} z_k(i)\sum_{k=1}^{n} z_k(j)\right] \tag{3}$$

where,

C is the covariance matrix

i,j are (i,j)-th elements in the covariance matrix

n is the total number of pixels in the image

k is the k-th pixel in the image

z is a feature matrix

4.4   Multi-class Classifier — Support Vector Machine (SVM)

After generating the shape-based and region-based descriptions from the test image, our system requires these descriptions to be fed to the classifiers to determine if they contain any object-of-interest. We utilized two types of classifiers — multi-class SVM and binary class PCA classifiers. This subsection gives a description of our implementation of the SVM classifier. Our SVM classifiers (i.e. the shape- and region- based descriptions modules) are built upon LIBSVM [13].

Given a collection of data where each data point corresponds to a fixed-dimension vector (i.e. a fixed length description generated by either one of the above-mentioned internal feature description modules) and a class number, a SVM performs training by mapping the presented data into a higher dimension space and attempts to partition these mapped data point into their respective classes. A radial basis Gaussian kernel is used here [13] by taking into consideration the relatively large number of data points with respect to the number of dimensions (i.e. 31 and 20 for the shape-based and region-based description modules, respectively).

The partitioning process of the data in the feature space is based on determining the hyperplanes that maximize the distances between the classes. SVM developed in [11] is a binary class classifier but have been adapted to perform multi-class classification in LIBSVM using a one-against-one approach [23] and a voting-based selection of the final class. In addition, we utilize LIBSVM's option to generate the classification probability score to indicate the likelihood of a successful classification.

4.5   Binary Class Classifier — Principal Component Analysis (PCA)

PCA is used to provide a binary-class classification in our system. PCA has been widely used to classify patterns in high dimensional data. It calculates a set of eigenvectors from the covariance matrix of all the training images in each class and uses them to project a test image to a lower dimension space, thereby causing information loss during the dimension reduction, and then back-projecting it to its original number of dimensions. In the process, an error score can be calculated by computing either/both (i) the distance between the projected test image and the class in the lower dimension space or/and (ii) the difference between the back-projected image and the original test image (i.e. the reconstruction error). A test image is classified as a positive match if its error score is within a pre-defined threshold.

In our implementation, the colour information in the images was first discarded. We then performed histogram equalization to reduce the irregular illumination and Gaussian blur was then applied to reduce the noise in the images. To train each class, each image is resized to fixed dimensions, vectorized and combined to form a matrix where each row is the data represents a training image. This matrix is then mean-normalized with respect to the average of all the training images for the class. The covariance matrix for the pre-processed, resized and vectorized training images is then calculated and its corresponding eigenvalues and eigenvector were obtained. The eigenvalues, eigenvector and the mean image make up the generated training output. However, it is not necessary to store all the eigenvalue and eigenvector pairs as only the principal components (i.e. the eigenvectors with large eigenvalues) need to be retained. To choose the error threshold and number of principal components to retain, a PCA model for each class is built and the true positive and false negative rates were recorded for varying the number of principal components and error threshold. The 'best' set of parameters is used based on the closest classification result to the ideal scenario of having a true positive rate of 1 and false negative rate of 0 for a sample test set.

4.6   Decision Algorithm

The segmentation and classifiers modules were then integrated into the final system to perform the classification of merchandise images. In this subsection, we describe how the system decides the final assigned brand and its score.

Referring back to Figure 1, the image was segmented and the contours and regions were processed by the multi-classifiers to obtain a probability score in the classification. The scores returned by the multi-classifiers for each contour/region were then combined. In this case, an average score was computed for each of the classes. Based on the combined score, the top result(s) was sent to the corresponding binary classifier(s) for further verification. For each positive classification result by the binary class classifier(s), the score was adjusted accordingly while the assigned brand remained the same. In the case of a subsequent negative classification by the binary class classifier(s), the previously identified contour/region is regarded as not encompassing a logo.

5   Experiments

We developed the system and conducted logo classification experiments on logos of three brands (i.e. Louis Vuitton (LV), Chanel and Polo Ralph Lauren (PRL)) and images without any logo of interest. The training datasets were randomly collected from the internet. The logos were collected from the images of products including bags, shoes, shirts, etc. The negative collections are images which do not have any logo of interest here. These are termed as negative images. The number of positive contours used for training the LV, Chanel, PRL and Others (i.e. negative) SVM shape-based classifier models were 2516, 1078, 1314 and

16709, respectively. The number of extracted positive regions used for training the LV, Chanel, PRL and Others SVM region-based classifier models were 3135, 3237, 3004 and 31570, respectively.

The test dataset was collected from the Ebay website. We used the Ebay search engine to search for the name of the brand and obtain the first 100 images containing the logo of each brand, and 100 more images which did not contain any logo of interest. The 400 test images were verified to be not within the training dataset and were sent to the system for classification. In the experiments, we returned only the top 1 classification result for each image.

The results are shown in Table 1 and 2. A classification is considered as a true positive if the merchandise image is correctly detected as containing the relevant logo of interest, while a false negative refers to the merchandise image incorrectly detected as not containing the logo. A false positive classification refers to an image classified wrongly as containing the logo of interest.

Table 1. Classification Results

Brand	Classified as LV	Classified as Chanel	Classified as PRL	Classified as Others
LV	81	4	0	15
Chanel	0	55	3	42
PRL	0	1	84	15
Others	4	9	1	86

Table 2. True Positive, False Positive and False Negative Rates

	LV	Chanel	PRL
True Positive	81/100	55/100	84/100
False Positive	4/300	15/300	4/300
False Negative	19/100	45/100	16/100

We observed that LV and PRL are classified with a low false positive rate and a high accuracy, despite the low quality of the merchandise images. However, Chanel suffers from a low true positive rate. The lower true positive rate is due to the Chanel logo responding poorly to our contour extraction, while the higher false positive rate is due to the less distinctive shape and composition, compared to the other two logos. The Chanel logo is also better represented and defined by its shape rather than its region features. However, the usual appearances of this logo on the merchandise have either an extremely low contrast from its background (i.e. merchandise item) or a high metalic and reflective nature, resulting in a difficult-to-extract contour. Therefore, applying the current adaptive blurring technique in the segmentation module results in the logo being even harder to extract given its nature of appearance.

To further improve the results and strengthen the system, we plan to conduct further research on the description modules in our future work. The classification results can also be further improved with a larger training dataset and optimized blurring techniques in the segmentation module through knowledge gained from the design characteristics of the merchandise and brand logo.

6   Conclusion

In this paper, we proposed a novel modular framework and system for the detection of noisy logos of interest to support the forensics investigation of online fraud and counterfeits trading. For most of the brands, the intra-class variations of the logo images are considerably large. Further more, the quality of many realistic product images used in E-Commerce are very low. When trying to perform logo detections on those product images, the training and operation approach should be able to deal with these noisy training data. The major contributions of this paper are the design of a modular SVM-based logo classification framework, its internal segmentation module, two new feature extraction modules, and the integrated decision algorithm to perform noisy logo detection and classification.

Through the experiments carried out on three brand logos, we showed that our system is capable of classifying the LV, Chanel and PRL merchandise images, and negative images at a success rate of 81%, 55%, 84%, and 86%, respectively. The true positive rate of the Chanel merchandise images is shown to be low. The reason is mainly due to the intrinsic design characteristics of the Chanel logo on the merchandise. For future work, we plan to enhance the system by incorporating additional description modules to increase the true positive rates, optimize the blurring techniques in the segmentation module through knowledge gained from the design characteristics of the merchandise, and other forms of binary classifiers to further improve outlier filtering.

References

1. International Authentication Association, "Counterfeit statistics." (2010), http://internationalauthenticationassociation.org/content/counterfeit_statistics.php
2. Otim, S., Grover, V.: E-commerce: a brand name's curse. Electronic Markets 20(2), 147–160 (2010)
3. Zhu, G., Doermann, D.: Automatic document logo detection. In: Proc. 9th Int. Conf. Document Analysis and Recognition (ICDAR 2007), pp. 864–868 (2007)
4. Zhu, G., Doermann, D.: Logo matching for document image retrieval. In: Proceedings of the 2009 10th International Conference on Document Analysis and Recognition, pp. 606–610 (2009)
5. Wang, H., Chen, Y.: Logo detection in document images based on boundary extension of feature rectangles. In: Proceedings of the 2009 10th International Conference on Document Analysis and Recognition, pp. 1335–1339 (2009)
6. Rusinol, M., Llados, J.: Logo spotting by a bag-of-words approach for document categorization. In: Proceedings of the 2009 10th International Conference on Document Analysis and Recognition, pp. 111–115 (2009)

7. Li, Z., Schulte-Austum, M., Neschen, M.: Fast logo detection and recognition in document images. In: Proceedings of the 2010 20th International Conference on Pattern Recognition, pp. 2716–2719 (2010)
8. Sun, S.-K., Chen, Z.: Robust logo recognition for mobile phone applications. J. Inf. Sci. Eng. 27(2), 545–559 (2011)
9. Viola, P., Jones, M.: Rapid object detection using a boosted cascade of simple features. In: IEEE Computer Society Conference on Computer Vision and Pattern Recognition, vol. 1, pp. 511–518 (2001)
10. Dalal, N., Triggs, B.: Histograms of oriented gradients for human detection. In: IEEE Computer Society Conference on Computer Vision and Pattern Recognition, vol. 1, pp. 886–893 (2005)
11. Cortes, C., Vapnik, V.: Support-vector networks. Machine Learning 20, 273–297 (1995)
12. Joachims, T.: Making large-scale svm learning practical. In: Schlkopf, B., Burges, C., Smola, A. (eds.) Making large-Scale SVM Learning Practical. Advances in Kernel Methods - Support Vector Learning. MIT-Press (1999)
13. Chang, C.-C., Lin, C.-J.: LIBSVM: A library for support vector machines. ACM Transactions on Intelligent Systems and Technology 2, 27:1–27:27 (2011), http://www.csie.ntu.edu.tw/~cjlin/libsvm
14. Lowe, D.G.: Object recognition from local scale-invariant features. In: The Proceedings of the Seventh IEEE International Conference on Computer Vision, vol. 2, pp. 1150–1157 (1999)
15. Deng, H., Zhang, W., Mortensen, E., Dietterich, T.: Principal curvature-based region detector for object recognition. In: IEEE Computer Society Conference on Computer Vision and Pattern Recognition, pp. 1–8 (2007)
16. Suzuki, S., Abe, K.: Topological structural analysis of digitized binary images by border following. Computer Vision, Graphics, and Image Processing 30, 32–46 (1985)
17. Canny, J.F.: A computational approach to edge detection. IEEE Transactions on Pattern Analysis and Machine Intelligence 8, 679–698 (1986)
18. Avrithis, Y.S., Xirouhakis, Y., Kollias, S.D.: Affine-invariant curve normalization for shape-based retrieval. In: 15th International Conference on Pattern Recognition, vol. 1, pp. 1015–1018 (2000)
19. Zhang, D., Lu, G.: A comparative study on shape retrieval using fourier descriptors with different shape signatures. Journal of Visual Communication and Image Representation 14, 41–60 (2003)
20. Turk, M., Pentland, A.: Eigenfaces for recognition. Journal of Cognitive Neuroscience 3, 71–86 (1991)
21. Tuzel, O., Porikli, F., Meer, P.: Region Covariance: A fast Descriptor for Detection and Classification. In: Leonardis, A., Bischof, H., Pinz, A. (eds.) ECCV 2006, Part II. LNCS, vol. 3952, pp. 589–600. Springer, Heidelberg (2006)
22. Rodgers, J.L., Nicewander, A.W.: Thirteen ways to look at the correlation coefficient. The American Statistician 42, 59–66 (1988)
23. Hsu, C.-W., Lin, C.-J.: A comparison of methods for multiclass support vector machines. IEEE Transactions on Neural Networks 13, 415–425 (2002)

Using Agent in Virtual Machine for Interactive Security Training

Yi-Ming Chen, Cheng-En Chuang[*], Hsu-Che Liu,
Cheng-Yi Ni, and Chun-Tang Wang

Department of Information Management, National Central University, Taiwan
Department of Computer Science, National Central University, Taiwan
cym@cc.ncu.edu.tw, {ChengEn.Chuang,HsuChe.Liu}@gmail.com,
{nichy,chuntang}@dslab.csie.ncu.edu.tw

Abstract. With the lack of security awareness, people are easy to become malicious programs' target. Hence, it is important to educate people to know how the hackers intrude the systems. In this paper, we propose a platform that combining agent and virtualization technologies to build an interactive security training platform with which people can easily get security training. In our system, all malicious programs are contained in virtual machines, and by installing an agent in the virtual machine, our system can record trainee's operations to the malicious program, then decide what situation the trainee may face and what steps should follow up to accomplish attack or defense in hands-on labs according to the results of trainee's previous operations. This kind of interactivity as well as the individualized learning experience will decrease the disadvantage of "single size fit all" which is generally associated with traditional security training courses.

Keywords: Agent, Interactivity, Security training, Virtual machine.

1 Introduction

Security training is an important element for whom need their IT infrastructure keeping in secure. As cyber warfare is growing, the demand for training both college students and on-job-professional is increasing too [9]. However, to fulfill such demand usually faces two challenges. First, building up a security training environment is not an easy task. For example, as time passing by, lots of classic security exploit examples are disappeared due to the upgrading of the operating systems and network devices. Moreover, amount of expense may be needed to reconstruct the scale of exploit example's environment as we considering about the restraints of physical resources existing in university and training organizations. Second, security trainee usually needs a lot of background knowledge (including OS, networks, programming, database, etc.) to comprehend the training material. As a

---

[*] Corresponding author.

T.-h. Kim et al. (Eds.): SecTech 2011, CCIS 259, pp. 65–74, 2011.

result, when a trainee is practicing in hands-on labs, a human tutor is usually needed to tell the trainee the implications of the operations he/she performs and what steps should follow up to complete the labs. However, assigning a tutor for each trainee is not practical for general security training programs.

To solve the problems mentioned above, in this paper we propose an interactive security training platform, named Cloud Security Experiment Platform (CSEP), using both virtualization and agent technologies. According to the classification proposed by Franklin S. *et al.* [3], the agent in this paper is fall into the class of *task-specific agent*. It means our agent is in fact a process in the virtual machine and it is responsible to communicate with a CSEP server so that the system can know exactly operations the trainee is performing.

The contributions of this paper are in three aspects:

(1) We introduce how to combine the virtualization and agent technologies to build a security training platform.
(2) We present how to construct a document which can give trainee the individualized learning experience.
(3) We present a demonstrative SQL injection case to show the usefulness of our system.

This paper is divided into 6 sections. In Section 2, we review some related work. The system requirements are listed in Section 3. Section 4 describes the design and implementation of the platform. In the Section 5, we will demonstrate the use of the platform by a SQL injection training case. Finally we give conclusions and future research directions in Section 6.

2   Related Work

There have been many security training or experiment platforms proposed [2][7][8][12]. In this section, we will introduce two of them.

WebGoat [12] is a J2EE web application which is developed by the OWASP to teach web application security. WebGoat can be installed and run on any platform with a JVM, and there are over 30 lessons. Once it has been downloaded and run, a lightweight Apache Tomcat web server will be run in the local machine. Then the user can access the local web server and choose the lesson he/she wants to learn. WebGoat has an interactive training web interface. But the user has to download and run it in local machine. In addition, WebGoat focuses on the web security and thus lacks the training of many other important security topics, such Spam mail, DDoS, etc.

SWEET [1] is a set of modules which include documents and a training environment. Both documents and training environment can be downloaded from the SWEET's web site. Though each module contains a security lesson and has its own document, all the modules duplicate the same virtual machine based training environment. SWEET needs trainees to install the virtualization environment in their own machines [5]. Moreover, running a virtual machine in local environment will spend many resources like CPU time memory space. Neither can it support trainees to perform a large scale experiment like DDoS.

3   System Requirements

One requirement of CSEP is the support of interactivity. Interactivity means every time the trainee decide to perform operations, e.g. enter some exploit string to a web form, our system will give different next instruction depending on the result of the trainee's decision. We believe this kind of personalized practicing experience can enhance the trainee's impression on the contents of security lessons.

Another system requirement is security. To isolate the security experimental network from the Internet, many security experiment frameworks using virtual private network (VPN) for user remote access. Unfortunately, most of them use only one VPN for all trainees. As all trainees share the same VPN account and password, once a malicious Trainee A enters the VPN, there is no further protection to prevent Trainee A from accessing Trainee B's nodes in the same VPN (see Fig. 1). Therefore, security is also an important requirement we need to address when we design our system.

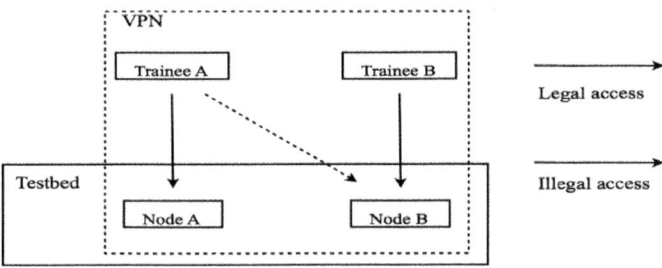

Fig. 1. The risk of using single VPN in security training platform

4   System Design and Implementation

4.1   System Overview

The CSEP is implemented by Django web framework [10] and Xen [13]. Its main modules are shown in Fig. 2. This figure also illustrates how the CSEP handles a trainee's request and provides the interactive training.

Dispatcher is in charge of trainee's http requests and initiates a set of operations to fulfill trainee's requests. For example, when it receives a "Booting up a virtual machine" request from trainee (Step 1 in Fig. 2), it will call the VMController to communicate with Virtualization Platform's API to start a virtual machine (Step 2 to Step 4). After the virtual machine has been boot up successfully, Vagent will be run up automatically. After that, Vagent server will build up a *waypoint* in Step 5 (the detail of waypoint will be described in Section 4.3). Then the trainee can connect to the virtual machine through *waypoint* in Step 6. Finally, when Vagent needs to pass some new information about the virtual machine (e.g. the trainee has exploited the web server on the virtual machine) to the trainee, the information will be pushed through WebSocket [4].

In next subsection, we will describe how the CSEP achieves security and interactivity requirement which we mentioned in Section 3.

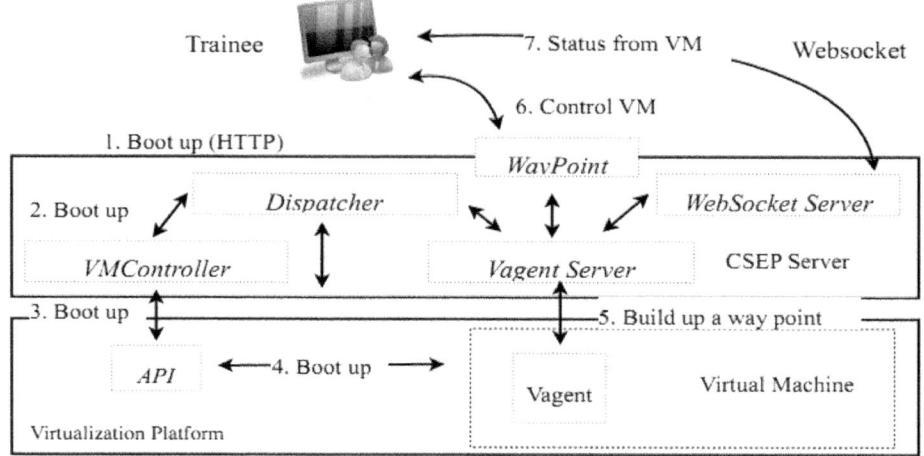

Fig. 2. System architecture

4.2   Security Design and Implementation

As we have mentioned in Section 3, the security requirement of CSEP is to prevent the trainee from interfering each other or the Internet. This interference can be eliminated by providing individual VPN for each trainee. However, a new problem called asymmetric network problem arises.

Assume there are two nodes, one of them in at the Internet and the other node is in a NAT server or behind a firewall. We denote them as the Node A and Node B respectively. Node B can connect to node A at anytime. But node A can not do that vice versa because node B is behind NAT or firewall (refer to Fig. 3).

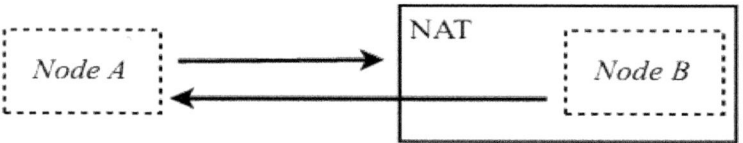

Fig. 3. Asymmetric network

To allow Node B to reach Node A, we have to setup a waypoint [6] which is a machine at somewhere in the Internet (see Fig. 4). When Node B connects to the waypoint, the waypoint will establish a connection to a service on Node B, e.g. the SSH service, which Node B wants to share with Node A. While SSH service on Node B listening to the waypoint, Node A can establish SSH connection to Node B through the waypoint which handles the traffic forwarding between Node A and Node B.

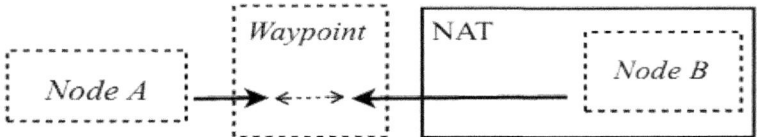

Fig. 4. Waypoint forwards the traffic between node A and node B

In our CSEP, the waypoint is located in the CSEP server and is implemented within the Vagent server module by reverse tunneling technique. The Vagent module resides in the virtual machine represents the Node B while the trainee's machine represents Node A. The operations of reverse tunneling are described as follows (refer to Fig. 5).

First, Vagent connects back to Vagent server. Second, Vagent server binds and listens to a random port P on the CSEP server. The port number P will be pushed to trainee's machine by WebSocket so that the latter knows the virtual machine is now ready to be connected. Third, when the trainee's machine tries to connect to the port P of CSEP server, the Vagent server (which is inside the CSEP server) will set up a waypoint to forward the traffic.

Finally, as soon as the waypoint needs to pass traffic from the trainee's machine to the virtual machine, the Vagent server will connect to the remote control service port of the latter, and forward the traffic to the virtual machine accordingly.

The security of above design comes from that once the traffic flow through the waypoint is over, the reverse tunnel will be closed. Next time the building of reverse tunnel will adopt another random port. As a result, a malicious trainee has difficulty to guess the new random port to access the virtual machine of another trainee, even he/she know the account and password of the latter. Trying to access another trainee's virtual machine by brute force, e.g. through port scanning, will be easily noticed and be blocked by the CSEP server.

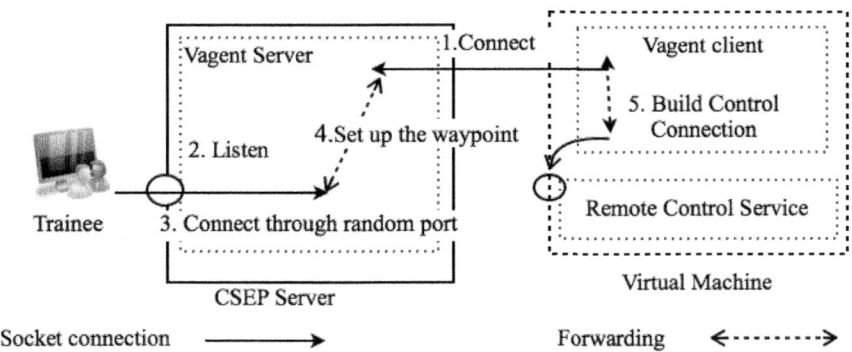

Fig. 5. Build up a reverse tunnel

4.3   Design and Implementation of Interactivity Support

To achieve the interactivity support, we need to rewrite the training documents so that they can cooperate with CSEP system to provide individual guidance to trainees. In general, a document is the training material for each security experiment, and the trainee will read and follow the instructions inside the documents to practice experiments. All of our documents have the following sections:

- Introduction: Give an overview of a specific security topic.
- Goal: Describe the learning goal that we hope the trainee will obtained after practicing the experiment.
- Principle: Explaining why and how the specific security issue will happen.
- Setting: List the tools that will be used later, and the environment such as network topology.
- Experiment: The experiment is divided into attack and defense parts. Each part contains instructions for trainee to follow up. .

The CSEP's interactivity is through the addition of JavaScript in the trainee machine's browser and checkpoints in the vulnerable or malicious programs installed in the virtual machines. The function of checkpoints is to get the results of the operations performed by the trainee during the experiments. To practice a hands-on lab, a trainee follows the instructions inside a document and passes a checkpoint to get next part of instructions and continue this process until the completion of the lab.

The implementation of checkpoints can be achieved by injecting some codes into vulnerable or malicious programs. An example is injecting some PHP codes into a vulnerable web application. The major design issue is where to place the checkpoints within the programs. One option is to place the checkpoint at the code which receives inputs from the trainee. Checkpoint which receives input from the trainee can judge if the trainee has sent the right input, e.g. a checkpoint can use the regular expression "/(\%27)|(\')|(\-\-)|(\%23)|(#)/ix" to examine if there is a SQL injection happening. Another option is to place the checkpoint at the code where some programs use it to handle trainee's click action. For instance, after we add check point code into the tbl_replace.php in the phpMyAdmin's source code, so that checkpoint will be triggered if trainee clicks some database insert button on the web page.

In the following paragraphs, we will give a simple example to show how we provide interactivity support in the CSEP documents.

SQL injection is a well known and popular web application's security issue [11]. To learn about this issue, our SQL injection training document will list instructions to ask trainee to connect to the vulnerable web server running in the virtual machine. After this connection is established, the web server will show some input form through which the trainee can submit data to a vulnerable web application. Once the trainee inject a SQL input pattern of ' or '1'='1 into the *account* variable of the SQL query *SELECT * FROM `user` where `name` = ' " + account + "';"*, then the authentication of the SQL application will be bypassed.

To check whether the trainee has input the correct string to exploit the vulnerable SQL application, we need to insert some codes into the vulnerable web application.

For example, if we want to use the SQL injection vulnerability to create a *cmd.php* file in the web application's file system, we need to insert some php code as shown in below.

```
if(file_exists("C:/AppServ/www/cmd.php")){
    $fp = fsockopen("localhost", vagent_listen_port);
    $out = "next step signal";
    fwrite($fp, $out);
}
```

This code first examine whether the trainee has successful injected the file (i.e. successfully exploit the SQL injection vulnerability), if so, it will send *"next step signal"* string to the port *vagent_listen_port* which the Vagent is always listening on. This string tells the Vagent that trainee has finished the current instruction and now goes to next experiment stage.

After receiving the signal string sent by the vulnerable SQL application, Vagent will pass this string back to the CSEP server which in turn will pass it to the trainee's browser to show the next part of documentation. During these operations, there is one issue is how can the CSEP server know which trainee it needs to pass the signal string. Our solution is that after the CSEP server gets the string from the Vagent, it will look up the Vagent server's correspondence table in which we keep the record of the IP address to whom boot this virtual machine up. Once CSEP server find the one who boot the virtual machine up, it will use WebSocket to push the string to the trainee's browser to instruct the JavaScript with signal for the Websocket to show the next part of documentation. Fig. 6 illustrates our implementation.

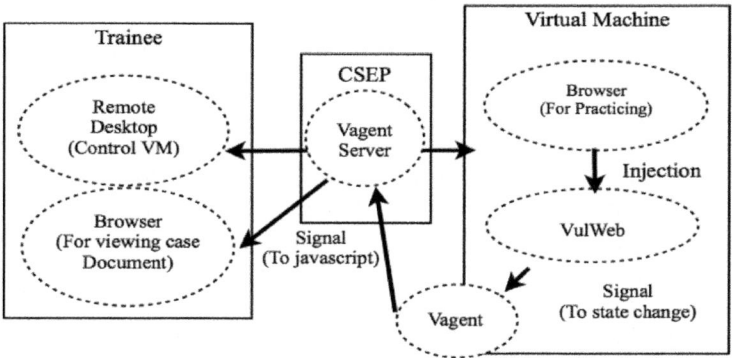

Fig. 6. The modules to support interactivity in the SQL injection case

The final action is updating the document's experiment step in client's browser. We split the all steps into several parts. As soon as the browser receives the signal from the virtual machine, the JavaScript within the training document will show the appropriate experiment steps needed to be followed up. Fig. 7 describes that the JavaScript will show the second part of document when the signal 2 arrived to the trainee's machine.

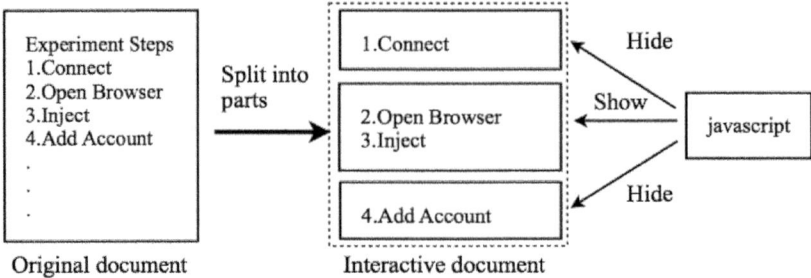

Fig. 7. Display second part when server received signal 2

5   Platform Application Example

In this section, we will show how a trainee using CSEP to learn SQL injection.

Firstly, trainee can use the reverse tunnel to connect to the vulnerable web server. As soon as connecting to the CSEP's waypoint at CSEP server (140.115.x.y:random port), trainee's connection will be forwarding to the virtual machine inside the NAT of which the IP address is 192.168.198.131.

Then the trainee will follow the instructions on the web page (see Fig. 8(a)). The instruction will tell him/her to open the browser and connect to the vulnerable web application in the virtual machine and enter some input, such as following line:

```
';select '<?php $a = $_GET[\'cmd\']; echo `$a`; ?>' into
outfile 'C:/AppServ/www/cmd.php'#
```

to the web form in Fig. 8(b) so that SQL injection will happen, as we have insert checkpoints in the vulnerable web application, the CSEP can determine whether the trainee inject above string successfully or not. Once the input is correct, the success signal will be sent back to the trainee's browser so that the next part of training document (Fig. 8(e)) will be shown correspondingly according to the part which signal is asking for in the documents. Note that there are several options the trainee may leverage to perform the SQL injection. For example, there are two ways to conduct SQL inject by the instructions shown in Fig. 8(a). Different trainee may select different option according to his/her background knowledge about IT security, so that getting different results. An example is shown in Fig. 8(c) where the trainee select the first instruction of Fig. 8(a) to create a new database account, while in Fig. 8(d) the trainee inject a new file to the system directory of victim computer by using the second instruction of Fig. 8(a). Moreover, trainees will see different instructions in their browser if they make different decisions during security experiments, as shown in Fig. 8(e)(f).

By allowing trainee to select more than one option and get different feedback will enhance his/her understanding of the meaning of security topics. In this case, the trainee will understand how and what condition to create a database account or insert a file to a victim's computer successfully, then what consequence will occur after this attack performed.

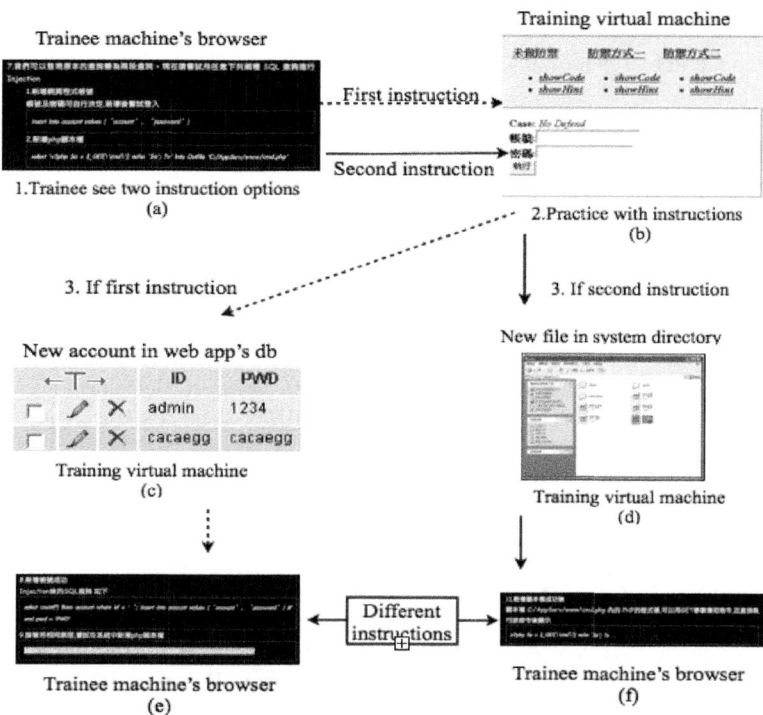

Fig. 8. Interactive security training support in CSEP

6   Conclusion

In this paper, we propose an interactive security training platform using virtualization technology. Virtualization can easily bring back lots of classic security examples. In particular, we use agent in virtual machines. The agent brings two main benefits. One is the improvement of security. As our agent can cooperate with CSEP server to build a waypoint by using reverse tunnel, we can eliminate the interference between trainees and avoid the spreading of malicious program from training platform to the Internet. The other benefit is interactivity support. As agent can stay in the virtual machine and detect the status change of the virtual machine and send back the new status to the trainee's browser, the JavaScript in the trainee's machine can then show different instructions according to his/her previous operations. This kind of interactivity can increase the learning effectiveness of security hands-on labs.

According to our current experience in constructing the CSEP, we find that the smaller the granularity of the document parts, the better the interactivity support. So our future work will focus on how make agent to more precisely monitor the virtual machine's state so that we can have better granularity.

Acknowledgements. This work was partially supported by the National Science Council of Taiwan, R.O.C. under Grant No. 99-2218-E-008-013 and the Software Research Center of National Central University.

References

1. Chen, L.C., Tao, L.: Hands on Teaching Modules for Secure Web Application Development. In: ACM SIGCSE Workshop, p. 27 (2011)
2. Du, W., Wang, R.: SEED: A Suite of Instruction Laboratories for Computer Security Education. Journal on Educational Resources in Computing 8 (2008)
3. Franklin, S., Graesser, A.: Is It an Agent, or Just a Program?: A Taxonomy for Autonomous Agents. In: Jennings, N.R., Wooldridge, M.J., Müller, J.P. (eds.) ECAI-WS 1996 and ATAL 1996. LNCS, vol. 1193, pp. 21–35. Springer, Heidelberg (1997)
4. HyBi Working Group:The Web Socket protocol, IETF, Standards Track, pp. 1--69 (2011), http://tools.ietf.org/html/draft-ietf-hybi-thewebsocketprotocol-10
5. Tao, L., Chen, L.C., Lin, C.T.: Virtual Open-Source Labs for Web Security Education. In: International Conference on Education and Information Technology, WCECS 2010, San Francisco, vol. I, pp. 280–285 (2010)
6. Tschudin, C., Gold, R.: Network pointers. In: 1st ACM Hotnets Workshop ACM SIGCOMM Computer Communication Review, New York, vol. 33, pp. 23–28 (2003)
7. Volvnkin, A., Skormin, V.: Large-scale Reconfigurable Virtual Testbed for Information Security Experiments, Conference of Testbeds and Research Infrastructure for the Development of Networks and Communities, Florida (2007)
8. Willems, C., Dawoud, W., Klingbeil, T., Meinel, C.: Protecting Tele-Lab – attack vectors and countermeasures for a remote virtual IT security lab. International Journal of Digital Society 1, 113–122 (2010)
9. Yang, T.A.: Computer security and impact on computer science education. Journal of Computing Sciences in Colleges 16, 233–246 (2001)
10. Django Software Foundation, https://www.djangoproject.com/
11. OWASP, Top 10 for (2010), https://www.owasp.org/index.php/Category:OWASP_Top_Ten_Project
12. The Open Web Application Security Project (OWASP) WebGoat Project, https://www.owasp.org/
13. Xen, http://xen.org

Information Technology Security Governance Approach Comparison in E-banking

Theodosios Tsiakis, Aristeidis Chatzipoulidis,
Theodoros Kargidis, and Athanasios Belidis

Alexander Technological Educational Institute of Thessaloniki,
Dept. of Marketing, Thessaloniki
{tsiakis,kargidis,abelidis}@mkt.teithe.gr,
hatzipoulidis@gmail.com

Abstract. Banks' have constantly been looking for channels as means to lower operational costs and reach a greater market share. This opportunity has been achieved through electronic banking channels capable to offer services that add value to the business. However, the increasing reliance on Information Technology (IT) has caused an array of risks that need to be mitigated before damage the system reputation and customer records. For this role, the Information Technology Security Governance (ITSG) implementation is to protect the most valuable assets of an organization. In this paper, we describe the components of an e-banking environment, clarify congruent terminology used in achieving Information Security Governance (ISG) objectives and evaluate most reputed ITSG approaches to help banks choose which approach best fits the e-banking environment.

Keywords: Electronic banking, information technology security governance, risk management.

1   Introduction

Electronic banking (e-banking) is a service that has received high attention from many researchers and practitioners because of the great potential it possess. Along with the opportunities e-banking presents such as lower operational costs, access to new customers, increase in the quality of services and new business prospects, it carries along a variety of risks which if not managed appropriately can damage an otherwise infallible e-banking system. This paper focuses on managing e-banking risks from an Information Technology Security Governance (ITSG) perspective due to the increasing demand in compliance with industry-related standards and also due to the strong requirement for exchanging secure information and keeping customers records safe [4,14].

In this respect, society and experts created a discipline that can effectively add value to the business and also manage and mitigate Information Technology (IT) risks [26,27]. ITSG is a newly developed term requiring the attention of Boards of Directors and Executive Management for effective information security. This paper

T.-h. Kim et al. (Eds.): SecTech 2011, CCIS 259, pp. 75–84, 2011.

focuses on current ITSG approaches applicable to complex systems, such as e-banking, to show shortcomings and benefits each approach delivers in an attempt to help financial institutions achieve a holistic view to Information Security (IS). In this regard, this paper is organized as follows; in the next section we review the literature about e-banking and ITSG and in section 3 we evaluate the most reputed ITSG approaches for e-banking based on ISG objectives. The paper ends with a conclusion about the future for e-banking services.

2   Literature Review

Before getting into detail about e-banking risks and current ITSG approaches it is wise to review e-banking and ITSG as separate concepts. Therefore, e-banking can be regarded as a service with intense operational activity that relies heavily on IT to acquire, process, and deliver the information to all relevant users [7]. In essence, the term e-banking is used as an umbrella term to describe banking applications, including products and services, with the use of technology. Specifically, the proliferation of Internet technology have led the development of new products such as aggregation of services, bill presentment and personalized financial services. The primary motivation for the increasing role of technology in e-banking has been to a) reduce costs, b) eliminate uncertainties, c) increase customer satisfaction and d) standardize e-banking services by reducing the heterogeneity prevalent in the typical employee/customer encounter [1]. In this respect, banks have moved quickly to invest in technology as a way of controlling costs, attracting new customers, and meeting the convenience and technical innovation expectations of their customers. Banks use e-banking because this service can create competitive advantage, improve image and reputation of the financial institution and increase customer loyalty. According to [2] there are a number of retail banking services, distribution channels and target markets in an e-banking environment (see figure 1) but three major types distinguish depending on the channel by which the transactions are performed: (1) Internet banking, (2) Phone banking, (3) Mobile banking.

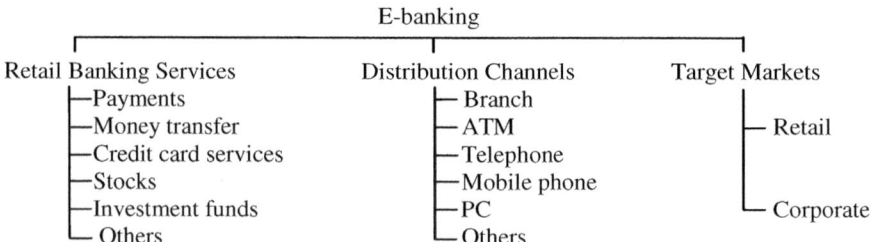

Source: Adopted from [2]

Fig. 1. Retail banking services and distribution channels

(1) Internet banking (or web banking), refers to the use of Internet as a remote delivery channel for banking services, such as transferring funds, electronic bill presentment and payment [3]. Another definition [10] describe Internet banking as a direct connection through a modem via which people can access their banks and conduct transactions 24 h a day, with reduced costs and increased convenience.

(2) Phone banking, as it name implies, is the service conducted via a phone device that is not mobile. This service is divided [1] into two categories a) manually via real-person contact and b) automatically through IVR (Interactive Voice Response) systems where the customer responds to voice messages.

(3) Mobile banking (m-banking) is a relative new channel where the service is conducted via a mobile phone device. However, this channel has not reached its full potential and the main reasons are customer acceptance/trust for m-banking, regulatory issues and bank participation towards this channel [5].

Moreover, e-banking is considered an electronic financial service that belongs to the wider e-commerce area [19]. Electronic commerce (EC) is the process of electronically conducting all forms of business between entities in order to achieve the organization's objectives [18]. E-commerce consists of two broad categories namely a) e-finance, a term which included financial services via e-channels and b) e-money, a term that includes all the mechanisms for stored value or pre-paid payment. The main difference between e-money and e-banking is that the former uses financial information that are not stored in a financial account but are depicted instantly as digital money. Examples of e-money are usually the direct deposit and virtual currency. E-finance is a broad term including e-banking and other financial services and products such as insurance and online brokering. The figure below summarizes this notion.

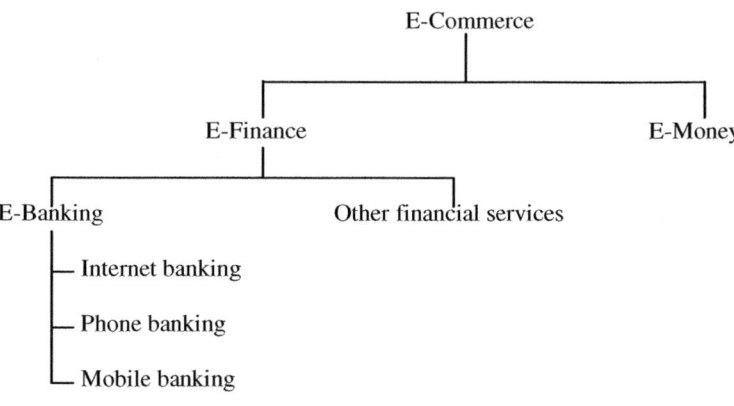

Source: Adopted from [19]

Fig. 2. Position of e-banking in relation to e-commerce

E-banking depends heavily on the role of IT to perform. Consequently, IT security is important to safeguard information such as customer records and financial data. Particularly, IT security is a subset of IS, a concept which has become an integral part of daily life and banks need to ensure that the information exchanged are adequately secured [24]. For this reason and because e-banking necessitates the involvement of different stakeholders, from the Board of Directors to regular users, IT security should be regarded as an operational and management issue rather than a solely technical issue [28]. In this respect, IT security has been moving strongly towards the use of documents and guidelines based on so called Best standards, Risk Management methods, internal controls and Codes of Practice for governing and managing IS.

In literature there exist a confusion among experts about the use of congruent terms related to IT security that usually overlap in objectives. In this regard, the purpose of ITSG, a term that has its roots in the ITG (Information Technology Governance) discipline, is to describe the roles and responsibilities of those involved in an IT system. Particularly, [23] use a number of references to define ITG: *"specifying the decision rights and accountability framework to encourage desirable behavior in the use of IT"*, and as: *"the organizational capacity exercised by the Board, executive management and IT management to control the formulation and implementation of IT strategy and in this way ensuring the fusion of business and IT"*. Particularly, [17] define ITSG as the establishment and maintenance of the control environment to manage the risks relating to the confidentiality, integrity and availability of information and its supporting processes and systems. Others [15,22] use the term Information Security Governance (ISG) to describe not only the operational (managerial) and strategic but also the technological environment in an organization.

Moreover, [12] argues that ITSG is compliment to ISG consisting of a set of responsibilities various stakeholders possess with the goal of providing strategic direction, ensuring that risks and resources are managed efficiently. In addition, [23] describe ISG as a decision-making process including protection of stakeholder value and the most valuable resources of a financial institution, including IT assets. Similar to the ITSG concept lies the Corporate Governance (CG), a term which is used to identify and describe the relationships between, and the distribution of rights, information and responsibilities among, the four main groups of participants in a corporate body naming 1. Board of directors, 2. Managers, 3. Employees, and 4. Various stakeholders. CG can also be defined as the process in which business operations are directed and controlled [9].

Complementary to CG lies the Enterprise Government (EG) term. EG refers to the organizational structures and processes that aim to ensure that the organization's business objectives and IT sustains and delivers business value to the financial institution and stakeholders [11]. The noticeable difference between EG and CG is that CG refers more to the combined beliefs, values, procedures in an industry or in a sector (e.g. financial sector) whereas EG refers more to the activities of an organization. EG also supports relevant aspects of ISG including accountability to stakeholders, compliance with legal requirements, setting clear security policies, spreading security awareness and education, defining roles and responsibilities, contingency planning and instituting best practice standards. The ISG objectives according to [25] are summarized in the next bullets:

- *Strategic alignment*: aligning security activities with business strategy to support organizational objectives
- *Risk Management*: actions to manage risks to an acceptable level
- *Business process assurance/convergence*: integrating all relevant assurance processes to maximize the effectiveness and efficiency of security activities
- *Value delivery*: optimizing investments in support of business objectives
- *Resource management*: using organizational resources efficiently and effectively
- *Performance measurement*: monitoring and reporting on security processes

However, there are sound examples that ISG has failed to live up to expectations due to high visibility failures such as Enron, Tyco, WorldCom, and Arthur Andersen [21]. For this reason, the need for ITSG has become apparent in an attempt to support ISG achieve its role. At its core, ITSG is concerned with two things a) delivery of value to the business and b) mitigation of IT risks [16]. A comprehensive definition of ITSG [25] is as an integral part of enterprise (corporate) governance consisting of the leadership and organizational structures that ensure the organization's IT infrastructure sustains and extends the organization's strategies and objectives. Taking into consideration all the discussed literature on ITSG and congruent terminology, we conclude that the role of ITSG in e-banking is as a *"cognitive process that adds value to the business and IT infrastructure resulting in a set of actions among several stakeholders towards managing e-banking risks"*.

3   ITSG Approach Comparison

In this section, we will consider the most reputed methods used to describe the ISG objectives [8,9,12,13]. Therefore, in our quest for which approach can "better" define objectives for ITSG, we evaluate a number of approaches (table 1) to help define a desired state of security. Here "better" means "in a more holistic way".

3.1   Sherwood Applied Business Security Architecture

SABSA is a "security architecture" tool capable to provide a framework within which complexity of modern business can be managed successfully. Particularly, it can offer simplicity and clarity through layering and modularization of business functions. It has been developed to address issues such as the design, management, implementation, and monitoring of business activities against security incidents. The approach is a framework that is compatible with and can utilize other IT Governance frameworks such as CobiT as well as ITIL and ISO/IEC 27001. The SABSA Model comprises of six layers each layer representing the view of a different player in the process of specifying, designing, constructing, and using business systems.

3.2   Control Objectives for Information and Related Technology

CobiT [20] is an IT governance framework that can be used in ensuring proper control and governance over information and the systems that create, store, manipulate, and retrieve it. CobiT 4.1 is organized with 34 IT processes, giving a complete picture of how to control, manage, and measure each process. CobiT also appeals to different users namely from Executive management (to obtain value from IT investments and balance risk and control investment), to auditors (to validate their opinions and provide advice to management on internal controls). In particular, high level processes such as ME 1 and ME 4 and DS 5 are referring to Monitoring, Surveillance and Evaluating respectively.

3.3   Capability Maturity Model

CMM is used to measure two things: the maturity of processes (specific functions) that produce products (e.g., identified vulnerabilities, countermeasures, and threats) and the level of compliance as a process with respect to the IATRP (InfoSec Assurance Training and Rating Program) methodology. In other words, CMM measures the level of assurance that an organization can perform a process consistently. In this respect, CMM identifies nine process areas related to performing information security assurance services.

3.4   ISO/IEC 27002:2005

This standard is an industry benchmark code of practice for information security practice. Formally known as ISO/IEC 17799:2005, this standard can support useful governance guidance and can also be effectively used to establish the current state of security for an organization. It supports ISO/IEC 27001:2005, a standard known as an ISMS process. An ISMS is a management system for dealing with IS risk exposures namely, a framework of policies, procedures, physical, legal, and technical security controls forming part of the organization's overall Risk Management processes. ISO 27001 incorporates Deming's Plan-Do-Check-Act (PDCA) cycle have to be continually reviewed and adjusted to incorporate changes in the security threats, vulnerabilities and impacts of information security failures. The organization who adapts ISO 27001 can receive certification by an accredited certification body. ISO 27002 (aka ISO 17799) is used to describe two distinct documents: ISO 27002, which is a set of security controls (a code of practice), and ISO 27001 (formerly BS7799-2), which is a standard ''specification'' for an Information Security Management System (ISMS). This standard and code of practice can serve to provide an approach to information security governance (ISG), although, to some extent by inference. That is, ISO 27001 is a management system with a focus on control objectives, not a strategic governance approach.

3.5   National Cyber Security Summit Task Force Corporate Governance Framework

CGTF is an ISG framework towards organizational compliance. In particular, item 3 in the framework refers to the security responsibilities for the Board, Senior management and workforce towards compliance and governance objectives. The details described in the framework can be used to identify whether the security conditions exist, to what extend and how can the organization reach a higher level of compliance.

3.6   Basel Committee on Banking Supervision

The Basel Committee objective is to formulate broad supervisory standards and guidelines about the banking industry in the areas of system supervision and regulation. The Committee does not possess any formal supranational supervisory authority and does not enforce any kind of compliance however it offers comprehensive coverage of Risk Management and ISG issues relating to e-banking such as operational Risk Management, outsourcing, business continuity management, anti-money laundering, privacy of customer information and audit procedures.

3.7   The Joint Forum

The Joint Forum is considered as an advisory group formed under the guidance of the Bank for International Settlements, Basel, Switzerland and consists of three members namely the Basel Committee on Banking Supervision, the International Organization of Securities Commissions (IOSCO) and the International Association of Insurance Supervisors (IAIS). The Joint Forum mainly provides recommendations for the insurance, securities, and banking industries worldwide setting high level principles including risk assessment guidelines. Relevant principles refer to outsourcing of e-banking activities and the need for a Business Continuity Planning (BCP).

3.8   Operationally Critical Threat, Asset and Vulnerability Assessment

OCTAVE [13] is an asset-driven method and represents visually the range of threats during the evaluation in tree structures. Currently, there exist three variations of the OCTAVE method namely the original OCTAVE method as a comprehensive suite of tools, the OCTAVE-S for smaller organizations and the OCTAVE-Allegro as a streamline approach for IS and assurance. OCTAVE is based on interactive workshops to accumulate the different knowledge perspectives of the employees, the Board and Executives and other stakeholders for the purpose to measure current organization security practices and develop security improvement strategies and risk mitigation planning. The OCTAVE approach is driven by operational risk and security practices. Technology is examined only in relation to security practices. The OCTAVE also characterizes certain criteria as set of principles, attributes, and outputs. Important principles among others are the fundamental concepts driving the nature of the evaluation, for example, self direction, integrated management and open communication.

In table 1 we provide an approach features evaluation under a scale: "yes", "partial" and "no" - levels of fulfillment. For example, the Basel Committee of Banking Supervision for e-banking provides guidelines for monitoring and reporting however, it does not provide performance measurement in the sense of exact metrics. Most of the aforementioned frameworks, best standards, Risk Management methods suggest security policies, procedures, and guidelines as the key components to implement information security in order to provide management, support compliance and direct employees with what is expected as behavior. Every single approach has its own strengths and weaknesses but none covers all ITSG objectives. Therefore, according to literature [8,22] customization is pertinent to appropriately fit within the e-banking environment.

Table 1. ITSG approach comparison

ITSG Approach / ITSG Objectives	Basel Committee	Joint Forum	ISO 27002	COBIT	OCTAVE	CGTF	SABSA	CMM
Strategic alignment	✓	✓	✓	✓	✓	✓	✓	✓
Risk Management	✓	✓	✓	✓	✓	✓	✓	✓
Business process assurance	✓	x	✓	✓	✓	✓	✓	✓
Value delivery	✓	x	✓	✓	✓	✓	✓	✓
Resource management	✓	x	✓	✓	✓	✓	✓	✓
Performance measurement	/	x	✓	✓	✓	✓	✓	✓
User awareness & training	✓	x	/	✓	✓	✓	✓	✓
Certification	x	x	✓	✓	x	x	✓	x
Internal audit	✓	x	✓	x	✓	✓	✓	✓
Best practice	✓	x	✓	✓	x	✓	✓	✓
Corporate governance	✓	✓	✓	✓	✓	✓	✓	✓
Incident management	✓	/	✓	x	✓	✓	✓	✓
Business continuity planning	✓	✓	✓	✓	✓	✓	✓	✓
Ethical codes	✓	x	/	x	x	x	/	x
Compliance	✓	x	✓	✓	✓	✓	✓	✓

Legend

✓ = yes   / = partial   x = no

According to the table results there is no single approach that encompasess all the range of ITSG objectives. Based on the summary of attributes (derived from the evaluation results) for a desired state of security, we conclude that the first step in choosing and adapting to an ITSG approach is to fulfill the ISG objectives, namely the first six components of the ITSG objectives. However, ISG objectives alone may not satisfy the security needs of an e-banking system. For example, user awareness and training is a paramount factor in adopting e-banking services [2,6]. Moreover, receiving certification for attaining an approach can prove beneficial by elevating the professional stature of the e-banking system through proven experience and expertise. In addition, conformity to ethical codes is crucial for competence in the area of user interaction with the e-banking system [1]. In this respect, the bank in search for a desired state of security, should choose a combination of approaches in order to build a holistic ITSG framework around the e-banking system. Priority is to satisfy strategic, operational and technical sytem parameters and to ensure most of the evaluated ITSG objectives are fullfilled.

4   Conclusion

Banking has traditionally been built on the branch-banking model, however technology has offered tremendous opportunities for banks to surpass geographical, commercial and demographic barriers. Therefore, the success of e-banking is now determined by its ability to successfully secure financial and customer's data. In this respect, it has become all the more critical for banks to have flexible and responsive ITSG processes that recognize, address and manage e-banking risks in a prudent manner according to the challenges of e-banking services. Based on this paper's research, customization is pertinent according to each e-banking system unique environment. Each method encompasses a set of traits for a proper framework to govern the IS in an e-banking system however, there are benefits and shortcomings. Current ISG is often based on a centralized decision derived from the Board of Directors taken from risk management approaches to IS. However, there is a role for more corporate governance and improved organizational security practices in the e-banking domain. The implementation and adaption of a particular ITSG approach depends on the size, financial strength, culture, core competencies and overall security strategy the bank employs in accordance with the business objectives.

References

1. Aggelis, V.G.: The bible of e-banking. New Technologies Publications, Athens (2005) (in Greek)
2. Akinci, S., Aksoy, S., Atilgan, E.: Adoption of Internet banking among sophisticated consumer segments in an advanced developing country. The International Journal of Bank Marketing 22(3), 212–232 (2004)
3. Aladwani, A.M.: Online banking: a field study of drivers, development challenges, and expectations. International Journal of Information Management 21, 213–225 (2001)
4. Angelakopoulos, G., Mihiotis, A.: E-banking: challenges and opportunities in the Greek banking sector. Electronic Commerce Research, 1–23 (2011)
5. Barnes, S.J., Corbitt, B.: Mobile banking: concept and potential. Author: International Journal of Mobile Communications 1(3), 273–288 (2003)
6. Basel Committee on Banking Supervision: Risk Management Principles for Electronic banking (2003), http://www.bis.org/publ/bcbs98.pdf (retrieved July 20, 2011)
7. Baten, M.A., Kamil, A.A.: E-Banking of Economical Prospects in Bangladesh. Journal of Internet Banking and Commerce 15(2) (2010)
8. Brotby, K.: Information Security Governance, A Practical Development and Implementation Approach. Wiley (2009)
9. Da Veiga, A., Eloff, J.H.P.: An Information Security Governance Framework. Information Systems Management 24(4), 361–372 (2007)

10. Ho Bruce, C.T., Wu, D.D.: Online banking performance evaluation using data evelopment analysis and principal component analysis. Computers & Operations Research 36, 1835–1842 (2009)
11. IFAC: Enterprise governance: getting the balance right, International Federation of Accountants, Professional Accountants in Business Committee (2004),
    http://www.ifac.org/Members/DownLoads/
    EnterpriseGovernance.pdf (retrieved July 20, 2011)
12. IT Governance Institute: Information Security Governance, Guidance for Boards of Directors and Executive Management, 2nd edn. Rolling Meadows, IL (2006)
13. IT Governance Institute: COBIT 4.1 Excerpt: Executive Summary – Framework (2007),
    http://www.isaca.org/KnowledgeCenter/cobit/Documents/
    COBIT4.pdf (retrieved July 20, 2011)
14. Kondabagil, J.: Risk Management in electronic banking: concepts and best practices. Wiley Finance (2007)
15. Kritzinger, E., von Solms, S.H.: E-learning: incorporating information security governance. Issues in Informing Science and Information Technology 3, 319–325 (2006)
16. Moreira, E., Martimiano, L.A.F., Brandao, A.J., Bernardes, M.C.: Ontologies for information security management and governance. Information Management & Computer Security 16(2), 150–165 (2008)
17. Moulton, R., Coles, R.S.: Applying Information Security Governance. Computers & Security 22(7), 580–584 (2003)
18. Mustaffa, S., Beaumont, N.: The effect of electronic commerce on small Australian enterprises. Technovation 24(2), 85–95 (2004)
19. Nsouli, S.M., Schaechter, A.: Challenges of the E-banking revolution. International Monetary Fund: Finance & Development 39(3) (2002),
    http://www.imf.org/external/pubs/ft/fandd/2002/09/nsouli.htm
    (retrieved July 20, 2011)
20. OCTAVE - Operationally Critical Threat, Asset, and Vulnerability Evaluation (2003),
    http://www.cert.org/octave/approach_intro.pdf (retrieved July 20, 2011)
21. Poore, R.S.: Information Security Governance. EDPACS 33(5), 1–8 (2005)
22. Rao, H.R., Gupta, M., Upadhyaya, S.J.: Managing Information Assurance in Financial Services. IGI Publishing (2007)
23. Rastogi, R., Von Solms, R.: Information Security Governance a Re-definition. IFIP, vol. 193. Springer, Boston (2006)
24. Saint-Gemain, R.: Information security management best practice based on ISO/IEC 17799. Information Management Journal 39(4), 60–65 (2005)
25. Solms, S.H., von Solms, R.: Information Security Governance. Springer, Heidelberg (2009)
26. Southard, P.B., Siau, K.: A survey of online e-banking retail initiatives. Communications of The ACM 47(10) (2004)
27. Tan, T.C.C., Ruighaver, A.B., Ahmad, A.: Information Security Governance: When Compliance Becomes More Important than Security. In: Proceedings of the 25th IFIP TC 11 International Information Security Conference, pp. 55–67 (2010)
28. Tanampasidis, G.: A Comprehensive Method for Assessment of Operational Risk in E-banking. Information Systems Control Journal 4 (2008)

A Fast and Secure One-Way Hash Function

Lamiaa M. El Bakrawy[1], Neveen I. Ghali[1],
Aboul ella Hassanien[2], and Tai-Hoon Kim[3]

[1] Al-Azhar University, Faculty of Science, Cairo, Egypt
nev_ghali@yahoo.com
[2] Cairo University, Faculty of Computers and Information, Cairo, Egypt
aboitcairo@gmail.com
[3] Hannam University, Korea
taihoonn@hannam.ac.kr

Abstract. One way hash functions play a fundamental role for data integrity, message authentication, and digital signature in modern information security. In this paper we proposed a fast one-way hash function to optimize the time delay with strong collision resistance, assures a good compression and one-way resistance. It is based on the standard secure hash function (SHA-1) algorithm. The analysis indicates that the proposed algorithm which we called (fSHA-1) is collision resistant and assures a good compression and pre-image resistance. In addition, the executing time compared with the standard secure hash function is much shorter.

1 Introduction

Hash functions were introduced in cryptography to provide data integrity, message authentication, and digital signature [1, 2]. A function that compresses an input of arbitrary large length into a fixed small size hash code is known as hash function [3,4]. The input to a hash function is called as a message or plain text and output is often referred to as message digest, the hash value, hash code, hash result or simply hash. Hash function is defined as: A hash function H is a transformation that takes an input m and returns a fixed size string, which is called the hash value h. One-way hash function must have the following properties: (1) **one-way resistance:** for any given code h, it is computationally infeasible to find x such that
$H(x) = h$, (2) **weak collision resistance:** for any given input x, it is computationally infeasible to find: $H(y) = H(x), y \neq x$, and **strong collision resistance:** it is computationally infeasible to find any pair (x,y) such that $H(y) = H(x)$. We have to note that for normal hash function with an m-bit output, it requires 2^m operations to find the one way and weak collision resistance and the fastest way to find a collision resistance is a birthday attack, which needs approximately $2^{m/2}$ operations [6,7].

The SHA-1 is called secure because it is computationally infeasible to find a message which corresponds to a given message digest, or to find two different messages which produce the same message digest. Any change to a message in transit will, with very high probability, result in a different message digest, and the signature will fail to verify

T.-h. Kim et al. (Eds.): SecTech 2011, CCIS 259, pp. 85–93, 2011.
© Springer-Verlag Berlin Heidelberg 2011

[6,7]. In this paper, a fast hash one-way function is proposed to optimize the time delay with strong collision resistance, assures a good compression and one-way resistance feature.

The remainder of this paper is organized as follows. Section (2) reviews the related works. Section (3) discusses the proposed hash function. Section (4) shows the experimental results. Conclusions are discussed in Section (5).

2   Related Works

The secure hash algorithm (SHA) was developed by National Institute of Standards and Technology (NIST) along with National Security Agency (NSA) and published as a federal information processing standard (FIPS 180) in 1993 [9]. This version is often referred to as SHA-0. It was withdrawn by NSA shortly after publication. The NSA suggested minimal changes to the standard because of security issues. The NSA did not disclose any further explanations. A revised version was issued as FIPS 180-1 in 1995 and is generally referred to as SHA-1 [9]. The actual standards document is entitled secure hash standard. SHA-1 differs from SHA-0 only by a single bitwise rotation in the message schedule of its compression function. SHA-0 and SHA-1 both produce a 160 bit message digest from a message with maximum size of 264 bits [10,11,12].

In 2002 NIST developed three new hash functions SHA- 256, 384 and 512 whose hash value sizes are 256, 384 and 512 bits respectively. These hash functions are standardized with SHA-1 as SHS(Secure Hash Standard),and a 224-bit hash function, SHA-224, based on SHA-256,was added to SHS in 2004 but moving to other members of the SHA family may not be a good solution, so efforts are underway to develop improved alternatives [6,13].

Szydlo and Lisa in [10] presented several simple message pre-processing techniques and show how these techniques can be combined with MD5 or SHA-1, so that applications are no longer vulnerable to the known collision attacks. Sugita et al. in [14] presented an improved method for finding collision on SHA-1. To do so, they use algebraic techniques for describing the message modification technique and propose an improvement. Both methods improved the complexity of an attack against 58-round SHA-1 and they found many new collisions.

Tiwari and Asawa in [6] presented hash function similar to SHA-1 but the word size and the number of rounds are same as that of SHA-1. In order to increase the security aspects of the algorithm the number of chaining variables is increased by one (*six working variables*) to give a message digest of length 192 bits. Also, a different message expansion is used in such a way that, the message expansion becomes stronger by generating more bit difference in each chaining variable. The extended sixteen 32 bit into eighty 32 bit words are given as input to the round function and some changes have been done in shifting of bits in chaining variables. They proposed a new message digest algorithm based on the previous algorithm that can be used in any message integrity or signing application but they couldn't optimize time delay.

In this paper, a fast hash one-way function is proposed to optimize the time delay with strong collision resistance, assures a good compression and one-way resistance.

3   Description of the Proposed Hash Function

The proposed hash function (fSHA-1) is algorithmically similar to SHA-1, as well as the word size and the number of rounds but it is more cheaper in time compared with SHA-1. This section discusses the proposed function in details, including a brief introduction of the basic terminology we used in this paper including the bit strings and integers, operations on words, and message padding.

3.1   Bit Strings and Integers

Here we define some basic terminology related to the proposed hash function.

1. A hex digit is an element of the set $0, 1, .., 9, A, ..F$. A hex digit is the representation of a 4-bit string. For example (7= 0111, A = 1010).
2. A word equals a 32-bit string which may be represented as a sequence of 8 hex digits. To convert a word to 8 hex digits each 4-bit string is converted to its hex equivalent as described before. For example, (1010 0001 0000 0011 1111 1110 0010 0011 = A103FE23).
3. An integer between 0 and $2^{32} - 1$ inclusive may be represented as a word. The least significant four bits of the integer are represented by the right-most hex digit of the word representation. For example, the integer $291 = 2^8 + 2^5 + 2^1 + 2^0 = 256 + 32 + 2 + 1$ is represented by this hex word (=00000123).
   We have to note that, If z is an integer, $0 <= z < 2^{64}$, then $z = (2^{32})x + y$ where $0 <= x < 2^{32}$ and $0 <= y < 2^{32}$. Since x and y can be represented as words X and Y, respectively, the z can be represented as the pair of words (X, Y).
4. A block may be represented as a sequence of 16 words.

3.2   Operations on Words

The following logical operators will be applied to the words:

– Bitwise logical word operations given as follows:
   - X AND Y = bitwise logical "and" of X and Y.

   - X OR Y = bitwise logical "inclusive-or" of X and Y.

   - X XOR Y = bitwise logical "exclusive-or" of X and Y.

   - NOT X = bitwise logical "complement" of X.

– The operation $X + Y$ is defined as follows: words X and Y represent integers x and y, where $0 <= x < 2^{32}$ and $0 <= y < 2^{32}$. For positive integers n and m, let n mod m be the remainder upon dividing n by m, and then compute the value of z using the following form:

$$z = (x + y) \quad mod \quad 2^{32} \tag{1}$$

Where $0 \leq z < 2^{32}$.

Then, by converting the value z to a word (i.e. Z) and define Z using the following form:

$$Z = X + Y \tag{2}$$

– The circular left shift operation $S^{n(X)}$, where X is a word and n is an integer with $0 <= n < 32$, is defined by:

$$S^{n(X)} = (X << n)OR(X >> 32 - n) \tag{3}$$

$X << n$ is obtained as follows: discard the left-most n bits of X and then pad the result with n zeroes on the right (i.e., the result will still be 32 bits).

$X >> n$ is obtained by discarding the right-most n bits of X and then padding the result with n zeroes on the left. Thus, $S^{n(X)}$ is equivalent to a circular shift of X by n positions to the left

3.3   Message Padding

The proposed function (fISH-1) is used to compute a message digest for a message or data file that is provided as input. The message or data file should be considered to be a bit string. The length of the message is the number of bits in the message (the empty message has length 0). If the number of bits in a message is a multiple of 8, for compactness we can represent the message in hex. The purpose of message padding is to make the total length of a padded message a multiple of 512. fISH-1 sequentially processes blocks of 512 bits when computing the message digest. The following specifies how this padding shall be performed. As a summary, a "**1**" followed by **m** "**0**"s followed by a 64- bit integer are appended to the end of the message to produce a padded message of length $512 * n$. The 64-bit integer is the length of the original message. The padded message is then processed by the fISH-1 as n 512-bit blocks.

Suppose a message has length $l < 2^{64}$ and the message is padded on the right as the following rules:

1. **"1" is appended.**

    if the original message is "01010000", this is padded to "010100001".

2. **"0"s are appended.** The number of "0"s will depend on the original length of the message. The last 64 bits of the last 512-bit block are reserved for the length l of the original message.

Example 1. *Suppose the original message is the bit string= 01100001 01100010 01100011 01100100 01100101, gives 01100001 01100010 01100011 01100100 01100101 1.*

Since $l = 40$, the number of bits in the above is 41 and 407 "0"s are appended, making the total now 448. This gives (in hex):
61626364 65800000 00000000 00000000
00000000 00000000 00000000 00000000
00000000 00000000 00000000 00000000
00000000 00000000.

3. Obtain the 2-word representation of l, the number of bits in the original message. If $l < 2^{32}$ then the first word is all zeroes. Append these two words to the padded message.
   Suppose the original message is as given in Example (1). Then $l = 40$ (note that l is computed before any padding). The two-word representation of 40 is hex 00000000 00000028.
   Hence the final padded message is the following hex:
   [61626364 65800000 00000000 00000000
   00000000 00000000 00000000 00000000
   00000000 00000000 00000000 00000000
   00000000 00000000 00000000 00000028.]

The padded message will contain $16 * n$ words for some $n > 0$ and its regarded as a sequence of n blocks $[M(1), M(2)]$ which represent the first character (or bits) of the message.

3.4   Functions and Constants Used

A sequence of logical functions $f(0), f(1), \ldots, f(79)$ is used in the proposed hash function. Each $f(t), 0 \leq t \leq 79$, operates on three 32-bit words B, C, D and produces a 32-bit word as output. Then, the $f(t; B, C, D)$ is defined as given in the following definition:

Definition 1 $(f(t; B, C, D))$. *For words B, C, D*
$f(t; B, C, D) = (BANDC)OR((NOTB)ANDD)(0 \leq t \leq 19))$
$f(t; B, C, D) = BXORCXORD(20 \leq t \leq 39)$
$f(t; B, C, D) = (BANDC)OR(BANDD)OR(CANDD)(40 \leq t \leq 59)$
$f(t; B, C, D) = BXORCXORD(60 \leq t \leq 79)$.

A sequence of constant words $K(0), K(1), \ldots, K(79)$ is used in the proposed hash function. In hex form, these sequence are given by:

1. $K(t) = 5A827999(0 \leq t \leq 19)$
2. $K(t) = 6ED9EBA1(20 \leq t \leq 39)$
3. $K(t) = 8F1BBCDC(40 \leq t \leq 59)$
4. $K(t) = CA62C1D6(60 \leq t \leq 79)$

3.5   Computing the Message Digest

The message digest is computed using the message padded as described before. The computation is described using two buffers, each consisting of five 32-bit words, and a sequence of eighty 32-bit words. The words of the first 5-word buffer are labeled A, B, C, D, E. The words of the second 5-word buffer are labeled $H0, H1, H2, H3, H4$. The words of the 80-word sequence are labeled $W(0), W(1), ..., W(79)$. A single word buffer TEMP is also employed.

To generate the message digest, the 16-word blocks $M(1), M(2), ..., M(n)$ defined in before are processed in order. The processing of each $M(i)$ involves 80 steps before processing any blocks, the Hs are initialized as follows: in hex,

H0 = 67452301
H1 = EFCDAB89
H2 = 98BADCFE
H3 = 10325476
H4 = C3D2E1F0.

Now, $M(1), M(2), ..., M(n)$ are processed. Algorithm (1) shows the computation of $M(i)$.

Algorithm 1. Computation of $M(i)$

1: Divide $M(i)$ into 16 words $W(0), W(1), ..., W(15)$
    Where $W(0)$ is the left-most word.
2: **for** t= 16 to 39 **do**
3:      Set $W(t) \leftarrow S^{(1W(t-16))}$
4: **end for**
5: **for** t= 40 to 79 **do**
6:      Set $W(t) \leftarrow (W(t-3)XOR(K(t-1))XOR(W(t-17)))$ This transformation keeps all operands 64-bit aligned and it reduce the time of implementing of the algorithm instead of
7: **end for**
8: **for** t = 16 to 79 **do**
9:      Set
        $W(t) \leftarrow S^{(W(t-3)XOR(W(t-8))XOR(W(t-14))XOR(W(t-16)))}$
10: **end for**
11: Set $A \leftarrow H0, B \leftarrow H1, C \leftarrow H2, D \leftarrow H3, E \leftarrow H4$.
12: **for** t = 0 to 79 **do**
13:     TEMP = $S^{5(A)} + f(t; B, C, D) + E + W(t)$ instead of
14:     TEMP = $S^{5(A)} + f(t; B, C, D) + E + W(t) + K(t-1)$
15:     $E = D; D = C; C = S^{30(B)}; B = A; A = TEMP;$
16:     Set H0 = H0 + A, H1 = H1 + B, H2 = H2 + C, H3 = H3 + D, H4 = H4 + E.
17:     **Output:** the message digest is the 160-bit string represented by the 5 words $H0\ H1\ H2\ H3\ H4$.
18: **end for**

---

4   Experimental Results

We have presented a new dedicated hash function (fISH-1) based on SHA-1 scheme. Simulation results of text data are shown in Table (I). It indicates that suggested algorithm needs little time to generate a message digest when compared with SHA-1 because in proposed algorithm there is deferent complexity of the address computations as we explained in proposed hash function. It produces message digest of length 160 bits similar to the SHA-1. Even with the small change in the input algorithm produces greater change in the output. Fig. 1. and Fig. 2. show the computation time of the proposed hash function (fISH-1) against (SHA-1). It shows that the proposed hash function is much cheaper than fISH-1.

Table 1. Message digest for certain messages

Message	SHA-1	Time	fISH-1	Time
a	86f7e437 faa5a7fc e15d1ddc b9eaeaea 377667b8	0.178 Sec	DE5DE041 7D0F94D5 98BADCFE 10325476 43D2E1F0	0.153 Sec
abc	a9993e36 4706816a ba3e2571 7850c26c 9cd0d89d	0.171 Sec	69EFD901 2C031F55 98BADCFE 10325476 43D2E1F0	0.153 Sec
ABCDE FGHIJ KLMNO PQRST UVWXYZ	80256F39 A9D30865 0AC90D9B E9A72A95 62454574	0.165 Sec	3A8EDFF1 FFF4DA95 98BADCFE 10325476 43D2E1F0	0.144 Sec
abcdef ghijklm nopqrstuv wxyz	32D10C7B 8CF96570 CA04CE37 F2A19D84 240D3A89	0.172 Sec	F0802E71 1A059B95 98BADCFE 10325476 43D2E1F0	0.159 Sec

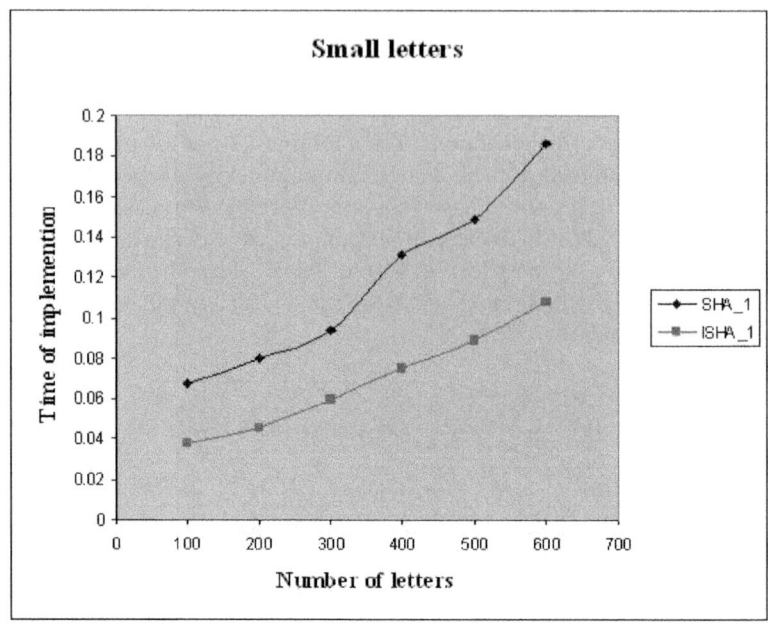

Fig. 1. Time for certain messages with different numbers of small letters

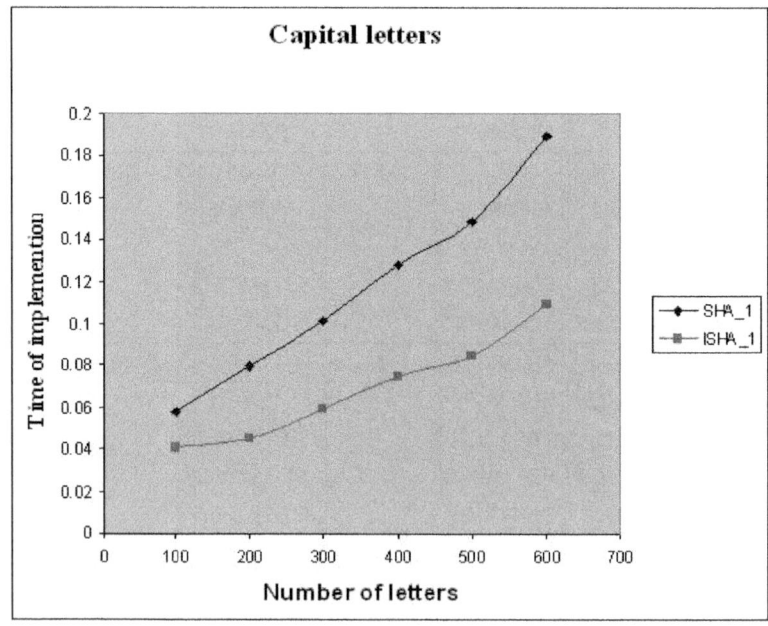

Fig. 2. Time for certain messages with different numbers of capital letters

5   Conclusions

In this paper, we proposed a new message digest algorithm basis on Standard Secure Hash Function SHA-1 that can be used in any message integrity or signing application. Experimental results indicate that the proposed hash function is collision resistant and assures a good compression and preimage resistance. Also it reduces the time of implementation comparing to Standard Secure Hash Function. Moreover, the difference in time between SHA-1 and fISH-1 increases by increasing the number of letters in message since the over time of implementation of fISH-1 is limited compared to the over time of implementation of SHA-1.

References

1. He, W., Peng, X., Qin, W., Meng, X.: The keyed optical hash function based on cascaded phase-truncated fourier transforms. Optics Communications 283, 2328–2332 (2010)
2. Zhen, W., Guo, Z., Hong, W., Yu, Z., Lei, L., Yu, Z.: Design theory and method of multivariate hash function. Information Sciences 53, 1977–1987 (2010)
3. Andreeva, E., Preneel, B.: A Three-Property-Secure Hash Function. In: Avanzi, R.M., Keliher, L., Sica, F. (eds.) SAC 2008. LNCS, vol. 5381, pp. 228–244. Springer, Heidelberg (2009)
4. Seoa, M., Haitsmab, J., Kalkerb, T., Yooa, C.: A robust image fingerprinting system using the radon transform. Signal Processing: Image Communication 19(4), 325–339 (2004)
5. Tiwari, H.: Cryptographic hash function: an elevated view. European Journal of Scientific Research 43, 452–465 (2010)
6. Tiwari, H., Asawa, K.: A secure hash function MD-192 with modified message expansion. International Journal of Computer Science and Information Security VII(II) (2010)
7. Eastlake, D., Jones, P.: US secure hash algorithm 1 (SHA-1), Network Working Group, Category: Informational, pp.1-22 (2001)
8. Pongyupinpanich, S., Choomchuay, S.: An architecture for a SHA-1 applied for DSA. In: Proceeding of 3rd Asian International Mobile Computing Conference (AMOC), Thailand, May 26-28, pp. 8–12 (2004)
9. Secure hash standard, United States of American, National Institute of Science and Technology, Federal Information Processing Standard (FIPS) 180-1 (April 1995)
10. Szydlo, M., Yin, Y.L.: Collision-Resistant Usage of MD5 and SHA-1 via Message Preprocessing. In: Pointcheval, D. (ed.) CT-RSA 2006. LNCS, vol. 3860, pp. 99–114. Springer, Heidelberg (2006)
11. Wang, X., Yu, H., Yin, Y.L.: Efficient Collision Search Attacks on SHA-0. In: Shoup, V. (ed.) CRYPTO 2005. LNCS, vol. 3621, pp. 1–16. Springer, Heidelberg (2005)
12. Cochran, M.: Notes on the wang et al. 2^{63} SHA-1 differential path. Cryptology ePrint Archive, Report 2007/474 (2007), http://eprint.iacr.org/
13. Secure hash standard, National Institute of Science and Technology (NIST), Federal Information Processing Standards Publications (FIPS PUB) 180-2 (2002)
14. Sugita, M., Kawazoe, M., Perret, L., Imai, H.: Algebraic cryptanalysis of 58-round SHA-1. In: Biryukov, A. (ed.) FSE 2007. LNCS, vol. 4593, pp. 349–365. Springer, Heidelberg (2007)

CLAPTCHA- A Novel Captcha

Rahul Saha[1], G. Geetha[1], and Gang-soo Lee[2]

[1] Department of Computer Science and Engineering
Lovely Professional University, Phagwara, India
{Rsahaaot,gitaskumar}@yahoo.com
[2] Department of Computer Engineering, Hannam University, Korea
gslee@hun.kr

Abstract. In this paper we have introduced a new form of captcha named CLAPTCHA. This Claptcha we believe can reform a new world of image and imagination based captcha. In this Claptcha, we have to find the English alphabets (alpha). Its efficiency is also proven here to be better than normal image based captchas or imagination captchas. Claptchas will be also more user friendly and enjoying.

Keywords: CLAPTCHA, captcha, naming, efficiency, user-friendly, usability.

1   Introduction

With an increasing number of free services on the internet, we have found a pronounced need to protect these services from abuse. Attackers hijack secondary victim systems using them to wage a coordinated large-scale attack against primary victim systems. To thwart automated attacks, services often ask users to solve a puzzle before being given access to a service. These puzzles, first introduced by von Ahn et al. in 2003 [1], were CAPTCHAs: Completely Automated Public Turing Tests to Tell Computers and Humans Apart (CAPTCHAs) are one of the important branches of HIP systems. This technology is now almost a standard security mechanism for addressing undesirable or malicious Internet bot programs (such as those spreading junk emails and grabbing thousands of free email accounts instantly) and has found widespread application on numerous commercial web sites including Google, Yahoo, and Microsoft's MSN. It is widely accepted that a good CAPTCHA must be both robust and usable. The robustness of a CAPTCHA is its strength in resisting adversarial attacks, and this has attracted considerable attention in the research community (e.g. [2,3,4,5]). Attackers are constantly developing new methods to circumvent these countermeasures, so the puzzles get still harder and more burden is placed on humans.

CAPTCHA was introduced to address the availability problem but it in turn pose accessibility problem to users who are blind, who have low vision, or have a learning disability such as dyslexia. In [6], [7] K.Chellapilla et al have discussed about the design of a user friendly CAPTCHA. However, solving a CAPTCHA requires a substantial human cognitive effort. Based on the type of cognitive effort required to

T.-h. Kim et al. (Eds.): SecTech 2011, CCIS 259, pp. 94–100, 2011.

solve CAPTCHA, CAPTCHAs can be classified into three categories which are listed below.

Text based CAPTCHAs require users to read and type distorted text rendered in an image.

Audio based CAPTCHAs rely on sound or speech recognition by the users.

Image based CAPTCHAs ask users to perform an image recognition task.

The *naming* of our CLAPTCHA is also interesting. The origin of the word CLAPTCHA comes from two words CAPTCHA and ALPHA. We can see that all the characters in the later word exist in the former one except L. So, we have just inserted the L in the word captcha and have got our idea as CLAPTCHA means "a captcha of appreciation."

2   How Claptcha Works?

Our claptcha basically consists of animation based environments. In this environment we have embedded some alphabets in such a way that the alphabets also seem to be parts of the corresponding environment. Now, users have to type the letters, they assume to be present in the environment, in the given text box. Then click the Submit button. It is difficulty and time consuming to identify all the alphabets. So we shall maintain a permit level like 70 % success ratio. If a user is able to complete this level he or she can be allowed for using services on internet else try again. A user can try at most four times after which the service will be blocked to prevent unauthorized tasks.

The screenshots of our project are given below to show the working process of CLAPTCHA.

Fig. 1. Screenshot 1   **Fig. 2.** Screenshot

Fig. 1 shows that user assumes some alphabets in the environment given and types in the given text box and Fig. 5 shows that a message is displayed to the user if the identification of alphabets is wrong.

Fig. 3. Screenshot 3   **Fig. 4.** Screenshot 4

Fig.3 shows where the user retries Claptcha test and Fig.4. Shows if the identification of the letters are appropriate the positioning of the alphabets are shown in the picture environment and clapping starts.

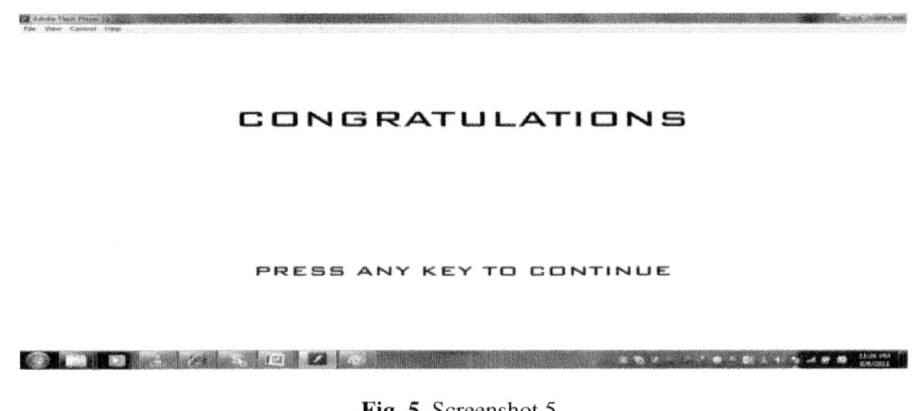

Fig. 5. Screenshot 5

This will continue up to maximum 4 time in case of unsuccessful attempts after which the service will be blocked for the user to take security measures.

3   Testing Our Claptcha

We have gone through a survey on our new idea among different kind of people with respect to sex, age with more than 100 samples. The results are shown below.

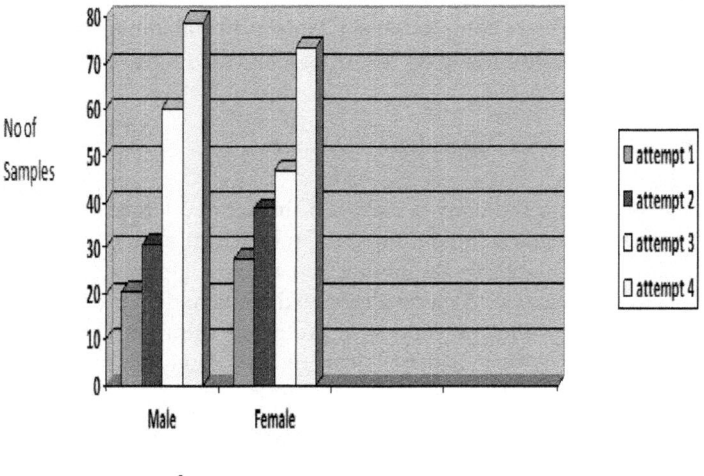

Fig. 6. Analysis of Survey 1

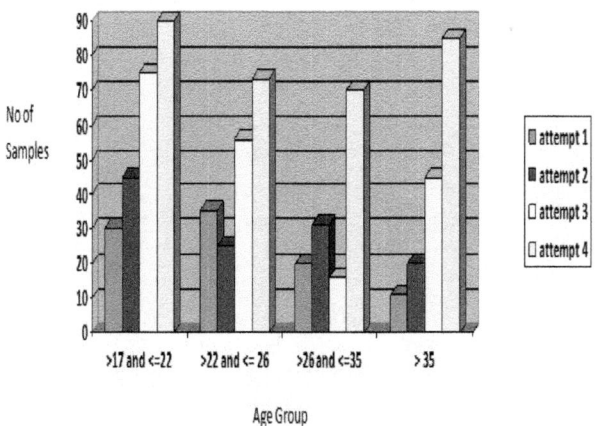

Fig. 7. Analysis of Survey 2

In our survey of Claptcha, we have found the following reasons for supporting our Claptcha.

Firstly, the environment of claptcha is animated or real environment which users find interesting and amusing.

Secondly, it looks like a game and users are interested to solve game.

Thirdly, there is no monotony like text captcha.

Fourth, to solve a Claptcha a user must have observation factor which is needed for supporting security issues.

Fifth, though it is a little time consuming but unauthorized prevention factor is more than the other type of captchas.

The analysis of our two surveys easily give a view that all the users whether different in sex or age can complete our Claptcha in maximum four attempts which has helped us to fix the attempt level for using Claptcha to prevent unauthorized tasks.

4   Dos Attack v/s Claptcha

DoS attack is dealt with the unavailability of the service intended for. The malicious node or the intruder sends a huge number of requests at a time to the service so that the service gets unavailable to the authorized users. Claptcha gives a maximum of four attempts to pass the test. As a result the malicious node did not get chance to pass the test after fourth try and the service is protected from getting DoS attacked. For practical implementation in real life we can rethink about the maximum permissible level.

5   Evaluation

We have compared our new captcha- CLAPTCHA with all the other existing captchas according to the result of the previous surveys done in past in the basis of some factors which is shown in the graph.

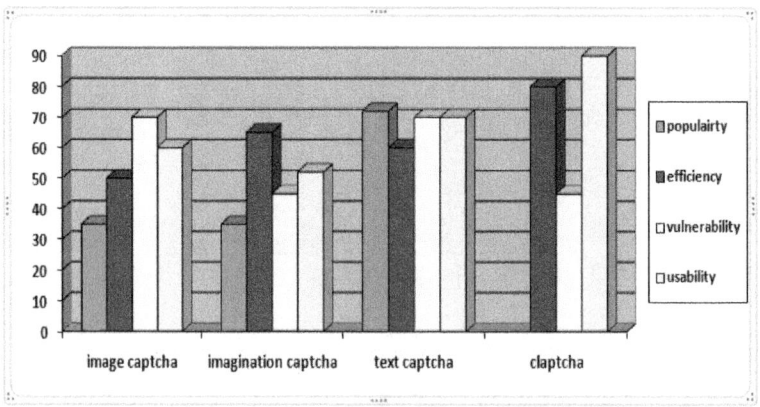

In our chart, we can notice that the popularity bar for Claptcha is null as it is not introduced till in applications.

The reasons that our Claptcha is powerful than others are listed below.

Firstly, users have interest to solve Claptcha that we have found from our survey of Claptcha.

Secondly, though vulnerability level of imagination captcha and our Claptcha is same but from the perspective of users' choice Claptcha is better.

Thirdly, efficiency is higher than any other of captchas.

6   Conclusion

As technology advances, human is being replaced by machines for different tasks. It also includes misuse of technology progress that deals with unauthorized access of services on internet which some time leads to some severe attacks like DoS, desynchronization of request-response etc. Our novel captcha- Claptcha is therefore introduced to help this crisis.

In our future work, we wish to apply some sound applications to our Claptcha to make it general even also for different physically disabled users.

Acknowledgement. This work was supported by the Security Engineering Research Center, granted by the Korea Ministry of Knowledge Economy.

References

1. von Ahn, L., Blum, M., Langford, J.: Telling Humans and Computer Apart Automatically. CACM 47(2) (2004)
2. Mori, G., Malik, J.: Recognising Objects in Adversarial Clutter: Breaking a Visual CAPTCHA. In: IEEE Conference on Computer Vision and Pattern Recognition
3. Yan, J., El Ahmad, A.S.: Breaking Visual CAPTCHAs with Naïve Pattern Recognition Algorithms. In: Proc. of the 23rd Annual Computer Security Applications Conference (ACSAC 2007), FL, USA, pp. 279–291. IEEE Computer Society (December 2007)
4. Yan, J., El Ahmad, A.S.: A Low-cost Attack on a Microsoft CAPTCHA. School of Science Technical Report, Newcastle University, England (February 2008)
5. Yan, J., El Ahmad, A.S.: Is cheap labour behind the scene? - Low-cost automated attacks on Yahoo CAPTCHAs. School of Computing Science Technical Report, Newcastle University, England (April 2008)
6. Chellapilla, K., Larson, K., Simard, P., Czerwinski, M.: Designing Human friendly human interaction proofs. In: ACM CHI 2005 (2005)
7. Chellapilla, K., Larson, K., Simard, P.Y., Czerwinski, M.: Building Segmentation Based Human-Friendly Human Interaction Proofs (HIPs). In: Baird, H.S., Lopresti, D.P. (eds.) HIP 2005. LNCS, vol. 3517, pp. 1–26. Springer, Heidelberg (2005)
8. Baird, H.S., Moll, M.A., Wang, S.-Y.: A Highly Legible CAPTCHA that Resists Segmentation Attacks. In: Baird, H.S., Lopresti, D.P. (eds.) HIP 2005. LNCS, vol. 3517, pp. 27–41. Springer, Heidelberg (2005)
9. Chew, M., Baird, H.S.: BaffleText: a human interactive proof. In: Proc. of 10th IS&T/SPIE Document Recognition & Retrieval Conference (2003)
10. Converse, T.: CAPTCHA Generation as a Web Service. In: Baird, H.S., Lopresti, D.P. (eds.) HIP 2005. LNCS, vol. 3517, pp. 82–96. Springer, Heidelberg (2005)
11. Nielsen, J.: Usability 101: Introduction to Usability (2003),
    http://www.useit.com/alertbox/20030825.html

12. Elson, J., Douceur, J.R., Howell, J., Saul, J.: Asirra: a CAPTCHA that exploits interest-aligned manual image categorization. In: Proceedings of the 14th ACM Conference on Computer and Communications Security, CCS (2007)
13. Ragavi, V., Geetha, G.: An Analysis of IMAGINATION CAPTCHA. In: 2nd International Conference on Signal and Image Processing, ICSIP 2009, pp. 649–651 (August 2009)
14. Yan, J., El Ahmad, A.S.: Usability of CAPTCHAs or usability issues in CAPTCHA design. In: SOUPS 2008: Proceedings of the 4th Symposium on Usableprivacy and Security, pp. 44–52. ACM, New York (2008)

An Approach to Provide Security in Wireless Sensor Network Using Block Mode of Cipher

Gulshan Kumar[1], Mritunjay Rai[2], and Gang-soo Lee[3]

[1,2] Department of Computer Science, Lovely Professional University, Jalandhar, India
gulshan_acet@yahoo.com, raimritunjay@gmail.com
[3] Department of Computer Engineering, Hannam University, Korea
jslee@hannam.ac.kr

Abstract. Wireless sensor network (WSN) is gaining an importance in variety of Applications. The security in the sensor network communication is highly recommended to provide data confidentiality and authentication. Existing security approaches in Wireless Sensor networks is basically based on some particular assumptions about the participating nodes and the network environment combined for a specific application. In Sensor networks there is resource constraint as the nodes work on battery and therefore low energy consumption is needed. In our paper for the purpose of security in Sensor networks we have shown an approach to apply encryption algorithms like DES, Blowfish using CBC block cipher mode. This approach will achieve high data confidentiality and authentication.

Keywords: Wireless Sensor network, Security, Blowfish, DES, Confidentiality.

1 Introduction

Wireless sensor network is a wireless network comprised of automated sensor devices that are geographically installed to sense physical or environmental factors like temperature, pressure, vibrations, sound etc. Wireless Sensor Networks have variety of applications including healthcare, military surveillance, logistics, energy plants, inventory etc. A sensor is distributed among three different parts: a radio transceiver, a battery and a micro controller (Sink node). The radio transceiver transmits data whereas microcontroller accumulates and processes the data and battery is the only resource that provides power for transceiver and microcontroller. The data transmitted through the various nodes of a WSN needs to be protected from active and passive attacks. The intruder is aware of the data transmission between sensor nodes and easily eavesdrop those data. Sensor nodes should be preventive enough against these attacks. The sensors nodes are dependent on battery thus low power consumption should be there to make it active for long duration.

To provide security in sensor networks we can apply Data Encryption Standard (DES) and Blowfish algorithm. Both the standards follow symmetric key encryption which is more efficient as compare to that of public key encryption.

T.-h. Kim et al. (Eds.): SecTech 2011, CCIS 259, pp. 101–112, 2011.
© Springer-Verlag Berlin Heidelberg 2011

Table 1. Component Description

Componet		Description
Sensor Node	MICAz	Mote module
	MDA300CA	Data acquisition board
	Echo20	Soil moisture sensor
Sink Node	MIB510	Serial interface board
	Terminal	A single board computer

2   Various Attacks on Wireless Sensor Network

2.1   Denial of Service Attack

The main aim of this kind of attack is to make the service or resources unavailable to the authorized users. It is mainly occurred due to the sending of unnecessary data packets in huge amount to the victim node such that it gets exhausted and the network gets disrupted. In a wireless sensor network DoS can be of several forms: in physical layer it takes the form of jamming and tampering; at link layer it is like collision, exhaustion; at network layer it is neglect and greed, homing, misdirection, black hole; at transport layer it takes the form of flooding and desynchronization.

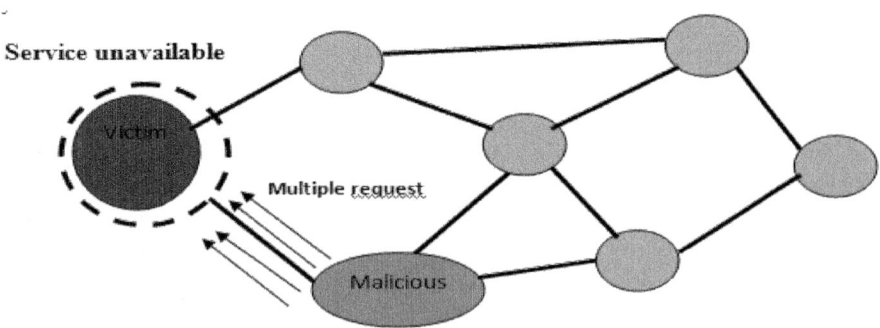

Fig. 1. Denial of service

2.2   Sinkhole Attack

In a sensor network, sensor nodes monitor their surroundings, take input of sensor data readings and forward them to a base station. In a sinkhole attack, malicious node makes itself attractive to its surrounding nodes with false routing information so that all the data destined to the base station can pass through that malicious node using a high quality route. It then performs alteration or selective forwarding.

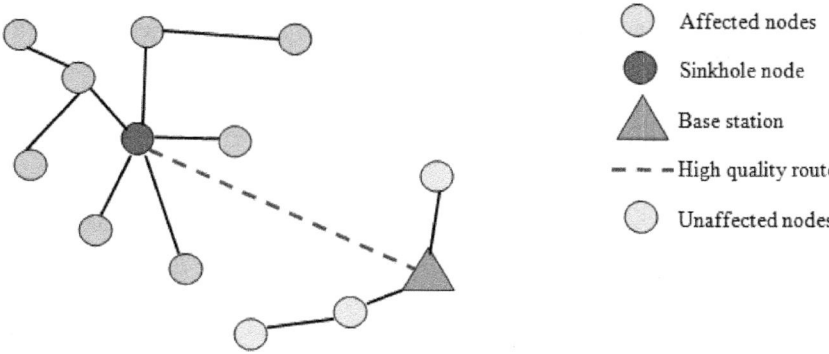

Fig. 2. Sinkhole Attack

2.3   Wormhole Attack

It is basically a partnership attack where attackers may be more than one in number and work together to forge the targeted node. This is the most serious attack on WSN. A high speed network is also used here. Source sends data which are falsely passed through the attackers' zone. The attacker or malicious nodes then pass these data to destination through a high-speed link faster than any other link from source to destination. As the requests come faster through the false high speed link, the destination node also selects the same path to send its reply. When replies are arrived at the source through the attackers' zone source node also starts sending its data through the path in which the attackers are included without being aware of it. As a result all the data passes through the malicious nodes.

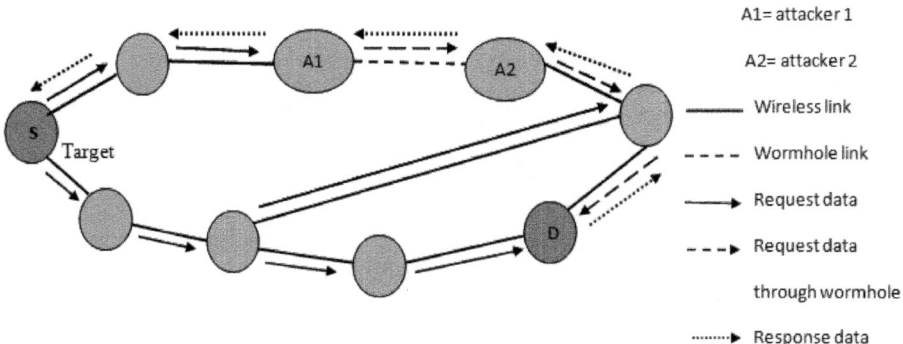

Fig. 3. Wormhole Attack

2.4   Sybil Attack

In this attack a faulty or malicious node appears to be a group of nodes i.e. it has the capability of presenting itself as different identities in a WSN to function as distinct nodes. It can send false information like position of nodes, strength of signal, node formation to a node. By masquerading and disguising as multiple identities, a malicious node can gain control over a sensor network.

2.5   Passive Information Gathering

In this attack, the intruder gets equipped with strong receiver and well designed antenna to intercept the data stream transmitting to and fro in a sensor network. A lot of information, therefore, can be easily accessed and used in further direct attacks to the network. It also makes the intruder capable of locating and destroying the sensors in the network.

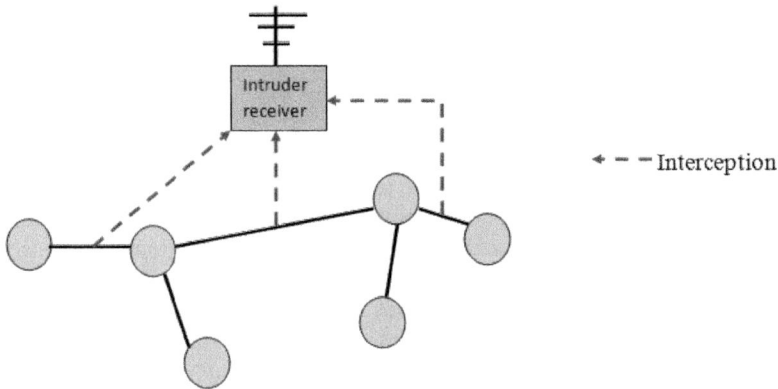

Fig. 4. Passive Information Gathering

3   Security on Wireless Sensor Network

Authentication confirms the identity of the parties participating in a connection. It can be classified into two types. *Peer entity authentication* provides identity proofs at establishment or at runtime of a data transfer phase in a connection. *Data origin authentication* confirms the identity of the source that generates a data or a message.

Confidentiality ensures the protection of the data being transmitted between sender and receiver such that the data will never be disclosed to a third party.

Data Integrity means that the data sent by the sender should remain same while it reaches to the receiver and there should not be any sort of alteration or fabrication during the transmission.

Non repudiation deals with the fact that that both the sender and the receiver must keep the proof of data transmission and reception so that neither of the communicating parties can deny the responsibility of its own.

Availability ensures the presence of network services in spite of the security attacks.

4   Data Encryption Standard (DES)

4.1   Encryption

Data Encryption Standard (DES) is one of the encryption techniques used for the block cipher. It takes 64 bits data block as input with 56 bit key (after randomly generated from 64 bits). DES is comprised of three stages. Firstly, an initial permutation is done on the 64 bits input block which generates a permuted input to work with further. The second stage deals with the 16 rounds of iteration of same function with randomly generated keys at each round and a pre-output is generated. The third stage consists of an inverse initial permutation that gives us our desired cipher block. We shall now explain each stage in the following.

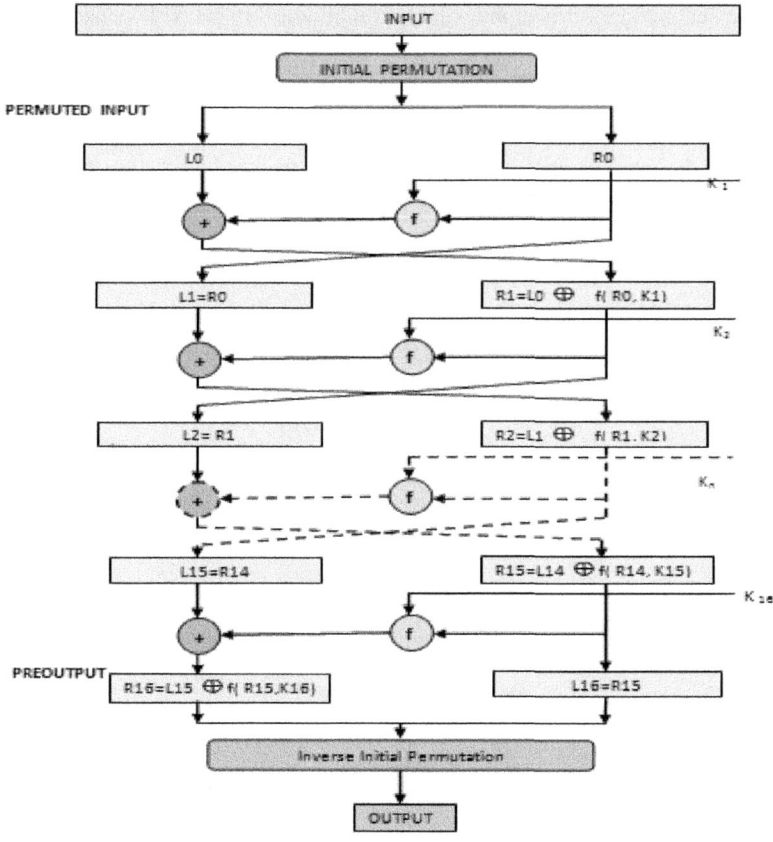

Fig. 5. DES algorithm

Initial Permutation (IP)
It is the first stage of data block computation. IP reorders the bits in the data block. It arranges the even bits in left half L0 and odd bits in right half R0. In this permutation, the data bits are permuted in the following pattern.

Table 2. Initial Permutation

58	50	42	34	26	18	10	2	
60	52	44	36	28	20	12	4	Even bits as L0
62	54	46	38	30	22	14	6	
64	56	48	40	32	24	16	8	
57	49	41	33	25	17	9	1	
59	51	43	35	27	19	11	3	Odd bits as R0
61	53	45	37	29	21	13	5	
63	55	47	39	31	23	15	7	

Round Structure

This is the second stage for cipher block computation in DES. It consists of 16 same rounds each of which takes input of two halves of data block L_{i-1} and R_{i-1} and randomly generated key K_i where i= 1 to 16. In each round, the 32 bit right half of the previous round and the 48 bit key is given input to a function f whose output and the left half is XOR ed. The right half directly and the output of the XOR function is then interchanged to get the left and right halves respectively for the next round. The formulae for left and right halves are given below.

$$L_i = R_{i-1}$$
$$R_i = L_{i-1} \oplus F(R_{i-1}, K_i), \text{ for i= 1 to 16}$$

The function f takes input of 32 bits right half and 48 bits sub key. The 32 bits right half is expanded to make it 48 bits to work in the following way. After the expansion,

Table 3. Initial Permutation

32	1	2	3	4	5
4	5	6	7	8	9
8	9	10	11	12	13
12	13	14	15	16	17
16	17	18	19	20	21
20	21	22	23	24	25
24	25	26	27	28	29
28	29	30	31	32	1

All the numbers signify bit positions

Expanded 32 bits

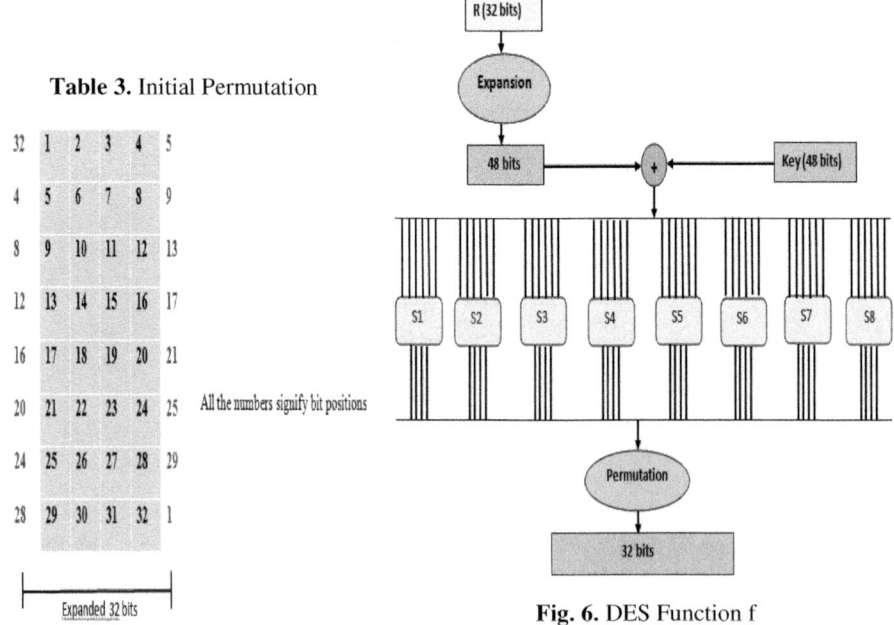

Fig. 6. DES Function f

the 48 bits are XOR ed with 48 bits of sub key. The resultant 48 bits are then sub divided into 8 substitution box. Each of them takes 6 bits input and gives 4 bits of output. As a result, we get total 32 bits of output which is again permuted and we get 32 bits from the function f.

The output of the function f is XOR ed with the left half of the data and the output of the XOR and the right half are interchanged to get the right half and left half for the next round. Thus, 16 rounds occur.

Inverse Initial Permutation (IP -1)
The output of the 16 rounds, called *PREOUTPUT* is then inversely permuted according to the table 4. Thus we get 64 bit encrypted data block.

Table 4. Inverse Permutation Table

40	8	48	16	56	24	64	32
39	7	47	15	55	23	63	31
38	6	46	14	54	22	62	30
37	5	45	13	53	21	61	29
36	4	44	12	52	20	60	28
35	3	43	11	51	19	59	27
34	2	42	10	50	18	58	26
33	1	41	9	49	17	57	25

4.2   Key Generation

At first 64 bit key is given as input in which every 8th bit is ignored. So, key input becomes from 64 bits to 56 bits. This 56 bit key is first subjected to a permutation

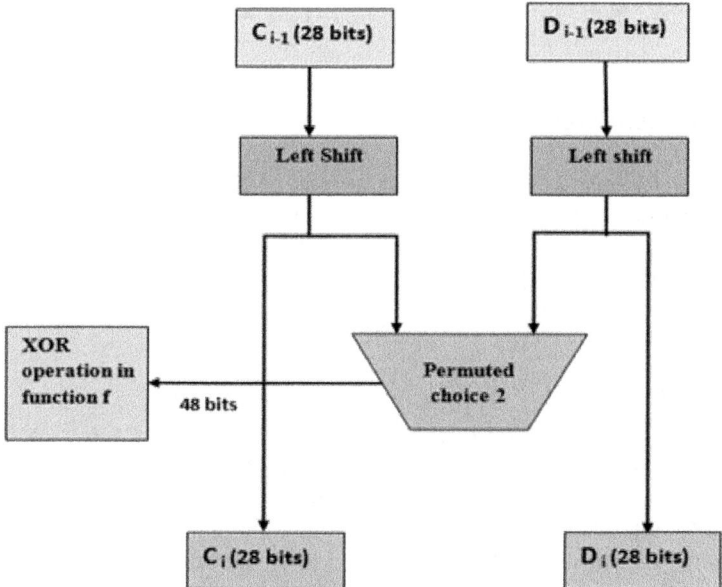

Fig. 7. Key generation

called Permuted Choice 1 according to a permutation table PC 1. After this permutation 56 bits are divided into two parts C_{i-1} and D_{i-1} where i= 1 to 16 rounds. At each round, both the halves of 56 bits separately undergo the circular left shift of 1 bit for round number 1, 2 ,9, 16 respectively and 2 bits for rest of the rounds. These shifted values serve as the inputs for the next round as well as go for the next step of permutation called Permutation Choice 2 according to the table of PC 2, which produces 48 bit subkey for each round used in the function f.

4.3   Decryption in DES

The decryption technique in the DES is the same as encryption one with the only the difference that the application of the sub keys are reversed.

Table 5. PC-1   **Table 6.** PC-2

57	49	41	33	25	17	9
1	58	50	42	34	26	18
10	2	59	51	43	35	27
19	11	3	60	52	44	36
63	55	47	39	31	23	15
60	62	54	46	38	30	22
14	6	61	53	45	37	29
21	13	5	28	20	12	4

Permuted Choice 1 (PC 1)

[Numbers signify bit positions]

14	17	11	24	1	5	3	28
15	6	21	10	23	19	12	4
26	8	16	7	27	20	13	2
41	52	31	37	47	55	30	40
51	45	33	48	44	49	39	56
34	53	46	42	50	36	29	32

Permuted Choice 2 (PC 2)

[Numbers signify bit positions]

5   Blowfish Algorithm

Blowfish a symmetric key block cipher. It uses 64 bits of data blocks and a variable size key maximum up to 448 bits. It is a version of Feistel Network having 16 times of iteration of a simple encryption function. The main features of Blowfish algorithm is that it includes key dependent S-boxes and has a complex key schedule which makes the algorithm stronger.

5.1   Encryption

The data block of 64 bits are first divided into two halves of 32 bits each. Each line in the diagram of the Blowfish algorithm represents 32 bit data. This algorithm uses two sub key arrays 18-entry P-array and 256-entry S-boxes. The S-boxes maps the 8 bit input into 32 bits output. One entry of P-array is compulsory for each of 16 rounds. The remaining 2 entries of P-array are used after the final round to separately XOR the outputs of each of the halves of the data block.

In the function F, four S-boxes are used and two types of bit operations: XOR and addition of modulo 2^{32} are used. The function divides the input of 32 bits into four S-boxes of 8 bits each. The outputs of first and second S-boxes are first added to modulo 2^{32} and the output of the addition is XOR ed with the output of third S-box output. The result of XOR operation and the output of fourth S-box is finally added to modulo 2^{32} to get the final output from the function F.

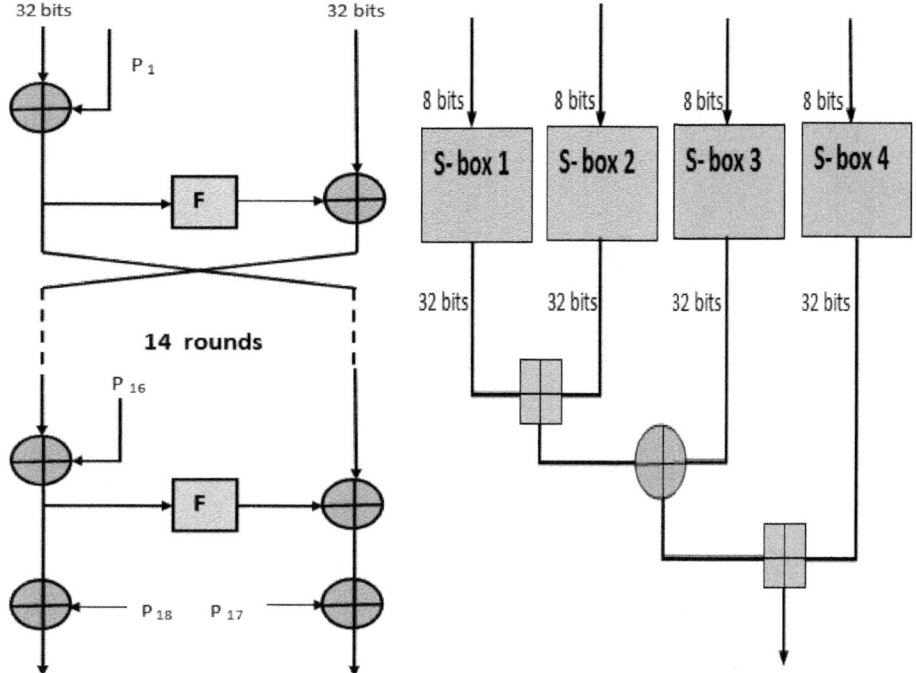

Fig. 8. Blowfish algorithm   **Fig. 9.** Function of S-box

The key schedule of Blowfish algorithm starts by initializing the P-array and S-boxes with values derived from the hexadecimal value of pi. The secret key is then byte wise XOR-ed with all the P-entries in order. Because the P-array is 576 bits long (18 P-entries * 32 bits) and the bytes are XOR-ed with all these bits, many implementations may support 576 bit key size.

5.2   Decryption

Decryption is exactly the same as encryption technique except the P1, P2 ……. P18 are used in reverse order.

6   Cipher Block Chaining (CBC) Mode

CBC is the most commonly used block mode operation for generating cipher blocks using fixed size of plaintext blocks of 64 bits. In CBC, an initialization vector (IV) is

used for the first block of plaintext. While encryption each block of plaintext is XOR
-ed with the previous cipher text block before being encrypted and while decryption
the XOR is done after the decryption of the cipher text block. Two formulae are used
here for encryption and decryption.

$$C_i = E_k(P_i) \oplus C_{i-1}, \ C0 = IV \ [\ \text{Encryption} \ ] \tag{2}$$

$$P_i = D_k(C_i) \oplus C_{i-1}, \ C0 = IV \ [\ \text{Decryption} \ ]$$

The data i.e. the plaintext that is to be sent is firstly divided into small blocks of 8
bytes or 64 bits each. The final block is to be padded to get the complete 8 bytes
block. The final n bytes plaintext (data) $0 \le n \le 7$ are to be followed by $(8 - n)$ bytes
for padding. It means that each block of plaintext must be of 64 bits for the encryption
purpose.

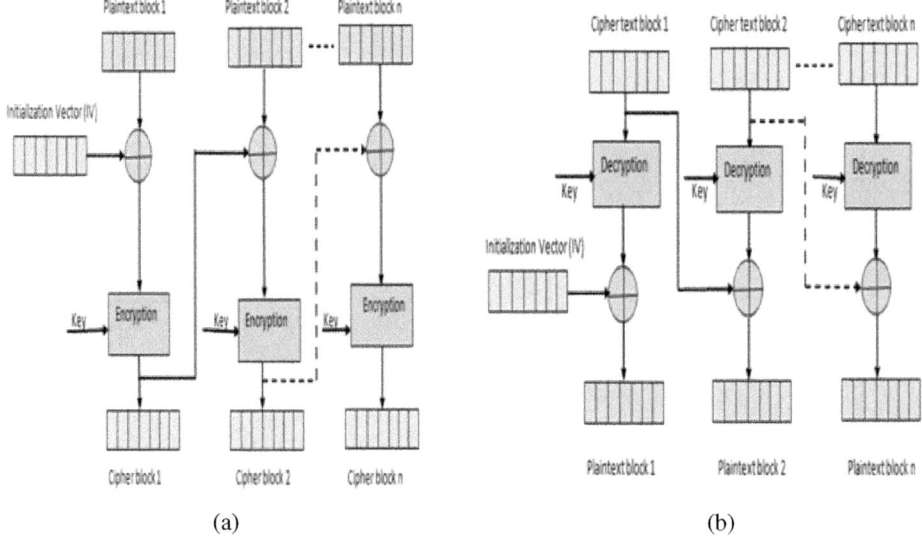

(a)   (b)

Fig. 10. (a) CBC (Encryption) (b) CBC (Decryption)

7   Results

As it is important to secure our network from malicious activities performed by
intruders, encryption algorithms plays an important role for achieving that goal. To
have an effective encryption algorithm we must evaluate the algorithms with different
issues like speed, throughput, efficiency etc. Here, we have tested our algorithms for
speed and battery consumption with the parameters of 64 bit plaintext block, 64 bit
key and 16 rounds of iteration in both cases. The results are shown below.

7.1   Based on Speed

The above graph shows clearly that Blowfish algorithm gives better throughput of generating encrypted packets than that of the DES algorithm.

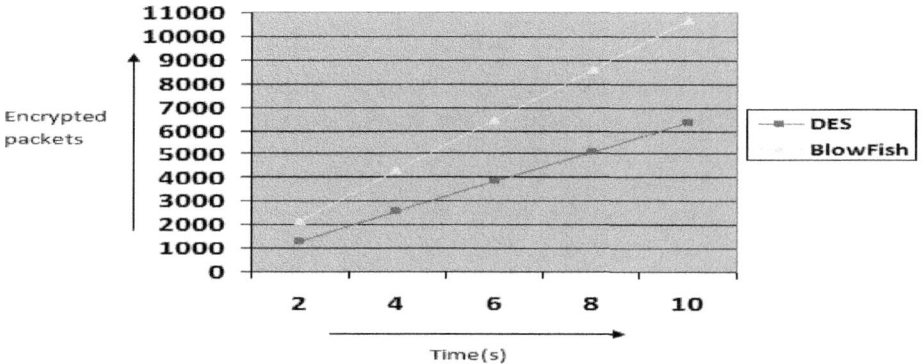

Fig. 11. DES v/s Blowfish (speed)

7.2   Based on Battery Consumption

The above analysis shows that Blowfish and DES both the algorithms consume almost same amount of battery power at same levels.

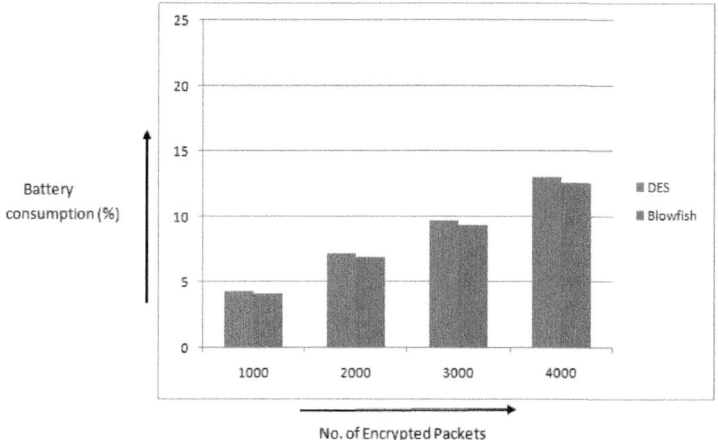

Fig. 12. DES v/s Blowfish (battery consumption)

8   Conclusion

As per the above discussion we can state that the throughput i.e. the capability of generating encrypted packets and battery consumption is efficient using block cipher mode encryption. Our approach also provides more security, confidentiality, authentication as Blowfish algorithm is strong enough to break. As using Block cipher encryption it is hard to break the security by intruder as compare to that of stream cipher. Also CBC block cipher mode of operation is most efficient as it effectively scrambles the plaintext prior to each encryption steps. In our future work we shall try to apply other block cipher encryption algorithms to optimize the security services in a sensor network.

Acknowledgement. This work was supported by the Security Engineering Research Center, granted by the Korea Ministry of Knowledge Economy.

References

[1] Salama, Elminaam, A., et al.: Evaluating The Performance of Symmetric Encryption Algorithms. International Journal of Network Security 10(3), 216–222 (2010)
[2] Ahmed, S., Beg, R., Abbas, Q.: Energy Efficient Sensor Network Security Using Stream Cipher Mode of Operation. In: ICCCT 2010, pp. 348–354 (2010)
[3] Nadeem, M.Y.J.: A performance comparison of data encryption algorithms. In: First International Conference on Information and Communication Technologies, pp. 84–89 (2005)
[4] Schneier: The Blowfish Encryption Algorithm (October 25 (2008),
    http://www.schneier.comlblow-sh.html
[5] Stallings, W.: Cryptography and Network Security, 4th edn., pp. 58–309. Prentice Hall (2005)
[6] Ekdahl, P., Johansson, T.: A new version of the stream Cipher SNOW (2002),
    http://www.it.lth.se/cryptology/snow/
[7] Nadeem, A., Javed, M.Y.: A performance comparison of data encryption algorithms. In: Information and Communication Technologies, ICICT 2005, pp. 84–89 (2005)
[8] Elminaam, D.S.A., Kader, H.M.A., Hadhoud, M.M.: Performance Evaluation of Symmetric Encryption Algorithms. IJCSNS International Journal of Computer Science and Network Security 8(12), 280–286 (2008)

Microscopic Analysis of Chips

Dominik Malcik and Martin Drahansky

Faculty of Information Technology, Brno University of Technology, Bozetechova 2,
61266 Brno, Czech Republic
xmalci00@stud.fit.vutbr.cz, drahan@fit.vutbr.cz

Abstract. Nowadays many different types of chips are used virtually everywhere in the real world. Sometimes, it is necessary to ensure that a certain chip meets specific requirements. For this reason, it is essential to examine various properties of chips; one of those can be, e.g., the chip security with respect to its physical structure. This paper provides description of a proven chip decapsulation process (the presented process can be used to obtain bare chips for further analysis) and some additional information concerning analysis of the chips. Finally, a prototype of our application designated for later semiautomatic analysis is also briefly presented.

Keywords: microscope, chip, chip package, leadframe, decapsulation, bare chip, analysis of chips.

1 Introduction

The current trend is increasing constantly the concentration of different electronic systems. These can be found, without exaggeration, almost everywhere. In certain situations, we expect a definite level of security or specific features in general to be guaranteed. We are therefore always forced to invent new ways to provide all the needed properties of these chip modules. The new methods have to be analysed and tested properly.

This article is the first result of our effort to develop semiautomatic application for supporting the chips analysis and testing. The main goal is not only the application itself, but also the whole process, starting with obtaining chips up to the evaluations of the results. Last year, we established a new laboratory specifically for this purpose. Next year, we shall attempt to extend the department with new equipment and with more research workers to get more precise results.

2 Obtaining the Chips

The process of obtaining the chips is usually not difficult, because we can mostly obtain standalone, encapsulated chips for experiments very easily: either by buying them or by getting them from manufacturers. However, sometimes it is necessary to obtain the chips from PCBs (Printed Circuit Boards) and in this case,

T.-h. Kim et al. (Eds.): SecTech 2011, CCIS 259, pp. 113–122, 2011.

there are, of course, more than one possible techniques how to get the demanded separate chips [1]. The often-used method is to unsolder the chips. It is almost exactly a reversed process to the original PCB manufacturing process (soldering chips onto the PCB). When using this method, it is recommended to keep in mind the following rules to preserve the chip functionality after detaching it from the PCB [2]:

- the temperature of the soldering iron tip should be max. 250 °C,
- the increase or the decrease in the soldering iron tip temperature should not exceed 25 °C/s,
- the soldering process duration should be 6 seconds max.

The new types of chip packages are usually better protected against simple unsoldering, because the leads are hidden below the package body (BGA, FlipChip) or there are other ways of attaching them to the PCB (DCA – Direct Chip Attach, WLP – Wafer Level Packaging, 2D and 3D packages) [1]. It can be therefore very uncomfortable or even impossible to get the necessary heat exactly to the right place. In certain cases, we can use a heat gun instead of an iron solder. It is recommended to use the heat gun with a thin head that aims the heat to the very narrow space to achieve the required efficiency and to protect the chip functionality. The principle of working with a heat gun is the same as that of working with an iron solder, but one has to be very careful as the heat gun heats a larger area and this could be undesirable in most situations (naturally, overheating is undesirable).

It is definitely not the only way, how to acquire separate encapsulated chips. Due to modern requirements, the pitch of chip packages leads is still decreasing, and hence the contemporary classic packages (with bare leads on sides) contain many very thin leads. We can call this a fine pitch package – the pitch between the leads is smaller than 1 mm. Due to that, we can sometimes simply use a sharp knife to cut out the chosen chips or, rather, the packaged chips from the PCB. There is no need to use heat with this method, and it can therefore be considered a safer technique. On the other hand, it is essential to pay attention to the thickness or, rather, thinness of the leads and to work very carefully with the blade to avoid any physical damage to these. It should also be borne in mind that not all chips can be obtained by using this method.

3   Decapsulation

It would be appropriate to discuss all the types of chip packages, but it is not possible to fulfil this task within a single article. There are several books dealing especially with the chip packages and the related topics, e.g. [2], [3], [4], [5]. It is a very wide area, with many important aspects of knowledge.

It can be said, very briefly, that there are three main types of common chip packages regarding their material – metal, ceramic and plastic. The most important category for us is the plastic one. These packages are widely used and are often suitable for most of ordinary integrated circuits, at a low price. The metal and ceramic packages do not occur as often as the plastic ones, so the effective approach to obtain a bare chip out of the plastic package with the use of sulphuric and nitric acid is described herein.

3.1 Chip Preparation

It is recommended to prepare some holders for chips, to be able to manipulate with these in the beaker containing the acids. For better image, see Fig. 1 where the BGA-type package with a tinplated copper holder can be seen. The quality of soldered connection between the chip package and the holder is bad, because the BGA-type ball leads are usually protected by special compound with a feature of keeping the solder away [1]. Other types of chip packages connected to copper holders will be dealt with later in this section (see Fig. 3).

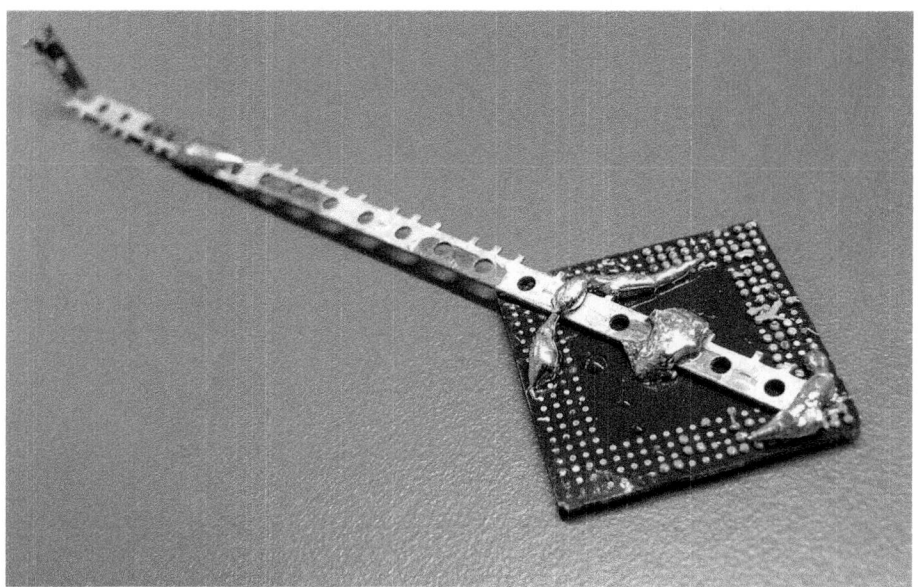

Fig. 1. Chip package BGA with a soldered copper holder

3.2 Chip Package Decapsulation

The plastic packages differ one from another. Due to this fact, a certain package provides unique features suitable for a particular purpose. However, the composition is usually considerably similar and that is why the same process can be used to remove almost all types of such moulding compounds. For better illustration of the presented decapsulation process see Fig. 2.

A chemical laboratory equipped with a fume cupboard and a chemical sink should be visited for the safe performance of the etching process. It is also automatically assumed that a personal protection equipment (gloves, glasses, protective clothes etc.) is used.

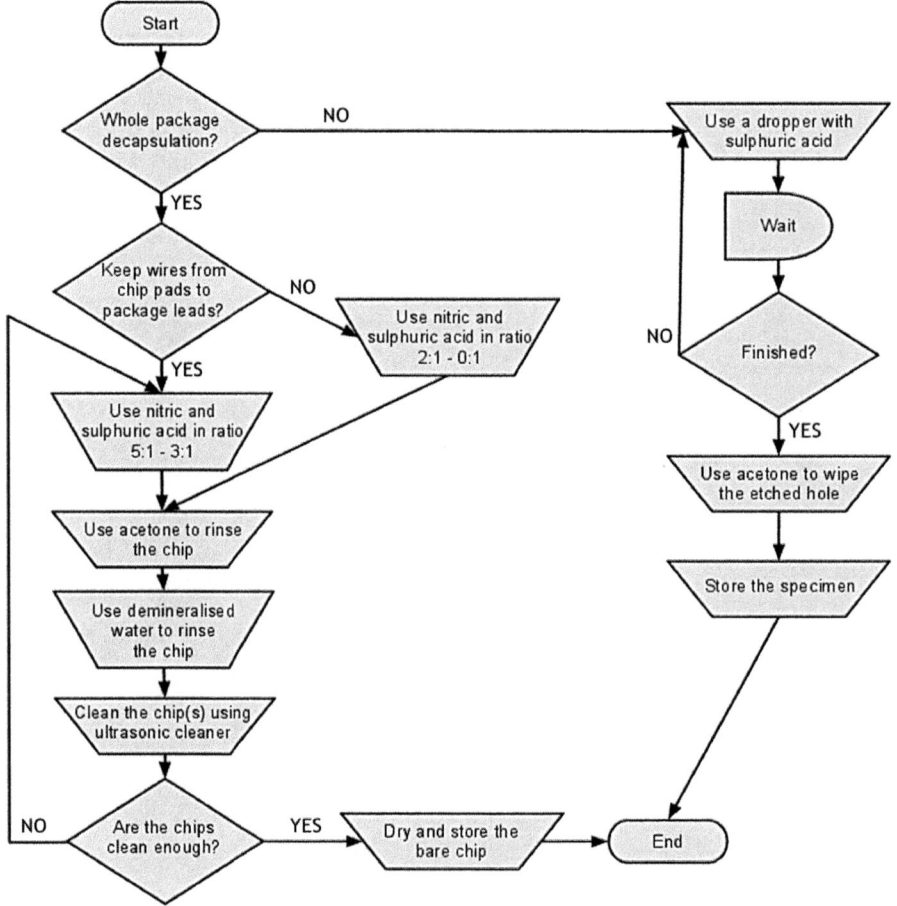

Fig. 2. Illustration of the presented decapsulation process

Basic Equipment. This part provides a list of items needed to complete the process of decapsulation [1].

- Sulphuric acid (H_2SO_4 – concentration 96 % or more).
- Nitric acid (HNO_3 – concentration 96 % or more).
- Acetone (C_3H_6O).

- Demineralised water or distilled water (in the worst case tap water).
- Ultrasonic cleaner.
- Cooker.
- Fume cupboard.
- Beakers (at least four pieces).
- Tweezers.
- Filter paper or nitrogen flow.
- Personal protection equipment (gloves, glasses, protective clothes etc.).

Additional Convenient Equipment. For more comfortable work it is recommended to prepare also these items:

- Microscope or magnifier.
- Double-sided tape with weak adhesive.
- Box to place the chips in.

Ratio of Nitric Acid to Sulphuric Acid. The ratio is always stated as nitric acid to sulphuric acid (the recommended approx. temperature is mentioned in brackets) [1].

- 5 : 1 - 3 : 1 (ca. 90-94 °C) – preservation of wire bonds from leadframe to the chip.
- 2 : 1 - 1 : 1 (ca. 90-94 °C) – faster, cheaper and a more aggressive decapsulation.
- 0 : 1 (up to ca. 270 °C) – to etch very resistant moulding compounds, very aggressive.

Whole-Package Decapsulation Process. It is strongly recommended to proceed very cautiously, while observing the chemical laboratory rules to avoid any injuries or damage to the laboratory equipment or to the chips.

First, the four beakers should be prepared. Two beakers should be half-filled with the acids in a correct ratio. The third beaker should be half-filled with acetone and the last one with demineralised water. The cooker must be placed into the fume cupboard. Other recommended equipment should be placed nearby the fume cupboard or even inside it, if there is enough room for all the items. Only the beakers with acids must be placed on the cooker to reach the desired working temperature, the other steps of the whole process should take place out of the cooker.

The major etching should be performed in the first beaker with acids. The acids will become non-transparent soon due to the presence of etched moulding compounds. The recommendation is to inspect periodically the level of decapsulation during the process. Ideally in intervals of approx. thirty seconds. When the process is almost complete, it is better to use the second beaker with acids to do the fine etching. It is necessary to monitor the progress permanently then, and transparent acid is ideal for this purpose. When the chip is bared, it should be washed in the beaker with acetone, then with flowing demineralised water and it should be put inside the beaker with demineralised water afterwards.

The beaker with demineralised water and a chip or chips, as the case may be, should be placed into ultrasonic cleaner for up to two minutes in the case that there is only one chip in the beaker or thirty seconds in the case there are more chips in that beaker (with exaggeration, the chips act as emery paper). Then a final check should take place. If everything seems to be all right, the chips should be dried with filter paper or nitrogen flow, and properly stored. If there is any problem with cleanness of the chip surface or similar, the entire process can be repeated. [1]

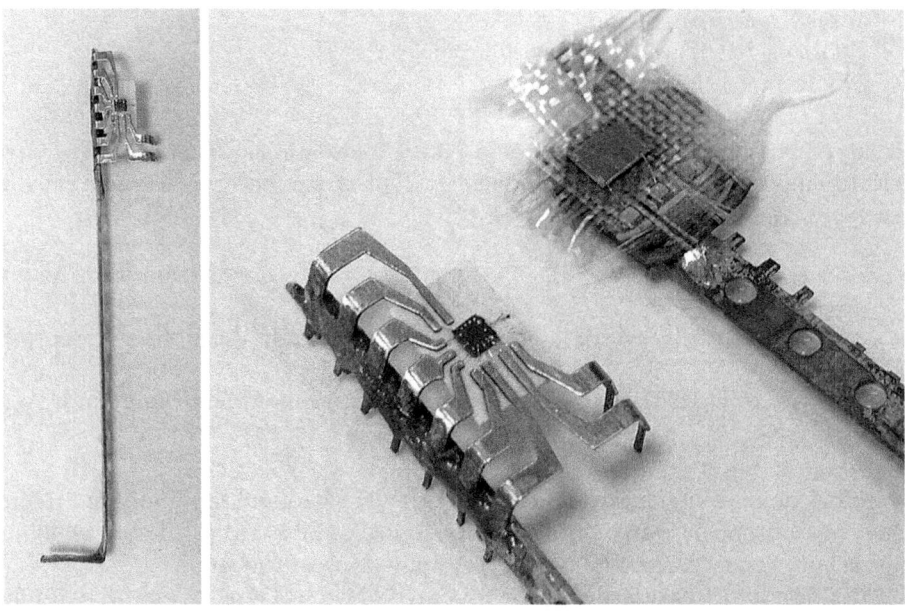

Fig. 3. Bare chips with copper holders after the whole decapsulation process

Etching of Specific Packaging Part. Useful approach is to etch only a specific part of the chip package. The entire chip is preserved and hence it can be attached to other components as usual. This is needed when some measurements have to occur or only when it is necessary to preserve the whole structure of the chip. The chip surface can be still observed via an etched aperture. This is the preferred method for observing the new unknown chips, because the risk of damaging the specimen is smaller.

This process is more demanding, because of manual dosing of acid drops to the specific area via a dropper. First, a little hollow is made in the surface of the chip (approx. in the centre of the area designated for etching). Then the drops of sulphuric acid are manually applied to the chosen place (usually, nitric acid is not used in this approach). There has to be a short period of inactivity between applications of the acid drops, to allow reaction with the surface. It is undesirable to apply more acid than it is imperative, because the reaction is not under a perfect control in that case, and therefore the result cannot be predicted or even guarantied. [1]

3.3   Process Results

A very brief demonstration of the whole package decapsulation process can be seen in Fig. 3 [1]. In case that the process is done correctly (especially the duration of the etching step has to be adequate), the holders and the entire structure of the chip is preserved. That is convenient, because the holders can still be used for an easy manipulation.

3.4   Other Methodologies of Decapsulation

It is not possible to present a complete overview of decapsulation methodologies within a such paper. However, other different approaches in decapsulation exist. Some of them make use of the same acids, but mostly in a different manner. And some of them are totally dissimilar. Representative examples are mentioned below. One example is from the group of similar procedures, one is naturally from the group of dissimilar procedures.

One of the similar approaches was presented by Nick Chernyy in [7]. There are the following differences:

1. only a sulphuric acid is used for etching of the moulding compounds (instead of specific acid mixture; consequence: worse control of a fine etching process),
2. after the etching part of the whole process, water is used to rinse a chip (instead of acetone),
3. ultrasonic cleaning is done with a beaker filled with acetone (instead of demineralised water; consequence: worse final results).

We propose to use acetone to rinse the bared chips first and then demineralised water for ultrasonic cleaning. This proposal followed from results of trying different order of the liquids. [1]

Another technique is based on using resin instead of acids (briefly described in [6]). However, to achieve desired results it takes a lot of time. And in fact, it is not recommended to follow this approach, because resin vapour can foul up an exhaust. Moreover, the temperature of resin during the etching process should be really high, ca. 350 °C. On the other hand, the use of dangerous acids is unnecessary. Therefore, the process can be practically performed somewhere outside of a building to avoid a necessity of using any exhaust. In that case, the work can be done without any proper chemical laboratory. Considering the price of resin and the fact that storing resin is safe, this approach may be sometimes appropriate.

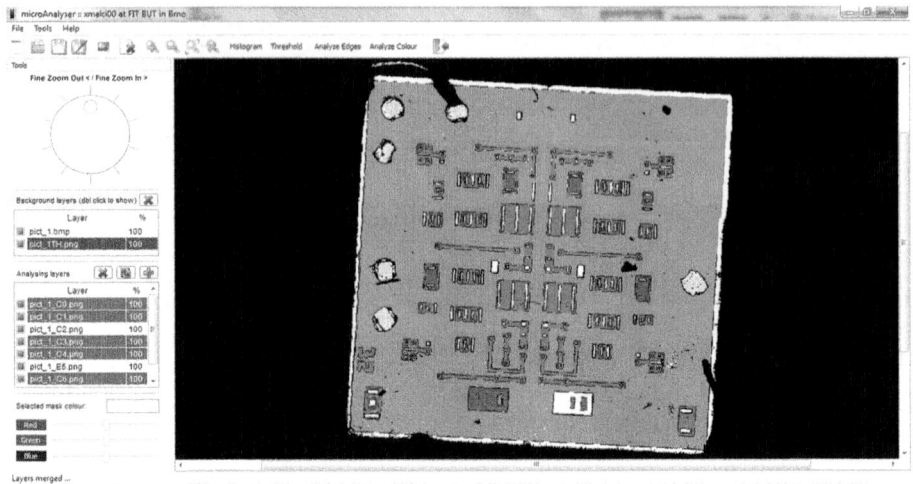

Fig. 4. Demonstration of the microAnalyser application. No disturbing background is present. Some layers are switched off (white areas).

4 Introduction to Analysis

The work with microscope is not dealt with in this paper, because each laboratory is equipped with a different equipment with certain features and limitations. It is assumed that pictures of the chips can be taken by personnel in every laboratory.

A performance of any analysis of a chip surface with the only one picture available is virtually impossible. Every contemporary chip is made of different layers. Decomposition of a chip will be presented in another paper.

4.1 Application

The layer structure is important also from the application point of view. In consequence, the application must be able to handle several layers and it should also provide corresponding functionality.

Our prototype - microAnalyser (screenshot can be seen in Fig. 4) - is based on the above-mentioned principals. We are aware that there is still a lot of work to be done, but some basic features have already been developed:

- handling large images,
- working with layers (see Fig. 5),
- colour-based analysis,
- simple edge detectors,
- ability to save and load entire projects containing several layers,
- cooperation with OpenCV library.

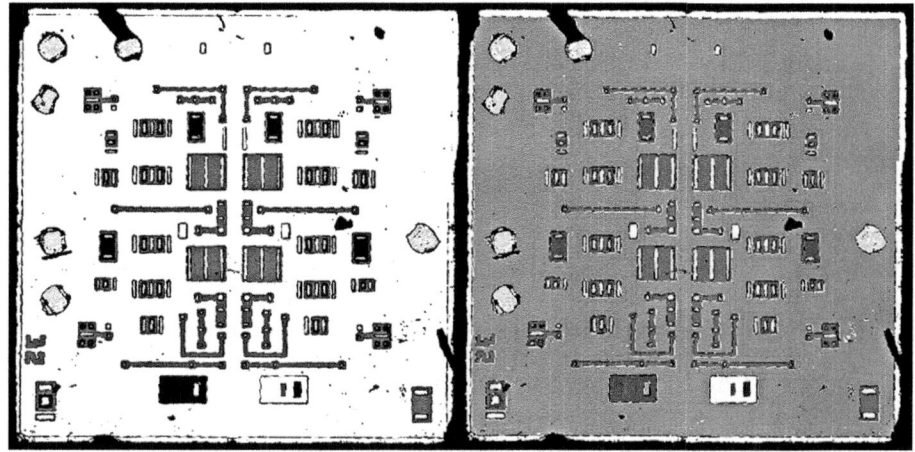

Fig. 5. Examples of the same chip with different layers turned on

The application should provide many more functions later on – semiautomatic analysing tools (searching for specific structures, comparing picture data with a library of common blocks, searching for repeating occurrence of the selected block, support for making schemes on the basis of analysed pictures of chips) as well as the painting functions for modifying the picture data and for making notes. The layer basis will be also upgraded to a very similar concept as that used in the programs such as the GIMP or Photoshop.

The goal is to develop a complex application for general use in this field of analysing and testing the known and even unknown structures. The lack of such a program can be felt significantly, because nowadays it is necessary to combine several programs, and even to put a pen to a paper [6]. We would like to simplify the whole process and to have all the data arranged in some sort of a database, for valuable and very fast use by computers and by researchers too. [1]

5   Conclusion

Nowadays a following paper concerning chip layer decomposition and picture data analysis is being prepared. After finishing this paper we would be able to get all the necessary picture data of particular chips. The very first significant picture data analysis of a specific chip and a comprehensive description of the whole process will be worked out consequently. Afterwards a next version of microAnalyser application prototype with an ability to extract some relevant information from pictures of chips' layers will be released.

The further goal of our effort is to improve the whole process as much as possible to be allowed to use the methodologies and the microAnalyser application with many types of chips in general.

Acknowledgment. This work is partially supported by the research plan *"Security-Oriented Research in Information Technology"*, MSM0021630528 (CZ), by the grant *"Advanced secured, reliable and adaptive IT"*, FIT-S-11-1 (CZ) and by the grant *"Information Technology in Biomedical Engineering"*, GD102/09/H083.

References

1. Malcik, D.: Microscopic analysis of chips security, Diploma thesis, Faculty of Information Technology, Brno University of Technology (2011)
2. Szendiuch, I.: Zaklady technologie mikroelektronickych obvodu a systemu. VUTIUM (2006) ISBN 80-214-3292-6
3. Chung, D.: Materials for electronic packaging. Butterworth-Heinemann (1995) ISBN 978-0750693141
4. Tummala, R.: Fundamentals of Microsystems Packaging. McGraw Hill Professional (2001) ISBN 978-0071371698
5. Blackwell, G.R.: The Electronic Packaging Handbook. CRC Press (1999) ISBN 978-0849385919
6. Schobert, M.: All Chips Reversed. Die Datenschleuder 94, 17–36 (2010) ISSN 0930-1054
7. Chernyy, N.: HOW TO: write an IC Friday post (2008), http://microblog.routed.net/2008/07/15/how-to-write-an-ic-friday-post/

An ID-Based Broadcast Signcryption Scheme Secure in the Standard Model[*]

Bo Zhang

School of Computer Science and Engineering, University of Jinan,
250022, Jinan, Shandong, P.R. China
zhangbosdu@gmail.com

Abstract. Broadcast signcryption is a cryptographic primitive which combines the concepts of broadcast encryption and signcryption together to provide private and authenticated communications to several different receivers in the open channel. In this paper, we propose a concrete identity-based broadcast signcryption scheme in the standard model. The proposed scheme satisfies the message confidentiality and unforgeability.

Keywords: signcryption, identity based cryptography, broadcast signcryption.

1 Introduction

Identity-based (ID-based) cryptosystems were introduced by Shamir [1] in 1984. Its main idea is that the public keys of a user can be easily derived from arbitrary strings corresponding to his identity information such as name, telephone number or email address. The corresponding private key can only be derived by a trusted Private Key Generator (PKG).Encryption and signature are basic cryptographic tools to achieve private and authenticity. In 1997, Zheng [2] firstly proposed the notion of signcryption, which can perform digital signature and public key encryption simultaneously at lower computational costs and communication overheads than sign-then-encrypt. By combining ID-based cryptology and signcryption, Malone-Lee [3] gave the first ID-based signcryption scheme. Since then, quite a few ID-based signcryption schemes have been proposed.

In some network applications, we have to distribute same message to several different members. A simple approach for achieving this goal is that the sender encrypts or signcrypts the message for each member of the receiver group respectively. Obviously, the cost of using the approach in large group is very high. Broadcast encryption [4] considers this problem of broadcasting digital contents to a large set of authorized users. Such applications include paid-TV systems, copyrighted CD/DVD distributions, and fee-based online databases. The broadcaster encrypts the message and only the authorized users have the decryption keys to recover the data. In this type of scheme the sender encrypts a message for some subset of receivers and sends the ciphertext by the broadcast over Internet.

---

[*] This work is supported by the Doctor Foundation of University of Jinan.

T.-h. Kim et al. (Eds.): SecTech 2011, CCIS 259, pp. 123–127, 2011.
© Springer-Verlag Berlin Heidelberg 2011

Any receiver in the designated subset can use his private key to decrypt the ciphertext. However, nobody outside the subset can get any information about the contents of the broadcast. In 2004, Mu et al. [5] proposed an ID-based broadcast authenticated broadcast encryption scheme. In 2008, Li et al. [6] proposed an ID-based broadcast signcryption scheme. But these two scheme were show that Mu et al.'s scheme is insecure with respect to unforgeability, Li et al.'s scheme can be totally broken(with respect to both semantic security and unforgeability). In [7] ,a new ID-based broadcast signcryption scheme was proposed. The security of the scheme was proven secure in the random oracle model [8]. Although the model is efficient and useful, it has been shown that when random oracles are instantiated with concrete hash functions, the resulting scheme may not be secure [9]. Therefore, it is an important research problem to construct an ID-based anonymous signcryption scheme secure in the standard model.

Our Contribution. In this paper, we give an ID-based broadcast signcryption scheme secure in the standard model. The proposed scheme satisfies the message confidentiality and unforgeability. We also give the formal security proof on its message confidentiality under the hardness of Decisional Bilinear Diffie-Hellman problem and its unforgeability under the Computational Diffie-Hellman assumption.

2   Preliminaries

Let G and G_T be two cyclic multiplicative groups of prime order p and g be a generator of G.

2.1   Bilinear Pairings

The map $e : G \times G \to G_T$ is said to be an admissible bilinear pairing if the following conditions hold true.
   (1) e is bilinear, i. e. $e(g^a, g^b) = e(g, g)^{ab}$ for all $a, b \in Z_p$.
   (2) e is non-degenerate, i. e. $e(g, g) \neq 1_{G_T}$.
   (3) e is efficiently computable.
   We refer the reader to [10] for more details on the construction of such pairings.

2.2   Complexity Assumptions

Decisional Bilinear Diffie-Hellman (DBDH)Assumption. The challenger chooses $a, b, c, z \in Z_p$ at random and then flips a fair binary coin . If $\beta = 1$ it output the tuple $(g, A = g^a, B = g^b, C = g^c, Z = e(g, g)^{abc})$. Otherwise, if $\beta = 0$, the challenger outputs the tuple $(g, g, A = g^a, B = g^b, C = g^c, Z = e(g, g)^z)$. The adversary must then output a guess β' of β.

   An adversary has at least an ε advantage in solving the decisional BDH problem if

$$|Pr[B(g, g^a, g^b, g^c, e(g, g)^{abc}) = 1] - Pr[B(g, g^a, g^b, g^c, e(g, g)^z) = 1]| \geq \varepsilon$$

where the probability is over the randomly chosen a, b, c, z and the random bits consumed by the adversary.

Definition 1. *The decisional (t, ε)-DBDH assumption holds if no t-time adversary has at least ε advantage in solving the above game.*

Computational Diffie-Hellman (CDH) Assumption. The challenger chooses $a, b \in Z_p$ at random and outputs $(g, A = g^a, B = g^b)$. The adversary then attempts to output $g^{ab} \in G$. An adversary has at least an ε advantage if $Pr[B(g, g^a, g^b) = g^{ab}] \geq \varepsilon$ where the probability is over the randomly chosen a, b and the random bits consumed by the adversary.

Definition 2. *The computational (t, ε)-CDH assumption holds if no t-time adversary has at least ε advantage in solving the above game.*

3   ID-Based Broadcast Signcryption Scheme(IBBSC Scheme)

3.1   Concrete IBBC Scheme

In this section, we propose an concrete IBBSC scheme. Our concrete scheme is motivated from Waters' ID-based encryption scheme [11] and the signature schemes in [12]. We follow the framework of a general ID-based broadcast signcryption scheme presented by [7] . The algorithms are as following:

Setup. Choose groups G and G_T of prime order p such that an admissible pairing $e : G \times G \to G_T$ can be constructed and pick a generator g of G.

Now, pick a random secret $\alpha \in Z_p$, compute $g_1 = g^\alpha$ and pick $g_2 \leftarrow_R G$. Furthermore, pick elements $u', m' \leftarrow_R G$ and vectors $\mathcal{V}_U, \mathcal{V}_M$ of length n_u and n_m, respectively, whose entries are random elements from G. Let H, H_u, H_m be a cryptography hash functions where $H : G_T \to \{0, 1\}^{l_t}$, $H_u : \{0, 1\}^* \to \{0, 1\}^{n_u}$, $H_m : \{0, 1\}^{l_t} \times \{0, 1\}^* \times G_T \to \{0, 1\}^{n_m}$ where l_t is the length of plaintext. The public parameters are $P = (G, G_T, e, g, g_1, g_2, u', \mathcal{V}_U, m', \mathcal{V}_M, H, H_u, H_m)$ and the master secret S is g_2^α.

Extract. Let $\mathcal{U}$ be a bit string of length n_u representing an identity and let $\mathcal{U}[i]$ be the i-th bit of $\mathcal{U}$. Define $U' \subset \{1, \ldots, n_u\}$ to be the set of indices i such that $\mathcal{U}[i] = 1$.

To construct the private key d_u of the identity $\mathcal{U}$, pick $r_u \leftarrow Z_p$ and compute:

$$d_u = (g_2^\alpha (u' \prod_{i \in U'} u_i)^{r_u}, g^{r_u})$$

Signcrypt. To signcrypt a message m to t of users with identities $L = \{ID_1, ID_2, \ldots, ID_t\}$,a broadcaster with identity ID_s who's private key is

$$d_s = (d_{s1}, d_{s2}) = (g_2^\alpha (u' \prod_{j \in U'_s} u_j)^r, g^r)$$

does the following.

He picks $r_m \in Z_p$ randomly.

(1) Compute $U_j = u' \prod_{i \in U_j'} u_i$ (for $j = 1, 2, ..., t$),

(2) Compute $\omega = e(g_1, g_2)^{r_m}$

(3) Compute $c = m \oplus H(\omega)$

(4) Compute $\sigma_1 = \{R_j = U_j^{r_m} | j = 1, 2, ..., t\}$

(5) Compute $\sigma_2 = g^{r_m}$

(6) Compute $M = H_m(m, L, \omega), \sigma_3 = d_{s1} \cdot (m' \prod_{j \in M'} m_j)^{r_m}$

($M' \subset \{1, 2, ..., n_m\}$ be the set of indices j such that $m[j] = 1$, where $m[j]$ is the jth bit of M).

The resultant ciphertext is $L, \sigma = (c, \sigma_1, \sigma_2, \sigma_3, d_{s2})$.

Unsigncrypt. The receiver with index j in L decrypts the ciphertext as follows:

(1) Compute $U_s = u' \prod_{j \in U_s'} u_j$

(2) Compute $\omega = e(d_{j1}, \sigma_2)/e(d_{j2}, R_j)$

(3) Compute $m = c \oplus H(\omega)$

(4) Compute $M = H_m(m, L, \omega)$

The receiver accepts the message if and only if the following equality holds:

$$e(\sigma_3, g) = e(g_1, g_2)e(U_s, d_{s2})e(m' \prod_{j \in M'} m_j, \sigma_2)$$

3.2   Correctness

The correctness of the scheme can be directly verified by the following equations.

$$e(\sigma_3, g) = e(d_{s1} \cdot (m' \prod_{j \in M'} m_j)^{r_m}, g)$$

$$= e(g_2^\alpha U_s^r, g)e((m' \prod_{j \in M'} m_j)^{r_m}, g)$$

$$= e(g_2^\alpha, g)e(U_s^r, g)e((m' \prod_{j \in M'} m_j)^{r_m}, g)$$

$$= e(g_1, g_2)e(U_s, d_{s2})e(m' \prod_{j \in M'} m_j, \sigma_2)$$

3.3   Security

Theorem 1. *The concrete IBBSC scheme is secure against any IND-IBBSC-CCA2 adversary if the Decisional Bilinear Diffie-Hellman problem is hard.*

Theorem 2. *Under the CDH assumption, the proposed IBBSC scheme is existentially unforgeable against adaptive chosen message attack.*

Due to space limitations, the security proof will present in a full version of this paper.

4   Conclusions

We have proposed an IBBSC scheme that satisfy the message confidentiality and unforgeability. It remains an open problem to construct a much more efficient scheme that is secure in the standard model with constant size signcryption ciphertext while removing all limitations on the size of group.

References

1. Shamir, A.: Identity-Based Cryptosystems and Signature Schemes. In: Blakely, G.R., Chaum, D. (eds.) CRYPTO 1984. LNCS, vol. 196, pp. 47–53. Springer, Heidelberg (1985)
2. Zheng, Y.: Digital Signcryption or How to Achieve Cost (Signature & Encryption) $<<$ cost(Signature) + cost(Encryption). In: Kaliski Jr., B.S. (ed.) CRYPTO 1997. LNCS, vol. 1294, pp. 165–179. Springer, Heidelberg (1997)
3. Malone-Lee, J.: Identity based signcryption, Cryptology ePrint Archive. Report 2002/098
4. Fiat, A., Naor, M.: Broadcast Encryption. In: Stinson, D.R. (ed.) CRYPTO 1993. LNCS, vol. 773, pp. 480–491. Springer, Heidelberg (1994)
5. Mu, Y., Susilo, W., Lin, Y.-X., Ruan, C.: Identity-Based Authenticated Broadcast Encryption and Distributed Authenticated Encryption. In: Maher, M.J. (ed.) ASIAN 2004. LNCS, vol. 3321, pp. 169–181. Springer, Heidelberg (2004)
6. Li, F., Xin, X., Hu, Y.: Indentity-based broadcast signcryption. Computer Standards and Interfaces 30(1-2), 89–94 (2008)
7. Selvi, S.S.D., Vivek, S.S., Gopalakrishnan, R., Karuturi, N.N., Rangan, C.P.: Cryptanalysis of mu et al.'s and li et al.'s Schemes and a Provably Secure ID-based Broadcast Signcryption (IBBSC) Scheme. In: Chung, K.-I., Sohn, K., Yung, M. (eds.) WISA 2008. LNCS, vol. 5379, pp. 115–129. Springer, Heidelberg (2009)
8. Bellare, M., Rogaway, P.: Random oracles are practical: a paradigm for designing efficient protocols. In: Proc. CCS 1993, pp. 62–73 (1993)
9. Canetti, R., Goldreich, O., Halevi, S.: The random oracle methodology, revisited (preliminary version). In: Proc. STOC 1998, pp. 209–218 (1998)
10. Boneh, D., Franklin, M.: Identity-Based Encryption from the Weil Pairing. In: Kilian, J. (ed.) CRYPTO 2001. LNCS, vol. 2139, pp. 213–229. Springer, Heidelberg (2001)
11. Waters, B.: Efficient Identity-Based Encryption without Random Oracles. In: Cramer, R. (ed.) EUROCRYPT 2005. LNCS, vol. 3494, pp. 114–127. Springer, Heidelberg (2005)
12. Paterson, K.G., Schuldt, J.C.N.: Efficient Identity-Based Signatures Secure in the Standard Model. In: Batten, L.M., Safavi-Naini, R. (eds.) ACISP 2006. LNCS, vol. 4058, pp. 207–222. Springer, Heidelberg (2006)

Robust Audio Watermarking Scheme Based on Short Time Fourier Transformation and Singular Value Decomposition

Pranab K. Dhar[1], Mohammad I. Khan[1],
Sunil Dhar[1], and Jong-Myon Kim[2,*]

[1] Chittagong University of Engineering and Technology, Chittagong, Bangladesh
[2] University of Ulsan, Usan, Korea
{pranab_cse,muhammad_ikhancuet,sdhar03}@yahoo.com,
jongmyon.kim@gmail.com

Abstract. Digital watermarking has been widely used for copyright protection of digital contents. This paper proposes a new watermarking scheme based on short time Fourier transformation and singular value decomposition. In our proposed watermarking scheme, spectrum of the original audio signal is computed first by short-time Fourier transformation (STFT). Prominent spectral peaks are detected from the frequency spectrum of each frame using a peak detection algorithm. Singular value decomposition (SVD) is applied to the selected prominent peaks of each frame represented in matrix form. Watermarks are then embedded into the highest singular value of each matrix of the selected prominent peaks of each frame. Watermarks are extracted by performing the inverse operation of watermark embedding process. Simulation results indicate that the proposed watermarking scheme is highly robust against various kinds of attacks such as noise addition, cropping, re-sampling, re-quantization, MP3 compression, and achieves similarity values ranging from 28 to 32. In addition, our proposed scheme achieves signal-to-noise ratio (SNR) values ranging from 20 to 31 dB.

Keywords: Copyright Protection, Sound Contents, and Fast Fourier Transformation, Singular Value Decomposition.

1   Introduction

Digital watermarking is a process of embedding watermarks into digital contents such as audio, video or image for copyright protection. A digital watermark is an invisible signature embedded into an audio signal which should be perceptually imperceptible to prevent obstruction of the original audio. A significant number of techniques that create robust and imperceptible audio watermarks have been reported in recent years. *Wang et al.* [1] proposed a method based on the Reduced Singular Value

---

* Corresponding author.

T.-h. Kim et al. (Eds.): SecTech 2011, CCIS 259, pp. 128–138, 2011.

Decomposition (RSVD). Watermark bits are embedded into the selected singular values of each frame represented in matrix form. Lei and Lo [2] described a blind audio watermarking scheme in the DCT domain based on Singular Value Decomposition (SVD). A binary image permuted by the Piecewise Affine Markov Map (PWAM) is embedded as watermark into the host audio signal. The block-based method is applied to the DCT coefficients by modifying the largest singular values after the SVD transformation. Xiang and Huang [3] presented a watermarking system using the insensitivity of the audio histogram shape and the modified mean of time scale modification. Lie and Chang [4] proposed a method of embedding watermarks into audio signals in the time domain. Their algorithm exploits the differential average-of-absolute-amplitude relations within each group of audio samples to represent one-bit information. It uses low-frequency amplitude modification to scale the amplitudes in selected sections of the samples so that the time domain waveform envelope can be almost completely preserved. Wang and Zhao [5] described a blind audio watermarking scheme for protection against a synchronization attack. The multi-resolution characteristics of discrete wavelet transformation (DWT) and the energy compression characteristics of the discrete cosine transformation (DCT) are combined in this scheme to improve the transparency of the watermark. The watermark is then embedded into low frequency components by using adaptive quantization according to human auditory system. Liu and Lin [6] proposed a blind watermarking scheme that takes the advantages of the attack-invariant feature of the cepstrum domain and the error-correction capability of BCH code to increase the robustness as well as the imperceptibility of audio watermarking. The authors of [7] proposed a blind audio watermarking system which embeds watermarks into audio signal in the time domain. The strength of the audio signal modifications is limited by the necessity to produce an output signal for watermark detection. The watermark signal is generated using a key, and watermark insertion depends on the amplitude and the frequency of audio signal that minimizes the audibility of the watermarked signal. In the method of Cox's *et al.* [8], watermark sequence is embedded in the n highest DCT coefficient of the whole sound excluding the DC component. The watermark sequence is extracted by performing the inverse operation of watermark embedding process.

In this paper, we propose a new watermarking scheme based on short time Fourier transformation and singular value decomposition for audio copyright protection. Initially, spectrum of the original audio signal is computed by short-time Fourier transformation (STFT). Prominent spectral peaks are detected from the frequency spectrum of each overlapping frame using a peak detection algorithm. Singular value decomposition (SVD) is applied to the selected prominent peaks of each frame represented in matrix form. Watermarks are then embedded into the highest singular value of each matrix of the selected prominent peaks of each frame. Watermarks are extracted by performing the inverse operation of watermark embedding process. Simulation results indicate that the proposed watermarking scheme shows strong robustness against various kinds of attacks such as noise addition, cropping, re-sampling, re-quantization, MP3 compression, and achieves similarity values ranging from 28 to 32. In addition, its signal-to-noise ratio (SNR) values range from 20 to 31 dB.

The rest of this paper is organized as follows. Section 2 provides background information including short time Fourier transformation and singular value decomposition. Section 3 introduces our proposed watermarking scheme including watermark embedding process and watermark detection process. Section 4 discusses the performance of our proposed scheme in terms of imperceptibility as well as robustness. Finally, section 5 concludes with the brief summary of the key points.

2   Background Information

2.1   Short Time Fourier Transformation

The Short-Time Fourier Transform (STFT) is a powerful general-purpose tool for audio signal processing. It defines a particularly useful class of time-frequency distributions which specify complex amplitude versus time and frequency for any signal. It extracts the frequency spectrum of the signal through short-time windows. Mathematically, STFT can be written as follows:

$$X_m(w) = \sum_{n=-\infty}^{\infty} x(n)w(n-mR)e^{-jwn} = DTFT_w(x.SHIFT_{mR}(w)) \tag{1}$$

where $x(n)$ is the input signal at time n, $w(n)$ is the length (M) of the window function, $X_m(w)$ is the DTFT (Discrete Time Fourier Transformation) of windowed data centered about time mR, and R is the hope size in samples between successive DTFTs.

2.2   Singular Value Decomposition

Singular value decomposition (SVD) is a mathematical tool which is mainly used to analyze matrices. In SVD, a given matrix A is decomposed into three matrices such that, $A=U\Sigma V^T$ where U and V are orthogonal matrices and $UU^T=I$, $VV^T=I$, I is an identity matrix. The diagonal entries of Σ are called the singular values of A where $\Sigma = diag (\sigma_1, \sigma_2, \ldots, \sigma_n)$, the columns of U are called the left singular vectors of A, and the columns of V are called the right singular vectors of A. This decomposition is known as the singular value decomposition (SVD) of matrix A represented by the following equation:

$$A = \begin{pmatrix} U_{1,1} & \cdots & \cdots & U_{1,n} \\ U_{2,1} & \cdots & \cdots & U_{2,n} \\ \vdots & & & \vdots \\ U_{n,1} & \cdots & \cdots & U_{n,n} \end{pmatrix} \begin{pmatrix} \sigma_{1,1} & 0 & 0 & 0 \\ 0 & \sigma_{2,n} & 0 & 0 \\ \cdots & & & \\ 0 & 0 & 0 & \sigma_{n,n} \end{pmatrix} \begin{pmatrix} V_{1,1} & \cdots & \cdots & V_{1,n} \\ V_{2,1} & \cdots & \cdots & V_{2,n} \\ \vdots & & & \vdots \\ V_{n,1} & \cdots & \cdots & V_{n,n} \end{pmatrix}^T \tag{2}$$

3   Proposed Watermarking Scheme

In this section, we present an overview of our basic watermarking scheme which consists of watermark embedded process and watermark detection process. In this study, a watermark consists of a sequence of real numbers $\mathbf{X}=\{x_1, x_2, x_3,..., x_n\}$. We create a watermark where each value of x_i is chosen independently according to $N(0,1)$ where $N(\mu, \sigma^2)$ denotes a normal distribution with mean μ and variance σ^2.

3.1   Watermark Embedding Process

The proposed watermark embedding process is shown in Fig. 1. The embedding process is implemented in the following seven steps:

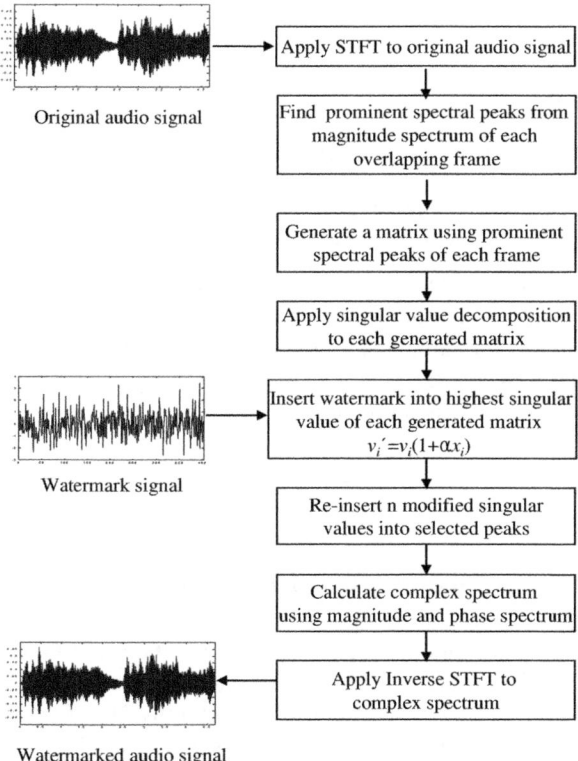

Fig. 1. Watermark embedding process

1) Spectrum of the original audio signal is computed by short-time Fourier transformation (STFT).

2) Prominent spectral peaks are detected from the frequency spectrum of each frame using a peak detection algorithm.

3) Singular value decomposition (SVD) is applied to the selected prominent peaks of the magnitude spectrum of each frame represented in matrix form.

4) Place watermarks into the highest singular value of each matrix of the selected prominent peaks to obtain watermarked peaks $V' = \{v_1', v_2', v_3',..., v_n'\}$. This ensures that the watermark is located at the most significant perceptual components of the audio. When we insert the watermark X into V to obtain V', we specify a scaling parameter α, which determines the extent to which X alters V, shown in the following equation:

$$v_i' = v_i(1 + \alpha x_i) \tag{3}$$

5) Insert back the highest modified singular value of each matrix of the selected prominent peaks into the magnitude spectrum of each overlapping frame.

6) The complex spectrum of each overlapping frame is calculated by using magnitude and phase spectrum.

7) The inverse STFT of the complex spectrum is taken to obtain the watermarked audio signal.

3.1   Watermark Detection Process

The proposed watermark detection process is shown in Fig. 2. The detection process is implemented in the following three steps:

1) Calculate the STFT of the attacked watermark audio frame.

2) Extract the highest singular value of each matrix of the selected prominent peaks which are located at the same position in the pre-embedding process.

3) Extract the watermark sequence by performing the inverse operation of (3) represented by the following equation:

$$x_i^* = (\frac{v_i^*}{v_i} - 1)/\alpha \tag{4}$$

4   Simulation Results and Discussion

In this section, we evaluate the performance of our watermarking scheme for four different types of 16 bit mono audio signals sampled at 44.1 kHz: (a) the song 'Let it Be,' by the Beatles; (b) the beginning of 'Symphony No. 5' in C Minor, Op. 67, by Ludwig van Beethoven; (c) an instrumental song, 'Hey Jude,' played by a Korean traditional musical instrument called the Gayageum; (d) a human voice providing TOEIC (Test of English for International Communication) listening test instruction. Each audio file contains 262,000 samples (duration 5.94 sec). By considering a frame size of 512 samples, we have 1024 overlapping frames for each audio sample. From each frame we detect 64 most prominent peaks which can be represented by an 8×8 matrix. Singular value decomposition (SVD) is applied to each of these matrices. Watermarks are embedded into the highest singular value of each of these matrices. Here, the length of the watermark sequence is 1024.

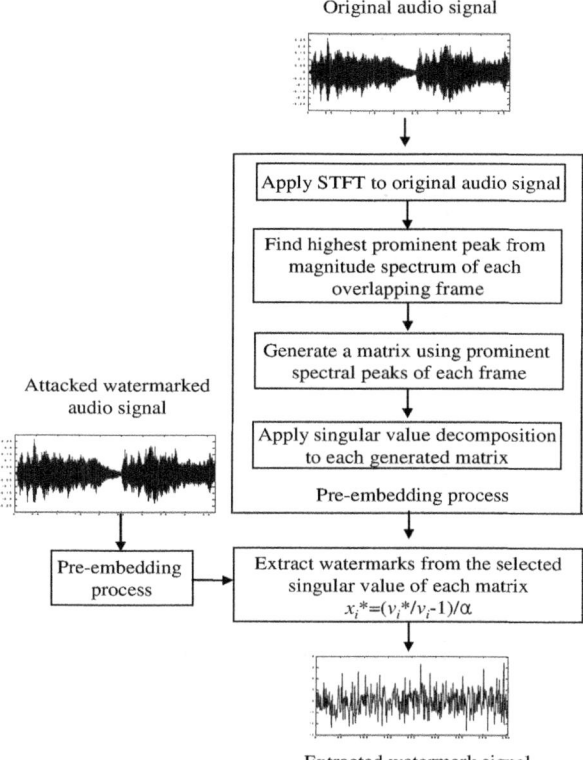

Fig. 2. Watermark detection process

In order to evaluate the performance of the proposed watermarking scheme, the correlation coefficient between the original watermark X and the extracted watermark X^* is calculated by the following similarity SIM(X, X^*) formula:

$$SIM(X, X^*) = \frac{X \cdot X^*}{\sqrt{X^* \cdot X^*}}$$ (5)

It is highly unlikely that X^* will be identical to X. To decide whether X and X^* match, we determine whether the SIM(X, X^*) > T, where T is a detection threshold. In this study, the selected detection threshold (T) value is 6 [8].

Figure 3 shows a qualitative evaluation of the original audio with a watermarked audio in which the watermarks are imperceptible using the proposed scheme. In order to evaluate the quality of watermarked signal, the following signal-to-noise ratio (SNR) equation is used:

$$SNR = 10\log_{10} \frac{\sum_{n=1}^{N} S^2(n)}{\sum_{n=1}^{N} \left[S(n) - S^*(n) \right]^2}$$ (6)

where $S(n)$ and $S^*(n)$ are original audio signal and watermarked audio signal respectively. After embedding watermark, the SNR of all selected audio signals using the proposed method are above 20 dB which ensures the imperceptibility of our proposed scheme.

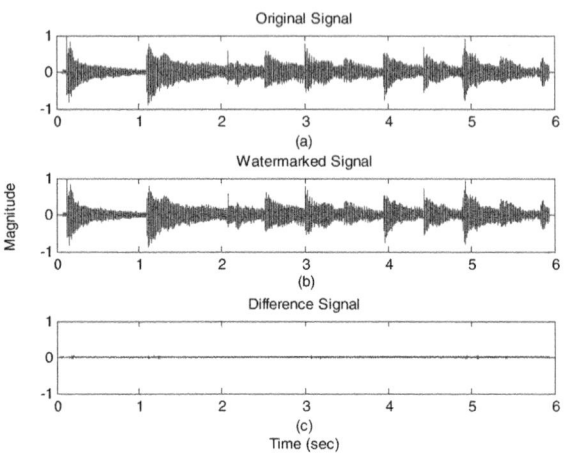

Fig. 3. Imperceptibility of watermarked audio using the proposed scheme: (a) Original audio signal 'Hey Jude' (b) watermarked audio signal 'Hey Jude' (c) difference between original and watermarked audio signal

Figure 4 shows the STFT representation of the original audio signal 'Let it be'. Figure 5 shows the peak detection of the selected frame for the original audio signal 'Let it be'. In our proposed scheme, watermarks are embedded into the highest singular value of each of the matrix of the selected prominent peaks which provides high robustness against different kinds of attacks as well as good SNR values for different watermarked sounds. This is because slight variations of the highest singular values can not affect the quality of the sound and also these values can change very little against different types of attacks.

4.1   Imperceptibility Test

A subjective listening test was applied to the original and watermarked audio signals to determine their quality. Ten people carefully listened to the signals and could not distinguish between the original and watermarked ones. This indicates that the proposed watermarking scheme does not affect the perceived quality of the audio signal, meaning that the embedded watermarks are imperceptible. Table 1 shows the SNR result of the proposed scheme for the four selected different watermarked sounds. Our proposed method achieves SNR values ranging from 20 to 31 dB for different watermarked sounds.

4.2   Robustness Test

Table 2 shows the similarity results of the proposed scheme when no attack is applied to four different types of watermarked audio signals for α=0.3.

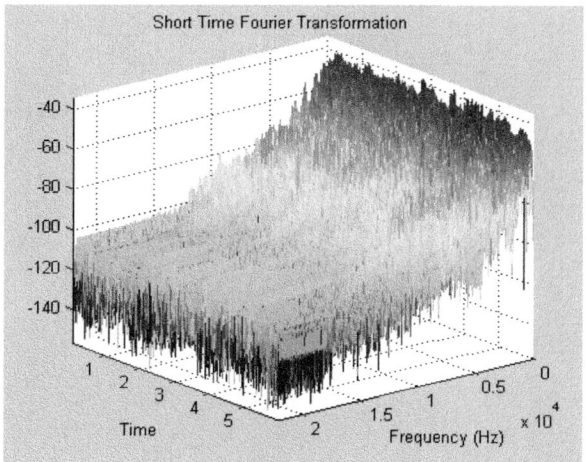

Fig. 4. STFT representation of the original audio signal 'Let it be'

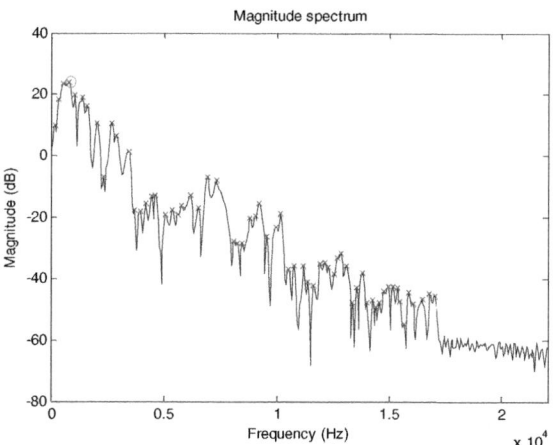

Fig. 5. Peak detection of the selected frame of the audio signal 'Let it be'

Table 1. SNR results of the proposed method for different watermarked sounds

Types of signal	SNR		
	α=0.1	α=0.2	α=0.3
Let it Be	31.342	25.741	21.457
Symphony No 5	30.471	24.938	20.362
Hey Jude	31.143	24.553	21.822
Human Voice	30.853	24.240	20.935

Table 2. Watermark detection results of the proposed scheme against no attack

Types of signal	SIM
Let it Be	32.256
Symphony No 5	32.256
Hey Jude	32.256
Human Voice	32.256

Figure 6 shows the response of the watermark detector to 1000 randomly generated watermarks where correct watermark is at the 500th position when no attack is applied to the watermarked sound 'Let it be' for α=0.3 using the proposed scheme.

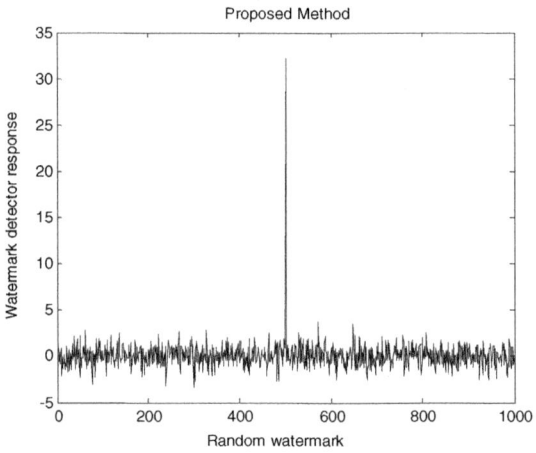

Fig. 6. Watermark detector response using proposed scheme against no attack

In order to test the robustness of our proposed scheme, five different types of attacks, summarized in Table 3, were performed to the watermarked audio signal.

Table 3. Attacks used in this study for watermarked sound

Attacks	Description
Noise addition	Additive white Gaussian noise (AWGN) is added with the watermarked audio signal.
Cropping	We removed 10% samples from the beginning of the watermarked signal and then replaced these samples by the original signal.
Re-sampling	The watermarked signal originally sampled at 44.1 kHz is re-sampled at 22.050 kHz, and then restored by sampling again at 44.1 kHz.
Re-quantization	The 16 bit watermarked audio signal is quantized down to 8 bits/sample and again re-quantized back to 16 bits/sample.
MP3 Compression	MPEG-1 layer 3 compression with 128 kbps is applied to the watermarked signal.

Figure 7 shows the response of the watermark detector to 1000 randomly generated watermarks where correct watermark is at the 500th position against re-sampling attack for α=0.3 using the proposed scheme.

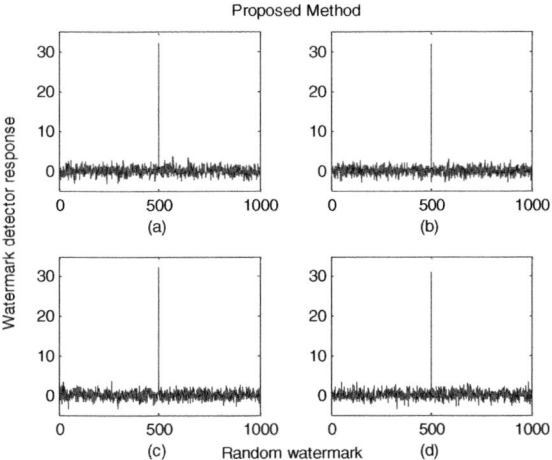

Fig. 7. Watermark detector response against re-sampling attack using the proposed method: (a) Let it be, (b) Symphony No. 5, (c) Hey Jude, (d) Human Voice

Table 4 shows the similarity results of the proposed scheme in terms of robustness against several kinds of attacks applied to four different types of watermarked audio signal 'Let it be', 'Symphony No 5', 'Hey Jude', and 'human voice' respectively for $\alpha=0.3$.

Table 4. Similarity results of proposed scheme against several attacks

Types of Attack	Types of Signal	SIM
Noise addition	Let it be	31.251
	Symphony No 5	31.564
	Hey Jude	30.932
	Human Voice	30.345
Cropping	Let it Be	31.267
	Symphony No 5	31.489
	Hey Jude	30.985
	Human Voice	31.427
Re-sampling	Let it Be	32.179
	Symphony No 5	32.132
	Hey Jude	32.183
	Human Voice	31.167
Re-quantization	Let it Be	32.134
	Symphony No 5	32.165
	Hey Jude	32.180
	Human Voice	31.644
MP3 Compression	Let it Be	30.143
	Symphony No 5	29.237
	Hey Jude	29.834
	Human Voice	28.635

5   Conclusion

In this paper, a new watermarking scheme based on short time Fourier transformation and singular value decomposition was introduced for copyright protection of audio data. Experimental results indicate that our proposed watermarking scheme shows strong robustness against several kinds of attacks such as noise addition, cropping, re-sampling, re-quantization, and MP3 compression and achieves similarity values ranging from 28 to 32. Moreover, our proposed scheme achieves SNR values ranging from 20 to 31 dB for different watermarked sounds. This is because we embed watermarks into the highest singular value of each matrix of the selected prominent peaks and slight variations of the highest singular values can not affect the quality of the sound and also these values can change very little against different types of attacks. These results demonstrate that our proposed watermarking scheme is a suitable means of copyright protection for audio data.

Acknowledgement. This work was supported by the National Research Foundation of Korea (NRF) grant funded by the Korea government (MEST) (No. 2011-0017941).

References

1. Wang, J., Healy, R., Timoney, J.: A Novel Audio Watermarking Algorithm Based on Reduced Singular Value Decomposition. In: 6th IEEE International Conference on Intelligent Information Hiding and Multimedia Signal Processing (IIH-MSP-2010), pp. 143–146 (2010)
2. Lei, B.Y., Lo, K.T.: Hybrid SVD-based Audio Watermarking Scheme. In: International Conference on Communications, Circuits and Systems (ICCCAS 2010), pp. 428–432 (2010)
3. Xiang, S., Huang, Z.: Histogram-based audio watermarking against time-scale modification and cropping attacks. IEEE Transactions on Multimedia 9(7), 1357–1372 (2007)
4. Lie, W.N., Chang, L.C.: Robust and High-Quality Time-Domain Audio Watermarking Based on Low-Frequency Amplitude Modification. IEEE Transaction on Multimedia 8(1), 46–59 (2006)
5. Wang, X.Y., Zhao, H.: A Novel Synchronization Invariant Audio Watermarking Scheme Based on DWT and DCT. IEEE Transaction on Signal Processing 54(12), 4835–4840 (2006)
6. Liu, S.C., Lin, S.D.: BCH Code Based Robust Audio Watermarking in the Cepstrum Domain. Journal of Information Science and Engineering 22, 535–543 (2006)
7. Bassia, P., Pitas, I., Nikolaidis, N.: Robust Audio Watermarking in the Time domain. IEEE Transaction on Multimedia 3(2), 232–241 (2001)
8. Cox, I., Killian, J., Leighton, F., Shamoon, T.: Secure Spread Spectrum Watermarking for Multimedia. IEEE Transactions on Image Processing 6(12), 1673–1687 (1997)

A Study on Domain Name System as Lookup Manager for Wireless/Mobile Systems in IPv6 Networks

Sunguk Lee[1], Taeheon Kang[2], Rosslin John Robles[3],
Sung-Gyu Kim[3], and Byungjoo Park[3,*]

[1] Research Institute of Industrial Science and Technology,
Pohang, Gyeongbuk, 790-330, Korea
sunguk@rist.kr
[2] Chang Shin Infotel, Galma2-dong, Seo-gu,
Daejeon, Korea
thk0512@csinfotel.com
[3] Department of Multimedia, Hannam University, Ojeong-dong, Daedeok-gu,
Daejeon 306-791, Korea
rosslin_john@yahoo.com, {sgkim,bjpark}@hnu.kr

Abstract. Mobile IPv6 (MIPv6) is a protocol developed as a subset of Internet Protocol version 6 (IPv6) to support mobile connections. MIPv6 allows a mobile node to transparently maintain connections while moving from one subnet to another. Each device is identified by its home address although it may be connecting to through another network. When connecting through a foreign network, a mobile device sends its location information to a home agent, which intercepts packets, intended for the device and tunnels them to the current location. If a node is a web server, and another node will try to access it, it is very easy if it knows the IP address of the web server. As practiced, we use the domain name when searching for websites other than the IP address. This paper suggests an IP lookup in Mobile IPv6 environment. This method utilizes the DNS lookup.

Keywords: Mobile IPv6, DNS, Reverse DNS, Look-Up.

1   Introduction

Mobile IPv6 brings a lot of benefits. In Mobile IPv6, even though the mobile node changes locations and addresses, the existing connections through which the mobile node is communicating are maintained. To accomplish this, connections to mobile nodes are made with a specific address that is always assigned to the mobile node, and through which the mobile node is always reachable. Mobile IPv6 provides Transport layer connection survivability when a node moves from one link to another by performing address maintenance for mobile nodes at the Internet layer. Each node in Mobile IPv6 has its own home address. A node hosting a website also has its own

---

* Corresponding author.

T.-h. Kim et al. (Eds.): SecTech 2011, CCIS 259, pp. 139–145, 2011.

address. It is possible to locate this node utilizing the home address. However, for a common user, memorizing the home address is very difficult. That's why web sites have their own domain name, a name that is easy to memorize like "www.hnu.ac.kr". It is easier to remember compared to 202.30.54.67 which is the IP address.

In Mobile IPv6, home address is used to locate nodes. Common web users use the domain name to search or browse a site. Because of this we suggest the use of Reverse Domain Name lookup. The Domain Name System is maintained by a distributed database system, which uses the client-server model. The nodes of this database are the name servers. Each domain or sub-domain has one or more authoritative DNS servers that publish information about that domain and the name servers of any domains subordinate to it.

The top of the hierarchy is served by the root name-servers: the servers to query when looking up (resolving) a top-level domain name (TLD). DNS refers to Domain Name System and represents a powerful Internet technology for converting domain names to IP addresses. Its special mission is to be a mediator between the IP addresses, the system-side names of the websites and their respective domains, and their user-side alpha-numeric titles. Another important function of the DNS is to control the delivery of email messages.

2   Related Work

2.1   Standard Mobile IPv6 (MIPv6)

MIPv6 is an extensible and modular implementation of IPv6-based mobility mechanisms. The original objective was to develop a RFC 3775 compliant system but the platform was extended and the objectives redefined to support additional solutions such as Hierarchical MIPv6 and other local-mobility architectures such as those involved in the on-going efforts of the NETLMM IETF group. [1]

MIPv6 uses care-of address or CoA as source address in foreign links. And to support natural route optimization, the Correspondent node uses IPv6 routing header than the IP encapsulation. The following are the benefits of Mobile IPv6 over Mobile IPv4.

IPv6 utilizes Route Optimization. It is a built-in feature for Mobile IPv6. In mobile IPv4, this feature was available via an optional set of extensions that was not supported by all nodes.

There is no requirement of foreign Agents in Mobile IPv6. As mentioned previously, Neighbor Discovery and Address Auto-configuration features enable mobile nodes to function in any location without the services of any special router.

No ingress filtering problem in Mobile IPv6. In Mobile IPv4 this happens because the correspondent node puts its home address as the source address of the packet. In Mobile IPv6, the correspondent node puts the care-of address as the source address and having a Home Address Destination option, allows the use of the care-of address to be transparent over the IP layer.

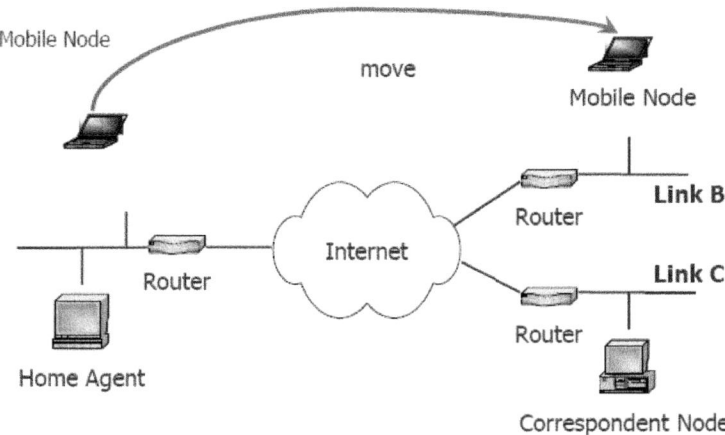

Fig. 1. MIPv6 Senario

2.2   DNS

The Domain Name System or DNS is a hierarchical naming system for computers, services, or any resource participating in the Internet. It associates information with the domain names assigned to each of the participants. It translates domain names meaningful to humans into the numerical or binary identifiers associated with networking equipment for the purpose of locating and addressing these devices world-wide. The Domain Name System serves as the "phone book" for the Internet by translating human-friendly computer hostnames into IP addresses. For example, www.websitename.com translates to 213.77.185.123.

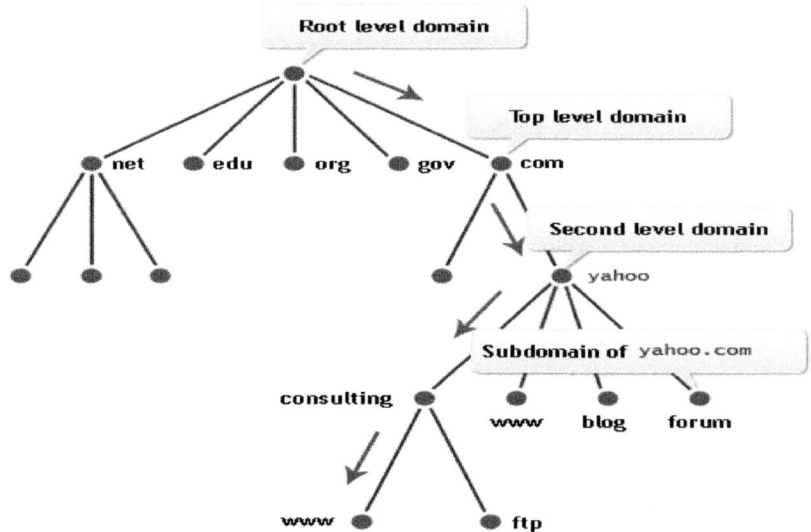

Fig. 2. Hierarchy of Domain Names

DNS makes it possible to assign domain names to groups of Internet users in a meaningful way, independent of each user's physical location. Because of this, World-Wide Web (WWW) hyperlinks and Internet contact information can remain consistent and constant even if the current Internet routing arrangements change or the participant uses a mobile device. Internet domain names are easier to remember than IP addresses such as 2001:db8:1f70::999:de8:7648:6e8. People take advantage of this when they recite meaningful URLs and e-mail addresses without having to know how the machine will actually locate them.

The DNS distributes the responsibility of assigning domain names and mapping those names to IP addresses by designating authoritative name servers for each domain. Authoritative name servers are assigned to be responsible for their particular domains, and in turn can assign other authoritative name servers for their sub-domains.

The process of finding the host name (or domain name) from an IP address involves sending a message to the IP address and requesting the computer located at that IP address to return its name. Usually this will be the same as the domain name. However, many computers host many domains so the host name may be one of the domain names hosted or it could be something totally different.

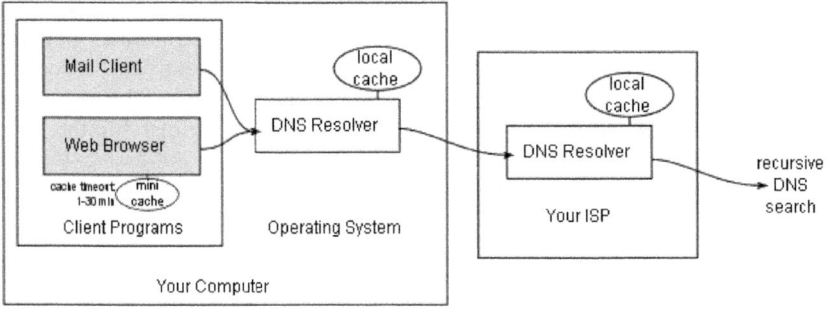

Fig. 3. DNS Resolving

There are some special IP addresses. 127.0.0.1 is always the IP address of every computer. No matter which computer you use, it will always have an IP address of 127.0.0.1 and a name of 'localhost'. In addition, a computer can have more than one IP address. In order to connect to other computers it will have an IP address that is known to other computers.

DNS lookup refers to the process of searching for the unique IP address and DNS records that a certain domain name is associated with. Since the domain name is only the user-side title of a website, whose main purpose is to make it easily findable among the pool of web pages online, it does not provide sufficient information for the website administration process. Website owners may often need to know what the system-side name of a domain is while managing their websites and the best way to find out is through a DNS lookup tool.

2.3   Reverse DNS Look-Up

Reverse DNS lookup or reverse DNS resolution (rDNS) is the determination of a domain name that is associated with a given IP address using the Domain Name System (DNS) of the Internet. It is also used to refer to the overall capability of mapping IP addresses to host names, and "reverse tree" the portions of the DNS that provide the functionality. [6]

Computer networks use the Domain Name System to determine the IP address that is associated with a given domain name. This process is also known as forward DNS resolution. Reverse DNS lookup is the inverse process of this, the resolution of an IP address into its designated domain name.

The reverse DNS database of the Internet is rooted in the Address and Routing Parameter Area (arpa) top-level domain of the Internet. IPv4 uses the in-addr.arpa domain and the ip6.arpa domain is delegated for IPv6.

The process of reverse resolving an IP address is facilitated with the pointer DNS record type (PTR record).

Reverse DNS lookups for IPv6 addresses use the special domain ip6.arpa. An IPv6 address appears as a name in this domain as a sequence of nibbles in reverse order, represented as hexadecimal digits as subdomains. For example, the pointer domain name corresponding to the IPv6 address 4321:0:1:2:3:4:567:89ab is b.a.9.8.7.6.5.0.4.0.0.0.3.0.0.0.2.0.0.0.1.0.0.0.0.0.0.0.1.2.3.4.ip6.arpa.

Internet standards documents [4] specify that "Every Internet-reachable host should have a name" and that such names are matched with a reverse pointer record. When a domain name has a valid Reverse DNS, it can also be accessed by just using the IP address – if you type "202.30.54.67" in your browser, you will be directed to the Hannam University Website.

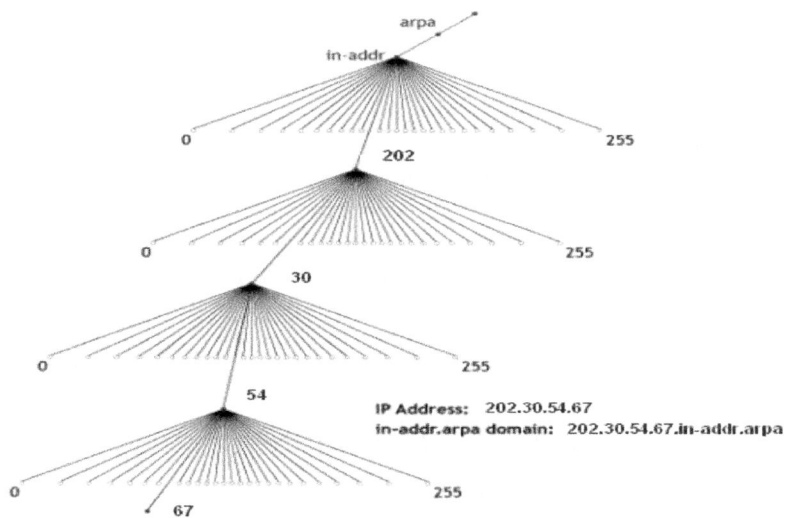

Fig. 4. Reverse Mapping

Reverse DNS is required by some Internet protocols and by extensions to some other Internet protocols. Without reverse DNS, you will experience trouble with r-commands, IRC, some SMTP servers, most enterprise management systems, and many network backup systems.

Troubleshooting problems caused by faulty or non-existant reverse DNS can take considerable time and effort. It is much better to ensure that reverse DNS is configured correctly from the beginning.

3   DNS Look-Up in MIPv6

In IPv6 all devices have its own specific IPv6 address therefore it is easier to develop a list of IPv6 addresses with there corresponding domain name address. All nodes have its own IPv6 address so if one node is a webserver, so if one mobile node or the Home Agent will communicate with it, its IPv6 address should be used. Problem is it is very difficult for a common user to memorize IPv6 address that is why a domain name address can be used.

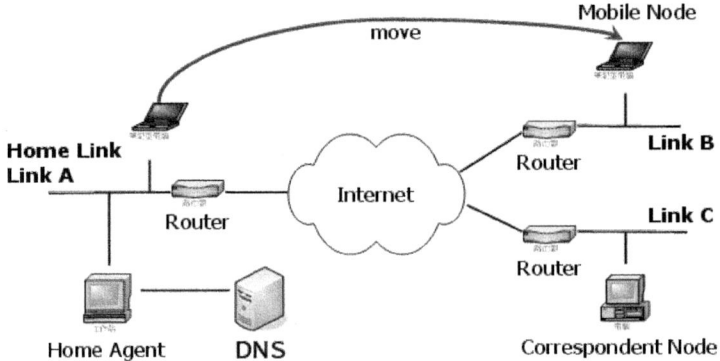

Fig. 5. DNS on the Home Agent

Reverse DNS in MIPv6 will be done by attaching a Domain Name Server (DNS) on the home agent. When a mobile node tries to request information from a web server (say a corresponding node) it can send the domain name to the home address. In the home address, it will resolve or find the IPv6 address of the web server utilizing the reverse DNS lookup technique. After finding the IPv6 address of the corresponding node, it will use that address to communicate with the web server and route the data back to the requesting mobile node.

4   Advantages DNS Look-Up in MIPv6

A DNS lookup in MIPv6 is handy for several applications. [7]

- it is a quick way to check on the availability of a domain name that an individual or company wants to acquire.

- it is a great way to research the business operations of another entity.
- it is a great way to investigate the origin of unwanted electronic communications, and possibly be able to put a stop to them.
- it can be used to check if the node in which the domain resides is active.
- it makes it easier for the users to access websites without memorizing the IPv6 address of the node.

5   Conclusion

MIPv6 is an extensible and modular implementation of IPv6-based mobility mechanisms. The original objective was to develop a RFC 3775 compliant system but the platform was extended. Mobile IPv6 brings a lot of benefits. In Mobile IPv6, even though the mobile node changes locations and addresses, the existing connections through which the mobile node is communicating are maintained. In this paper suggests an IP lookup in Mobile IPv6 environment. We suggested the use of DNS lookup. DNS lookup is the process of searching for the IPv6 address and DNS records that a certain domain name is associated with.

Acknowledgments. This research was supported by the Security Engineering Research Center, granted by the Korea Ministry of Knowledge Economy (No. 11-8).

References

[1] MIPv6, an IPv6 mobility framework, http://fivebits.net/proj/mipv6/ (accessed: June 2009)
[2] Soliman, H.: Mobile IPv6: Mobility in a Wireless Internet (2004)
[3] Wikipedia - DNS, http://en.wikipedia.org/wiki/Domain_Name_System (accessed: June 2009)
[4] RFC 1033
[5] RFC 1922 Section 2.1
[6] Senie, D., Amaranth Networks Inc., A. Sullivan, Command Prompt Inc. Considerations for the use of DNS Reverse Mapping (March 2008)
[7] How do I Perform a DNS Lookup?, http://www.tech-faq.com/dns-lookup.shtml

An Information-Theoretic Privacy Criterion for Query Forgery in Information Retrieval⋆

David Rebollo-Monedero, Javier Parra-Arnau, and Jordi Forné

Department of Telematics Engineering, Technical University of Catalonia (UPC),
E-08034 Barcelona, Spain
{david.rebollo,javier.parra,jforne}@entel.upc.edu

Abstract. In previous work, we presented a novel information-theoretic privacy criterion for query forgery in the domain of information retrieval. Our criterion measured privacy risk as a divergence between the user's and the population's query distribution, and contemplated the entropy of the user's distribution as a particular case. In this work, we make a twofold contribution. First, we thoroughly interpret and justify the privacy metric proposed in our previous work, elaborating on the intimate connection between the celebrated method of entropy maximization and the use of entropies and divergences as measures of privacy. Secondly, we attempt to bridge the gap between the privacy and the information-theoretic communities by substantially adapting some technicalities of our original work to reach a wider audience, not intimately familiar with information theory and the method of types.

1 Introduction

During the last two decades, the Internet has gradually become a part of everyday life. One of the most frequent activities when users browse the Web is submitting a query to a search engine. Search engines allow users to retrieve information on a great variety of categories, such as hobbies, sports, business or health. However, most of them are unaware of the privacy risks they are exposed to [1]. The literature of information retrieval abounds with examples of user privacy threats. Those include the risk of user profiling not only by an Internet search engine, but also by location-based service (LBS) providers, or even corporate profiling by patent and stock market database providers. In this context, query forgery, which consists in accompanying genuine with forged queries, appears as an approach, among many others, to preserve user privacy to a certain extent, if one is willing to pay the cost of traffic and processing overhead.

In a previous work [2], we presented a novel information-theoretic privacy criterion for query forgery in the domain of information retrieval. Our criterion

---

⋆ This work was partly supported by the Spanish Government through projects Consolider Ingenio 2010 CSD2007-00004 "ARES", TEC2010-20572-C02-02 "Consequence" and by the Government of Catalonia under grant 2009 SGR 1362. D. Rebollo-Monedero is the recipient of a Juan de la Cierva postdoctoral fellowship, JCI-2009-05259, from the Spanish Ministry of Science and Innovation.

T.-h. Kim et al. (Eds.): SecTech 2011, CCIS 259, pp. 146–154, 2011.

measured privacy risk as a divergence between the user's and the population's query distribution, and contemplated the entropy of the user's distribution as a particular case. In this work, we make a twofold contribution. First, we thoroughly interpret and justify the privacy metric proposed in our previous work, elaborating on the intimate connection between the celebrated method of entropy maximization and the use of entropies and divergences as measures of privacy. Secondly, we attempt to bridge the gap between the privacy and the information-theoretic communities by substantially adapting some technicalities of our original work to reach a wider audience, not intimately familiar with information theory and the method of types.

2 Background

A variety of solutions have been proposed in information retrieval. Some of them are based on a trusted third party (TTP) acting as an intermediary between users and the information service provider [3]. Although this approach guarantees user privacy thanks to the fact that their identity is unknown to the service provider, in the end, user trust is just shifted from one entity to another.

Some proposals not relying on TTPs make use of perturbation techniques. In the particular case of LBS, users may perturb their location information when querying a service provider [4]. This provides users with a certain level of privacy in terms of location, but clearly not in terms of query contents and activity. Further, this technique poses a trade-off between privacy and data utility: the higher the perturbation of the location, the higher the user's privacy, but the lower the accuracy of the service provider's responses. Other TTP-free techniques rely on user collaboration. In [5, 6], a protocol based on query permutation in a trellis of users is proposed, which comes in handy when neither the service provider nor other cooperating users can be completely trusted.

Query forgery stands as yet another alternative to the previous methods. The idea behind this technique is simply to submit original queries along with false queries. Despite its plainness, this approach can protect user privacy to a certain extent, at the cost of traffic and processing overhead, but without the need to trust the information provider or the network operator. Building upon this principle, several protocols have been put forth. In [7, 8], a solution is presented, aimed to preserve the privacy of a group of users sharing an access point to the Web while surfing the Internet. The authors propose the generation of fake accesses to a Web page to hinder eavesdroppers in their efforts to profile the group. Privacy is measured as the similarity between the actual profile of a group of users and that observed by privacy attackers [7].

One of the most popular privacy criteria in database anonymization is k-anonymity [9], which can be achieved through the aforementioned microaggregation procedure. This criterion requires that each combination of key attribute values be shared by at least k records in the microdata set. However, the problem of k-anonymity, and of enhancements [10, 11, 12, 13] such as l-diversity, is their vulnerability against skewness and similarity attacks [14]. In order to overcome these deficiencies, yet another privacy criterion was considered in [15]: a dataset is said to satisfy t-closeness if for each group of records sharing a combination of key attributes, a certain measure of divergence between the within-group distribution of confidential attributes and the distribution of those attributes for the entire dataset does not exceed a threshold t. An average-case version of the worst-case t-closeness criterion, using the Kullback-Leibler divergence as a measure of discrepancy, turns out to be equivalent to a mutual information, and lend itself to a generalization of Shannon's rate-distortion problem [16, 17]. A simpler information-theoretic privacy criterion, not directly evolved from k-anonymity, consists in measuring the degree of anonymity observable by an attacker as the entropy of the probability distribution of possible senders of a given message [18, 19]. A generalization and justification of such criterion, along with its applicability to information retrieval, is provided in [2, 20].

3   Statistical and Information-Theoretic Preliminaries

This section establishes notational aspects, and recalls key information-theoretic concepts assumed to be known in the remainder of the paper. The measurable space in which a *random variable* (r.v.) takes on values will be called an *alphabet*, which, with a mild loss of generality, we shall always assume to be finite. We shall follow the convention of using uppercase letters for r.v.'s, and lowercase letters for particular values they take on. The *probability mass function* (PMFs) p of an r.v. X is essentially a *relative histogram* across the possible values determined by its alphabet. Informally, we shall occasionally refer to the function p by its value $p(x)$. The *expectation* of an r.v. X will be written as $\mathrm{E}\, X$, concisely denoting $\sum_x x\, p(x)$, where the sum is taken across all values of x in its alphabet.

We adopt the same notation for information-theoretic quantities used in [21]. Concordantly, the symbol H will denote entropy and D relative entropy or Kullback-Leibler (KL) divergence. We briefly recall those concepts for the reader not intimately familiar with information theory. All logarithms are taken to base 2. The *entropy* $\mathrm{H}(p)$ of a discrete r.v. X with probability distribution p is a measure of its uncertainty, defined as

$$\mathrm{H}(X) = -\,\mathrm{E}\,\log p(X) = -\sum_x p(x)\log p(x).$$

Given two probability distributions $p(x)$ and $q(x)$ over the same alphabet, the *KL divergence* or *relative entropy* $\mathrm{D}(p\,\|\,q)$ is defined as

$$\mathrm{D}(p\,\|\,q) = \mathrm{E}_p\,\log\frac{p(X)}{q(X)} = \sum_x p(x)\log\frac{p(x)}{q(x)}.$$

The KL divergence is often referred to as *relative entropy*, as it may be regarded as a generalization of entropy of a distribution, relative to another. Conversely, entropy is a special case of KL divergence, as for a uniform distribution u on a finite alphabet of cardinality n,

$$\mathrm{D}(p\,\|\,u) = \log n - \mathrm{H}(p). \tag{1}$$

Although the KL divergence is not a distance in the mathematical sense of the term, because it is neither symmetric nor satisfies the triangle inequality, it does provide a measure of discrepancy between distributions, in the sense that $D(p \parallel q) \geq 0$, with equality if, and only if, $p = q$. On account of this fact, relation (1) between entropy and KL divergence implies that $H(p) \leqslant \log n$, with equality if, and only if, $p = u$. Simply put, *entropy maximization* is a special case of *divergence minimization*, attained when the distribution taken as optimization variable is identical to the *reference distribution*, or as "close" as possible, should the optimization problem appear accompanied with *constraints* on the desired space of candidate distributions.

4   Entropy and Divergence as Measures of Privacy

In this paper we shall interpret entropy and KL divergence as privacy criteria. For that purpose, we shall adopt the perspective of Jaynes' celebrated *rationale on entropy maximization methods* [22], which builds upon the *method of types* [21, §11], a powerful technique in large deviation theory whose fundamental results we proceed to review.

The first part of this section will tackle an important question. Suppose we are faced with a problem, formulated in terms of a model, in which a probability distribution plays a major role. In the event this distribution is unknown, we wish to assume a feasible candidate. What is the most likely probability distribution? In other words, what is the "probability of a probability" distribution? We shall see that a widespread answer to this question relies on choosing the distribution *maximizing the Shannon entropy*, or, if a reference distribution is available, the distribution *minimizing the KL divergence* with respect to it, commonly subject to feasibility constraints determined by the specific application at hand.

Our review of the maximum entropy method is crucial because it is unfortunately not always known in the privacy community, and because the rest of this paper constitutes a sophisticated illustration of its application, in the context of the protection of the privacy of user profiles. As we shall see in the second part of this section, the key idea is to model a user profile as a histogram of relative frequencies across categories of interest, regard it as a probability distribution, apply the maximum entropy method to measure the likelihood of a user profile either as its entropy or as its divergence with respect to the population's average profile, and finally take that likelihood as a measure of anonymity.

4.1   Rationale behind the Maximum Entropy Method

A wide variety of models across diverse fields have been explained on the basis of the intriguing principle of entropy maximization. A classical example in physics is the Maxwell-Boltzmann probability distribution $p(v)$ of particle velocities V in a gas [23, 24] of known temperature. It turns out that $p(v)$ is precisely the probability distribution maximizing the entropy, subject to a constraint on the temperature, equivalent to a constraint on the average kinetic energy, in turn equivalent to a constraint on $E V^2$. Another well-known example, in the field of electrical engineering, of the application of the maximum entropy method, is Burg's spectral estimation method [25]. In this method, the power spectral density of a signal is regarded as a probability distribution of power across frequency, only partly known. Burg suggested filling in the unknown portion of the power spectral density by choosing that maximizing the entropy, constrained on the partial knowledge available. More concretely, in discrete case, when the constraints consist in a given range of the crosscorrelation function, up to a time shift k, the solution turns out to be a kth order Gauss-Markov process [21]. A third and more recent example, this time in the field of natural language processing, is the use of log-linear models, which arise as the solution to constrained maximum entropy problems [26] in computational linguistics.

Having motivated the maximum entropy method, we are ready to describe Jaynes' attempt to justify, or at least interpret it, by reviewing the method of types of large deviation theory, a beautiful area lying at the intersection of statistics and information theory. Let $X_1, \ldots, X_k$ be a sequence of k i.i.d. drawings of an r.v. uniformly distributed in the alphabet $\{1, \ldots, n\}$. Let k_i be the number of times symbol $i = 1, \ldots, n$ appears in a sequence of outcomes $x_1, \ldots, x_k$, thus $k = \sum_i k_i$. The *type* t of a sequence of outcomes is the relative proportion of occurrences of each symbol, that is, the *empirical distribution* $t = \left(\frac{k_1}{k}, \ldots, \frac{k_n}{k} \right)$, not necessarily uniform. In other words, consider tossing an n-sided fair dice k times, and seeing exactly k_i times face i. In [22], Jaynes points out that

$$\mathrm{H}(t) = \mathrm{H} \left(\frac{k_1}{k}, \ldots, \frac{k_n}{k} \right) \simeq \frac{1}{k} \log \frac{k!}{k_1! \cdots k_n!} \quad \text{for } k \gg 1.$$

Loosely speaking, for large k, the size of a *type class*, that is, the number of possible outcomes for a given type t (permutations with repeated elements), is approximately $2^{k \mathrm{H}(t)}$ in the exponent. The fundamental rationale in [22] for selecting the type t with maximum entropy $\mathrm{H}(t)$ lies in the approximate equivalence between entropy maximization and the maximization of the number of possible outcomes corresponding to a type. In a way, this justifies the infamous *principle of insufficient reason*, according to which, one may expect an approximately equal relative frequency $k_i/k = 1/n$ for each symbol i, as the uniform distribution maximizes the entropy. The principle of entropy maximization is extended to include constraints also in [22].

Obviously, since all possible permutations count equally, the argument only works for uniformly distributed drawings, which is somewhat circular. A more general argument [21, §11], albeit entirely analogous, departs from a prior knowledge of an arbitrary PMF $\bar{t}$, not necessarily uniform, of such samples $X_1, \ldots, X_k$. Because the empirical distribution or type T of an i.i.d. drawing is itself an r.v., we may define its PMF $p(t) = P\{T = t\}$; formally, the PMF of a random PMF. Using indicator r.v.'s, it is straightforward to confirm the intuition that $E T = \bar{t}$. The general argument in question leads to approximating the probability $p(t)$

of a type class, a fractional measure of its size, in terms of its relative entropy, specifically $2^{-k\,\mathrm{D}(t\,\|\,\bar{t})}$ in the exponent, i.e.,

$$\mathrm{D}(t \,\|\, \bar{t}) \simeq -\frac{1}{k}\,\log p(t) \quad \text{for } k \gg 1,$$

which encompasses the special case of entropy, by virtue of (1). Roughly speaking, the likelihood of the empirical distribution t exponentially decreases with its KL divergence with respect to the average, reference distribution $\bar{t}$.

In conclusion, the most likely PMF t is that minimizing its divergence with respect to the reference distribution $\bar{t}$. In the special case of uniform $\bar{t} = u$, this is equivalent to maximizing the entropy, possibly subject to constraints on t that reflect its partial knowledge or a restricted set of feasible choices. The application of this idea to the establishment of a privacy criterion is the object of the remainder of this work.

4.2   Measuring the Privacy of User Profiles

We are finally equipped to justify, or at least interpret, our proposal to adopt Shannon's entropy and KL divergence as measures of the privacy of a user profile. Before we dive in, we must stress that the use of entropy as a measure of privacy, in the widest sense of the term, is by no means new. Shannon's work in the fifties introduced the concept of *equivocation* as the conditional entropy of a private message given an observed cryptogram [27], later used in the formulation of the problem of the wiretap channel [28, 29] as a measure of confidentiality. More recent studies [18, 19] rescue the suitable applicability of the concept of entropy as a measure of privacy, by proposing to measure the degree of anonymity observable by an attacker as the entropy of the probability distribution of possible senders of a given message. More recent work has taken initial steps in relating privacy to information-theoretic quantities [2, 17, 16, 15].

In the context of this paper, an intuitive justification in favor of entropy maximization is that it boils down to making the apparent user profile as uniform as possible, thereby hiding a user's particular bias towards certain categories of interest. But a much richer argumentation stems from Jaynes' rationale behind entropy maximization methods [22, 30], more generally understood under the beautiful perspective of the method of types and large deviation theory [21, §11], which we motivated and reviewed in the previous subsection.

Under Jaynes' rationale on entropy maximization methods, the entropy of an apparent user profile, modeled by a relative frequency histogram of categorized queries, may be regarded as a measure of privacy, or perhaps more accurately, anonymity. The leading idea is that the method of types from information theory establishes an approximate monotonic relationship between the likelihood of a PMF in a stochastic system and its entropy. Loosely speaking and in our context, the higher the entropy of a profile, the more likely it is, and the more users behave according to it. This is of course in the absence of a probability distribution model for the PMFs, viewed abstractly as r.v.'s themselves. Under this interpretation, entropy is a measure of anonymity, *not* in the sense that the user's identity remains unknown, but only in the sense that higher likelihood of an apparent profile, believed by an external observer to be the actual profile, makes that profile more common, hopefully helping the user go unnoticed, less interesting to an attacker assumed to strive to target peculiar users.

If an aggregated histogram of the population were available as a reference profile, the extension of Jaynes' argument to relative entropy, that is, to the KL divergence, would also give an acceptable measure of privacy (or anonymity). Recall from Sec. 3 that KL divergence is a measure of discrepancy between probability distributions, which includes Shannon's entropy as the special case when the reference distribution is uniform. Conceptually, a lower KL divergence hides discrepancies with respect to a reference profile, say the population's, and there also exists a monotonic relationship between the likelihood of a distribution and its divergence with respect to the reference distribution of choice, which enables us to regard KL divergence as a measure of anonymity in a sense entirely analogous to the above mentioned. In fact, KL divergence was used recently in our own work [2, 20] as a generalization of entropy to measure privacy, although the justification used built upon a number of technicalities, and the connection to Jaynes' rationale was not nearly as detailed as in this manuscript.

5   Conclusion

In this work, we make a twofold contribution. First, we thoroughly interpret and justify the privacy metric proposed in [2], elaborating on the intimate connection between the celebrated method of entropy maximization and the use of entropies and divergences as measures of privacy. Measuring privacy enables us to optimize it, drawing upon powerful tools of convex optimization. The entropy maximization method is a beautiful principle amply exploited in fields such as physics, electrical engineering and even natural language processing.

Secondly, we attempt to bridge the gap between the privacy and the information-theoretic communities by substantially adapting some technicalities of our original work to reach a wider audience, not intimately familiar with information theory and the method of types. As neither information theory nor convex optimization are fully widespread in the privacy community, we elaborate and clarify the connection with privacy in far more detail, and hopefully in more accessible terms, than in our original work.

Although our proposal arises from an information-theoretic quantity and it is mathematically tractable, the adequacy of our formulation relies on the appropriateness of the criteria optimized, which ultimately depends on the particular application at hand.

References

1. Fallows, D.: Search engine users, Pew Internet and Amer. Life Project, Res. Rep. (January 2005)
2. Rebollo-Monedero, D., Forné, J.: Optimal query forgery for private information retrieval. IEEE Trans. Inform. Theory 56(9), 4631–4642 (2010)

3. Mokbel, M.F., Chow, C., Aref, W.G.: The new Casper: query processing for location services without compromising privacy. In: Proc. Int. Conf. Very Large Databases, Seoul, Korea, pp. 763–774 (2006)
4. Duckham, M., Mason, K., Stell, J., Worboys, M.: A formal approach to imperfection in geographic information. Elsevier Comput., Environ., Urban Syst. 25(1), 89–103 (2001)
5. Rebollo-Monedero, D., Forné, J., Subirats, L., Solanas, A., Martínez-Ballesté, A.: A collaborative protocol for private retrieval of location-based information. In: Proc. IADIS Int. Conf. e-Society, Barcelona, Spain (February 2009)
6. Rebollo-Monedero, D., Forné, J., Solanas, A., Martínez-Ballesté, T.: Private location-based information retrieval through user collaboration. Elsevier Comput. Commun. 33(6), 762–774 (2010),
   http://dx.doi.org/10.1016/j.comcom.2009.11.024
7. Elovici, Y., Shapira, B., Maschiach, A.: A new privacy model for hiding group interests while accessing the web. In: Proc. ACM Workshop on Privacy in the Electron. Society, pp. 63–70. ACM, Washington, DC (2002)
8. Shapira, B., Elovici, Y., Meshiach, A., Kuflik, T.: PRAW – The model for PRivAte Web. J. Amer. Soc. Inform. Sci., Technol. 56(2), 159–172 (2005)
9. Samarati, P., Sweeney, L.: Protecting privacy when disclosing information: k-Anonymity and its enforcement through generalization and suppression. SRI Int., Tech. Rep (1998)
10. Sun, X., Wang, H., Li, J., Truta, T.M.: Enhanced p-sensitive k-anonymity models for privacy preserving data publishing. Trans. Data Privacy 1(2), 53–66 (2008)
11. Truta, T.M., Vinay, B.: Privacy protection: p-sensitive k-anonymity property. In: Proc. Int. Workshop Privacy Data Manage (PDM), Atlanta, GA, p. 94 (2006)
12. Machanavajjhala, A., Gehrke, J., Kiefer, D., Venkitasubramanian, M.: l-Diversity: Privacy beyond k-anonymity. In: Proc. IEEE Int. Conf. Data Eng (ICDE), Atlanta, GA, p. 24 (April 2006)
13. Jian-min, H., Ting-ting, C., Hui-qun, Y.: An improved V-MDAV algorithm for l-diversity. In: Proc. IEEE Int. Symp. Inform. Processing (ISIP), Moscow, Russia, pp. 733–739 (May 2008)
14. Domingo-Ferrer, J., Torra, V.: A critique of k-anonymity and some of its enhancements. In: Proc. Workshop Privacy, Security, Artif. Intell. (PSAI), Barcelona, Spain, pp. 990–993 (2008)
15. Li, N., Li, T., Venkatasubramanian, S.: t-Closeness: Privacy beyond k-anonymity and l-diversity. In: Proc. IEEE Int. Conf. Data Eng (ICDE), Istanbul, Turkey, pp. 106–115 (April 2007)
16. Rebollo-Monedero, D., Forné, J., Domingo-Ferrer, J.: From t-Closeness to PRAM and Noise Addition Via Information Theory. In: Domingo-Ferrer, J., Saygın, Y. (eds.) PSD 2008. LNCS, vol. 5262, pp. 100–112. Springer, Heidelberg (2008)
17. Rebollo-Monedero, D., Forné, J., Domingo-Ferrer, J.: From t-closeness-like privacy to postrandomization via information theory. IEEE Trans. Knowl. Data Eng. 22(11), 1623–1636 (2010),
   http://doi.ieeecomputersociety.org/10.1109/TKDE.2009.190
18. Díaz, C., Seys, S., Claessens, J., Preneel, B.: Towards Measuring Anonymity. In: Dingledine, R., Syverson, P.F. (eds.) PET 2002. LNCS, vol. 2482, pp. 54–68. Springer, Heidelberg (2003)
19. Díaz, C.: Anonymity and privacy in electronic services. Ph.D. dissertation, Katholieke Univ. Leuven (December 2005)

20. Parra-Arnau, J., Rebollo-Monedero, D., Forné, J.: A Privacy-Preserving Architecture for the Semantic Web Based on Tag Suppression. In: Katsikas, S., Lopez, J., Soriano, M. (eds.) TrustBus 2010. LNCS, vol. 6264, pp. 58–68. Springer, Heidelberg (2010)
21. Cover, T.M., Thomas, J.A.: Elements of Information Theory, 2nd edn. Wiley, New York (2006)
22. Jaynes, E.T.: On the rationale of maximum-entropy methods. Proc. IEEE 70(9), 939–952 (1982)
23. Brillouin, L.: Science and Information Theory. Academic-Press, New York (1962)
24. Jaynes, E.T.: Papers on Probability, Statistics and Statistical Physics. Reidel, Dordrecht (1982)
25. Burg, J.P.: Maximum entropy spectral analysis. Ph.D. dissertation, Stanford Univ. (1975)
26. Berger, A.L., Della Pietra, J., Della Pietra, A.: A maximum entropy approach to natural language processing. MIT Comput. Ling. 22(1), 39–71 (1996)
27. Shannon, C.E.: Communication theory of secrecy systems. Bell Syst., Tech. J. (1949)
28. Wyner, A.: The wiretap channel. Bell Syst., Tech. J. 54 (1975)
29. Csiszár, I., Körner, J.: Broadcast channels with confidential messages. IEEE Trans. Inform. Theory 24, 339–348 (1978)
30. Jaynes, E.T.: Information theory and statistical mechanics II. Phys. Review Ser. II 108(2), 171–190 (1957)

A Distributed, Parametric Platform for Constructing Secure SBoxes in Block Cipher Designs

Panayotis E. Nastou[1] and Yannis C. Stamatiou[2,3]

[1] Dept. of Mathematics, University of Aegean, Samos, Greece
pnastou@aegean.gr
[2] Dept. of Mathematics, University of Ioannina, Ioannina, Greece
stamatiou@uoi.gr
[3] Computer Technology Institute and Press ("Diophantus"), Patras, 26504, Greece

Abstract. Many of the network security protocols employed today utilize symmetric block ciphers (DES, AES and CAST etc). The majority of the symmetric block ciphers implement the crucial substitution operation using look up tables, called substitution boxes. These structures should be highly nonlinear and have bit dispersal, i.e. avalanche, properties in order to render the cipher with resistant to cryptanalysis attempts, such as linear and differential cryptanalysis. Highly secure substitution boxes can be constructed using particular Boolean functions as components that have certain mathematical properties which enhance the robustness of the whole cryptoalgorithm. However, enforcing these properties on SBoxes is a highly computationally intensive task. In this paper, we present a distributed algorithm and its implementation on a computing cluster that accelerates the construction of secure substitution boxes with good security properties. It is fully parametric since it can employ any class of Boolean functions with algorithmically definable properties and can construct SBoxes of arbitrary sizes. We demonstrate the efficiency of the distributed algorithm implementation compared to its sequential counterpart, in a number of experiments.

Keywords: Symmetric Block Ciphers, Distributed SBox Construction, NonLinearity, SAC criterion, Bent Functions.

1 Introduction

Many of the network security protocols employed today utilize symmetric block ciphers. *IPSec*, for example, which is a widely used *Virtual Private Network* protocol (VPN), employs in the encapsulation mode the triple *DES*, *AES* in various modes, *CAST* and many other symmetric block ciphers. Many of the employed symmetric block ciphers are based on the *Feistel* block cipher structure, which is actually a product cipher that alternates, in a number of rounds, the operations of bit substitutions and permutations on the input data and key bits.

For a block cipher design based on the Feistel structure the block and key sizes, the number of rounds, the key schedule and the round function determine

T.-h. Kim et al. (Eds.): SecTech 2011, CCIS 259, pp. 155–166, 2011.

the security properties of the design. An important operation performed at each round of operation of a block cipher is the *substitution operation*, which is based on a look up table called *Substitution Box* or SBox for short. If V_n is the vector space of dimension n over the field F_2, a $n \times m$ SBox S, is a mapping of $n - bit$ strings to $m - bit$ strings, i.e. $S : V_n \rightarrow V_m$. Alternatively, an $n \times m$ SBox can be considered as a set $S(x) = \{C_{m-1}(x), \ldots, C_0(x)\}$ of m Boolean functions $C_i(x)$ on V_n, that is $C_i : V_n \rightarrow F_2$, where $0 \leq i < m$. A Boolean function C_i of an SBox is called SBox column. Various SBox sizes considered in a number of well known block ciphers are 6×4 for DES, 8×8 for AES, and 8×32 for CAST.

In order to construct block ciphers which are resistant to currently known cryptanalytic attacks, such as linear and differential cryptanalysis, the employed SBoxes should be highly nonlinear and have a certain bit dispersal, i.e. avalanche, properties. In [7], a formal method that generates SBoxes according to certain mathematical properties of Boolean functions and their linear combinations is presented. Although this method provides cryptographically strong SBoxes, its main disadvantage is that it is computationally intensive. In general, for large values of n and m constructing cryptographically strong SBoxes may be an intractable problem. In the literature (see, e.g., [2,3,4]) for $n = 8$, the space of all Boolean functions is considered large and consequently its exhaustive exploration for discovering functions with good cryptographic properties is considered a computationally intensive task.

In this paper, we present a distributed algorithm and its implementation on a computing cluster that accelerates the construction of secure substitution boxes with good security properties. Using this implementation, a block cipher designer can use any class of algorithmically definable Boolean functions in order to construct, within a reasonable time span, an SBox that satisfies a set of desirable properties. It is tunable and parametric: it can accept as input (the algorithmic definition of) any class of Boolean functions, the target SBox dimensions n and m, as well as the target properties that should be satisfied by the SBox. With regard to the structure of the paper, Sect. 2 presents a brief introduction of the basic theory of cryptographically strong SBoxes while Sects 3 and 4 present a distributed algorithm and its implementation on a computing cluster, for the (computational demanding) task of the generation of secure SBoxes. Experimental results that demonstrate the efficiency of the distributed implementation over its sequential counterpart are presented in Sect. 5. Finally, in Sect. 6 we discuss the obtained results and provide pointers for future research.

2   Background

With the notation $x \in V_n$ we mean the binary vector on n Boolean variables $x = (x_{n-1} \ldots x_0)$. The sequence of values of a Boolean function f of n variables, i.e. the sequence $(f(0), f(1), \ldots, f(2^n - 1))$, is called the *truth table* of function f. The *linear combination* of two Boolean functions f and g on V_n is defined by $(f \oplus g)(x) = f(x) \oplus g(x)$ where $\oplus$ is the XOR operation.

A Boolean function f on V_n is called *affine* if for every $x = (x_{n-1} \ldots x_0)$ it holds $f(x) = (w \cdot x) \oplus y$ where $w = (w_{n-1} \ldots w_0) \in V_n$, $y \in F_2$ and $w \cdot x =$

$w_{n-1} \cdot x_{n-1} \oplus \ldots \oplus w_0 \cdot x_0$. If $y = 1$, the inner product $w \cdot x$ on a specific value of x is simply inverted, while for $y = 0$ there is no effect on the inner product and f is called *linear*.

The *Hamming weight* $wt(f)$ of a Boolean function f is defined as the number of $1s$ in the truth table of f. A Boolean function f on V_n is *balanced* if $wt(f) = 2^{n-1}$, i.e. half of the values in the truth table of f are equal to 1. The *sign function* $\hat{f} : V_n \rightarrow R^*$ of a Boolean function f is defined as $\hat{f}(x) = (-1)^{f(x)}$.

The *autocorrelation function* r_f of a Boolean function f on V_n and the auto-correlation function of its sign function $\hat{f}$ are defined as

$$r_f(a) = \sum_{x \in V_n} f(x) \oplus f(x \oplus a). \tag{1}$$

$$\hat{r}_{\hat{f}}(a) = \sum_{x \in V_n} \hat{f}(x) \cdot \hat{f}(x \oplus a). \tag{2}$$

for all $a \in V_n$. It is, easy to derive the equation that correlates $r_f(a)$ and $\hat{r}_{\hat{f}}(a)$:

$$r_f(a) = 2^{n-1} - \frac{1}{2}\hat{r}_{\hat{f}}(a). \tag{3}$$

2.1 Nonlinearity of a Boolean Function

The *non-linearity* of a function f on V_n is defined by $nl(f) = \min_{g \in A_n} wt(f \oplus g)$, where A_n is the class of all affine Boolean functions on V_n. Intuitively, nonlinearity measures the *minimum distance* of a function f from all affine functions. The computation of the nonlinearity of a function f can be performed efficiently by the use of the *Walsh-Hadamard* transform [2]. The Walsh-Hadamard transform of the sign function $\hat{f}$ of a Boolean function f on V_n is a function $W_{\hat{f}} : V_n \rightarrow R^*$ and is defined as

$$W_{\hat{f}}(w) = \sum_{x \in V_n} \hat{f}(x) \cdot (-1)^{w \cdot x}. \tag{4}$$

The Walsh Transform of the sign function $\hat{f}$ can be computed by multiplying the truth table of $\hat{f}$, represented by $[\hat{f}(0), \ldots \hat{f}(2^n - 1)]$, with the Hadamard matrix H_n of order n ([2]):

$$W_{\hat{f}} = [\hat{f}(0), \ldots, \hat{f}(2^n - 1)] \times \begin{bmatrix} H_{n-1} & H_{n-1} \\ H_{n-1} & -H_{n-1} \end{bmatrix}. \tag{5}$$

The nonlinearity of a function f can be computed efficiently using the equation of the theorem below ([2]):

Theorem 1. *The nonlinearity of a Boolean function f on V_n is determined by the Walsh transform of its sign function $\hat{f}$ by the following equation:*

$$nl(f) = 2^{n-1} - \frac{1}{2} \max_{w \in V_n} |W_{\hat{f}}(w)|. \tag{6}$$

A crucial result for the nonlinearity of a Boolean function is presented in [2] and [4]:

Theorem 2. *The nonlinearity of any Boolean function f on V_n satisfies*

$$nl(f) \leq 2^{n-1} - 2^{\frac{n}{2}-1} \ . \tag{7}$$

Since an SBox is a set of Boolean functions, its columns, if C is the set of all nontrivial linear combinations of the SBox columns, then the nonlinearity of an SBox S is defined as $nl_S = \min_{f \in C} nl(f)$.

2.2   Strict Avalanche Criterion

Another important property of a Boolean function f on V_n is the *Strict Avalanche Criterion* or SAC for short. A Boolean function f on V_n is said to satisfy SAC if changing one of the n bits in the binary representation of its input x, the function value $f(x)$ changes for exactly half of 2^n possible values of x ([2]). The SAC property is particularly useful in cryptography since it is easy to see that a small change in the input of a function causes a massive change in the output behavior of the function (avalanche effect). Based on the definition of the autocorrelation function of a Boolean function f the following result follows ([2]):

Lemma 1. *A Boolean function f on V_n is SAC if and only if for the autocorrelation function it holds that $r_f(a) = 2^{n-1} \ \forall a \in V_n$ with $wt(a) = 1$.*

Based on (3), the criterion that $r_f(a) = 2^{n-1} \ \forall a \in V_n$ with $wt(a) = 1$ in Lemma 1 can be stated differently, as $\hat{r}_{\hat{f}}(a) = 0 \ \forall a \in V_n$ with $wt(a) = 1$. In [2] the theorem of Wiener and Khintchine is discussed that correlates the spectrum of the sign function of a Boolean function f with its autocorrelation function:

Theorem 3. *A Boolean function on V_n satisfies $W_{\hat{r}_{\hat{f}}}(w) = W_{\hat{f}}^2(w) \ \forall w \in V_n$.*

From the above theorem, a value of the autocorrelation function $\hat{r}_{\hat{f}}$ can be obtained by computing the inverse Walsh transform of $W_{\hat{r}_{\hat{f}}}(w)$, which is computed from the Walsh spectrum of the sign function $\hat{f}$.

2.3   Bent Functions

Rothaus in [4] defined a class of Boolean functions f on V_n with n even, such that $W_{\hat{f}}(w) = \pm 2^{\frac{n}{2}}, \forall w \in V_n$ which is called the class of *bent* Boolean functions and is denoted by B_n. It follows from the definition that *energy* spectrum coefficients $W_{\hat{f}}^2(w)$ are all the same. A Boolean function f on V_n has *linear* structures if the function $g(x) = f(x) \oplus f(x \oplus a)$ is constant for a nonzero $a \in V_n$. In [2], the definition of perfect nonlinear functions is presented, as given by Meier and Staffelbach:

Definition 1. *A Boolean function f on V_n is called perfect nonlinear if for every nonzero $a \in V_n$ the values $f(x \oplus a)$ and $f(x)$ are equal for exactly half of the values of arguments $x \in V_n$.*

Rothaus discovered in [4] that the concept of perfect nonlinearity is equivalent to the Bent property of Bent functions. Thus, the nonlinearity of a Bent function is the maximum nonlinearity according to Theorem 2. The oldest methods for the construction of Bent functions are due to Rothaus ([4]), Maiorana ([3] and [2]), McFarland ([2]), Dillon ([2]) and Dobbertin ([2]) while new methods are described by Adams and Tavares in [1] and by Carlet in [2]. In [2], the Maiorana-McFarland function (MM) is defined to be any function $f(x, y)$ on V_n of the form:

$$f(x, y) = \phi(x) \cdot y \oplus g(x). \tag{8}$$

where $x = (x_{s-1} \ldots x_0)$ and $y = (y_{t-1} \ldots y_0)$ such that $n = s + t$, $\phi(x)$ is any mapping from V_s to V_t and $g(x)$ is any function on V_s. If $s = t = \frac{n}{2}$ and $\phi(x)$ is any permutation $\pi(x)$ on $V_{\frac{n}{2}}$, the Maiorana-McFarland is a Bent function.

3   Distributed Sbox Construction

An SBox of m columns can be constructed sequentially in an incremental fashion. Starting with an empty SBox, a function $f(x)$ on V_n that has certain properties, i.e. certain value range for nonlinearity, the SAC property and the desired algebraic degree, is generated and assigned as the first column of the SBox. At the second step, a new function with the same class of properties is generated. If the linear combination of these two functions has certain desirable properties (e.g. nonlinearity within some bounds) then the function is accepted as the second SBox column. As more columns are added, all possible linear combinations of the new function with previously inserted ones should be checked. This procedure is repeated until m columns have been produced. It is obvious that the procedure is computationally intensive since for large m the number of linear combinations that should be checked, each time a new function is inserted, is very large. Moreover, the procedure is likely to be computationally intractable for large values of n and m, as every linear combination of the sbox columns is required to satisfy a number of target properties.

For the generation of SBox columns, there are many methods given in [2]. We have adopted the generation method of Maiorana-McFarland Bent functions, as described in Sect. 2.3 as well as the generation method that is based on the linear combination of certain Maiorana-McFarland bent functions which are SAC and possess sufficiently high nonlinearity. In order to check every linear combination of the Boolean functions within SBox, a mechanism for the generation of every linear combination should be employed. In the sequential SBox construction algorithm, we employed a slightly modified version of the sequential *lazy counting* algorithm described in [3] for the linear combinations generation:

$nc = 0;$
While $(nc < m)$ do
    begin
        $C_{nc} = generateFunction();$
        PropertiesSatisfied=TRUE; $g = 0; i = 0;$

> While ($i < 2^{nc}$ AND PropertiesSatisfied) do
> > begin
> > > If $b_{nc-1} \ldots b_0$ is the binary reprsentation of i
> > > find the k-th bit position from right where $b_k = 1$
> > > $g = g \oplus C_k$;
> > > PropertiesSatisfied=validateLinearCombination(g);
> > > $i = i + 1$;
> > end
> > if PropertiesSatisfied $nc = nc + 1$;
> end

The number of linear combinations that should be checked by the sequential SBox construction method is very large even for small values of the counting variable nc. For instance, when the tenth column is about to enter SBox, i.e. when $nc = 10$, there are 1024 linear combinations that should be checked. This check requires the validation of a number of desirable properties, a task which may be highly time consuming. Thus, performing all these checks sequentially on a single processor based on the sequential lazy counting algorithm alone, slows down considerably the whole SBox construction process.

The SBox construction process can be accelerated by parallelizing the lazy counting algorithm. This can be achieved by partitioning the space of all 2^{nc} possible linear combinations into B non-overlapping subsets of linear combinations, each of them assigned for checking to a different processor from a pool of B available processors. The space of linear combinations can be efficiently partitioned into B non-overlapping sets based on Lemma 2. This lemma provides a relationship between the columns of the SBox that are involved in the $i - th$ linear combination and the binary representation of the value of the index variable i of the SBox construction algorithm described above (the variable i enumerates the linear combinations of the nc SBox columns).

Lemma 2. *If $b_{nc-1}b_{nc-2} \ldots b_0$ is the binary representation of the value of the variable i that enumerates the number of all possible linear combinations of the nc columns of an SBox then the following holds:*

(i) If l is the leftmost bit position of i that $b_l = 1$ ($0 \le l \le nc - 1$), then the i-th linear combination of the nc SBox columns contains the column C_l while it does not contain the columns C_k for $k > l$.

(ii) For any bit position l, $0 < l \le nc - 1$, if $b_l \ne b_{l-1}$ then the i-th linear combination of the nc SBox columns contains the column C_{l-1} otherwise it does not contain it.

Proof. We will proceed using induction on nc. We will, also, denote by S_i^{nc} the set of columns involved in the i-th linear combination of nc SBox columns generated by the sequential lazy counting method in the above SBox construction method. For $nc = 1$, (i) and (ii) hold as i and l assume only the value 1 and $S_i^{nc} = \{C_0\}$. Let us assume that they also hold for $nc \le nc_0$. We will prove that they hold for $nc = nc_0 + 1$. Note that if the leftmost bit position of i equal to 1 is position $l \leq nc_0 - 1$, (i) and (ii) hold from the induction hypothesis. Thus, we only have to prove them in the case where $l = nc_0$. The column C_{nc_0} belongs to the current linear combination since when the algorithm examines the first value of i such that the least significant bit position equal to 1 is the $l = nc_0$-th position, it includes C_{nc_0} to the current linear combination. Thus (i) holds.

In order to prove (ii), it suffices to consider the value $l = nc_0$ and only when this position is equal to 1 as, in the other cases, (ii) holds by induction hypothesis. If $b_{l-1} = 0$, while $b_l = 1$, then this means that column $nc_0 - 1$ has been considered for inclusion in the current linear combination in a previous step i. Thus, column C_{l-1} is involved to the linear combination. On the other hand, if $b_{l-1} = 1$ then C_{l-1} has been considered twice in the current linear combination: once when the l-th bit was equal to 0 and $(l-1)$-th bit was equal to 1 and secondly when later the l-th bit became 1 and after some steps the $l - 1$ bit became 1. But this means that C_{l-1} appears (implicitly) twice in the current linear combination and as the operation is XOR, C_{l-1} vanishes and, thus, it effectively disappears from the current linear combination.   □

Based on Lemma 2, the set of the 2^{nc} linear combinations of Sbox columns can be partitioned into B equally sized subsets of $\frac{2^{nc}}{B}$ linear combinations each, where each subset is determined by the index x_j ($1 \leq j \leq B$) of its first (i.e. lowest index) linear combination. The linear combination that corresponds to x_j is equal to the linear combination of the columns C_k for $k \leq l$, due to case (i) of the lemma, and b_k satisfies the condition given by case (ii), where l is the bit position of the most significant bit of the binary representation of x_j in which $b_l = 1$.

Based on this, our distributed lazy counting algorithm is based on partitioning to several processing elements the space of linear combinations of SBox columns, each time a new column is generated. More specifically, each time a new SBox column is generated, the space of linear combinations is partitioned into B subsets, where B is the number of available processors. The subset of linear combinations S_j and its corresponding index x_j are assigned to the j-th processor, which calculates the first linear combination LC_{x_j} of the subset. This means that the j-th processor sets variables g and i in the above SBox construction algorithm to LC_{x_j} and x_j respectively. After setting these variables, each processor enumerates linear combinations and checks if they satisfy the desirable properties. If every linear combination satisfies the desirable properties, then the generated Boolean function is accepted, otherwise it is discarded. This procedure is repeated until m SBox columns, whose linear combinations satisfy the target properties, have been generated.

4   Implementation of the Distributed Algorithm on a Computing Cluster

The domain of the distributed algorithm described in the previous section is the set of all possible linear combinations of the SBox columns. Based on Lemma 2,

the domain decomposition programming model and the message passing programming paradigm are suitable for the implementation of the distributed algorithm on a computing cluster. It was implemented using the Message Passing Interface (MPI, [6]) and was ran on the computing cluster named *Pythagoras* located in the Department of Mathematics of the Aegean University. The operational environment of Pythagoras is the *Rocks* Cluster Distribution on the CentOS Linux distribution. There are 32 processor cores available for computations distributed in 5 nodes and 4 cores for managing the computing cluster.

Assuming that $nProcs$ processors have been allocated, one processor is designated as the master of the computation while the remaining $nProcs - 1$ processors are the slaves. Initially, the master generates $IN = \lceil log_2(nProcs - 1) \rceil$ cryptographically strong Boolean functions, all linear combinations of which satisfy a set of target properties (e.g. nonlinearity greater than a given value, SAC property, etc). This initial subset of SBox columns is saved in a file and the master broadcasts a message to the $nProcs - 1$ slaves in order to trigger them to read it through NFS. Each slave, while waiting to receive a new function from the master, i.e. to have $nc = IN + 1$, determines its subset of linear combinations and the first linear combination that corresponds to this subset. Then, it waits for the reception of a new Boolean function for evaluation.

Figures 1 and 2 show the communication and computation steps of both the master and the slave processors during the SBox computation. After the completion of the initial phase described above, the master generates a new cryptographically strong Boolean function and broadcasts it to slaves (Column Generation and $MPI\_Bcast : Column$ in Fig. 1). After receiving the column, each slave initiates a nonblocking receive process in order to get a message from the master that designates the final result of the validation procedure and starts the validation of its linear combinations (Combination Validation and $MPI\_IRecv : final\_result$ in Fig.2). The master is in the state labeled $MPI\_Recv : SlaveResults$ where it gets the results of the validation procedure from every slave processor. Each slave polls the status of the nonblocking receive process during certain intervals depending on the number of linear combinations.

If a slave processor, while enumerating its linear combinations, discovers a linear combination that does not satisfy the target properties, it completes the validation procedure prematurely and sends a failure message to the master ($MPI\_Send : its\_Result$ in Fig. 2). On the other hand, if every linear combination of a slave processor satisfies the properties it sends a success message to the master. After sending its result, a slave waits for the final decision of the master (MPI_Wait in Fig. 2). If it receives a success message, it recalculates the number of its linear combinations and the index of the first linear combination, (Parameter Calculation in Fig. 2), and waits for the next column, while in case of a failure it simply waits for the next column without any recalculation. The master, after receiving a failure message from a slave, sends a failure message to all slaves through a nonblocking send process ($MPI\_ISend : Failure$ in Fig. 1) since there is no reason to enumerate and check any more linear combinations. After receiving the failure message through the polling process described above,

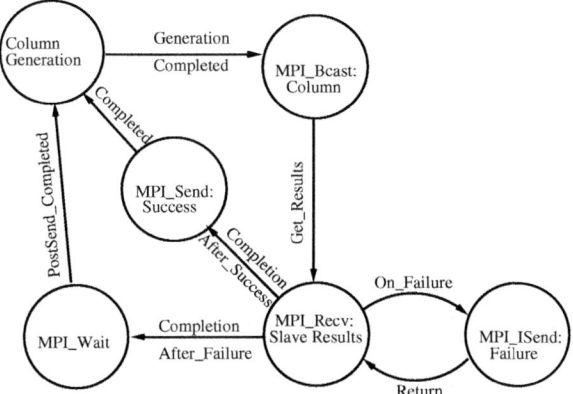

Fig. 1. Master State Diagram

the slaves terminate their validation procedure and send a failure message to the master, waiting for synchronization. The master, after receiving a message from every slave, waits for the nonblocking send to be completed and discards the function caused a failure. On the other hand, if the master receives a success message from every slave, then it sends a success message to every slave through a blocking send ($MPI\_Send : Success$ in Fig. 1). After its completion, the master starts the generation of the next SBox column. The described distributed computation is repeated until all the m SBox columns have been computed.

5   Experimental Results

Since the class of MM bent functions presented in Sect. 2.3 have maximum nonlinearity and satisfy the SAC property, it was selected for the evaluation of our distributed SBox construction algorithm. Functions on V_8 were selected for the evaluation of the algorithm. For the generation of an MM bent function, a permutation $\phi(x)$ on V_4 and a Boolean function $g(x)$ on V_4 are chosen at random. Before using this class of functions, the properties of linear combinations of two and three MM bent functions were examined with respect to its nonlinearity and the satisfaction of the SAC property. The probability distributions of the random variables NL_1 and NL_2, which represent the nonlinearities of the linear combinations of two randomly selected MM bent functions and three randomly selected MM bent functions respectively are graphically presented in Fig. 3. These distributions were produced after the examination of 10^9 pairs and triples of MM bent functions, a process which required 27 days. The most probable values for the nonlinearity of a linear combination of two and three MM bent functions are $96, 104, 112$ with 104 having the highest probability. Moreover, these probabilities are higher for the linear combinations of three MM functions and about 0.5% of 10^9 linear combinations also satisfy SAC. Thus, we constructed a subclass of Boolean functions on V_8 named TMM where each

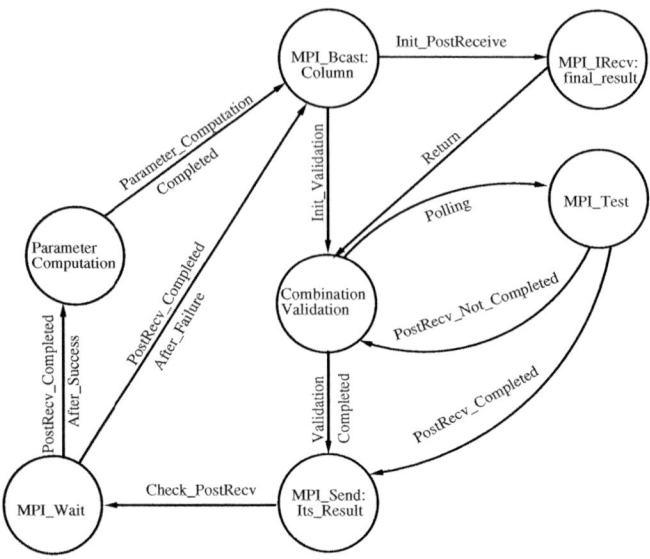

Fig. 2. Slave State Diagram

function is the linear combination of three MM bent functions with nonlinearity greater than 96 while it also satisfies SAC and its algebraic degree is 4 (i.e. $\frac{n}{2}$).

From the above description, it follows that the generation of an MM and a TMM function is a probabilistic procedure, in the sense that the constituent components of each function are randomly selected. In particular for the generation of a TMM function we choose randomly three MM functions and their linear combination is checked whether it satisfies the target nonlinearity value and the SAC property. This means that the execution time of the function generation procedure will be highly irregular. For example, running our construction procedure on one processor core using functions from the TMM class, the construction of an SBox of size 8×3 that has nonlinearity 104 (close to the maximum nonlinearity which is 120) and every linear combination of its columns satisfies SAC, took almost 8 days while running it on two cores required one and a half day only, which is a considerable improvement. Using functions from the MM class, the construction of an SBox with the same size and satisfying the same set of properties took 2450.53 secs using one core and 97.66 secs using two cores. Due to this variability in execution times, every experiment was run 10 times and the final execution time of the experiment was the average of the individual execution times.

Tables 1 and 2 present the execution times, in seconds, of the construction of SBoxes of various sizes and values of nonlinearity. They also show the speedup obtained, over the sequential execution i.e. running the same construction procedure on one processor core without partitioning the linear combination space, by the use of more than one cores. Table 1 presents the results obtained using only MM functions while Table 2 presents the results obtained by the use of

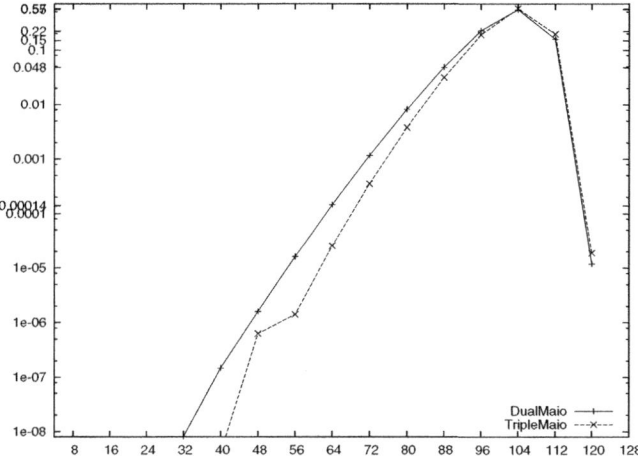

Fig. 3. Probability Distribution of NL_1 and NL_2 which are the nonlinearities of the linear combinations of two and three randomly selected MM bent functions respectively

only TMM functions. In the last column of these tables, the maximum percentage of linear combinations that satisfy SAC is presented. From a cryptographic point of view, both the MM and TMM classes lead to SBoxes with similar properties. As for the use of TMM functions, due to the fact that the execution time of the generation procedure is irregular, we have the curious result that the obtained speedup with the use of 8 cores in the construction of an SBox of size 8×6 with nonlinearity 104 is less than the speedup obtained by the use of 4 cores. This happened because the function generation is a highly irregular and computationally intensive task while each subset of linear combinations per core is relatively small. Consequently, the performance of the function generation procedure, the cardinality of each linear combinations subset and how much computational intensive is the procedure of checking each linear combination if it satisfies the target properties determine the number of cores that could provide the maximum efficiency and speedup. This means that the optimal number of cores for the construction of a cryptographically strong SBox depends on the above parameters of our SBox distributed construction algorithm.

Table 1. Performance of the construction of SBoxes using the MM class of functions

SBox Size	NL	cores=1 time	cores=4 time	speedup	cores=8 time	speedup	cores=16 time	speedup	%SAC
8×4	112	711.84	509.89	1.4	-	-	-	-	40
8×6	104	83.85	26.45	3.17	23.85	3.52	-	-	12.69
8×9	96	265.58	130.21	2.04	98.67	2.69	85.16	3.12	2.9
8×12	88	544.19	130.85	4.16	66.22	8.22	37.27	14.6	0.98

Table 2. Performance of the construction of SBoxes using TMM class of functions

SBox		cores=1	cores=4		cores=8		cores=16		
Size	NL	time	time	speedup	time	speedup	time	speedup	%SAC
8 × 6	104	7013.85	2697.72	2.6	3223.42	2.18	–	–	12.69
8 × 8	96	134.27	98.14	1.37	51.15	2.63	–	–	3.9
8 × 9	96	22077.39	17007.22	1.3	6969.54	3.17	5814.64	3.8	3.1

6   Conclusions

In this paper we have presented a distributed algorithm for the generation of cryptographically secure SBoxes and its implementation on a computing cluster. It was demonstrated that it can accelerate considerably the SBox construction process, which is a highly computationally intensive task. Our implementation is fully parametric since it uses as an input any class of Boolean functions, the SBox size parameters n and m and the properties that the SBox should satisfy and it can be employed as a tool by block cipher designers. It can be used for both the construction of secure SBoxes in a reasonable amount of time as well as the exploration of SBox properties containing functions from any Boolean function class. As a future research goal, we plan to construct SBoxes using more general Boolean function classes and explore the properties of the resulting SBoxes.

References

1. Adams, C.M., Tavares, S.: Generating and counting binary bent sequences. IEEE Transactions on Information Theory IT 36, 1170–1173 (1990)
2. Cusick, T.W., Stănică, P.: Cryptographic Boolean Functions and Applications. Academic Press, Elsevier (2009)
3. Mister, S., Adams, C.: Practical sbox design. In: Third Annual Workshop on Selected Areas in Cryptography, Kingston Ontario (1996)
4. Rothaus, O.: On bent functions. Journal of Combinatorial Theory 20(A), 300–305 (1976)
5. Seberry, J., Zhang, X.M., Zheng, Y.: Systematic generation of cryptographically robust s-boxes. In: Proceedings of the First ACM Conference on Computer and Communications Security, pp. 172–182 (1993)
6. Snir, M., Oto, S., Huss-Lederman, S., Walker, D., Dongarra, J.: MPI:The Complete Reference. The MIT Press, Cambridge (1996)
7. Stallings, W.: Cryptography and Security: Principles and Practice. Prentice Hall (1999)

Cryptanalysis of an Enhanced Simple Three-Party Key Exchange Protocol

Hae-Jung Kim[1] and Eun-Jun Yoon[2,*]

[1] College of Liberal Education, Keimyung University,
1000 Sindang-dong, Dalseo-Gu, Daegu 704-701, Republic of Korea
hjkim325@hanmail.net
[2] School of Computer Engineering, Kyungil University,
33 Buho-Ri, Hayang-Ub, Kyungsan-Si, Kyungsangpuk-Do 712-701, Republic of Korea
ejyoon@kiu.ac.kr

Abstract. A simple three-party password-based authenticated key exchange (S-3PAKE) protocols are extremely important to secure communications and are now extensively adopted in network communications. In 2009, Nam et al. pointed out that S-3PAKE protocol, by Lu and Cao for password-authenticated key exchange in the three-party setting, is vulnerable to an off-line dictionary attack. Then, they proposed some countermeasures how to eliminate the security vulnerability of the S-3PAKE. Nevertheless, this paper points out their enhanced S-3PAKE protocol is still vulnerable to undetectable on-line dictionary attacks and off-line dictionary attack unlike their claim.

Keywords: Authentication, 3PAKE, Password, Three-party key exchange, Network security, Dictionary attack.

1 Introduction

Three-party password-based authenticated key exchange (3PAKE) protocols are extremely important to secure communications and are now extensively adopted in network communications [1,2,3]. These 3PAKE protocols allow users to communicate securely over public networks simply by using easy-to-remember passwords. In the 3PAKE protocols, each user can exchange session keys with other users securely via the server. The server authenticates users by encrypting messages with passwords; only valid users can decrypt the messages with passwords and derive the correct session keys.

Since users usually choose easy-to-remember passwords, password-based protocols can be vulnerable to dictionary attacks. Unlike typical private keys, the password has limited entropy, and is constrained by the memory of the user. For example, one alphanumerical character has 6 bits of entropy, and thus the goal of the attacker, which is to obtain a legitimate communication party's password, can be achieved within a reasonable time. Therefore, the dictionary attacks on

---

* Corresponding author.

T.-h. Kim et al. (Eds.): SecTech 2011, CCIS 259, pp. 167–176, 2011.
© Springer-Verlag Berlin Heidelberg 2011

the password-based protocols should be considered a real possibility. In general, the dictionary attacks can be divided into three classes [4,5]:

- Detectable on-line dictionary attacks: an attacker attempts to use a guessed password in an on-line transaction. He/she verifies the correctness of his/her guess using the response from server. A failed guess can be detected and logged by the server.
- Undetectable on-line dictionary attacks: similar to above, an attacker tries to verify a password guess in an online transaction. However, a failed guess cannot be detected and logged by the server, as the server cannot distinguish between an honest request and an attacker's request.
- Off-line dictionary attacks: an attacker guesses a password and verifies his/her guess off-line. No participation of server is required, so the server does not notice the attack as a malicious one.

In 2007, Lu and Cao [6] proposed a simple 3PAKE protocol (in short, S-3PAKE) built upon the earlier two-party PAKE protocol due to Abdalla and Pointcheval [7]. However, it is founded out that S-3PAKE is vulnerable to various attacks according to recent works in [8,9,10]. Quite recently, Nam et al. [11] also pointed out that S-3PAKE protocol is vulnerable to an off-line dictionary attack. Furthermore, they proposed some countermeasures how to eliminate the security vulnerability of the S-3PAKE. They claimed that the enhanced S-3PAKE protocol (in short ES-3PAKE) is secure to various attacks like the off-line dictionary attack, man-in-the-middle attack, and unknown key-share attack. Nevertheless, this paper points out their ES-3PAKE protocol is still vulnerable to undetectable on-line dictionary attacks and off-line dictionary attack unlike their claim in which an attacker exhaustively enumerates all possible passwords in an on-line or off-line manner to determine the correct one.

The remainder of this paper is organized as follows. We subsequently review ES-3PAKE protocol in Section 2. The undetectable on-line dictionary attacks and off-line dictionary attack on ES-3PAKE protocol are presented in Section 3. Finally, we draw conclusions in Section 4.

Table 1. Notation used in protocol

A, B	Two communication parties.
S	A trusted server.
pw_A	The shared password between A and S.
pw_B	The shared password between B and S.
G, q, g	A cyclic group G of prime order q generated by an element g.
M, N	The elements in a represent group G.
$H_1(\cdot), H_2(\cdot)$	Cryptographic hash functions, where $H_1, H_2 : \{0,1\}^* \to G$.
$A \to B : M$	A sends message M to B.
$M_1 \| M_2$	M_1 is concatenated with M_2.

2   Review of Enhanced S-3PAKE Protocol

This section reviews the Nam et al.'s ES-3PAKE Protocol [11]. Throughout the paper, notations are employed in Table 1. Fig. 1 depicts the ES-3PAKE protocol, which works as follows.

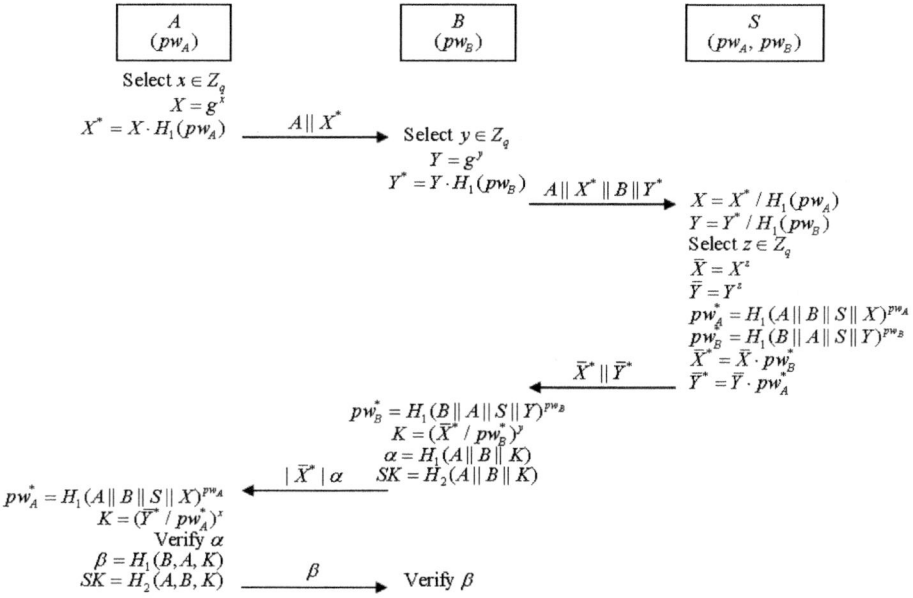

Fig. 1. Nam et al.'s ES-3PAKE protocol

1. $A \to B$: $A||X^*$
   A chooses a random number $x \in Z_q$, computes

$$X = g^x,$$

$$X^* = X \cdot H_1(pw_A),$$

   and sends $A||X^*$ to B.
2. $B \to S$: $A||X^*||B||Y^*$
   B selects a random number $y \in Z_q$, computes

$$Y = g^y,$$

$$Y^* = Y \cdot H_1(pw_B),$$

   and sends $A||X^*||B||Y^*$ to S.

3. $S \rightarrow B$: $\overline{X}^*||\overline{Y}^*$

Upon receiving $A||X^*||B||Y^*$, S first recovers X and Y by computing

$$X = X^*/H_1(pw_A),$$

$$Y = Y^*/H_1(pw_B).$$

Next, S selects a random number $z \in Z_q$ and computes $\overline{X} = X^z$ and $\overline{Y} = Y^z$. S then computes

$$pw_A^* = H_1(A||B||S||X)^{pw_A},$$

$$pw_B^* = H_1(B||A||S||Y)^{pw_B},$$

$$\overline{X}^* = \overline{X} \cdot pw_B^*,$$

$$\overline{Y}^* = \overline{Y} \cdot pw_A^*,$$

and sends $\overline{X}^*||\overline{Y}^*$ to B.

4. $B \rightarrow A$: $Y^*||\alpha$

After having received $\overline{X}^*||\overline{Y}^*$, B computes

$$pw_B^* = H_1(B||A||S||Y)^{pw_B},$$

$$K = (\overline{X}^*/pw_B^*)^y = g^{xyz},$$

$$\alpha = H_1(A||B||K),$$

and sends $Y^*||\alpha$ to A.

5. $A \rightarrow B$: β

After having received $Y^*||\alpha$, A computes

$$pw_A^* = H_1(A||B||S||X)^{pw_A},$$

$$K = (\overline{Y}^*/pw_A^*)^x = g^{xyz},$$

and verifies that α is equal to $H_1(A||B||K)$. If the verification fails, then A aborts the protocol. Otherwise, A computes the session key $SK = H_2(A||B||K)$ and sends $\beta = H_1(B||A||K)$ to B.

6. B verifies the correctness of β by checking that β is equal to $H_1(B||A||K)$. If it holds, then B computes the session key $SK = H_2(A||B||K)$. Otherwise, B aborts the protocol.

3   Cryptanalysis of ES-3PAKE Protocol

This section shows that Nam et al.'s ES-3PAKE protocol [11] is not secure to undetectable on-line dictionary attacks by any other user and off-line dictionary attacks. First, we define the security term needed for security problem analysis of the ES-3PAKE protocol as follows:

Definition 1. *A weak secret (password pw_i) is a value of low entropy Weak(k), which can be guessed in polynomial time.*

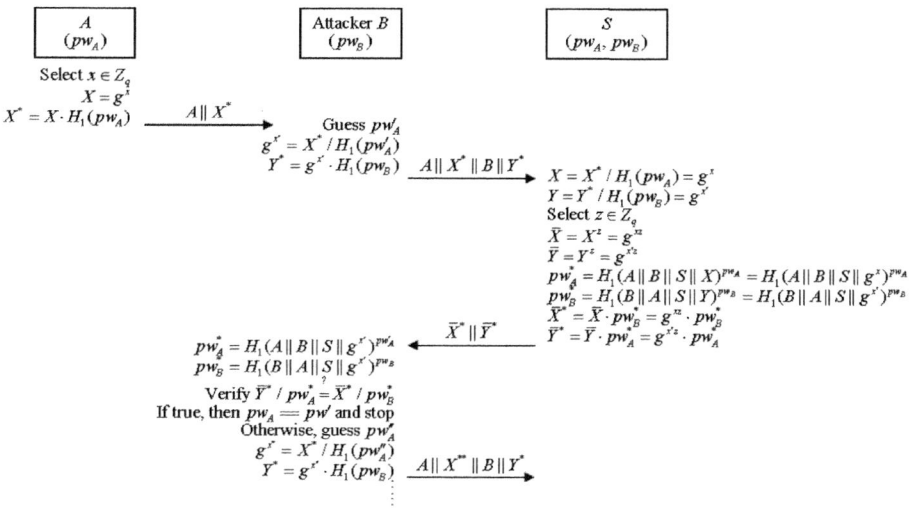

Fig. 2. Undetectable on-line dictionary attack 1 scenario

3.1 Undetectable On-Line Dictionary Attack 1

The *undetectable on-line dictionary attack 1* scenario is outlined in Fig. 2. A malicious user B with helping a legal user A can perform the following "undetectable on-line dictionary attack 1".

1. $A \rightarrow B$: $A||X^*$
   A operates as specified in the protocol in the first step.
2. $B \rightarrow S$: $A||X^*||B||Y^*$
   Let B be a malicious user mediating between S and A. Upon intercepting $A||X^*$ form the user A in flow (1) of the ES-3PAKE protocol in Fig. 1. B guesses a password pw'_A, and establishes an authenticated and private channel with S. B first computes

$$g^{x'} = X^*/H_1(pw'_A)$$

   for an unknown element $x' \in Z_q$. Then, B computes

$$Y^* = g^{x'} \cdot H_1(pw_B)$$

   and sends $A||X^*||B||Y^*$ to S.
3. $S \rightarrow B$: $\overline{X}^*, \overline{Y}^*$
   Upon receiving $A||X^*||B||Y^*$, S first will recover X and Y by computing

$$X = X^*/H_1(pw_A) = g^x,$$

$$Y = Y^*/H_1(pw_B) = g^{x'}.$$

Next, S will select a random number $z \in Z_q$ and compute

$$\overline{X} = X^z = g^{xz},$$

$$\overline{Y} = Y^z = g^{yz}.$$

S then will compute

$$pw_A^* = H_1(A||B||S||\overline{X})^{pw_A} = H_1(A||B||S||g^x)^{pw_A},$$

$$pw_B^* = H_1(B||A||S||\overline{Y})^{pw_B} = H_1(B||A||S||g^{x'})^{pw_B},$$

$$\overline{X}^* = \overline{X} \cdot pw_B^* = g^{xz} \cdot pw_B^*,$$

$$\overline{Y}^* = \overline{Y} \cdot pw_A^* = g^{x'z} \cdot pw_A^*,$$

and will send $\overline{X}^*||\overline{Y}^*$ to B.

4. When B receives $\overline{X}^*, \overline{Y}^*$, B uses his/her password pw_B, the guessed password pw_A', and $g^{x'}$ to obtain

$$pw_A^* = H_1(A||B||S||g^{x'})^{pw_A'},$$

$$pw_B^* = H_1(B||A||S||g^{x'})^{pw_B}.$$

B checks if the following equation holds or not

$$\overline{Y}^*/pw_A^* \overset{?}{=} \overline{X}^*/pw_B^*.$$

If the check passes, then B confirms that the guessed password pw_A' is the correct one.

5. Otherwise, B repeatedly performs the steps (2)-(5) without being noticed by S. For example, B guesses another password pw_A'', and computes $g^{x''} = X^*/H_1(pw_A'')$ and $Y^{**} = g^{x''} \cdot H_1(pw_B)$. Then, B sends $A||X^*||B||Y^{**}$ to S.

It is clear that if $pw_A' = pw_A$, then

$$\overline{Y}^*/pw_A^* = g^{x'z} = \overline{X}^*/pw_B^* = g^{xz}.$$

Therefore, $g^x = g^{x'}$.

3.2   Undetectable On-Line Dictionary Attack 2

The *undetectable on-line dictionary attack 2* scenario is outlined in Fig. 3. A malicious user B without helping a legal user A can perform the following "undetectable on-line dictionary attack 2".

1. $B \rightarrow S$: $A||X^*||B||Y^*$
   Let B be a malicious user mediating between S and A. Without any contribution from A, B guesses a password pw_A', and establishes an authenticated and private channel with S. B computes

$$X^* = H_1(pw_A'),$$

$$Y^* = H_1(pw_B).$$

Finally, B sends $A||X^*||B||Y^*$ to S.

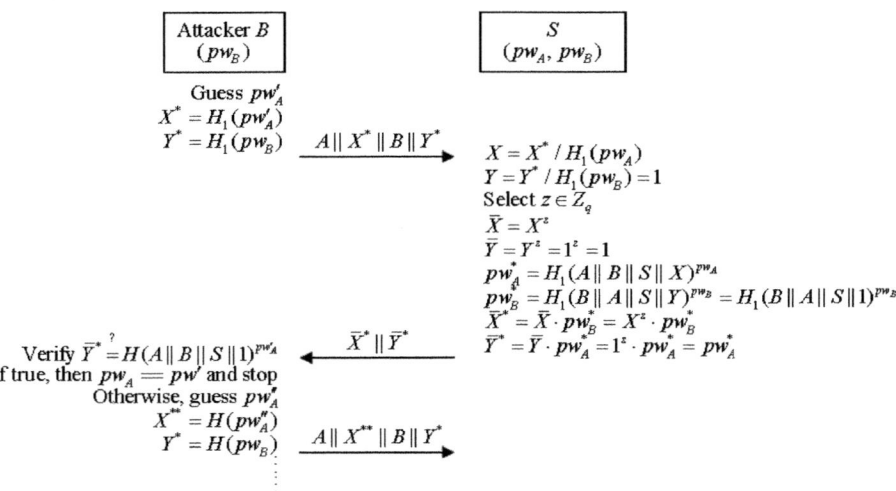

Fig. 3. Undetectable on-line dictionary attack 2 scenario

2. $S \rightarrow B$: $\overline{X}^*, \overline{Y}^*$

Upon receiving $A||X^*||B||Y^*$, S first will recover X and Y by computing

$$X = X^*/H_1(pw_A),$$

$$Y = Y^*/H_1(pw_B) = 1.$$

Next, S will select a random number $z \in Z_q$ and compute

$$\overline{X} = X^z,$$

$$\overline{Y} = Y^z = 1^z = 1.$$

S then will compute

$$pw_A^* = H_1(A||B||S||X)^{pw_A},$$

$$pw_B^* = H_1(B||A||S||Y)^{pw_B} = H_1(B||A||S||1)^{pw_B},$$

$$\overline{X}^* = \overline{X} \cdot pw_B^* = X^z \cdot pw_B^*,$$

$$\overline{Y}^* = \overline{Y} \cdot pw_A^* = 1 \cdot pw_A^* = pw_A^*,$$

and will send $\overline{X}^*||\overline{Y}^*$ to B.

3. When B receives $\overline{X}^*, \overline{Y}^*$, B uses the guessed password pw_A' to check if the following equation holds or not

$$\overline{Y}^* \stackrel{?}{=} H_1(A||B||S||1)^{pw_A'}.$$

If the check passes, then B confirms that the guessed password pw_A' is the correct one.

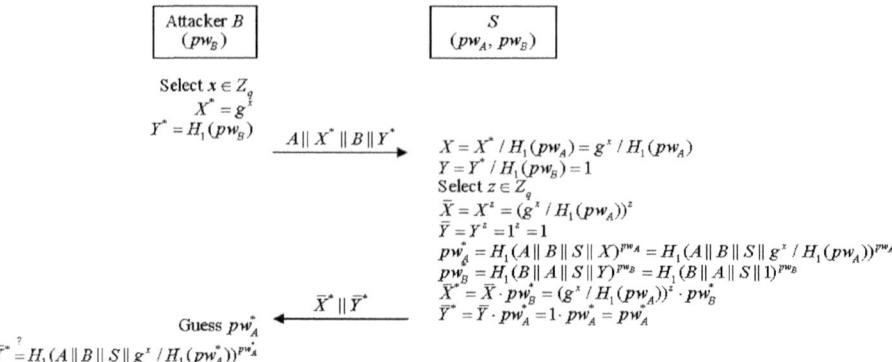

Fig. 4. Off-line dictionary attack scenario

4. Otherwise, B repeatedly performs the steps (1)-(3) without being noticed by S. For example, B guesses another password pw_A'', and computes $X^{**} = H_1(pw_A'')$ and $Y^* = H_1(pw_B)$. Then, B sends $A||X^{**}||B||Y^*$ to S.

It is clear that if $pw_A' = pw_A$, then

$$\overline{Y}^* = H_1(A||B||S||1)^{pw_A'} = pw_A^*.$$

Therefore, $X^* = H_1(pw_A)$.

3.3   Off-Line Dictionary Attack

The *off-line dictionary attack* scenario is outlined in Fig. 4. A malicious user B without helping a legal user A can perform the following "off-line dictionary attack".

1. $B \rightarrow S$: $A||X^*||B||Y^*$
   Let B be a malicious user mediating between S and A. Without any help of A, B choose $x \in Z_q$ randomly and establishes an authenticated and private channel with S. B lets

   $$X^* = g^x$$

   and computes

   $$Y^* = H_1(pw_B).$$

   Finally, B sends $A||X^*||B||Y^*$ to S.
2. $S \rightarrow B$: $\overline{X}^*, \overline{Y}^*$
   Upon receiving $A||X^*||B||Y^*$, S first will recover X and Y by computing

   $$X = X^*/H_1(pw_A) = g^x/H_1(pw_A),$$

   $$Y = Y^*/H_1(pw_B) = 1.$$

Next, S will select a random number $z \in Z_q$ and compute

$$\overline{X} = X^z = (g^x / H_1(pw_A))^z,$$

$$\overline{Y} = Y^z = 1^z = 1.$$

S then will compute

$$pw_A^* = H_1(A||B||S||X)^{pw_A} = H_1(A||B||S||g^x / H_1(pw_A))^{pw_A},$$

$$pw_B^* = H_1(B||A||S||Y)^{pw_B} = H_1(B||A||S||1)^{pw_B},$$

$$\overline{X}^* = \overline{X} \cdot pw_B^* = (g^x / H_1(pw_A))^z \cdot pw_B^*,$$

$$\overline{Y}^* = \overline{Y} \cdot pw_A^* = 1 \cdot pw_A^* = pw_A^*,$$

and will send $\overline{X}^* || \overline{Y}^*$ to B.

3. When B receives $\overline{X}^*, \overline{Y}^*$, B guesses a password pw_A' and checks if the following equation holds or not

$$\overline{Y}^* \stackrel{?}{=} H_1(A||B||S||g^x / H_1(pw_A'))^{pw_A'}.$$

If the check passes, then B confirms that the guessed password pw_A' is the correct one.

4. If it is not correct, B chooses another password pw_A'' and repeatedly performs above step (3) until

$$\overline{Y}^* \stackrel{?}{=} H_1(A||B||S||g^x / H_1(pw_A''))^{pw_A''}.$$

3.4   Real Applications for the Proposed Dictionary Attacks

In the modern life which the Internet has strong influence to people, passwords are the most common means of user authentication on the Internet. For practical applications, password-based authentication protocols are required when making use of Internet network services like E-learning, on-line polls, on-line ticket-order systems, roll call systems, on-line games, etc. Suppose that the password pw_A of user A can be revealed by the attacker due to the above described dictionary attacks. In real applications, users offer the same password as above to access several application servers for their convenience. Thus, an attacker may try to use the guessed password pw_A to impersonate the user A to login to other systems that the user A has registered with outside this ES-3PAKE protocol-based server. If the targeted outside server adopts the normal authentication protocol, it is possible that the attacker can successfully impersonate the user A to login to it by using the guessed password pw_A. Therefore, the password breach cannot be revealed by the attacker's actions.

4   Conclusions

Three-party authenticated key exchange technology has been widely deployed in various kinds of applications. Recently, Nam et al. proposed an enhanced simple three-party password-based authenticated key exchange (ES-3PAKE) protocol. However, we have demonstrated that ES-3PAKE protocol still falls prey to undetectable on-line dictionary attacks and and to off-line dictionary attacks by any other user. For this reason, ES-3PAKE protocol is insecure for practical application. It is important that security engineers should be made aware of this, if they are responsible for the design and development of three-party password-based authenticated key exchange systems.

Acknowledgements. This work was supported by Basic Science Research Program through the National Research Foundation of Korea(NRF) funded by the Ministry of Education, Science and Technology(No. 2010-0010106) and partially supported by the MKE(The Ministry of Knowledge Economy), Korea, under the ITRC(Information Technology Research Center) support program supervised by the NIPA(National IT Industry Promotion Agency (NIPA-2011-(C1090-1121-0002)).

References

1. Bellovin, S., Merritt, M.: Encrypted key exchange: password-based protocols secure against dictionary attacks. In: Proc. 1992 IEEE Symposium on Research in Security and Privacy, pp. 72–84 (1992)
2. Lee, T., Hwang, T., Lin, C.: Enhanced three-party encrypted key exchange without server public keys. Computers Security 23(7), 571–577 (2004)
3. Wen, H., Lee, T., Hwang, T.: Provably secure three-party password-based authenticated key exchange protocol using Weil pairing. IEE Proc. Com. 152(2), 138–143 (2005)
4. Kim, H., Choi, J.: Enhanced password-based simple three-party key exchange protocol. Computers & Electrical Engineering 35, 107–114 (2009)
5. Ding, Y., Horster, P.: Undetectable on-line password guessing attacks. ACM Operating Systems Review 29(4), 77–86 (1995)
6. Lu, R., Cao, Z.: Simple three-party key exchange protocol. Computers & Security 26(1), 94–97 (2007)
7. Abdalla, M., Pointcheval, D.: Simple Password-Based Encrypted Key Exchange Protocols. In: Menezes, A. (ed.) CT-RSA 2005. LNCS, vol. 3376, pp. 191–208. Springer, Heidelberg (2005)
8. Chung, H., Ku, W.: Three weaknesses in a simple three-party key exchange protocol. Inform. Sciences 178(1), 220–229 (2008)
9. Guo, H., Li, Z., Mu, Y., Zhang, X.: Cryptanalysis of simple threeparty key exchange protocol. Computers & Security 27(1), 16–21 (2008)
10. Phan, R., Yau, W., Goi, B.: Cryptanalysis of simple three-party key exchange protocol (S-3PAKE). Inform. Sciences 178(13), 2849–2856 (2008)
11. Nam, J., Paik, J., Kang, H., Kim, U., Won, D.: An off-line dictionary attack on a simple three-party key exchange protocol. IEEE Commun. Lett. 13(3), 205–207 (2009)

An Effective Distance-Computing Method
for Network Anomaly Detection

Guo-Hui Zhou

Department of Computer & Information Engineering, Guangxi Vocational & Technical
Institute of Industry, Nanning Guangxi, China 53001
zhgh1001@126.com

Abstract. Currently many traditional network anomaly detection algorithms are
proposed to distinguish network anomalies from heavy network traffic. However, most of them are based on data mining or machine learning methods, which
brings unexpected heavy computational cost and high false alarm rates. In this
paper, we propose a simple distance-computing algorithm for network anomaly
detection, which is able to distinguish network anomalies from normal traffic
using simple but effective distance-computing mechanism. Experimental results
on the well-known KDD Cup 1999 dataset demonstrate it can effectively detect
anomalies with high true positives, low false positives with acceptable computational cost.

Keywords: information security, anomaly detection, distance computing,
algorithm.

1   Introduction

Intrusion detection has two braches: signature based detection and anomaly detection.
As an important branch of intrusion detection field, anomaly detection has been an
active area of research in network security since it was originally proposed by Denning [1]. Therefore, a lot of data mining methods have been proposed for this hotspot
[2, 3, 9, 10, 11, 12]. Anomaly detection algorithms have the advantage over misuse
detection that they can detect new types of intrusions as deviations from normal
usage. In this problem, given a set of normal data to train from, and given a new piece
of test data, the goal of the intrusion detection algorithm is to determine whether the
test data belong to "normal" or to an anomalous behavior. However, anomaly detection methods suffer from a high rate of false alarms. This occurs primarily because
previously unseen (yet legitimate) system behaviors are also recognized as anomalies,
and hence flagged as potential intrusions. Moreover, if the training set is contami-
nated by the "noisy" data, the detection performance of anomaly detection methods
would deteriorate sharply.

In this paper, we present a distance-computing method for network anomaly detection. It is based on TCM-KNN (Transductive Confidence Machines for K-Nearest
Neighbors) algorithm, which is successfully applied to pattern recognition, fraud

T.-h. Kim et al. (Eds.): SecTech 2011, CCIS 259, pp. 177–182, 2011.
© Springer-Verlag Berlin Heidelberg 2011

detection and outlier detection [6,7]. It is based on simple distance computing and has better detection performance than the traditional anomaly detection methods in practice. A series of experiments on the well-known KDD Cup 1999 dataset demonstrate our method has higher detection rate and lower false alarm than the state-of-the-art anomaly detection methods.

2   A Distance-Computing Method

TCM-KNN (Transductive Confidence Machines for K-Nearest Neighbors) introduced the computation of the confidence using algorithmic randomness theory [5,6,7]. Unlike traditional methods in data mining, transduction can offer measures of reliability to individual points, and uses very broad assumptions except for the iid assumption (the training as well as new (unlabelled) points are independently and identically distributed). There exists a universal method of finding regularities in data sequences. This p-value serves as a measure of how well the data supports or not a null hypothesis (the point belongs to a certain class). The smaller the p-value, the greater the evidence against the null hypothesis (i.e., the point is an outlier with respect to the current available classes). Users of transduction as a test of confidence have approximated a universal test for randomness (which is in its general form, non-computable) by using a p-value function called strangeness measure [3,4]. The general idea is that the strangeness measure corresponds to the uncertainty of the point being measured with respect to all the other labeled points of a class.

3   Anomaly Detection Framework Based on TCM-KNN Algorithm

In standard TCM-KNN, we are always sure that the point we are examining belongs to one of the classes. However, in anomaly detection, we need not assign a point constructed from the network packets to a certain class, we only attempt to pinpoint the point in question is normal or abnormal.

Therefore, we propose to use a modified definition of α as follows:

$$\alpha_{iy} = \sum_{j=1}^{k} D_{ij}^{y} \tag{1}$$

This new definition will make the strangeness value of a point far away from the class considerably larger than the strangeness of points already inside the class. With respect to our anomaly detection task, there are no classes available, then the above test can be administered to the data as a whole (it all belonged to one class - normal). Therefore, it only requires a single α_i per point (as opposed to computing one per class), and the τ used directly reflects the confidence level ($1-\tau$) is required.

The process of our new simplified TCM-KNN algorithm for anomaly detection is depicted in Figure 1:

```
Parameters: k (the nearest neighbors to be used), m (size of training
dataset), τ (preset threshold), r (instance to be determined)

for i = 1 to m {

calculate Dᵢʸ for each one in training dataset and store;

calculate strangeness α for each one in training dataset and store;

            }

calculate the strangeness for r;

calculate the p-values for r;

if ( p≤τ )

determine r as anomaly with confidence 1−τ and return;

else

claim r is normal with confidence 1−τ and return;
```

Fig. 1. Distance-computing based algorithm for anomaly detection

We proposed an anomaly detection framework based on TCM-KNN algorithm. The framework includes two phases: training phase and detection phase. In the first phase, three important jobs should be considered:

a) Data collection for modeling: representative data for normal network behaviors should be collected for our method to modeling. It is worth noting here that as anomaly detection, attack data is no need for us to collect.

b) Feature selection & vectorlization: to meet the requirement of TCM-KNN which mainly depends on the distance calculation based on vectors, feature selection and vectorlization work should be employed. For instances, the duration time of a TCP connection, the ratio between the number of SYN packets, etc. might be selected for the features. They are mostly the same as those in KDD Cup 1999 dataset whose connections meta information have been extracted as 41 features.

c) Modeling by TCM-KNN algorithm: for the last step, TCM-KNN algorithm introduced in this paper then calculates the strangeness and p-value for each instance in the training dataset, thus to construct the anomaly detection engine.

For the detection phase, all the real-time data collected from the network also should be preprocessed to vectors according to the selected features having been acquired in training phase, then would be directed to the anomaly detection engine based on TCM-KNN, benign or malicious traffic would be determined.

4   Experimental Results

4.1   Dataset and Preprocess

In our experiments, we select the well-known KDD Cup 1999 dataset (KDD 99) [8] as our test dataset. It includes connections information summarized from the original TCP dump files. A connection is a sequence of TCP packets starting and ending at some well defined times, between which data flows to and from a source IP address to a target IP address under some well defined protocol. Each connection is labeled as either normal, or as an attack, with exactly one specific attack type. Each connection record consists of about 100 bytes. The attacks contain 24 different types of attacks that are broadly categorized in four groups such as Probes, DoS (Denial of Service), U2R (User to Root) and R2L (Remote to Local).

Before beginning our experiments, we preprocessed the dataset. First, we normalized the dataset. For the numerical data, in order to avoid one attribute will dominate another attribute, they were normalized by replacing each attribute value with its distance to the mean of all the values for that attribute in the instance space. For discrete or categorical data, we represent a discrete value by its frequency. That is, discrete values of similar frequency are close to each other, but values of very different frequency are far apart. As a result, discrete attributes are transformed to continuous attributes.

4.2   Experimental Results

In the contrast experiments between TCM-KNN and the most distinguished anomaly detection methods proposed by authors in [3, 9, 10], we used the sampled "noisy" dataset for training and test (it includes 93,675 normal instances and 10,030 attack instances). We adopted tenfold cross-validation approach to make the experiment. For the unsupervised anomaly detection algorithms, we set their parameters as the same in [3] for the convenience of comparison. For our TCM-KNN, k is set 200 and τ 0.05 (therefore, the confidence level is 0.95). Table 1 shows the comparison results of them. It is clear that our method demonstrates higher TP and especially the lower FP than the other three methods.

Moreover, we also use both "clean" dataset and "unclean" dataset for training, to test the adaptive performance of our TCM-KNN algorithm. The result is depicted in Table 2. It clearly shows that a little difference can be observed when we use the two types of training dataset. It strongly demonstrates the proposed TCM-KNN method can be a good candidate for anomaly detection in realistic network environment than the other three methods, because acquiring purely "clean" dataset for training is often impossible and the relatively "unclean" dataset is reasonable. Therefore, a robust detection performance in such a "noisy" network environment is a necessity for anomaly detection method. The results demonstrate our TCM-KNN method has such a good performance.

Table 1. Detection performance comparison results between TCM-KNN and the other distinguished anomaly detection methods

Algorithm Evaluation	Fixed width clustering	CSI-KNN	One-class SVM	TCM-KNN
TP	92.33%	93.48%	99.69%	99.54%
FP	9.18%	7.68%	5.36%	1.49%

Table 2. Running results using both "clean" and "unclean" training dataset

	clean dataset	unclean dataset
TP	99.78%	99.54%
FP	1.25%	1.49%

5 Conclusions

In this paper, we introduce a distance-computing method algorithm for effective network anomaly detection. Moreover, we design a series of experiments and the experimental results demonstrate its effectiveness and advantages over traditional methods. For our future work, we would compare our method with more mainstream methods, as well as optimize it for better performance.

References

1. Denning, D.E.: An Intrusion Detection Model. IEEE Transactions on Software Engineering, 222–232 (1987)
2. Lee, W., Stolfo, S.J.: Data Mining Approaches for Intrusion Detection. In: Proceedings of the 1998 USENIX Security Symposium (1998)
3. Eskin, E., Arnold, A., Prerau, M., Portnoy, L., Stolfo, S.J.: A Geometric Framework for Unsupervised Anomaly Detection: Detecting Intrusions in Unlabeled Data. In: Barbara, D., Jajodia, S. (eds.) Applications of Data Mining in Computer Security. Kluwer (2002)
4. Gammerman, A., Vovk, V.: Prediction algorithms and confidence measure based on algorithmic randomness theory. Theoretical Computer Science, 209-217 (2002)
5. Li, M., Vitanyi, P.: Introduction to Kolmogorov Complexity and its Applications, 2nd edn. Springer, Heidelberg (1997)
6. Proedrou, K., Nouretdinov, I., Vovk, V., Gammerman, A.: Transductive Confidence Machines for Pattern Recognition. In: Elomaa, T., Mannila, H., Toivonen, H. (eds.) ECML 2002. LNCS (LNAI), vol. 2430, pp. 381–390. Springer, Heidelberg (2002)
7. Barbará, D., Domeniconi, C., Rogers, J.P.: Detecting outliers using transduction and statistical testing. In: Proceedings of the 12th ACM SIGKDD International Conference on Knowledge Discovery and Data Mining, USA, pp. 55–64 (2006)
8. Knowledge discovery in databases DARPA archive. Task Description,
http://www.kdd.ics.uci.edu/databases/kddcup99/task.html

9. Kuang, L., Zulkernine, M.: An anomaly intrusion detection method using the CSI-KNN algorithm. In: Proc. of the 2008 ACM Symposium on Applied Computing, pp. 1362–1373 (2008)
10. Liao, Y., Vemuri, V.: Use of K-Nearest Neighbor classifier for intrusion detection. Computers & Security 21(5), 439–448 (2002)
11. Prerau, M.J., Eskin, E.: Unsupervised anomaly detection using an optimized K-nearest neighbors algorithm. Master's thesis
12. Skoudis, E., Liston, T., Reloaded, C.H.: A Step-by-Step Guide to Computer Attacks and Effective Defenses, 2nd edn. Prentice Hall PTR, Upper Saddle River (2005)

Formalization and Information-Theoretic Soundness in the Development of Security Architecture for Next Generation Network Protocol - UDT

Danilo V. Bernardo and Doan B. Hoang

i-Next, Faculty of Information Technology and Engineering
The University of Technology, Sydney
Australia
bernardan@gmail.com, dhoang@uts.edu.au

Abstract. The development and deployment of User Datagram Protocol (UDP)- based Data Transfer (UDT) is undoubtedly strongly reliant upon existing security mechanisms. However, existing mechanisms are developed for mature protocols such as TCP/UDP. We, therefore, developed proprietary mechanisms to form a security architecture for UDT. The primary objectives of the architecture include the management of messages through Authentication Option (AO) and cryptographic keys, the security of data communications, and the integration of data protection enhancing technologies across all the layers. Our approach is the result of our work which started in 2008. We verified each mechanism through formalisation to achieve information-theoretic soundness of the architecture. The results achieve the enhancement of existing schemes to introduce a novel approach to integrate mechanisms to secure UDT in its deployment. The architecture does include available and well-discussed schemes, which are used in other protocols, with proven computational intelligence which can be upgraded so as to provide improved security and primary protection in future extensive UDT deployments. In this work, we present UDT Security Architecture with suitable mechanisms to ensure preservation of data integrity in data transmission.

Keywords: Next Generation, Generic Security Service Application Program Interface (GSS-API), High Speed Bandwidth, User Datagram Protocol –Data Transfer (UDT), Authentication Option (AO), Host Identity Protocol (HIP), Cryptographically Generate Addresses (CGA), Simple Authentication Security layer (SASL), Datagram Transport Layer Security (DTLS).

1 Introduction

The emergence of high speed networks coincides with a burgeoning use of digital technology to deliver education, commerce, health care, national defense and many other endeavors that promise continued growth for decades.

In the past decades, these high speed networks were elusive and only available to governments and universities. A few decades later, they become increasingly available in the mainstreams.

T.-h. Kim et al. (Eds.): SecTech 2011, CCIS 259 pp. 183–194, 2011.

The use of high speed network such as Wide Optical Area Network (WOAN) addresses many of the problems we are facing; such as education disparity, high carbon emissions, slow delivery of e-health and many others. High speed network brings education closer to the regional homes; brings telemedicine and e-health into the mainstream and importantly, helps minimise carbon emissions by making most of the tele-video conferencing real-time streaming rather than travelling long distances, thus achieves environmental sustainability.

The transition from low speed networks to high speed networking in some sectors thus come at a time when societal reliance on networks is greater than its already significant level. Assured use and access of these networks, in a private, protected and reliable manner and with appropriate service guarantees, is very important and has motivated the study of the security of new network protocols.

High Speed networks have since pushed researchers to develop new protocols that support high density data transmissions in Wide Area Networks. Many of these protocols are Transmission Control TCP) protocol variants, which have demonstrated better performance in simulation and several limited network experiments but have limited practical applications because of implementation and installation difficulties. On the other hand, users who need to transfer bulk data (e.g., in grid/cloud computing) usually turn to application level solutions where these variants do not fair well. Among protocols considered in the application level solutions are UDP-based protocols, such as UDT (UDP-based Data Transport Protocol) for cloud /grid computing.

UDT was developed in a research laboratory at the National Center Data Mining Center, University of Illinois at Chicago [23].

Despite the promising development of protocols like UDT, what remains to be a major challenge that current and future network designers face is to achieve survivability and security of data and networks.

The development of future generation grid protocols such as UDT - a fast data transfer protocol for grid and cloud computing was successfully implemented by capturing data from outer space, gathering terabytes of information and transferring them across the continents in high speed network. This provides a compelling commercial promise in WOAN.   Whilst many types of protocols solve many of the problems in terms of achieving speed, performance and even address Climate Change by minimizing our carbon emissions, one common problem that adamantly remains: security.

Securing protocols, such as UDT, to achieve privacy, confidentiality and data integrity in wide optical area networks is a challenge against existing anomalies. The study of security of UDT is new, and presents interesting challenges. Many of the security problems present in the existing protocols such as (Transmission Control Protocol) TCP and (User Datagram Protocol) UDP are also applicable to UDT (UDP-data transfer protocol). Moreover, many of the traditional security mechanisms, such as end-to-end encryption may be applicable to UDT implementation and, in certain cases, may be even more necessary.

In this paper, we present the security architecture of UDT after 2 years of experiment, industrial implementation and deployment. We use the terms architecture and framework interchangeably as they yield and present the same and comprehensive unification of methodologies using various proven security schemes.

The outcome is the result of our extensive work over the years [8-17] concluding our experimental validation and implementation using UDT. Our objective is to use a common baseline architecture, which, in one hand, provides a sufficient level of protection of data and communication, and, on the other hand is practical and deployable to UDT and to other similar protocols in the future.

Our design relies on well-established and understood cryptographic primitives, which are fully scrutinized thus sufficiently trusted and implemented in various environments. Our framework allows flexibility in the deployment of UDT to accommodate more stringent requirements.

2   Framework Objectives

The important aspects that our architecture seeks to address are: authentication option through using a cryptographic key management for messages, privacy and data integrity, and secure communication. The architecture will focus on the upper layers, from (Internet Protocol) IP to the application layers of the stack.

It also seeks to address the basic fundamental design of UDT and introduce a security mechanism that is not available in the packet level.

Our design is fully drawn from the design of TCP and UDP and their reliant to existing security mechanisms that are applicable to UDT implementation and deployment. Our design for UDT is novel and applicable to future design of UDP reliant protocols.

3   Contributions

We present, for the first time, a practical security architecture for UDT that makes this attainable for other high speed data transfer protocols. We describe the mechanisms that are scalable and novel to achieve the desired protection.

To develop this architecture, we conducted extensive reviews and validations, and implementations of existing mechanisms on UDT. We developed our own security mechanisms for UDT and achieved proofs of their secrecy, authentication as well as their applicability. Our early work in 2008 on UDT Security [10] was proposed to IETF standard. We are progressing to proposing our work to IETF in the future.

The rationale is the architecture useful based on a few important theoretic and practical scenarios. The architecture is presented with supplemental information on the schemes which can provide a basis for basic if not comprehensive security of data flow specifically in the higher-level communication layers.

We present the following theoretical contributions to the security analysis of the developed and proposed security mechanisms specifically for UDT. These are first in the literature:

1. The Foundational development of these mechanisms for inductive analysis and automata of their security properties by proving connections between selected trace properties of execution and non-selected theoretic properties standard in the literature.
2. Formalisation of inductive properties in a set of newly introduced axioms and inference rules and proved soundness of the proposed mechanisms

over the widely used model with consideration on theoretic adversary and anomaly,

3. Formalisation of the proposed architecture through proofs of mechanisms and secrecy properties in data flow.

On the practical side, we apply the approach to the analysis of the real world UDT implementation with the proposed security mechanisms.

1. Proofs of authentication and secrecy properties of GSS-API UDT and Kerberos with both symmetric and public keys initialization in the given theoretic models, The analysis of GSS-API and proofs of Kerberos specifically for UDT leads to a change of UDT algorithm are first in the literature,
2. Proofs of secrecy and authentication properties of UDT-AO, UDT+DTLS in a real world test environment.
3. Development of a proprietary UDT visualisation tool in java.

We present in this paper the result of our work in developing a security architecture for UDT. We conducted practical implementations through extensive experimentations of the proposed mechanisms within UDT. Proofs of secrecy and authentication of the proposed mechanisms (specifically, UDT-AO, DTLS, GSS_API) and the formalization of the architecture through rewrite systems and automata for UDT data flow were performed to enhance applicability reliably based on theoretic and practical outcomes.

4   Overview

In this section we present a short overview of the schemes we presented in our previous works.

4.1   HIP (Host Identity Protocol)

We attempted implementing Host Identity Protocol (HIP) [1,25] which considered to be another possible way to secure UDT on top of UDP and IP. We confirmed that this protocol solves the problem of address generation in a different way by removing the dual functionality of IP addresses as both host identifiers and topological locations. However to achieve this, a new network layer called the Host Identity is required [1,2,25].

Securing IP addresses plays an important role in networking, especially in the transport layer. Generating a secure IP address can be achieved through HIP. It is considered the building block which is used in other protocols as well as a way to secure the address generation in practice [25].

4.2   CGA (Cryptographically Generated Addresses)

Solving the problems of address related attacks can be also be solved by using CGA for address and verification. Self-certifying are widely used and standardized, such as HIP [1,25] and Accountable Internet Protocol (AIP) [2].

CGA [3-4] is using the cryptographic hash of the public key. It is a generic method for self-certifying address generation and verification that can be used for specific purposes. In this paper, the conventions are used to either (Internet Protocol Version 4) IPv4 or (Internet Protocol Version 6) IPv6.

The interface identifier, which is required for CGA, is generated by taking the cryptographic hash [45] of the encoded public-key of the user. Modern cryptographic has functions produce message digest with more than required number of bits in CGA. The interface identifier is formed by truncation of the output of the cryptographic hash function to a specific number of bit depending on the leftmost number of bits that forms the subnet prefix, i.e., IPv6 addresses are 128-bit data blocks, therefore the leftmost bits is 64 and the rightmost bits is 64. The prefix is used to determine the location of each node in Internet topology and the interface identifier is used as an identity of the node. Using a cryptographic hash of the public-key is the most effective method to generate self-certifying addresses.

4.3   Combination of HIP-CGA

HIP introduces new namespace, which is cryptographic in nature, for host identifies. It introduces a way of separating the location and host identity information.

A hashed encoding of the Host Identity (HI), the HI, is used in protocols to represent the Host Identity. The HI is 128 bits long and has the following three properties [1,25]:

- it can be used in address-sized fields in APIs and protocols
- It is self-certifying (i.e., given a HI, it is computationally hard to find a Host Identity key that matches this HI)
- The probability of HI collision between two hosts is very low.

The HIs are self-certifying. This means no certificates are needed in practice. HIP uses base exchange protocol [3] to establish a pair of IPsec security associations between two host for further communication. The main challenge of implementing HIP is the requirement of a new network layer, called the Host Identity [1] which is difficult to run with existing networking protocols in use.

There are significant application and transport layer based authentication and end-to-end security options for UDT. Generic Security Service Application Program Interface (GSS-API) is one application layer based authentication.

4.4   GSS-API (Generic Security Service Application Program Interface)

The GSS-API is a generic (Application Program Interface) API for doing UDT client-server authentication. The motivation behind it is that every security system has its own API [34,54] and the effort involved with adding different security systems to applications is extremely difficult with the variance between security APIs. However, with a common API, application vendors could write to the generic API and it could work with any number of security systems, according to [34,54]. Vendors can use GSS-API during the UDT implementation. It is considered the easiest to use and implement and there exist implementations, such as Kerberos [41].

In summary, the protocol when used in UDT application can be viewed as:

- Authenticate (exchange opaque GSS context) through the user interface and (Congestion Control)CCC option of UDT.
- The utilize per-message token functions (GSS-API) to protect UDT messages during transmissions.

The GSS-API, however is a rather large API for some implementations, but for applications using UDT, one need only use a small subset of that API [54].

4.5   DTLS – Data Transport Layer Security

Another possible mechanism is Data Transport Layer Security (DTLS). DTLS [46] provides communications privacy for datagram protocols.   The protocol allows client/server applications to communicate in a way that is designed to prevent eavesdropping, tampering, or message forgery.   The DTLS protocol is based on the Transport Layer Security (TLS) [20] protocol and provides equivalent security guarantees.   Datagram semantics of the underlying transport are preserved by the DTLS protocol. DTLS is similar to TLS, but DTLS is designed for datagram transport.

High speed data transmission uses datagram transport such as UDP for communication due to delay-sensitive nature of transported data. The speed of delivery and behaviour of application running UDT are unchanged when DTLS is used to secure communication, since it does not compensate for lost or re-ordered data traffic when using applications using UDT running on top of UDP.

DTLS, however is susceptible to (Denial of Service) DoS attacks. Such attacks are launched by consuming excessive resources on the server by transmitting a series of handshake initiation requests, and by sending connection initiation messages with forged source of the victim. The server sends its next message to the victim machine, thus flooding it. In implementing DTLS, designers need to include cookie exchange with every hand shake during the implementation of applications using UDT and UDP.

4.6   IPsec - Internet Protocol Security

Most protocols for application security, such as DTLS operate at or above the transport layer.   This renders the underlying transport connections vulnerable to denial of service attacks, including connection assassination (Request for Comments - RFC 3552). IPsec offer the promise of protecting against many of denial of service attacks. It also offers other potential benefits.   Conventional software-based IPsec implementations isolate applications from the cryptographic keys, improving security by making inadvertent or malicious key exposure more difficult.   In addition, specialized hardware may allow encryption keys protected from disclosure within trusted cryptographic units.   Also, custom hardware units may well allow for higher performance.

4.7   AO -Authentication Option

The introduction of the proprietary mechanism UDT-Authentication Option (AO) is one of the main contributions of our work to secure UDP-based data transport. We introduced UDT extension within UDT to achieve security. We evaluated UDT-AO through the use of existing message authenticity for other protocols such as TCP. The existing message protection for transport protocols similarly acts like a signature for UDT segment incorporating information known only to the connection end points. Since UDT is operating on UDP for high speed data transfer, we attempted creating a new option in UDT that can significantly reduce the danger of attacks on applications running UDT. This can maintain message integrity during data transmissions on high speed networks. In the preceding sections, a few security mechanisms proposed are application and IP based. We aimed at presenting a unified scheme entailing the combination of existing security solutions for various layers [6-7,8-11] for UDT.

5   Architecture

Based on the schemes we reviewed, tested, and implemented, we present   the following layer to layer architecture for UDT.

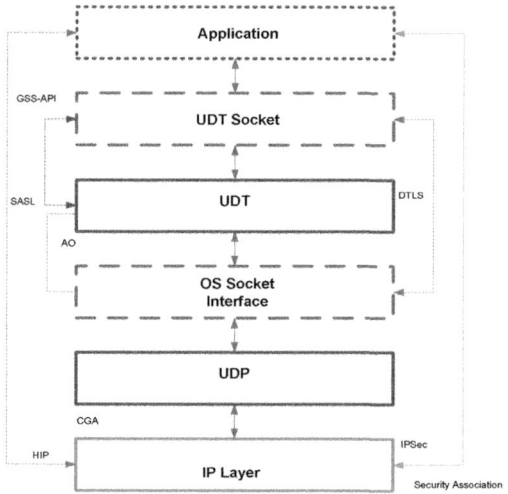

Fig. 1. Layer-to-Layer Architecture

Figure 7-1. Layer-to-Layer Architecture [23]. In our proposed architecture, the UDT layer provides transport functionalities to applications with security schemes that can be implemented, such as DTLS and SASL, for the upper layer. The layer above using UDT Socket can be implemented with GSS-API. UDT moreover, can be implemented with AO at the transport layer. The remaining lower layer can be protected using IPSec (securing end-to-end), HIP through the Application layer. CGA is specifically implemented on the IP layer provided HIP is not binding to the UDT socket.

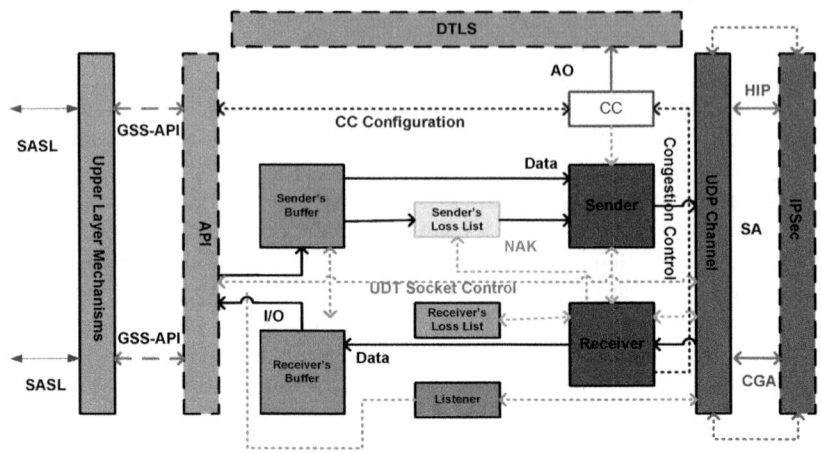

Fig. 2. Proposed UDT Security Architecture (improved version)

From Figure 1, detailed data flow with the proposed mechanisms is presented on Figure 2. With the introduction of IPSec, GSS-API, SA, SASL, a standard mechanism needed to manage secret encryption and authorisation keys, we proposed a generic key management API that can be used for IPSec and other existing security services. Similar to utilising sockets, this specific API creates new protocol family, the PF_Key domain. This must be constant that must be used with key management sockets, according to RFC 2367.

IPSec provides services to packets based on the security association (SA) which is stored for use in the security association database (SADB). This can be used for other routing protocols.

Key operations are supported on key management sockets, such as:

1. UDT can request a key from a key management daemon. The process /application that uses UDT can send a message to the kernel with open key management sockets by writing to a key management socket.
2. A process can read a message from the kernel (that UDT operates). The kernel uses this facility to request a key management daemon install an SA for new UDT connection.

We have introduced the security architecture after extensive review which included a design for security specific modular structure for UDT protocol that is practical for other data transfer protocols. To the best of our knowledge this is the first time this has been done.

We have presented our methods by using existing security mechanisms and developed one for UDT with the specification of TCP, UDP and UDT and Sockets API. Our design is the result of extensive experiments and implementations, and has broad coverage in terms of practical applications using existing high speed appliances to support our schemes.

6   Conclusion and Future Work

In our previous works [8-17], we highlighted the need to study UDT because of the following reasons, (1) It has great commercial promise (2) Fastest Data Transfer available at the present, and most importantly, it has no security to protect data transfer.

We presented an overview on securing UDT implementations in various layers. However securing UDT in application and other layers need to be explored in future UDT deployments in various applications.

There are application and transport layer based authentication and end-to-end security options for UDT.

In this paper, we present the results of our work by presenting an experimentally validated architecture to secure UDT. There are important areas the framework highlights:

- Security at the application and session layers via UDT extensions may require client and servers, and significant changes on applications to accommodate security features
- Formalisation and information-theoretic soundness of the introduced mechanisms.
- Security at the layer 3. The encryption be performed at the layer 3 (Network Layer), abstracted from the UDT application, e.g., via gateway-to-gateway, virtual private networks (VPNs), when security on the application layer becomes too complex to develop.
- Introduction of Internet Protocol Security (IPSEC) (part of layer 3), Cryptographically Generated Addresses (CGA), and Host Identity Protocol (HIP).

The architecture has been presented with notable schemes, and through formalisation to achieve information-theoretic soundness aiming to make it useful to users and designers of protocol modifications. The practicality of our design architecture for UDT suggests that similar designs should be practical, feasible and desirable for future protocol design, leading to a more secure-capable protocol with higher-quality implementation security schemes.

Future Work
There are many directions for future work based on our existing architecture and UDT specification.

While the mechanisms introduced to develop a comprehensive architecture for UDT has been subject to extensive validation and annotation, and eventually implementation and deployment, the architecture surely still requires improvement, and is not as clearly presented as it might be. We would be interested to see how it can be used to other fast data transfer protocols.

The architecture has been developed based on the particular implementations, and with reference to the UDT source code and existing mechanisms, but we have aimed to make it sufficiently flexible to admit other implementation and deployment schemes made on other protocols. It would be interesting to use the architecture to guide on fresh implementation and deployment of new protocols to determine how much implementation-security specific change is required.

UDT does not have a clear modular structure, but rather has increased functionality after the new versions were released, but still security mechanisms notably absent. Any improvement to this structure would be worthwhile. For instance, good security and modular structure would let introduce a better checksum and option security without redesigning the whole structure of a protocol when deploying in IPV6.

Our results can be useful for network and security investigators, designers, and users who need to take into account and include security when implementing UDT across wide area networks. These can also support security architectural designs of UDP-based protocols as well as assist in the future development of other state-of-the-art fast data transfer protocols.

Detailed work on formalisation and information-theoretic soundness of the mechanisms and the architecture itself will be presented in our future publication.

References

1. Al-Shraideh, F.: Host Identity Protocol. In: ICN/ICONS/MCL, p. 203. IEEE Computer Society (2006)
2. Andersen, D.G., Balakrishnan, H., Feamster, N., Koponen, T., Moon, D., Shenker, S.: Accountable Internet Protocol (AIP). In: Bahl, V., Wetherall, D., Savage, S., Stoica, I. (eds.) SIGCOMM, pp. 339–350. ACM (2008)
3. Aura, T.: Cryptographically Generated Addresses (CGA). In: Boyd, C., Mao, W. (eds.) ISC 2003. LNCS, vol. 2851, pp. 29–43. Springer, Heidelberg (2003)
4. Aura, T.: Cryptographically Generated Addresses (CGA). RFC 3972, IETF (March 2005)
5. Aura, T., Nagarajan, A., Gurtov, A.: Analysis of the HIP Base Exchange Protocol. In: Boyd, C., González Nieto, J.M. (eds.) ACISP 2005. LNCS, vol. 3574, pp. 481–493. Springer, Heidelberg (2005)
6. Bellovin, S.: Defending Against Sequence Number Attacks. RFC 1948 (1996)
7. Bellovin, S.: Guidelines for Mandating the Use of IPsec. Work in Progress. IETF (October 2003)
8. Bernardo, D.V., Hoang, D.: Empirical Survey: Experimentation and Implementations of High Speed Protocol Data Transfer for Grid. In: 25th IEEE AINA Workshop 2011, pp. 335–340 (2011)
9. Bernardo, D.V., Hoang, D.: A Conceptual Approach against Next Generation Security Threats: Securing a High Speed Network Protocol – UDT. In: Proc. IEEE the 2nd ICFN 2010, Shanya China (2010)
10. Bernardo, D.V., Hoang, D.: Security Requirements for UDT. IETF Internet-Draft – working paper (September 2009)
11. Bernardo, D.V., Hoang, D.: Network Security Considerations for a New Generation Protocol UDT. In: Proc. IEEE the 2nd ICCIST Conference 2009, Beijing China (2009)
12. Bernardo, D.V., Hoang, D.: A Security Framework and its Implementation in Fast Data Transfer Next Generation Protocol UDT. Journal of Information Assurance and Security 4, 354–360 (2009) ISN 1554-1010
13. Bernardo, D.V., Hoang, D.: Security Analysis of the Proposed Practical Security Mechanisms for High Speed Data Transfer Protocol. In: Kim, T.-H., Adeli, H. (eds.) AST/UCMA/ISA/ACN 2010. LNCS, vol. 6059, pp. 100–114. Springer, Heidelberg (2010)

14. Bernardo, D.V., Hoang, D.B.: End-to-End Security Methods for UDT Data Transmissions. In: Kim, T.-H., Lee, Y.-H., Kang, B.-H., Ślęzak, D. (eds.) FGIT 2010. LNCS, vol. 6485, pp. 383–393. Springer, Heidelberg (2010)
15. Bernardo, D.V., Hoang, D.: Securing data transfer in the cloud through introducing identification packet and UDT-authentication option field: a characterization. International Journal of Network Security & Its Applications (IJNSA) 2(4) (October 2010) CoRR abs/1010.4845:
16. Bernardo, D.V., Hoang, D.: Multi-layer Security Analysis and Experimentation of High Speed Protocol Data Transfer for GRID. International Journal o Grid and Utility Computing (in the press) (October 2011)
17. Bernardo, D.V., Hoang, D.: A Pragmatic Approach: Achieving Acceptable Security Mechanisms for High Speed Data Transfer Protocol- UDT SERSC. International Journal of Security and Its Applications 4(4) (October 2010)
18. Blumenthal, M., Clark, D.: Rethinking the Design of the Internet: End-to-End Argument vs. the Brave New World. In: Proc. ACM Trans Internet Technology, p.1 (August 2001)
19. Clark, D., Sollins, L., Wroclwski, J., Katabi, D., Kulik, J., Yang, X.: New Arch: Future Generation Internet Architecture, Technical Report, DoD – ITO (2003)
20. Dierks, T., Allen, C.: The TLS Protocol Version 1.0. RFC 2246 (January 1999)
21. Falby, N., Fulp, J., Clark, P., Cote, R., Irvine, C., Dinolt, G., Levin, T., Rose, M., Shifflett, D.: Information assurance capacity building: A case study. In: Proc. 2004 IEEE Workshop on Information Assurance, U.S. Military Academy, pp. 31–36 (June 2004)
22. Gorodetsky, V., Skormin, V., Popyack, L. (eds.): Information Assurance in Computer Networks: Methods, Models, and Architecture for Network Security. Springer, St. Petersburg (2001)
23. Gu, Y., Grossman, R.: UDT: UDP-based Data Transfer for High-Speed Wide Area Networks. Computer Networks 51(7) (2007)
24. Hamill, J., Deckro, R., Kloeber, J.: Evaluating information assurance strategies. Decision Support Systems 39(3), 463–484 (2005)
25. H. I. for Information Technology, H. U. of Technology, et al. Infrastructure for HIP (2008)
26. Harrison, D.: RPI NS2 Graphing and Statistics Package, http://networks.ecse.rpi.edu/~harrisod/graph.html
27. Jokela, P., Moskowitz, R., Nikander, P.: Using the Encapsulating Security Payload (ESP) Transport Format with the Host Identity Protocol (HIP). RFC 5202, IETF (April 2008)
28. Joubert, P., King, R., Neves, R., Russinovich, M., Tracey, J.: Highperformance memory-based web servers: Kernel and user-space performance. In: USENIX 2001, Boston, Massachusetts (June 2001)
29. Jray, W.: Generic Security Service API Version 2:C-bindings, RFC 2744 (January 2000)
30. Kent, S., Atkinson, R.: Security Architecture for the Internet Protocol. RFC 2401 (1998)
31. Laganier, J., Eggert, L.: Host Identity Protocol (HIP) Rendezvous Extension. RFC 5204, IETF (April 2008)
32. Laganier, J., Koponen, T., Eggert, L.: Host Identity Protocol (HIP) Registration Extension. RFC 5203, IETF (April 2008)
33. Leon-Garcia, A., Widjaja, I.: Communication Networks. McGraw Hill (2000)
34. Linn, J.: Generic Security Service Application Program Interface Version 2, Update 1, RFC 2743 (January 2000)
35. Linn, J.: The Kerberos Version 5 GSS-API Mechanism, IETF, RFC 1964 (June 1996)
36. Mathis, M., Mahdavi, J., Floyd, S., Romanow, A.: TCP selective acknowledgment options. IETF RFC 2018 (April 1996)

37. Melnikov, A., Zeilenga, K.: Simple Authentication and Security Layer (SASL) IETF, RFC 4422 (June 2006)
38. Menezes, A.J., van Oorschot, P.C., Vanstone, S.A.: Handbook of Applied Cryptography. CRC Press (1997)
39. Moskowitz, R., Nikander, P.: RFC 4423: Host identity protocol (HIP) architecture (May 2006)
40. Moskowitz, R., Nikander, P., Jokela, P., Henderson, T.: Host Identity Protocol. RFC 5201, IETF (April 2008)
41. Neuman, C., Yu, T., Hartman, S., Raeburn, K.: Kerberos Network Authentication Service (V5), IETF, RFC 1964 (June 1996)
42. NIST SP 800-37, Guide for the Security Certification and Accreditation of Federal Information Systems (May 2004)
43. NS2, http://isi.edu/nsna/ns
44. PSU Evaluation Methods for Internet Security Technology (EMIST) (2004), http://emist.ist.psu.edu (visited December 2009)
45. Rabin, M.: Digitized signatures and public-key functions as intractable as Factorization. MIT/LCS Technical Report, TR-212 (1979)
46. Rescorla, E., Modadugu, N.: Datagram Transport Layer Security. RFC 4347, IETF (April 2006)
47. Rivest, R.L., Shamir, A., Adleman, L.M.: A method for obtaining digital signature and public-keycryptosystems. Communication of ACM 21, 120–126 (1978)
48. Schwartz, M.: Broadband Integrated Networks. Prentice Hall (1996)
49. Stewart, R. (ed.): Stream Control Transmission Protocol, RFC 4960 (2007)
50. Stiemerling, M., Quittek, J., Eggert, L.: NAT and Firewall Traversal Issues of Host Identity Protocol (HIP) Communication. RFC 5207, IETF (April 2008)
51. Stoica, I., Adkins, D., Zhuang, S., Shenker, S., Surana, S.: Internet Indirection Infrastructure. In: Proc. ACM SIGCOMM (August 2002)
52. Szalay, A., Gray, J., Thakar, A., Kuntz, P., Malik, T., Raddick, J., Stoughton, C., Vandenberg, J.: The SDSS SkyServer - Public access to the Sloan digital sky server data. ACM SIGMOD (2002)
53. Wang, G., Xia,Y.: An NS2 TCP Evaluation Tool, http://labs.nec.com.cn/tcpeval.html
54. Williams, N.: Clarifications and Extensions to the Generic Security Service Application Program Interface (GSS-API) for the Use of Channel Bindings. RFC 5554 (May 2009)
55. Globus XIO, http://unix.globus.org/toolkit/docs/3.2/xio/index.html (retrieved on November 1, 2009)
56. Zhang, M., Karp, B., Floyd, S., Peterson, L.: RR-TCP: A reordering-robust TCP with DSACK. In: Proc. the Eleventh IEEE International Conference on Networking Protocols (ICNP 2003), Atlanta, GA (November 2003)

Bi-Layer Behavioral-Based Feature Selection Approach for Network Intrusion Classification

Heba F. Eid[1], Mostafa A. Salama[2], Aboul Ella Hassanien[3], and Tai-hoon Kim[4]

[1] Faculty of Science, Al-Azhar University, Cairo, Egypt
heba.fathy@yahoo.com
[2] Department of Computer Science, British University in Egypt, Cairo, Egypt
mostafa.salama@gmail.com
[3] Faculty of Computers and Information, Cairo University
aboitcairo@gmail.com
[4] Hannam University, Korea
taihoonn@hannam.ac.kr

Abstract. Feature selection is a preprocessing step to machine learning, used to reduce the dimensionality of the dataset by removing irrelevant data. Variety of feature selection methods have been developed in the literature in order to increas the learning accuracy and reduce its complexity. In this paper we proposed a Bi-Layer behavioral-based feature selection approach. The proposed approach consists of two layers, in the first layer information gain is used to rank the features and select a new set of features depending on a global maxima classification accuracy. Then, in the second layer a new set of features is selected from within the first layer redacted data by searching for a group of local maximum classification accuracy in order to increase the number of reduced features. To evaluate the proposed approach it is applied on NSL-KDD dataset, where the number of features is reduced from 41 to 34 features in the first layer. Then reduced from 34 to 20 features in the second layer, which leads to improve the classification accuracy.

Keywords: Redundancy, Feature selection, Information gain, Network Intrusion Classification.

1 Introduction

Intrusion detection system (IDS) is a major research problem in network security. The IDS goal is to dynamically identify unusual access or attacks to secure the networks [1,2]. Hence, Network-based IDS is a valuable tool for the defense in depth of computer networks. It looks for known or potential malicious activities in the network traffic and raises an alarm whenever a suspicious activity is detected.

One of the important research challenges for constructing high performance IDS is dealing with data containing large number of features. Irrelevant and redundant features of the dataset complex IDS and reduce the detection accuracy as well. Therefor, dataset dimensional reduction is an active research area

T.-h. Kim et al. (Eds.): SecTech 2011, CCIS 259, pp. 195–203, 2011.
© Springer-Verlag Berlin Heidelberg 2011

in the field of machine learning and pattern recognition [3,4,5]. The dimensionality reduction of the dataset can be achieved by feature extraction or feature selection. Feature selection aims to choose an optimal subset of features that are necessary to increase the predictive accuracy and reduce the complexity of learned results[6,7]. Different feature selection methods are proposed to enhance the performance of IDS [8]. One of the most common feature selection method is information gain[9].

In this paper, we propose a bi-layer behavioral-based feature selection approach with the aim to improve the network intrusion classification accuracy. The proposed approach consists of two layers, the first layer used information gain method to rank the features and select a new set of features depending on a global maxima classification accuracy . Followed by a second layer which select a new set of features from within the first layer redacted data by searching for a group of local maximum classification accuracy in order to increase the number of reduced features. To evaluate the performance of the proposed bi-layer behavioral-based feature selection approach several experiments are conducted on NSL-KDD datasets using J48 classifier. The results obtained show effectiveness of the proposed approach over single level feature selection method.

The rest of this paper is organized as follows: Section 2 gives an overview of data reduction and information gain. Section 3 describes the proposed Bi-layer behavioral-based feature selection approach. The experimental results and conclusions are presented in Section 4 and 5 respectively.

2   An Overview

This section gives a brief overview of feature selection and Information gain.

2.1   Data Reduction: Feature Selection

Data dimensionality reduction is a preprocessing step before classification. It is purpose is to improve the classification performance through the removal of redundant or irrelevant features. The dimensionality reduction can be achieved in two different ways feature extraction and feature selection. Feature extraction methods create a new set of features by linear or nonlinear combination of the original features. While, feature selection methods generate a new set of features by selecting only a subset of the original features.

Based on the evaluation criteria feature selection methods fall into two categories: filter approach [6,10] and wrapper [11,12] approach. Filter approaches evaluate and select the new set of features depending on the general characteristics of the data without involving any machine algorithm. The features are ranked based on certain statistical criteria, where features with highest ranking values are selected. Frequently used filter methods include chi-square test [13], information gain [9], and Pearson correlation coefficients [14].

Wrapper approaches use a predetermined machine algorithm and use the classification performance as the evaluation criterion to select the new features set.

Machine learning algorithms such as ID3 [15] and Bayesian networks [16] are commonly used as induction algorithm for wrapper approaches.

Advantages of the filter based approaches are the low computational cost and the independent of the learning algorithm. Thus, they can easily scale up to high-dimensional datasets and have proven to be more practical than wrapper approach for application of large datasets [17].

2.2   Information Gain

The information gain of a given attribute X with respect to the class attribute Y is the reduction in uncertainty about the value of Y, after observing values of X. It is given by

$$IG = Y \mid X \tag{1}$$

When Y and X are discrete variables that take values in $y_1...y_k$ and $x_1...x_l$ then the uncertainty about the value of Y is measured by its entropy

$$H(Y) = -\sum_{i=1}^{k} P(y_i) log_2(P(y_i)) \tag{2}$$

where $P(y_i)$ is the prior probabilities for all values of Y.

The uncertainty about the value of Y after observing values of X is given by the conditional entropy of Y given X

$$H(Y \mid X) - \sum_{j=l}^{n} P(x_j) \sum_{i=1}^{k} P(y_i \mid x_j) log_2(P(y_i \mid x_j)) \tag{3}$$

where $P(y_i \mid x_j)$ is the posterior probabilities of Y given the values of X.

Thus, the information gain is given by:

$$IG(Y \mid X) = H(Y) - H(Y \mid X) \tag{4}$$

Following this measure, an attribute X is regarded more correlated to class Y than attribute Z, if $IG(Y \mid X) > IG(Y \mid Z)$.

We can rank the correlations of each attribute to the class and select key attributes based on the calculated information gain [18].

3   Proposed Approach: Bi-Layer Behavioral-Based Feature Selection

In network intrusion detection problem, the number of selected features to train the IDS are still high after applying the conventional feature selection methods. Thus, a second feature selection layer should be added to decrease the number of features without affecting the classification accuracy.

The Bi-layer behavioral-based feature selection approach consists of two layers as shown in Fig.1. In the first layer information gain is used to rank the features, where the classification accuracy is tested sequentially starting from the top ranked features. Depending on a global maxima classification accuracy a new set of features is selected. Then, the second layer select a new set of features from within the first layer redacted data in order to increase the number of reduced features. It search for a group of local maximum classification accuracy depending on the variation of the classification accuracy. The proposed Bi-layer behavioral-based feature selection approach is based on a hypothesis that features that leads to classification accuracy less than or equal to the accuracy of previous ranked feature can be removed. Fig 2 shows the variation of the classification accuracy, where a global maxima accuracy is defined; within the global maxima area a set of local maxima is defined. Thus, the new features set will be the union of the shaded area under the locals maxima and global maxima.

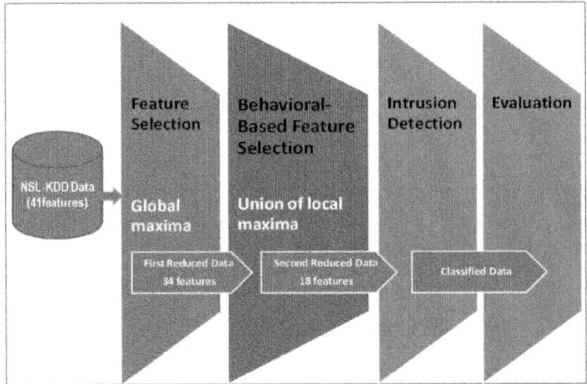

Fig. 1. Bi-layer behavioral-based feature selection approach

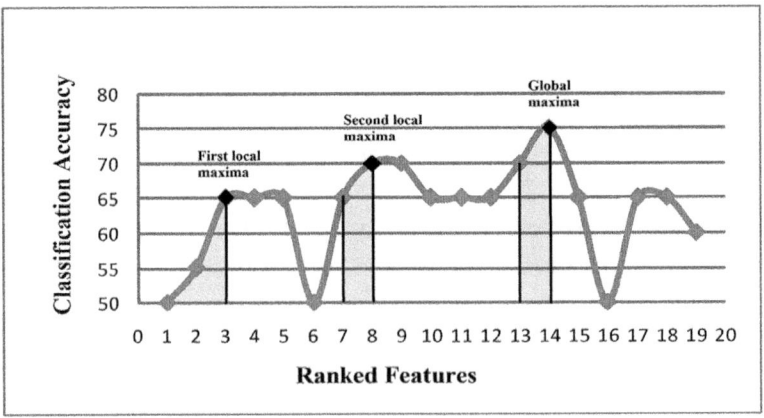

Fig. 2. The variation of the classification accuracy on ranked features

The algorithm of the proposed Bi-layer behavioral-based feature selection approach is given in algorithm 1:

Algorithm 1. Bi-layer behavioral-based feature selection approach

---

Input: set A of n selected features, sorted according the information gain ranked values.
Output: reduced set R of the selected features

    Define an array CA of n cells
    for $i = 1$ to n **do**
        Construct a data set that contains the first i features in the input data set
        Apply J48 classifier and assign the resulted accuracy to $CA[i]$
    end for
    Define a variable c to indicate the the current classification accuracy
    Define a variable p to indicate the the previous classification accuracy
    Define a variable max_c to indicate the maximum accuracy reached so far
    $max_c = 0$
    $p = 0$;
    for $i = 1$ to n **do**
      $c = CA[i]$
      if $c > p$ and $c > max_c$ **then**
        $A[i]$ to the set R
        $max_c = c$
      end if
      $p = c$
    end for

---

4 Experiments and Analysis

This section give a description for the network intrusion detection dataset used at the experimients and the performance measurements; and discusses the results of the proposed approach.

4.1 Network Intrusion Dataset Characteristics

NSL-KDD [19] is a dataset used for the evaluation of researches in network intrusion detection systems. NSL-KDD consists of selected records of the complete KDD'99 dataset [20]. Each NSL-KDD connection record contains 41 features have either discrete or continuous values, and is labeled as either normal or an attack. The training set contains a total of 22 training attack types, with additional to 17 types of attacks in the testing set. The attacks fall into four categories:DoS e.g Neptune, Smurf, Pod and Teardrop, R2L e.g Guess-password, Ftp-write, Imap and Phf, U2R e.g Buffer-overflow, Load-module, Perl and Spy, and Probing eg. Port-sweep, IP-sweep, Nmap and Satan.

It was found that not all the 41 features of NSL-KDD dataset are inportant for intrusion detection learning. Therefore, the performance of IDS may be improved by using feature selection methods [21].

4.2 Performance Measurements

The classification performance of an intrusion detection system depends on its True negatives (TN), True positives (TP), False positives (FP) and False negatives (FN). TN as well as True positives TP correspond to a correct prediction of the IDS. TN and TP indicates that normal and attacks events are successfully labeled as normal and attacks, respectively. FP refer to normal events being predicted as attacks; while FN are attack events incorrectly predicted as normal [22].

The classification performance is measured by the *precision, recall* and *F − measure*; which are calculated based on the confusion matrix given in Table 1.

Table 1. Confusion Matrix

		Predicted Class	
		Normal	Attake
Actual Class	Normal	True positives (TP)	False negatives (FN)
	Attake	False positives (FP)	True negatives (TN)

$$Recall = \frac{TP}{TP + FN} \tag{5}$$

$$Precision = \frac{TP}{TP + FP} \tag{6}$$

$$F - measure = \frac{2 * Recall * Precision}{Recall + Precision} \tag{7}$$

An IDS should achieve a high recall without loss of precision, where F-measure is a weighted mean that assesses the trade-off between them.

4.3 Bi-Layer Behavioral-Based Feature Selection Approach Results and Analysis

The NSL- KDD dataset are taken to evaluate the proposed Bi-layer behavioral-based feature selection approach. All experiments have been performed using Intel Core 2 Duo 2.26 GHz processor with 2 GB of RAM and weka software [23].

The 41 features of the NSL-KDD data set are evaluated and ranked according to the information gain method. Then, forward feature selection is applied to the ranked feature space, where classification accuracy is measured by j48 classifier. The variation of j48 classification accuracy is given in fig 3, as shown the classification accuracy leads to seven local maxima and a global maxima. In the conventional forward feature selection method all the 35 features before the

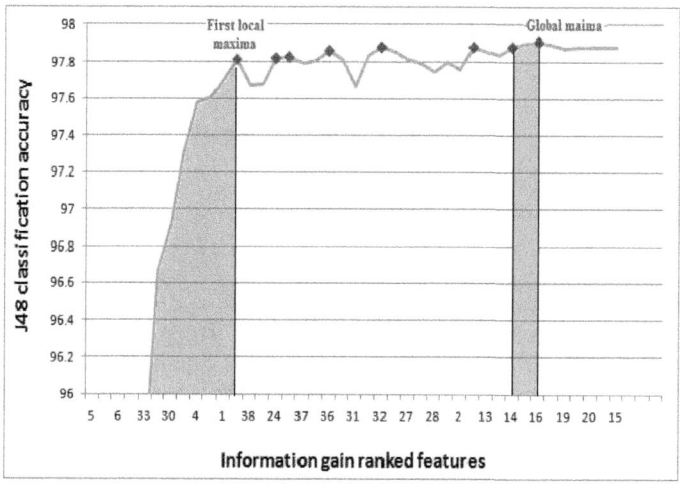

Fig. 3. Variation of J48 classification accuracy on ranked feature space

global maxima will be selected. However, in the proposed Bi-layer behavioral-based feature selection approach, only 20 features will be selected depending on the local maxima points.

Table 2 gives the $F - Measure$ comparison results based 10 fold cross-validation.

Table 2. $F - Measure$ comparison of proposed Bi-layer behavioral-based feature selection and conventional forward feature selection

Feature selection method	Number of features	F-Measure
Non	41	97.9 %
forward feature	35	98.6%
Bi-layer behavioral-based	20	99.2%

It is clear from table 2 that for Bi-layer behavioral-based feature selection the classification accuracy increased to 99.2 while the number of feature is decreased to 20 features.

5 Conclusion

This paper proposed a a Bi-Layer behavioral-based feature selection approach that depends on the behavior of the classification accuracy according to ranked feature. The proposed approach achieve better performance in terms of F-measure with reduced feature set. Experiments on well known NSL-KDD datasets are conducted to demonstrate the superiority of the proposed approach. The experiments shows that the proposed approach improved the accuracy to 99.2, while reducing the number of features from 41 to 20 features.

References

1. Tsai, C., Hsu, Y., Lin, C., Lin, W.: Intrusion detection by machine learning: A review. Expert Systems with Applications 36, 11994–12000 (2009)
2. Debar, H., Dacier, M., Wespi, A.: Towards a taxonomy of intrusion-detection systems. Computer Networks 31, 805–822 (1999)
3. Kuchimanchi, G., Phoha, V., Balagani, K., Gaddam, S.: Dimension reduction using feature extraction methods for real-time misuse detection systems. In: Fifth Annual IEEE Proceedings of Information Assurance Workshop, pp. 195–202 (2004)
4. Li, Y., Xia, J., Zhang, S., Yan, J., Ai, X., Dai, K.: An efficient intrusion detection system based on support vector machines and gradually feature removal method. Expert Systems with Applications 39, 424–430 (2012)
5. Amiri, F., Yousefi, M., Lucas, C., Shakery, A., Yazdani, N.: Mutual information-based feature selection for intrusion detection systems. Journal of Network and Computer Applications 34, 1184–1199 (2011)
6. Dash, M., Choi, K., Scheuermann, P., Liu, H.: Feature selection for clusteringa filter solution. In: Proceedings of the Second International Conference on Data Mining, pp. 115–122 (2002)
7. Koller, D., Sahami, M.: Toward optimal feature selection. In: Proceedings of the Thirteenth International Conference on Machine Learning, pp. 284–292 (1996)
8. Tsang, C., Kwong, S., Wang, H.: Genetic-fuzzy rule mining approach and evaluation of feature selection techniques for anomaly intrusion detection. Pattern Recognition 40, 2373–2391 (2007)
9. Ben-Bassat, M.: Pattern recognition and reduction of dimensionality. In: Handbook of Statistics II, vol. 1, pp. 773–791. North-Holland, Amsterdam (1982)
10. Yu, L., Liu, H.: Feature selection for high-dimensional data: a fast correlation-based filter solution. In: Proceedings of the Twentieth International Conference on Machine Learning, pp. 856–863 (2003)
11. Kim, Y., Street, W., Menczer, F.: Feature selection for unsupervised learning via evolutionary search. In: Proceedings of the Sixth ACM SIGKDD International Conference on Knowledge Discovery and Data Mining, pp. 365–369 (2000)
12. Kohavi, R., John, G.H.: Wrappers for feature subset selection. Artificial Intelligence 97, 273–324 (1997)
13. Jin, X., Xu, A., Bie, R., Guo, P.: Machine Learning Techniques and Chi-Square Feature Selection for Cancer Classification Using SAGE Gene Expression Profiles. In: Li, J., Yang, Q., Tan, A.-H. (eds.) BioDM 2006. LNCS (LNBI), vol. 3916, pp. 106–115. Springer, Heidelberg (2006)
14. Peng, H., Long, F., Ding, C.: Feature selection based on mutual information criteria of max-dependency, max- relevance,and min redundancy. IEEE Transactions on Pattern Analysis and Machine Intelligence 27, 1226–1238 (2005)
15. Quinlan, J.R.: Induction of Decision Trees. Machine Learning 1, 81–106 (1986)
16. Jemili, F., Zaghdoud, M., Ahmed, M.: Intrusion detection based on Hybrid propagation in Bayesian Networks. In: Proceedings of the IEEE International Conference on Intelligence and Security Informatics, pp. 137–142 (2009)
17. Veerabhadrappa, Rangarajan, L.: Bi-level dimensionality reduction methods using feature selection and feature extraction. International Journal of Computer Applications 4, 33–38 (2010)
18. Wang, W., Gombault, S., Guyet, T.: Towards fast detecting intrusions: using key attributes of network traffic. In: The Third IEEE International Conference on Internet Monitoring and Protection, Bucharest, pp. 86–91 (2008)

19. Tavallaee, M., Bagheri, E., Lu, W., Ghorbani, A.A.: A Detailed Analysis of the KDD CUP 99 Data Set. In: Proceeding of the 2009 IEEE Symposium on Computational Intelligence in Security and Defense Application, CISDA (2009)
20. KDD 1999 dataset Irvine, CA, USA (July 2010),
    http://kdd.ics.uci.edu/databases
21. Kayacik, H.G., Zincir-Heywood, A.N., Heywood, M.I.: Selecting features for intrusion detection: A Feature relevance analysis on KDD 99 intrusion detection datasets. In: Proceedings of the Third Annual Conference on Privacy, Security and Trust, PST 2005 (2005)
22. Duda, R.O., Hart, P.E., Stork, D.G.: Pattern Classification, 2nd edn. JohnWiley & Sons, USA (2001)
23. Weka: Data Mining Software in java, http://www.cs.waikato.ac.nz/ml/weka/

A Parameterized Privacy-Aware Pub-sub System in Smart Work

Yuan Tian, Biao Song, and Eui-Nam Huh

Department of Computer Engineering
KyungHee University Global Campus ICNS Lab
Suwon, South Korea
{ytian,bsong,johnhuh}@khu.ac.kr

Abstract. Ubiquitous and pervasive computing contribute significantly to the quality of life for dependent people by providing personalized services in smart environments. Due to the sensitive nature of home scenario, and the invasive nature of surveillance, the deployment of those services still require privacy and trust issues for dependent people. Various technologies have been proposed to address the privacy issue in smart home, however, they rarely consider the feasibility and possibility of their privacy strategies. Given that a huge batch of data is captured and processed in smart home system, it may not be easily implemented as issues related to data sharing and delivery may arise. Our work seeks to aid pub/sub mechanisms in smart home environment with the ability to handle parameterized constraints, simultaneously ensuring users' privacy and solves emergency tasks efficiently.

Keywords: Smart Home Technology, Pub-sub System, Privacy Preference.

1 Introduction

The concept of smart homes, also named intelligent homes, has been used for years to describe the networking devices and equipments in the house. Smart digital home technology is a way used to make all electronic devices around a house act smart or more automated. The smart home technology [1,5] gives a totally different flexibility and functionality than does conventional installations and environmental control systems, because of the programming, the integration and the units reacting on messages submitted through the network. There are many popular features currently available to make houses smarter. The illumination may for example be controlled automatically, or lamps can be lit as other things happen in the house. It is also widely used for health and social care support in order to enhance residents' safety and monitor health conditions. For example, leading elderly people an independent lifestyle away from hospitals and also avoid having expensive caregivers [2], enabling disabled people though appropriate design of technology to facilitate their life [3], and detecting emergency cases like fire before it happens [7].

The basic operation of smart technology is to collect video, audio, or binary sensor data from the home environment and controlled remotely through the residential

T.-h. Kim et al. (Eds.): SecTech 2011, CCIS 259, pp. 204–214, 2011.
© Springer-Verlag Berlin Heidelberg 2011

gateways [4], while the publish/subscribe (pub/sub for short) paradigm is used to deliver those data from a source to interested clients in an asynchronous way[23]. Much research has been done in the context of designing Pub/Sub systems in smart works [21, 22, 24]. However, due to the sensitive nature of home, and the invasive nature of surveillance [8], privacy has also to be concerned when we design the pub-sub system for smart environment [9, 10].

Various technologies have been proposed to address the privacy issue in smart home. Simon et al.[8, 9] proposed a framework to implement privacy within a smart house environment which privacy policy is dynamically altered based on the situation or context. Liampotis et al. [11] elaborated a privacy framework aims to address all privacy issues that arise by providing facilities, which support multiple digital identities of personal self-improving smart spaces owners, and privacy preferences for deriving privacy policies based on the context and the trustworthiness of the third parties.

However, the previous approaches declared rules about how to leverage the privacy problems in smart home, whereas they did not consider about the feasibility and possibility of their proposed system. Given that a huge batch of data is captured and processed in smart home systems, issues related to data sharing and delivery may arise. The overhead produced from context and privacy protection hinders the efficiency of the proposed system as implementation of privacy will result in extra computational cost. For example, storing the static context and matching the rules with privacy preferences may cause response delay.

In order to address the privacy concern and to assure the system efficiency after applying the privacy strategy, in this paper, we describe a novel publish/subscribe system for a privacy-aware smart home environment, which provides high performance and scalability with parameterized attributes. Parameterized subscriptions are employed in our pub-sub system to improve the efficiency by updating the state variables in subscription automatically rather than having the subscriber re-submit his/her subscription repeatedly. We adopt privacy predicate in the proposed pub-sub system to provide context-based access control. The privacy predicate can be utilized by privacy manager and data subject as a more flexible way to maintain the privacy. The privacy predicate defined by privacy manager, as the privacy policy for access control, is combined with subscription and stored in pub-sub system. The privacy predicate defined by data subject, as the privacy preference for access control, is combined with event that needs to be matched with subscription. In our system, the parameterized technologies are also utilized by privacy manager and data subject to create dynamic privacy policy and preference which are self-adaptive against the change of context. Thus, the privacy management cost can be reduced since updating privacy policy and preference does not require the costly operation of cancelling and re-submitting.

The remainder of this article is structured as follows. Section 2 covers background materials. In section 3 we first motivate our approach by introducing distinctive use cases, and then present a component-based view of the proposed system and the design approach in section 4. In the end, we conclude our paper and present future work in Section 5.

2   Related Works

Our research is motivated by improving the efficiency of privacy-aware smart home environment through parameterized pub-sub system. Accordingly, the review in this section covers the following issues: (1) context-aware smart home and work related to achieving privacy preservation by means of such methods, (2) publish/subscribe system, (3) parameterized subscription.

2.1   Context-Awareness in Smart Environment

The concept of context was defined by Anind [17] as "any information that can be used to characterize the situation of an entity", while the entity can be a person, place, or object which relevant to the interaction between the user and application. Generally, three context dimensions [19] were categorized: physical context, computational context, and user context. Context awareness [10], which refers to the idea that computers can both sense, and react based on their environment, play a big role in developing and maintaining a smart home.

2.2   Publish/Subscribe System

Publish/subscribe system, also known as pub-sub in short, has been discussed extensively in the past [12-16]. A pub-sub system is a common communication system in large-scale enterprise applications, enabling loosely coupled interaction between entities whose location and behaviors may vary throughout the lifetime of the system. Subscribers who are interested in a set of attributes register their interests in the system. The list of these subscriptions is then indexed. Once a particular event occurs, it searches through its database of subscribers and finds all the subscribers who are interested in this event and notifies them that an event of their interest has occurred [13]. An entity may become both a publisher and subscriber, sending and receiving messages within the system. In the pub/sub model, subscribers typically receive only a subset of the total messages published. The process of selecting messages for reception and processing is called filtering. There are two common types of subscription schemes: topic-based subscription and content-based subscription. In a topic-based scheme, a message is published to one of a fixed set of "topics" or named logical channels. Subscribers in a topic-based system will receive all messages published to the topics to which they subscribe, and all subscribers to a topic will receive the same messages. The publisher is responsible for defining the classes of messages to which subscribers can subscribe. In a content-based system, messages are not necessarily belong to a particular topic. Instead, messages are only delivered to a subscriber if the attributes or content of those messages match constraints defined by the subscriber. The subscriber is responsible for classifying the messages. The advantage of a content-based scheme is its loosely-coupled: publishers are loosely coupled to subscribers, and do not even know of their existence.

2.3   Parameterized Subscription

Unlike traditional publish/subscribe system which commonly deal with static subscriptions, parameterized subscriptions [12] depend on one or more parameters, which the state varies or maintained automatically by the pub-sub servers over time. Several excellent features about parameterized subscriptions can be considered. For example, there is no need for the costly operation of cancelling and re-submitting the whole subscription when updating a subscription. Moreover, as the parameters are updated by the publish/subscribe system itself, thus it leverages existing machinery.

3   System Architecture

In smart home environment, a centralized publish/subscribe system works for a single family or a single building. Figure 1 shows our proposed pub/sub system. The system generally consists of several *Data Sources* (DS), *Subscribers* (SS), a central *Privacy Engine* (PE) and a *Matching Engine* (ME). The DSs, which are usually sensors, publish sensed data as events. The SS can be doctors or caregivers who require information from the smart environment. The events through PE and ME are routed to appropriate SSs which can be Doctors or caregivers. They are allowed to subscribe information through household electrical appliances, alarms, mobile, desktop applications, or web portals. In the following section, we will explain how the parameterized publish/subscribe system works through each component.

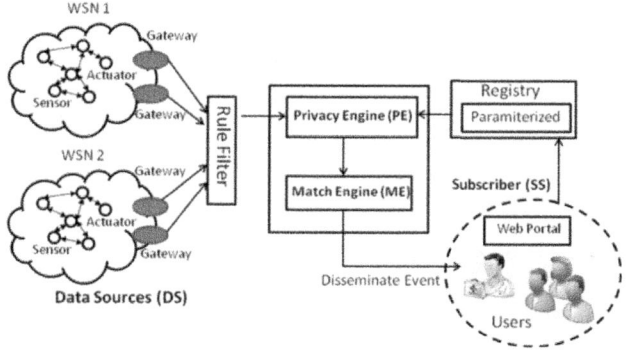

Fig. 1. Overall System Flow of the Proposed Privacy-aware Pub-sub System

4   Parameterized Publish/Subscribe Subscription and Event

In this section, we explain the static and parameterized publish/subscribe subscription as well as the parameterized event, each one is given an example in order to help illustrate what kinds of applications we want to support within a home environment, and roughly how they would work in our proposed system.

Let s_{ij} be the jth subscription published by SS_i. Once the subscription is published, it is first sent to PE which could generate and attach one or many privacy constraints on that subscription. Each constraint is expressed as a static or parameterized privacy point. We define ps_{ij} as the privacy-aware subscription generated from s_{ij}.

Let e represent an event which may contain a variety of predicates. For our discussion and example in this section, we refer to only one predicate $e.\gamma$. After an event e is generated, PE first receives the event and labels it with one or many privacy points. Also, for the simplicity of expression in this section, we refer to only one privacy point. Let pe represent the privacy-aware event generated from e, $pe.\rho$ be the privacy predicate and $pe.\gamma$ be the sensor data predicate. Here, $pe.\gamma$ equals to $e.\gamma$ and $pe.\rho$ contains the attached privacy point. When the event is understood, we just use ρ and γ to represent.

The basic form of a privacy-aware subscription is called a static subscription, which is defined and summarized as follows. We also provide several examples to explain each definition for a better understanding.

4.1   Static Privacy-Aware Subscription

A static privacy-aware subscription ps is defined by $ps : c(pe)$,where $c(pe)$ is a fixed predicate function defined on an event pe . Suppose SS_1 is a mobile application running on doctor Lee's cell phone. Since doctor Lee wants to monitor his patient Alice's body temperature information, through SS_1 he sends a subscription s_{11} to the publish/subscribe system in Alice's home.

Example 1

In this example, we assume that Alice is the only person lives in her house. As shown in Figure 2, the s_{11} subscribes those events in which $\gamma > 37.5$.

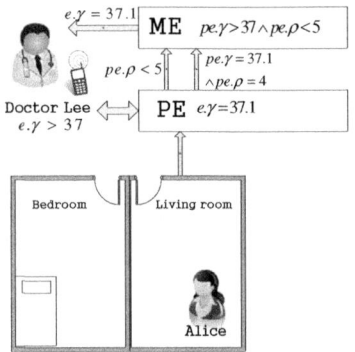

Fig. 2. Illustration of Example 1

Based on the role of subscriber doctor Lee, PE gives a privacy point to this subscription (suppose it is 5), generates ps_{11} and sends it to ME. Consequently, ps_{11} subscribes those events in which $ps : c(pe) \equiv (\gamma > 37.5 \wedge \rho < 5)$.

In Alice's living room, this is a body temperature sensor installed on a sofa. The sensor is considered as a DS in the system. Suppose at one moment Alice is sitting in the sofa and her body temperature is 38. To send this information to the system, the sensor generate an event e_1 where $e_1.\gamma = 38$. As the data is generated in living room, we suppose that PE decides the privacy point as 4. Thus PE produces pe_1 where $pe_1.\gamma = 38 \wedge pe_1.\rho = 4$. Then pe_1 is delivered to ME and matched with ps_{11} over there. By removing the privacy part, ME returns $e_1.\gamma = 38$ to SS_1.

Here we present another example when the event is not match with the subscription. Event e_2, where $e_2.\gamma = 37.7$, was generated by the sensors in Alice's bedroom. As bedroom is a place which needs more privacy protection than living room, the privacy point of this event is set to 6 by PE. Consequently, the privacy-aware event $pe_2(pe_2.\gamma = 37.7 \wedge pe_2.\rho = 6)$ cannot be matched with ps_{11} in ME and subscriber SS_1 cannot receive this event because $ps_{11} : c(pe_2) \equiv (pe_2.\gamma > 37.5 \wedge pe_2.\rho < 5) \equiv false$.

4.2   Parameterized Privacy-Aware Subscription

4.2.1   Sensor Data Parameterized Predicate

A parameterized privacy-aware subscription ps is defined by $ps : u[p_1, p_2, ..., p_k](pe)$ namely, a predicate function u whose evaluation depends on one or more parameters, p_1 through p_k. Each parameter p_i is in turn defined by $p_i : (v_0, f(pe))$ where v_0 is parameter p_i's initial value, and $f(pe)$ is the parameter update function, which specifies how p_i is to change over time.

In our model, some privacy related parameters can be defined by privacy manager, and updated by PE. When the central PE receives a parameterized privacy rule from the privacy manager, it allocates a state variable for each parameter p_i defined in the rule, and assigns it the initial value of $p_i.v_0$, as given in the parameter definition. Other parameters are defined by subscribers, and maintained by ME. Similarly, when subscriber publishes a parameterized subscription, the central ME allocates a state variable for each subscriber defined parameter and initiates the variable using the given initial value.

We use $p_i.v$ to denote the state variable for p_i. When a new privacy-aware event pe arrives, the value contained in $p_i.v$ at that time will be used to evaluate the predicate function u, which then to determine whether pe is a match for this privacy-aware subscription ps.

Example 2

We suppose now Dr. Lee wants to change his subscription to "the highest temperature". By using the static subscription, Dr. Lee's mobile application has to cache a variable saving the highest temperature information locally. Whenever this variable is changed, the mobile application needs to withdraw the previous subscription at the publish/subscribe system and publish a new one using the cached highest temperature information. This static approach is obviously inefficient since it wastes network resources and may result in rebuilt of matching indexes on the publish/subscribe server [1, 2].

To solve this problem, we can formulate it as a parameterized privacy-aware subscription (the privacy part remains same) $ps_{11} : u[p](pe) \equiv (pe.\gamma > p.v \wedge pe.\rho < 5)$ With $p : (0, p.v = (pe.\gamma > p.v ? pe.\gamma : p.v))$ where $pe.\gamma > p.v ? pe.\gamma : p.v$ returns $pe.\gamma$ when $pe.\gamma > p.v \equiv true$, or returns $p.v$ when $pe.\gamma > p.v \equiv false$.

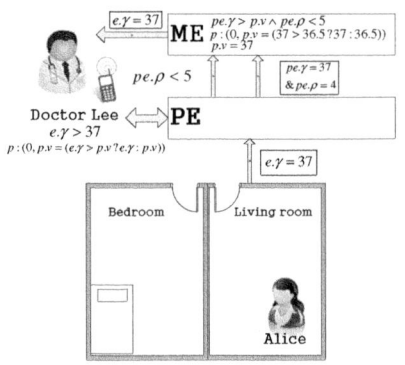

Fig. 3. Illustration of Example 2

Suppose that at a certain point in time ME caches a value of 36.5 for $p.v$ as shown in Figure 3. Assume then a new event pe_1 is generated with $pe_3.\gamma = 37 \wedge pe_3.\rho = 4$. Since $ps_{11} : u[p](pe_3) \equiv (37 > 36.5 \wedge 4 < 5) \equiv true$, pe_3 is said to be a match of ps_{11}. The temperature information contained in pe_3 will be sent to SS_1. Also, $p.v$ is automatically updated to 37 as $p : (0, p.v = (37 > 36.5 ? 37 : 36.5))$. After that, the events containing a γ less or equal to 37 cannot be matched with ps_{11}.

4.2.2 Privacy-Aware Parameterized Predicate

In the same "temperature monitor" scenario, we assume that Alice is ill abed with high body temperature.

Example 3

On Alice's bed, a sensor at a certain point in time generate an event $e_2 (e_2.\gamma = 39)$. As the event is generated in bedroom, *PE* generates a privacy-aware event

$pe_2(pe_2.\gamma = 39 \wedge pe_2.\rho = 6)$ containing a comparatively high privacy point $\rho = 6$. By default setting where Dr. Lee's privacy point is 5, he is not allowed to see this information because $ps_{11} : u[p](pe_2) \equiv (39 > 36.5 \wedge 6 < 5) \equiv false$.

However, the importance of privacy protection at that time should be degraded. We then suppose that privacy manager wants to change the privacy rule to make sure Dr. Lee can get Alice's body temperature information when Alice is sick. Rather than assigning a static privacy point to Dr. Lee's subscription, privacy manager defines a new rule to produce dynamic privacy point based on Alice's body temperature information. The rule can be implemented using a parameterized privacy-aware   subscription: $ps_{11} : u[p](pe) \equiv (pe.\gamma > 37 \wedge pe.\rho < p.v)$ with $p : (5, p.v = (pe.\gamma > 36.5?(5 + pe.\gamma - 36.5):5))$ where $pe.\gamma > 36.5?(5 + pe.\gamma - 36.5):5$ returns $(5 + pe.\gamma - 36.5)$ when $pe.\gamma > 36.5 \equiv true$,   or   returns   5   when $pe.\gamma > 36.5 \equiv false$. As p is a privacy related parameter, $p.v$ is cached by PE. In this case, PE can dynamically increase the privacy point for Dr. Lee's subscription when Alice's body temperature is higher than 36.5. The process is shown in Figure 4.

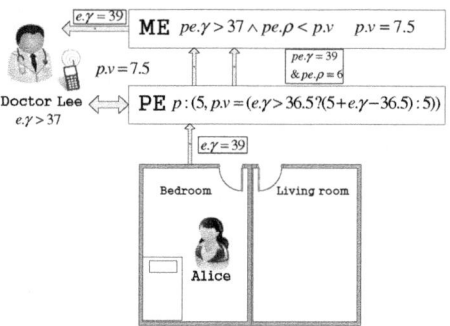

Fig. 4. Illustration of Example 3

According to the update function $f(pe_2)$, PE updates the privacy related parameter in ps_{11}. Since $p : (5, p.v = (39 > 36.5?(5 + 39 - 36.5):5))$, PE assigns 7.5 to $p.v$. This change makes sure that Dr. Lee is allowed to receive the event generated in bedroom since $ps_{11} : u[p](pe_2) \equiv (39 > 37 \wedge 6 < 7.5) \equiv true$.

4.3   A Parameterized Privacy-Aware Event

A parameterized privacy-aware event pe is defined by $pe = e \cup c[p_1, p_2, ..., p_k](e)$ where the privacy point calculator c depends on one or more parameters, p_1 through p_k. Unlike the predicate function which only provides a Boolean value, the privacy point calculator can generate a set of privacy points based on the parameters and the information contained in the event. Each parameter p_i is in turn defined by $p_i : (v_0, f(e))$ where v_0 is parameter p_i's initial value, and $f(e)$ is the parameter update function, which specifies how p_i is to change over time. When the central PE receives a parameterized privacy preference from the data subject, it allocates a state variable for each parameter p_i defined in the preference, and assigns it the initial value of $p_i.v_0$, as given in the parameter definition.

We also use $p_i.v$ to denote the state variable for p_i. When a new event e arrives, the value contained in $p_i.v$ at that time will be used to calculate one or many privacy points, which are then combined with the event e as the privacy-aware subscription pe.

As the system allows data subject to set privacy preference, we present another example showing that Alice can also assign dynamic privacy point to the events containing her body temperature information.

Example 4

In the same "temperature monitor" scenario, we assume that Alice sometimes takes exercise in her living room. Since her body temperature can be increased during that time, her privacy will be disclosed if any subscriber gets that information. To avoid this problem, Alice uses parameterized privacy-aware event to control her privacy. Particularly, Alice requests PE to maintain her lowest body temperature information using a parameter. Based on that, a parameterized privacy-aware event pe generated in her living room is defined by $pe = e \cup c[p](e)$ with the formula of privacy point calculator:

$$c[p](e) = (e.\gamma > p.v \,?(4 + e.\gamma - p.v) : 4)) \text{ and } p : (40, p.v = (e.\gamma < p.v \,? e.\gamma : p.v)) \,.$$

Suppose that at a certain point in time PE caches $p.v = 36.5$. Assume then a new event $e_3 (e_3.\gamma = 38)$ is generated. Using the privacy point calculator, we can get $c[p](e_3) = (38 > 36.5\,?(4 + 38 - 36.5) : 4)) = 5.5$. Then we have $pe_3(pe_3.\gamma = 38 \wedge pe_3.\rho = 5.5)$.

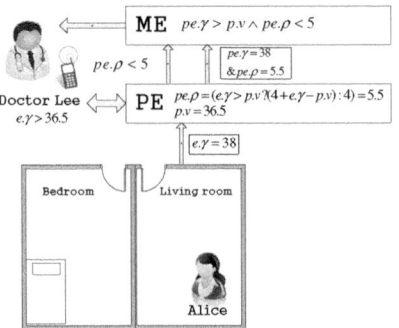

Fig. 5. Illustration of Example 4

Now we assume that Dr. Lee has published a subscription $ps_{11} : u[p](pe) \equiv (pe.\gamma > 36.5 \wedge pe.\rho < 5)$. Since Alice has made her privacy preference, event pe_3 cannot be matched with ps_{11} as $ps_{11} : u[p](pe_3) \equiv (38 > 36.5 \wedge 5.5 < 5) \equiv flase$. Alice's privacy sensitive data is successfully preserved by using parameterized privacy-aware event. The illustration is presented in Figure 5.

5 Conclusion

It has been shown that the current methods for privacy preserving in smart home are not easy to achieve for the lack of efficiency. This paper proposed a new approach for handling both privacy and efficiency in smart environment. We applied a publish/subscribe system with parameterized attributes, which solves emergency tasks efficiently. This work is still evolving and in the future work, we will apply prioritized attribute to the pub-sub system to assure that the important predicate and urgent subscription (with high priority) can be executed first. As the limitation of page, we could not present the experimental result of our work. We will also discuss about the evaluation result in our future work.

Acknowledgement. "This research was supported by the MKE(The Ministry of Knowledge Economy), Korea, under the ITRC(Information Technology Research Center) support program supervised by the NIPA(National IT Industry Promotion Agency)" (NIPA-2011-(C1090-1111-0001)).

References

1. Laberg, T., Aspelund, H., Thygesen, H.: Smart Home Technology, Planning and management in municipal services. Directorate for Social and Health Affairs
2. Jakkula, V.R., Cook, D.J., Jain, G.: Prediction Models for a Smart Home Based Health Care System. In: 21st International Conference on Advanced Information Networking and Applications Workshops (AINAW 2007), vol. 2, pp. 761–765 (2007)
3. Panek, P., Zagler, W.L., Beck, C., Seisenbacher, G.: Smart Home Applications for disabled Persons - Experiences and Perspectives. In: EIB Event 2001 - Proceedings, pp. 71–80 (2001)
4. Bierhoff, I., van Berlo, A., Abascal, J., Allen, B., Civit, A., Fellbaum, K., Kemppainen, E., Bitterman, N., Freitas, D., Kristiansson, K.: Smart home environment, pp. 110–156 (2009)
5. Robles, R.J., Kim, T.-H.: Applications, Systems and Methods in Smart Home Technology: A Review. International Journal of Advanced Science and Technology 15 (February 2010)
6. Bagüés, S.A.: Sentry@Home - Leveraging the Smart Home for Privacy in Pervasive Computing. International Journal of Smart Home 1(2) (July 2007)
7. Pesout, P., Matustik, O.: On the Way to Smart Emergency System. In: Proceedings of the 2010 Seventh International Conference on Information Technology: New Generations, ITNG 2010, pp. 311–316 (2010)
8. Moncrieff, S., Venkatesh, S., West, G.: Dynamic Privacy in a Smart House Environment. Multimedia and Expo., 2034–2037 (2007)

9. Moncrieff, S., Venkatesh, S., West, G.: Dynamic privacy assessment in a smart house environment using multimodal sensing. Transactions on Multimedia Computing, Communications, and Applications (TOMCCAP) 5(2), 10–27

10. Robles, R.J., Kim, T.-H.: Review: Context Aware Tools for Smart Home Development. International Journal of Smart Home 4(1) (January 2010)

11. Liampotis, N., Roussaki, I., Papadopoulou, E., Abu-Shaaban, Y., Williams, M.H., Taylor, N.K., McBurney, S.M., Dolinar, K.: A Privacy Framework for Personal Self-Improving Smart Spaces. In: CSE 2009, vol. 3, pp. 444–449 (2009)

12. Huang, Y., Garcia-Molina, H.: Parameterized subscriptions in publish/subscribe systems. Data & Knowledge Engineering 60(3) (March 2007)

13. Singh, M., Hong, M., Gehrke, J., Shanmugasundaram, J.: Pub-sub System, http://www.cis.cornell.edu/boom/2005/ProjectArchive/publish/ (accessed on January 2011)

14. Yoo, S., Son, J.H., Kim, M.H.: A scalable publish/subscribe system for large mobile ad hoc networks. Proceedings of Journal of Systems and Software 82(7) (July 2009)

15. Cugola, G., Frey, D., Murphy, A.L., Picco, G.P.: Minimizing the reconfiguration overhead in content-based publish-subscribe. In: Proceedings of the 2004 ACM symposium on Applied computing, SAC 2004, pp. 1134–1140 (2004)

16. Ordille, J.J., Tendick, P., Yang, Q.: Publish-subscribe services for urgent and emergency response. In: COMSWARE 2009, pp. 8.1–8.10 (2009)

17. Dey, A.K., Abowd, G.D.: Towards a better understanding of context and context-awareness. Technical Report GIT-GVU-99-22, Georgia Institute of Technology, College of Computing (1999)

18. Bettini, C., Brdiczka, O., Henricksen, K., Indulska, J., Niclas, D., Ranganathan, A., Riboni, D.: A survey of context modelling and reasoning techniques. Pervasive Mobile Computing (2009)

19. Bettini, C., Brdiczka, O., Henricksen, K., Indulska, J., Nicklas, D., Ranganathan, A., Riboni, D.: A survey of context modelling and reasoning techniques. Pervasive and Mobile Computing 6(2), 161–180 (2010)

20. Carzaniga, A., Rosenblum, D.S., Wolf, A.L.: Design and evaluation of a wide-area event notification service. Transactions on Computer Systems (TOCS) 19(3) (August 2001)

21. Zheng, Y., Cao, J.N., Liu, M., Wang, J.L.: Efficient Event Delivery in Publish/Subscribe Systems for Wireless Mesh Networks. In: Proceedings of Wireless Communications and Networking Conference, Hong Kong, China (2007)

22. Bhola, S., Strom, R., Bagchi, S., Zhao, Y., Auerbach, J.: Exactly-Once Delivery in a ContentBased Publish-subscribe System. In: Proceedings of Dependable Systems and Networks, Bethesda, MA, USA (2002)

23. Parra, J., Anwar Hossain, M., Uribarren, A., Jacob, E., El Saddik, A.: Flexible Smart Home Architecture using Device Profile for Web Services: a Peer-to-Peer Approach. International Journal of Smart Home 3(2), 39–55 (2009)

A Lightweight Access Log Filter of Windows OS Using Simple Debug Register Manipulation

Ruo Ando[1] and Kuniyasu Suzaki[2]

[1] National Institute of Information and Communication Technology,
4-2-1 Nukui-Kitamachi, Koganei, Tokyo 184-8795 Japan
ruo@nict.go.jp
[2] Advanced Industrial Science and Technology
1-1-1 Umezono Central-2, Tsukuba, Ibaraki, 305-8568, Japan

Abstract. Recently, leveraging hypervisor for inspecting Windows OS which is called as VM instospection has been proposed. In this paper, we propose a thin debugging layer to provide several solutions for current VM instrospection. First, out-of-the box monitoring has not been develoed for monitoring complicated event such as registry access of Windows OS. Second, logging inside guest OS is resource-intensive and therefore detactable. Third, shared memory should be prepared for notifying events which makes the system so complicated. To solve these problems, we emdded a simple debug register manipulation inside guest VM and modify its handler of hypervisor. In proposed system, we only change a few generic and debug register to cope with highly frequent events without allocating memory and generating file I/O. As a result, resource utilization of CPU, memory and I/O can be drastically reduced compared with commodity logging software inside Windows OS. In experiment, we have shown the result of tracking registry access of malware running on Windos OS. It is shown that proposed system can achive the same function of ProcMon of Windows OS with reasonable resource utilization. Particularly, we have achieved more than 84% of memory usage and 97% of disk access reduction compared with the case of using Proc-Mon.

1 Introduction

With the rapid advances of cloud computing, virtualization has become more pervasive. Also, diversity of desktop operating system and its environment makes virtualization more popular. For secure environment of cloud and personal computing, monitoring virtual machine is important.

VMM (virtual machine monitor) is a thin layer of software between the physical hardware and the guest operating system. The rapid increase of CPU performance enables VMM to run several operating system as virtual machine, multiplexing CPU, memory and I/O devices in reasonable processing time. Recent VMM is a successful implementation of micro kernels. Under the guest OS, VMM runs directly on the hardware of a machine which means that VMM can provides the useful inspection and interposition of guest OS. Recently,VMM introspection module is inserted as protection layer in XEN virtual machine monitor [3]. This is called VMI (Virtual Machine Introspection)[4] which solves traditional tradeoffs between two monitors.

T.-h. Kim et al. (Eds.): SecTech 2011, CCIS 259, pp. 215–227, 2011.

Recently, as well as virtualization technologies, debugging technology has been rapidly improved. Debuggers and development frameworks such as WinDBG and filter manager is provided to make debugging easier and make us monitor OS in more detailed. Also, DLL injection, filter driver of Windows OS could be helpful to debugging target software. Although VMI is not able to understand the event and semantics on guest OS, we can obtain information of event of guest OS with help of these debugging technologies.

In general, debugger is triggered in two events: software and hardware breakpoints. Software breakpoint is done by modifying debugee, In Intel architecture, INT03 is inserted in the point where breakpoint is set. Hardware breakpoint is activated when debug register is changed. In this paper, we apply hardware breakpoint for the lightweight implementation of VM intropsection.

2   Related Work

Proposed system is based on the concept of VMI (Virtual Machine Introspection). VMI has been introduced in [1]. VMI (Virtual machine introspection) is the ability of inspecting and understanding the events occurred inside virtual machine running on monitor. According to [1], Hypervisor based monitoring leverages three properties of VMM, isolation , inspection and interposition.

Recent researches of hypervisor based detection aims to solve semantic gap between VM and VMM to [10], [11] and [12] detect what is happening on VM. [10][11] propose the method to detect process and track its behavior on VM. [12] propose the modification of XEN to detect what kind of binary is executed on VM.

In generic, as current implementations of transferring information between VM and VMM, XEN has split kernel driver and XenAccess library. Split kernel driver is implementation of kernel module for XEN paravirtualization. The driver has shared memory of ring buffer and virtualized interruption mechanism. Split kernel module is implemented for network and block device. Specified for security, XenAccess is developed for memory introspection for virtual machines running on the Xen hypervisor.

3   Proposed System Overview

Proposed system is implemented in three steps: [1]modification of Windows OS using DLL injection and filter driver, [2]modification of debug register handler of virtual machine monitor and [3]putting visualization tool on host OS. Figure 1 is a brief illustration of proposed system. Our module extracts a sequence from Windows memory behavior and the sequence is transferred from VMM module to visualization tool on host OS. In following section, we also discuss modification of Windows OS. In this paper we propose visualization of memory behavior of full-virtualized Windows OS using virtual machine introspection. In proposed system, memory behavior of Windows OS is visualized by an application of the concept of virtual machine introspection. Proposed system extracts a sequence ofWindows memory behavior and transfers it to host OS by modifying the module of virtual machine monitor.

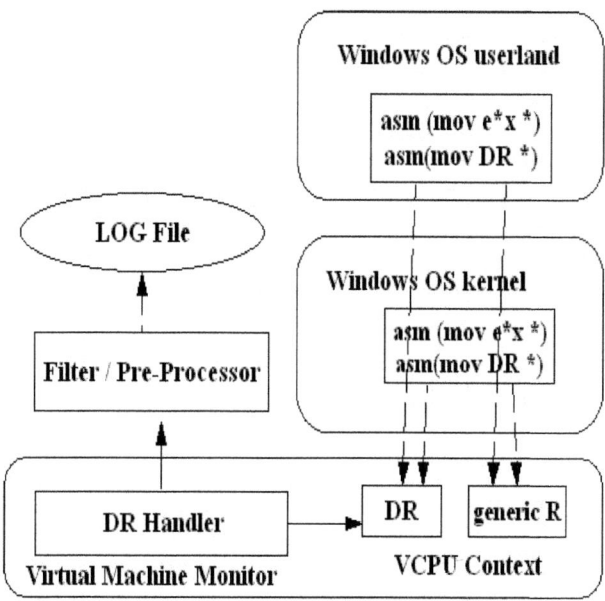

Fig. 1. Proposed system monitors DR (hardware) to be changed. When DR changes, proposed system reads generic register which is written by host OS to transfer information.

3.1   Modification of Windows OS

Although all hardware accesses pass through VMM, VMM is not able to understand semantics of guest OS, which means that VMM has no information about what kind of event is happened above. To detect events on virtualized OS correctly and achieve fine-grained monitoring, Windows OS need to be modified. Figure 2 shows the detailed illustration of proposed system, particularly the modification of Windows OS. Windows modification OS consists of three steps: [1]inserting DLL into user process, [2]inserting filter driver into kernel space, and [3]modifying IDT (interruption descriptor table) of daemon process. In this section we discuss library insertion (DLL injection) and filter driver injection.

3.2   Modificaiton of VMM

In this section discuss show the modification of XEN[3] and KVM[4]. Once the incident is detected on guest OS, the value of special register (DR/MSR) is changed. The context of virtualized CPU is stored in hypervisor stack. VMM can detect the incident of guest OS when domain context is switched because CPU context including the state of DR/MSR register is changed. Then, proposed system sends asynchronous notification to host OS. Figure 2 shows an implementation of proposed system in XEN. For asynchronous notification, software interruption is applied. Once the incident is detected in guest OS, special registers (DR/MSR) is changed (vector [1]). Then, the register handler caught this change (vector [2]) which is transferred to the host OS by software interruption generator by global pirq (vector [3]). When the host OS caught the pirq, memory snapshot is taken using facilities of QEMU I/O. Figure 3 shows an implementation of proposed system in KVM (Kernel Virtual Machine). KVM makes Linux as hypervisor. In implementation of KVM, a simple user defined signal is applied for the asynchronous notification. When the incident is detected by guest OS, the value of special registers is changed (vector [1]). When the system control is moved to VM root operation, the change is caught by register handler. Then, user defined signal is sent to QEMUmodules of KVM by control application or directly from kernel (vector [3][4][5]). Finally, signal handler invokes memory snapshot facilities using QEMU I/O module.

4 DR Based VM Introspection

For simple implementation of VMM side, proposed system only monitors the changes of DR (debug register). We have modified debug register handler to detect the change of debug register with mov instruction of guest OS. Also, some values is moved to generic registers such as EAX, EBX, ECX and EDX. A line of log is transferred for one character, byte by byte inserted into a generic register. We add some header such as string length, type of events using other generic registers.

4.1 Debug Register

In this paper we have constructed the system on KVM based on Intel x86 architecture. As we already know, x86 architecture has debug register DR0- DR6. Our system applies virtual machine introspection by monitoring these registers. Debug register is changed and accessed by register operation of MOV variants. When the CPU detects debug exception enabled, it sets low-order bits and then the debug register handler is activated. Among DR0-7, DR6 are never reset by the CPU.

4.2 Modification of Debug Register Handler

In this section discuss show the modification of modules debug register handler in virtual machine monitor. Once the incident is detected on guest OS, the value of special register (DR/MSR) is changed. The context of virtualized CPU is stored in hypervisor stack. VMM can detect the incident of guest OS when domain context is switched because CPU context including the state of DR/MSR register is changed. Then, proposed system sends asynchronous notification to host OS. In this paper we apply KVM (Kernel Virtual Machine)[2] for implementing our method. In implementation in KVM, a simple user defined signal is applied for the asynchronous notification. When the incident is detected by guest OS, the value of special registers is changed. When the system control is moved to VM root operation, the change is caught by register handler. Then, user defined signal is sent to QEMU modules of KVM by control application or directly from kernel. Finally, signal handler invokes memory snapshot facilities using QEMU I/O module.

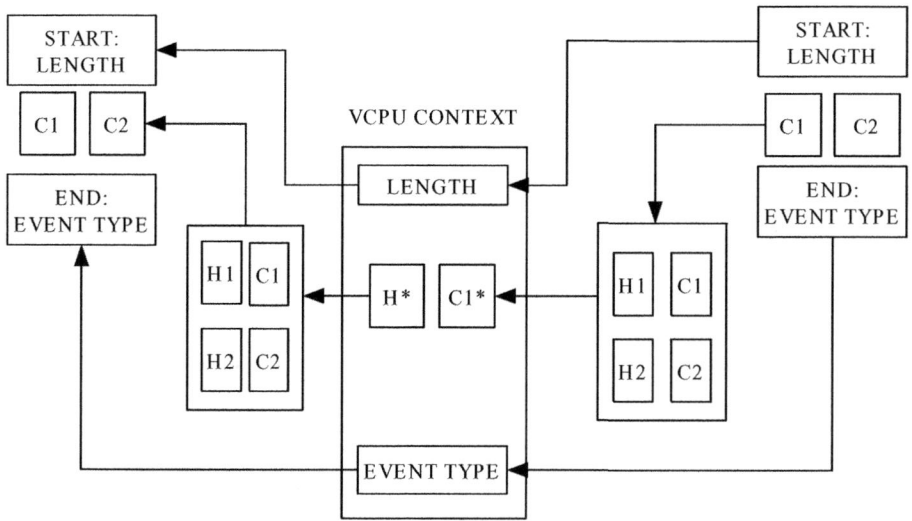

Fig. 2. Serial transfer of from guest OS to host OS using generic register debugger register. In addition to each character, header information such as length of strings and number of character is stored into generic register.

4.3   Transmission by Virtualized Register

In our systme we apply register operation to transmit information between guest and host OS instead of shared memoery. In HVM full-virtualization architecture, context switch between guest and host OS is occurred by VM entry / exit. VM entry / exit is invoked in many apects: system call, memory page fault and hardware change. Also the change of register invokes VM entry / exit. In the phase of VM entry called by debug register change, debug register handler is activated. On virtual machine monnitor side, we can obtain register of guest VM which is virtualized by this handler. Therefore proposed method of transmission by virtualized register is as follows:

```
step 1: guest VM devide log string into
one character and store the value into
register.
step 2: guest VM changes debug register.
step 3: VM Exit is occurred.
step 4: Processor control is moved to
debug register handler on virtual
machine montior.
step 5: host OS recieves the value byte
by byte.
```

In the next section, we discuss how the debug register handler needs to be modified.

4.4   Byte-by-Byte Transmission

Thrust of proposed system is only use register opeartion. Implementaion is simple. Proposed system does not use shared memory and ring buffer. Log information on guest Windows consists of strings which is transferred in byte-by-byte transmission by using generic registers. In previous work, Interface implementations between VM and VMM to transfer information have been proposed. In these implementations, shared memory and ring buffer is applied. In this paper we apply serial transfer by using generic and device driver. On guest OS, when the event we are intercepting is occurred, our system construct strings of the event and transfer these by putting it into generic register. And then, our system changes debug register to switch control to VMM. In the switching control to VMM, we add header information for each character. DR handler in VMM receives information by reading generic registers and construct string of the event. With this technique we can easily implement VMI and transfer information without allocating and managing shared memory and ring buffers.

Figure 2 show the byte-by-byte transmission. Proposed method is divided into three steps:

```
Step1: Sending the strength
    of each line.
Step2: Sending the character
    byte by byte.
        For generic register EAX,
    the number of character is stored.
        For generic register EBX,
    the character is stored.
Step3:  Sending the sign
    of strings end and type of event.
```

5   Windows Kernel Space Modification

In proposed system, we insert some debugging and monitoring layers to modify Windows kernel space. We apply three techniques: DLL inejection, filter driver and driver-supplied callback function.

5.1   DLL Injection

We apply DLL injection for inspecting illegal resource access of malicious process. DLL injection is debugging technology to hook API call of target process. Windows executable applies some functions from DLL such as kernel32. dll. Executable has import table to use the linked DLL. This table is called as import section. Among some techniques of DLL injection, modifying import table is useful because this technique is CPU-architecture independent. Figure 5 show the modification of import table. Address of function A on left side is changed to the address of inserted function on right side. In code table, some original functions are appended to executable. Modified address is pointed to code of inserted function. By doing this, when the function A is invoked, the inserted function is executed. In proposed system, the inserted function changes special registers (DR/MSR) to notify the events to VMM and control domain.

5.1.1   Search and Change IAT

After the module to be modified is determined, we need to change the address in IAT (Import Address Table) to our inserted DLL. ReplaceIATEntryInAllMods is available for changing the address of module. In this ReplaceIATEntry- Modues, ReplaceIA-TEntryInOneMod is invoked to get the address modules in import section table. Once the address of modules we try to insert our DLL, WriteProcessMemory is availabe for change the IAT.

5.1.2   Injecting DLL for All Process

To inject DLL for all running processes, SetWindowsHookEx is useful. For global hook, invoking SetWindowsHookEx maps DLL for all processes. Inject.dll call SetWindow-sHookEx Function to insert ReplaceIATEntryInAllMods ReplaceIATEntryINOneMod To use this API, avoiding hook for Inject.dll itself is required. In the case that the address of function to insert need to be hidden, LoadLibrary and GetProcAddress is hooked because these APIs can search the address of inserted function.

5.2   Filter Driver

Filter driver is an intermediate driver which runs between kernel and device driver. By using filter driver, we can hook events on lower level compared with library insertion technique on user land. In detail, System call table is modified to insert additional routine for original native API. In proposed system, filter driver is implemented and inserted for hooking events on file system.

5.3   Driver-Supplied Callback Function

To implement the proposal concept, we selected driver-based callback function, which is notified whenever an image is loaded for execution. Driver-based callback function is utilized for the identification of loading the target process. Highest-level system profiling drivers can call PsSetImageNotifyRoutine to set up their load-image notify routines. This could be declared as follows, particularly in Win32.

void LoadImageNotifyRoutine (
PUNICODE_STRING FullImageName,
HANDLE ProcessId,
PIMAGE_INFO ImageInfo);

Once the driver's callback has been registered, the operating system calls the callback function whenever an executable image is mapped into virtual memory. When the Load-ImageNotifyRoutine is called, the input FullImageName points to a buffered Unicode identifying the executable image file. The argument of list showing handle identities of process has been mapped when we call this function. But this handle is zero if the newly loading image is a driver. If FullImageName, which is input of LoadImageNotifyRoutine matches the name of target process, we go on to call the improved exception handler.

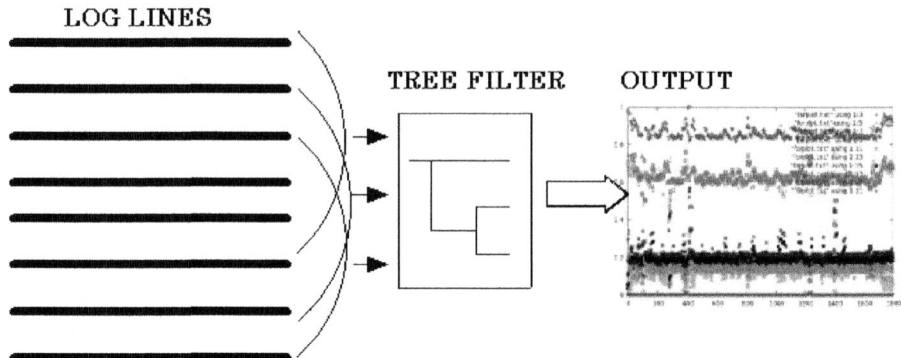

Fig. 3. Registry access log filter. We count some patterns composed as registry tree to retrieve matrix and graph for detecting malicious behavior.

6   Registry Access Log Filter

Windows registry access is one of the most important factors to check for detecting malicious or anomaly behaviors. Proposed system has registry access log filter which has tree structure to count some patterns of registry access. Figure 3 shows registry access filter. After obtaining log strings by DR based introspection of guest OS, we cut some lines of logs in a fixed interval (one to three seconds). And then we count some words of registry access according to tree structure such as one shown in Table 1 discussed in section 6. This filter is LIFO, suitable for streaming algorithm of which older logs are cut first. As we discuss in section 6, this filter is effective for retrieving the features of malware's behavior on guest Windows OS.

7   Experimental Results

7.1   Performance Measurements

In this section we show performance measurements. Proposed system monitors and filters access of registry, file and socket. According to these three items, we set ProcMon to monitor these three resource accesses. Figure shows the comparison of processor time aggregated in one hour. Proposed system is more lightweight because only registre opeartion and VM ENTER / EXIT has been occurred while memory allocation and file system operation has not been executed.

Figure shows the comparison of the number of paging file occurred in one hour. Proposed modules embedded into guest Windows OS are libraties and drivers executing register operation while ProcMon is the application which executes memory and file opeartion. As a result, propoposed system have reduced the number of paging file by 84%.

Figure and show disk read/write of proposed system and system running ProcMon. As we metioned, proposed system does not generate disk IO, only executes register operation which result in drastic reduce of disk IO compared with the system running ProcMon.

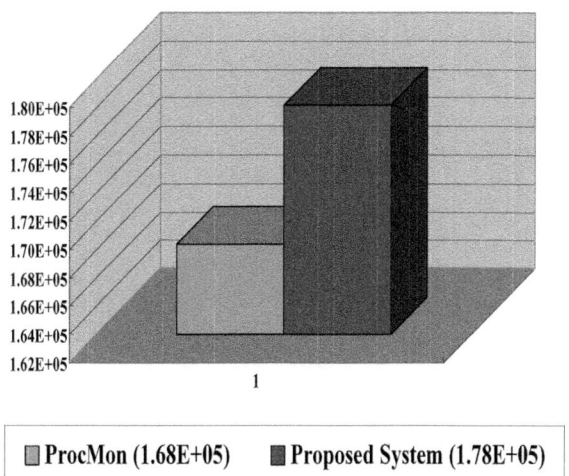

Fig. 4. Processor idle time (%) aggregated in one hour. Compared with the utilzation of ProcMon, proposed system reduces utilization by 94%.

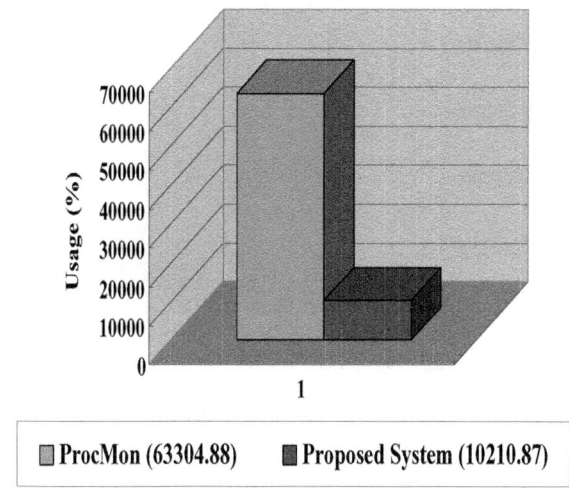

Fig. 5. Paging file (total) in one hour. Proposed system reduces paging file time by about 84 (%).

Disk Read (byte/sec) in one hour

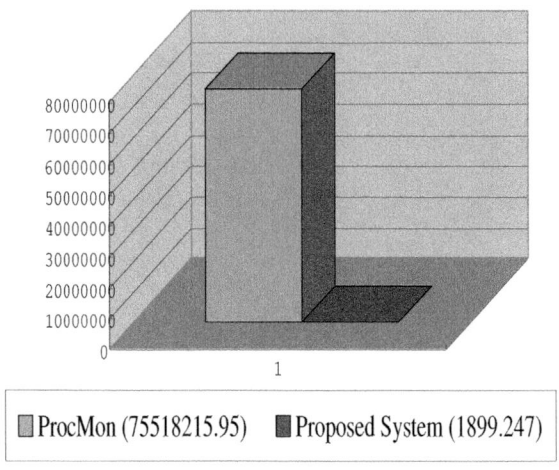

Fig. 6. Disk read in one hour

Disk Write (byte/sec) in one hour

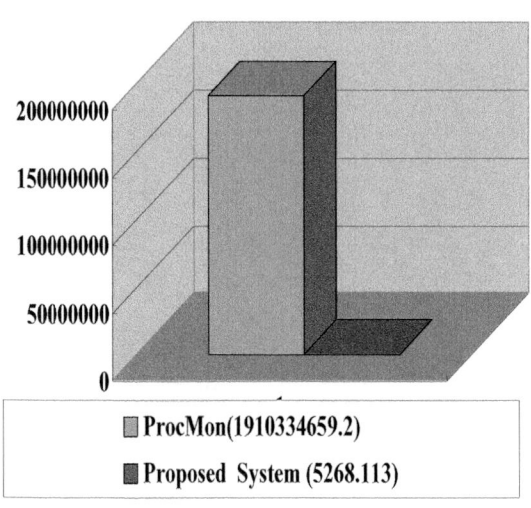

Fig. 7. Disk write in one hour

7.2   Filtering Registry Access for Malware Infection

Among all resource accesses in Windows OS, the registry access is the most changing sensitive to incidents. Compared with file and socket access, registry access is more frequently changing. Also, the regitstry access is more fine-grained event which means

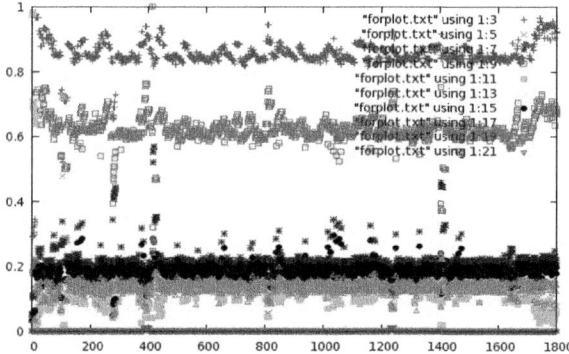

Fig. 8. Visualization of registry access of running Windows OS with no input. Registry access such as LKEY_LOCAL_MACHINE is filtered and aggregated for each line.

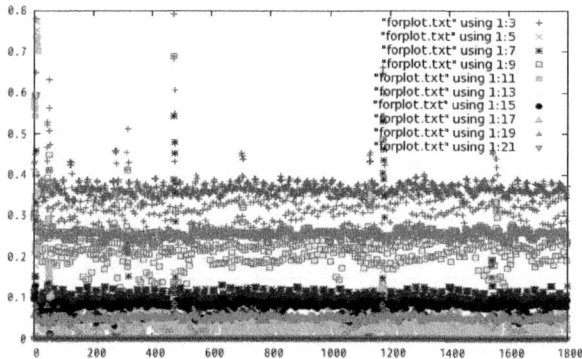

Fig. 9. Filtering and aggregation of Windows OS where the malware Sassar-A is executed

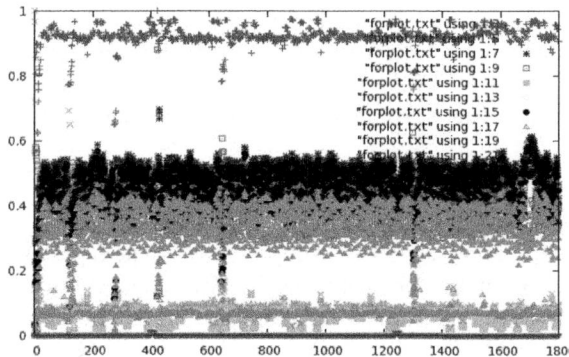

Fig. 10. Filtering and aggregation of Windows OS where the malware Sassar-A is executed

Table 1. Registry key tree for filtering log in section 7.2

Filter No	Key Name	Tree Depth
1	HKEY_LOCAL_MACHINE	0
2	HKEY_CURRENT_USER	0
3	HKEY_LOCAL_MACHINE/SOFTWARE	1
4	HKEY_LOCAL_MACHINE/SYSTEM	1
5	HKEY_LOCAL_USER/SOFTWARE	1
6	HKEY_LOCAL_USER/SYSTEM	1
7	HKEY_LOCAL_MACHINE/SOFTWARE/MICROSOFT/WINDOWS NT/CurrentVersion	4
8	HKEY_LOCAL_MACHINE/SOFTWARE/MICROSOFT/WINDOWS/CurrentVersion/run	5
9	HKEY_LOCAL_MACHINE/SYSTEM/CurrentControlSet/Services	3
10	HKEY_CURRENT_USER/SYSTEM/CurrentVersion/Services	3

Table 2. Registry key tree for filtering log in section 7.2

Filter No	No Input	Klez	Zeus
1	0.285714	0.841787	0.847437
2	0.142857	0.149786	0.14235
3	0.190476	0.336668	0.409672
4	0.0047619	0.527461	0.379102
5	0.0047619	0.100501	0.073626
6	0.0047619	0.001513	0.001115
7	0.0142857	0.239816	0.307894
8	0.0047619	0.210267	0.150901
9	0.0047619	0	0.135076
10	0.0047619	0.002955	0.002124

the registry access is sensitive to incidents. Registry acces is the best index for extarcting and detecting features of security incidents caused by malicious software. In this section we show the filtering registry access for detecting and extracting features of Windows OS infected by malicious software. We obtain the sequence of registry access per two seconds and aggregate the sequence accroding to the filter shown in Table 1. This is filter tree, consists of 10 fitlers, to genearte sequence from the sequence At the top level, tree has three items, HKEY_LOCAL_MACHINE, HKEY_CURRENT_USER, HKEY_LOCAL_USER/SOFTWARE. Lower the tree, we pick up sevaral branches from depth 1 to 5 to extract features from the behavior of malicious software.

8   Conclusions

Virtualization technologies have become important with the rapid improvement of both cloud and personal computing environment. However, current virtualization technologies mainly have two problems: First, semantic gap between host and guest OS. Second the virtualization of I/O has not been well developed. Fortunately, debugging technologies has been rapidly improved to provide solution for these problems in monitoring virtual machine. In this paper we propose a lightweight introspection module to leverage debugging technology on guest OS to provide solutions for semantic gap and I/O virtualization problem. Fine grained probing by embedding debugging modules into guest OS makes it possible to resolve semantic gap. As a result we can monitor and filter the events occurred on guest OS in real time. Also we apply debug register handler and generic register to transfer information from guest OS to host OS instead of share memory and its ring buffer. As a result, I/O throughput is drastically reduced compared with the case where monitoring software on guest OS. In experiment we show the result of filtering access log of guest OS from VMM (virtual machine monitor) side. Experiment shows that visual features can be extracted by our lightweight filtering system.

References

1. Garfinkel, T., Rosenblu, M.: A Virtual Machine Introspection Based Architecture for Intrusion Detection. In: The Internet Society's 2003 Symposium on Network and Distributed System Security (NDSS), pp. 191–206 (February 2003)
2. Nance, K., Bishop, M., Hay, B.: Virtual Machine Introspection: Observation or Interference? IEEE Security and Privacy 6(5), 32–37 (2008)
3. Barham, P., Dragovic, B., Fraser, K., Hand, S., Harris, T., Ho, A., Neugebauer, R., Pratt, I., Wareld, A.: Xen and the Art of Virtualization. In: Proceedings of the 19th ACM SOSP, pp. 164–177 (October 2003)
4. Waldspurger, C.A.: Memory resource management in VMware ESX server. In: Proceedings of the 5th Symposium on Operating Systems Design and Implementation, pp. 181–194 (December 2002)
5. Kernal Virtual Machine, http://sourceforge.net/projects/kvm
6. Dunlap, G.W., King, S.T., Cinar, S., Basrai, M., Chen, P.M.: ReVirt: Enabling intrusion analysis through virtual-machine logging and replay. In: Proceedings of the 2002 Symposium on Operating Systems Design and Implementation (OSDI 2002), Boston, MA (December 2002)
7. King, S., Dunlap, G., Chen, P.: Debugging Operating Systems with Time-Traveling Virtual Machines. In: Proc. Annual Usenix Tech. Conf., Usenix Assoc. (2005), www.usenix.org/events/usenix05/tech/general/king/king.pdf
8. Whitaker, A., et al.: Constructing Services with Interposable Virtual Hardware. In: Proc. 1st Symp. Networked Systems Design and Implementation (NSDI 2004) (March 2004)
9. Payne, B., et al.: Lares: An Architecture for Secure Active Monitoring Using Virtualization. In: Proc. IEEE Symp. Security and Privacy, pp. 233–247. IEEE CS Press (2008)
10. Jones, S., Arpaci-Dusseau, A., Arpaci-Dusseau, R.: VMM-based Hidden Process Detection and Identification Using Lycosid. In: Proc. ACM Int. Conf. Virtual Execution Environments (VEE 2008), pp. 91–100. ACM Press (2008)
11. Jones, S., Arpaci-Dusseau, A., Arpaci-Dusseau, R.: AntFarm: Tracking Processes in a Virtual Machine Environment. In: Proc. Annual Usenix Tech. Conf., Usenix Assoc., pp. 1–14 (2008)
12. Litty, L., Lagar-Cavilla, H.A.: Hypervisor Support for Identifying Covertly Executing Binaries. In: The 17th USENIX Security Symposium, Usenix 2008 (July - August 2008)
13. XenAccess, http://doc.xenaccess.org/

Diversity-Based Approaches to Software Systems Security

Abdelouahed Gherbi[1] and Robert Charpentier[2]

[1] Department of Software and IT Engineering
École de technologies supérieure, ÉTS
Montréal, Canada
[2] Defence Research and Development Canada - Valcartier
Québec, Canada

Abstract. Software systems security represents a major concern as cyber-attacks continue to grow in number and sophistication. In addition to the increasing complexity and interconnection of modern information systems, these systems run significant similar software. This is known as IT monoculture. As a consequence, software systems share common vulnerabilities, which enable the spread of malware. The principle of diversity can help in mitigating the negative effects of IT monoculture on security. One important category of the diversity-based software approaches for security purposes focuses on enabling efficient and effective dynamic monitoring of software system behavior in operation. In this paper, we present briefly these approaches and we propose a new approach which aims at generating dynamically a diverse set of lightweight traces. We initiate the discussion of some research issues which will be the focus of our future research work.

Keywords: Security, IT monoculture, Diversity, Dynamic monitoring.

1 Introduction

Security remains an extremely critical issue. This is evidenced by the continuous growth of cyber threats [22]. Cyber-attacks are not only increasing in number but also in sophistication and scale. Some attacks are now of nation/state class [24]. This observation can be explained by a combination of a multitude of contributing factors, which include the followings.

The increasing complexity of software systems makes it difficult to produce fault free software even though different quality controls are often part of the software development process. These residual faults constitute dormant vulnerabilities, which would eventually end up being discovered by determined malicious opponents and exploited to carry out cyber-attacks. Moreover, software systems are distributed and interconnected through open networks in order to communicate controls and data. This in turns increases tremendously the risk of attacks. Most importantly, the information systems are running significant similar software. This is called IT monoculture [17]. On one hand, IT monoculture presents

T.-h. Kim et al. (Eds.): SecTech 2011, CCIS 259, pp. 228–237, 2011.

several advantages including easier management, less configurations errors and support for inter-operability. On the other hand, IT monoculture has serious security concerns because similar systems share common vulnerabilities, and consequently, facilitates spread of viruses and malware.

The principle of diversity can be used to mitigate the effects of IT monoculture on software system. Diversity has been used to complement redundancy in order to achieve software systems reliability and fault tolerance. When it comes to security, the approach based on diversity seeks specifically to reduce the common vulnerabilities between redundant components of a system. As a result, it becomes very difficult for a malicious opponent to design one unique attack that is able to exploit different vulnerabilities in the system components simultaneously. Therefore, the resistance of the system to cyber attacks is increased. Moreover, the ability to build a system out of redundant and diverse components provides an opportunity to monitor the system by comparing the dynamic behavior of the diverse components when presented with the same input. This enables to endow the system with efficient intrusion detection capability.

In this paper we focus on how diversity can be used to generate dynamically a diverse set of light traces for the same behaviour of a software system. To this end, we define a setting which allows running in parallel several instances of a process. All these instances are provided with the same input. Each of these process instances runs on top of an operating system kernel which is instrumented differently to provide traces of the system calls pertaining to different important functionalities of the kernel. We raise in this paper some research questions that need to be addressed.

The remaining part of the paper is organized as follows: In Section 2, we introduce the main idea underlying the approaches using software diversity for security purposes. We devote Section 3 to review and evaluate the state-of-the-art approaches based on software diversity to mitigate the risk associated with the IT monoculture. We outline and discuss in Section 4 an approach which aims at enabling the dynamic generation of a *diverse* set of lightweight and complementary traces from a running software application. We conclude the paper in Section 5.

2   Diversity as a Software Security Enabler

Redundancy is a traditional means to achieve fault tolerance and higher system reliability. This has proven to be valid mainly for hardware because of the failure independence assumption as hardware failures are typically due to random faults. Therefore, the replication of components provides added assurance. When it comes to software, however, failures are due to design and/or implementation faults. As a result, such faults are embedded within the software and their manifestation is systematic. Therefore, redundancy alone is not effective against software faults.

Faults embedded in software represent potential vulnerabilities, which can be exploited by external interactive malicious fault (i.e. attacks) [2]. These attacks can ultimately enable the violation of the system security property (i.e. security failure) [2]. Therefore the diversity principle can potentially be used for security purposes. First, diversity can be used to decrease the common vulnerabilities. This is achieved by building a software system out of a set of diverse but functionally equivalent components. This in turns makes it very difficult for a malicious opponent to be able to break into a system with the very same attack. Second, the ability to build a system out of redundant and diverse components provides an opportunity to monitor the system by comparing the dynamic behavior of the diverse components when presented with the same input. This enables to endow the system with efficient intrusion detection capability.

Therefore, diversity has naturally caught the attention of the software security research community. The seminal work presented by Forrest et al. in [11] promotes the general philosophy of system security using diversity. The authors argue that uniformity represents a potential weakness because any flaw or vulnerability in an application is replicated on many machines. The security and the robustness of a system can be enhanced through the deliberate introduction of diversity. Deswarte et al. review in [9] the different levels of diversity of software and hardware systems and distinguish different dimensions and different degrees of diversity. Bain et al. [3] presented a study to understand the effects of diversity on the survivability of systems faced with a set of widespread computer attacks including the Morris worm, Melissa virus, and LoveLetter worm. Taylor and Alves-Foss report in [23] on a discussion held by a panel of renowned researchers about the use of diversity as a strategy for computer security and the main open issues requiring further research. It emerges from this discussion that there is a lack of quantitative information on the cost associated with diversity-based solutions and a lack of knowledge about the extent of protection provided by diversity.

3   Diversity-Based Approaches to Software Security

We have undertaken a comprehensive study to evaluate the state-of-the-art approaches based on the principle of software diversity to mitigate the risk of IT monoculture and enable software security [14]. These approaches can be classified into the three main following categories.

3.1   System Integration and Middlware

This category include proposals of software architectures which deploy redundancy combined with software diversity either by using integrating multiple Commercial-Off-The-Shelf (COTs) applications coordinated through a proxy component or by defining and using a middleware to achieve the same purpose.

The software architectures described in this section implement the architectural pattern depicted in Figure 1. This approach is ideal for a system integration of COTS components or legacy and closed applications aiming to deliver the services. The servers are shielded from the user side through proxies. Monitoring and voting mechanisms are used to check the health of the system, validate the results, and detect abnormal behavior. Examples of this approach include the Dependable Intrusion Tolerance (DIT) architecture [10][26], the Scalable Intrusion Tolerant Architecture (SITAR) [28], and Hierarchical Adaptive Control for QoS Intrusion Tolerance (HACQIT) [19].

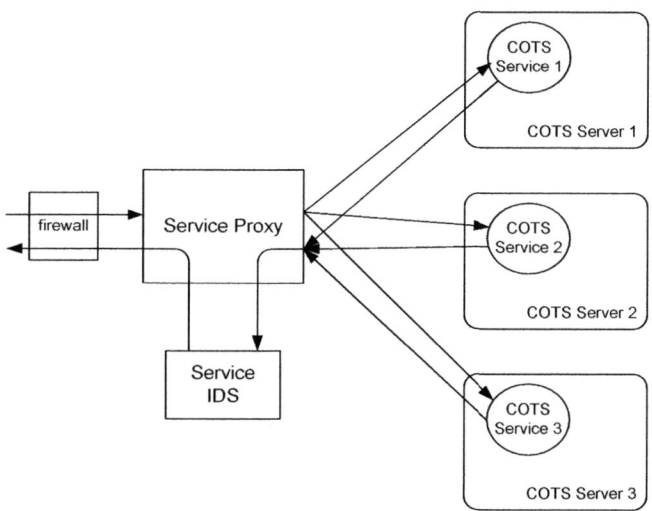

Fig. 1. General Pattern of Intrusion Tolerance Architecture

Middleware-based approaches are much richer since they can provide server co-ordination between multiple "diverse" applications while hiding the sub-system differences [20]. Several intrusion tolerant software architectures are part of this category. The Intrusion Tolerance by Unpredictable Adaptation (ITUA) architecture is a distributed object framework which integrates several mechanisms to enable the defense of critical applications [18]. The objective of this architecture is to enable the tolerance of sophisticated attacks aiming at corrupting a system. Malicious and Accidental Fault Tolerance for Internet Applications (MAFTIA) [27] is a European research project which targeted the objective of systematically investigating the tolerance paradigm in order to build large scale dependable distributed applications. The Designing Protection and Adaptation into a Survivability Architecture (DPASA) [1] [7] is a survivability architecture providing a diverse set of defense mechanisms. In this architecture diversity is used to achieve a defense in depth and a multi-layer security approach [7]. This architecture relies on a robust network infrastructure which supports redundancy and provides security services such as packet filtering, source authentication, link-level encryption, and network anomaly sensors. The detection of violations "triggers" defensive responses provided by middleware components in the architecture. Fault/instrusiOn REmoVal through Evolution and Recovery (FOREVER) [5] is a service which is used to enhance the resilience of intrusion-tolerant replicated systems. FOREVER achieves this goal through the combination of recovery and evolution. FOREVER allows a system to recover from malicious attacks or faults using time-triggered or event-triggered periodic recoveries.

3.2   Software Diversity through Automated Program Transformations

Diversity can be introduced in the software ecosystem by applying automatic program transformations, which preserve the functional behavior and the programming language semantics. They consist essentially in randomization of the code, the address space layout or both in order to provide a probabilistic defense against unknown threats. Three main techniques can be used to randomize software.

The Instruction Set Randomization (ISR) technique [4][16] changes the instruction set of the processor so that unauthorized code will not run successfully. The main idea underlying ISR is to decrease the attacker's knowledge about the language used by the runtime environment on which the target application runs. ISR techniques aim at defending against code injection attacks, which consist in introducing executable code within the address space of a target process, and then passing the control to the injected code. Code injection attacks can succeed when the injected code is compatible with the execution environment.

Address Space Randomization (ASR) [21] is used to increase software resistance to memory corruption attacks. These are designed to exploit memory manipulation vulnerabilities such as stack and heap overflows and underflows, format string vulnerabilities, array index overflows, and uninitialized variables. ASR consists basically in randomizing the different regions of the process address space such as the stack and the heap. It is worth noticing that ASR has been integrated into the default configuration of the Windows Vista operating system [30].

Data Space Randomization (DSR) is a different randomization-based approach which aims also at defending against memory error exploits [6]. In particular, DSR randomizes the representation of data objects. This is often implemented by applying a modification to the data representation, such as using an XOR operation for each data object in memory against randomly chosen mask values. The data are unmasked right before being used. This makes the results of using the corrupted data highly unpredictable. The DSR technique seems to have advantages over ASR, as it provides a broader range of randomization: on 32-bit architectures, integers and pointers are randomized over a range of 2^{32} values. In addition, DSR is able to randomize the relative distance between two data objects, addressing a weakness of the ASR technique.

3.3   Dynamic Behavior Monitoring

The ability to build a system combining redundant and diverse components provides new powerful capabilities in terms of advanced monitoring of the redundant system by comparing the behavior of the diverse replicas. This endows the system with efficient intrusion detection capabilities not achievable with standard intrusion detection techniques based on signatures or malware modeling. Moreover, with the introduction of some assessment of the behavioral advantages of one implementation over the others, a "meta-controller" can ultimately adapt the system behavior or its structure over time. Several experimental systems used output voting for the sake of detecting some types of server compromising. For example, the HACQIT system [19] uses the status codes of the server replica responses. If the status codes are different the system detects a failure. Totel et al. [25] extend this work to do a more detailed comparison of the replica responses. They realized that web server responses may be slightly different even when there is no attack, and proposed a detection algorithm to detect intrusions with a higher accuracy (lower false alarm rate). These research initiatives specifically target web servers and analyze only server responses. Consequently, they cannot consistently detect compromised replicas. N-variant systems provide a framework which allows executing a set of automatically diversified variants using the same input [8]. The framework monitors the behavior of the variants in order to detect divergences. The variants are built so that an anticipated type of exploit can succeed on only one variant. Therefore, such exploits become detectable. Building the variants requires a special compiler or a binary rewriter. Moreover, this framework detects only anticipated types of exploits, against which the replicas are diversified. Multi-variant code execution is a runtime monitoring technique which prevents malicious code execution [29]. This technique uses diversity to protect against malicious code injection attacks. This is achieved by running several slightly different variants of the same program in lockstep. The behavior of the variants is compared at synchronization points, which are in general system calls. Any divergence in behavior is suggestive of an anomaly and raises an alarm. The behavioral distance approach aims at detecting sophisticated attacks which manage to emulate the original system behavior including returning the correct service response (also known as mimicry attacks). These attacks are thus able to defeat traditional anomaly-based intrusion detection systems (IDS). Behavioral Distance achieves this defense using a comparison between the behaviors of two diverse processes running the same input. It measures the extent to which the two processes behave differently. Gao et al. proposed two approaches to compute such measures [12][13].

4   Towards a Diversity-Based Approach for Dynamic Generation of Lightweight Traces

The comprehensive dynamic monitoring of an operating system kernel such as Linux kernel is a daunting and challenging task. Indeed, it yields massive traces which are very difficult to be dealt with and in particular to be abstracted correctly to reach systematically meaningful information [15]. The principle of diversity can be potentially leveraged to address this issue. The main idea is to deploy a set of *redundant* Linux nodes running in parallel. This set can also includes deliberately a subset of replicas that are purposefully vulnerable. The diversity is introduced by the fact that the replicas are monitored differently. Indeed, the focus on each Linux kernel replica is put on different (predetermined) perspectives. These include the main kernel services such as memory management, file system management, networking sockets, interrupts, etc.

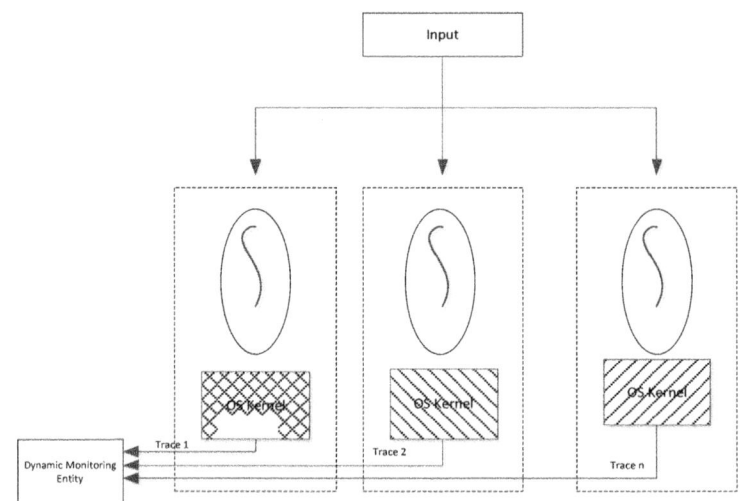

Fig. 2. Architecture for Diversity-based Dynamic Monitoring

The general software system architecture outlined Figure 2 aims at enabling the dynamic generation of a diverse set of traces of the behavior of a software application. Each of these traces is a sub-trace of the whole trace of the software application and it reflects a particular functionality of the operating system kernel. For an software application deployed in this setting N processes are spawn and run in parallel. Each of these processes runs in the environment of an operating system where the kernel has been instrumented to provide the trace of a particular functionality such as the memory management functionality, file management functionality, networking management, input/output drivers etc. All the instances of the application running are provided with the same input which might be a malicious input (i.e. an attack). The generated traces are collected by a monitoring entity which is in charge of analyzing and correlating them using techniques that need to be investigated as discussed in the following section.

This dynamic monitoring configuration would yield a diverse set of much more lightweight traces. The latter are are sub-traces of the comprehensive trace of the running application. We are interested in investigating several research questions which can be raised using this monitoring setting. These include the identification of correlations between the different traces both in normal (i.e. healthy and secure system) and abnormal situations (system under attack or intrusion) as well as the identification of malicious behavior patterns.

5   Conclusion

Software systems security is a critical issue. An important contributing factor to this issue is the significant similarity in the software used in such systems. This is called IT mono-culture. The mitigation of this issue consists in using diversity which aims at reducing the common vulnerabilities and consequently increasing the difficulty of breaking systems built with diversity in mind.

In this article we focus on how diversity can be deployed to enable software behaviour dynamic monitoring to the end of intrusion detection. We have presented a diversity based approach which aims at generating dynamically traces pertaining to different functionalities of the operating system kernel. These traces, which are the sub-traces of the comprehensive trace of the software application behaviour, are therefore smaller. We are interested to investigate the different correlations and patterns that we can discover between these sub-traces in situation where the software application is healthy and secure and when it is compromised.

References

1. Atighetchi, M., Rubel, P., Pal, P.P., Chong, J., Sudin, L.: Networking aspects in the dpasa survivability architecture: An experience report. In: Fourth IEEE International Symposium on Network Computing and Applications (NCA 2005), pp. 219–222. IEEE Computer Society (2005)
2. Avizienis, A., Laprie, J.C., Randell, B., Landwehr, C.E.: Basic concepts and taxonomy of dependable and secure computing. IEEE Trans. Dependable Sec. Comput. 1(1), 11–33 (2004)
3. Bain, C., Faatz, D.B., Fayad, A., Williams, D.E.: Diversity as a defense strategy in information systems. does evidence from previous events support such an approach? In: Gertz, M., Guldentops, E., Strous, L. (eds.) Fourth Working Conference on Integrity, Internal Control and Security in Information Systems, IICIS 2001. IFIP Conference Proceedings, vol. 211, pp. 77–94. Kluwer (2001)
4. Barrantes, E.G., Ackley, D.H., Palmer, T.S., Stefanovic, D., Zovi, D.D.: Randomized instruction set emulation to disrupt binary code injection attacks. In: Jajodia, S., Atluri, V., Jaeger, T. (eds.) Proceedings of the 10th ACM Conference on Computer and Communications Security, pp. 281–289. ACM (2003)
5. Bessani, A.N., Reiser, H.P., Sousa, P., Gashi, I., Stankovic, V., Distler, T., Kapitza, R., Daidone, A., Obelheiro, R.R.: Forever: Fault/intrusion removal through evolution & recovery. In: Douglis, F. (ed.) ACM/IFIP/USENIX 9th International Middleware Conference, pp. 99–101. ACM (2008)
6. Bhatkar, S., Sekar, R.: Data Space Randomization. In: Zamboni, D. (ed.) DIMVA 2008. LNCS, vol. 5137, pp. 1–22. Springer, Heidelberg (2008)
7. Chong, J., Pal, P.P., Atighetchi, M., Rubel, P., Webber, F.: Survivability architecture of a mission critical system: The dpasa example. In: 21st Annual Computer Security Applications Conference, ACSAC 2005, pp. 495–504. IEEE Computer Society (2005)
8. Cox, B., Evans, D., Filipi, A., Rowanhill, J., Hu, W., Davidson, J., Knight, J., Nguyen-Tuong, A., Hiser, J.: N-variant systems: a secretless framework for security through diversity. In: USENIX-SS 2006: Proceedings of the 15th conference on USENIX Security Symposium. USENIX Association, Berkeley (2006)

9. Deswarte, Y., Kanoun, K., Laprie, J.C.: Diversity against accidental and deliberate faults. In: Ammann, P., Barnes, B.H., Jajodia, S., Sibley, E.H. (eds.) Computer Security, Dependability, and Assurance: From Needs to Solutions, November 1998, pp. 171–181. IEEE Computer Press, Williamsburg (1998)
10. Deswarte, Y., Powell, D.: Intrusion tolerance for internet applications. In: Jacquart, R. (ed.) Building the Information Society, IFIP 18th World Computer Congress, pp. 241–256. Kluwer (2004)
11. Forrest, S., Somayaji, A., Ackley, D.H.: Building diverse computer systems. In: Workshop on Hot Topics in Operating Systems, pp. 67–72 (1997)
12. Gao, D., Reiter, M.K., Song, D.X.: Behavioral Distance Measurement Using Hidden Markov Models. In: Zamboni, D., Krügel, C. (eds.) RAID 2006. LNCS, vol. 4219, pp. 19–40. Springer, Heidelberg (2006)
13. Gao, D., Reiter, M.K., Song, D.X.: Behavioral Distance for Intrusion Detection. In: Valdes, A., Zamboni, D. (eds.) RAID 2005. LNCS, vol. 3858, pp. 63–81. Springer, Heidelberg (2006)
14. Gherbi, A., Charpentier, R., Couture, M.: Redundancy with diversity based software architectures for the detection and tolerance of cyber-attacks. Technical Memorandum TM-2010-287, Defence Reasearch and Development Canada - DRDC Valcartier (2010)
15. Hamou-Lhadj, A.: Measuring the complexity of traces using shannon entropy. In: Fifth International Conference on Information Technology: New Generations (ITNG 2008), pp. 489–494. IEEE Computer Society (2008)
16. Kc, G.S., Keromytis, A.D., Prevelakis, V.: Countering code-injection attacks with instruction-set randomization. In: Jajodia, S., Atluri, V., Jaeger, T. (eds.) Proceedings of the 10th ACM Conference on Computer and Communications Security, pp. 272–280. ACM (2003)
17. Lala, J.H., Schneider, F.B.: It monoculture security risks and defenses. IEEE Security & Privacy 7(1), 12–13 (2009)
18. Pal, P.P., Rubel, P., Atighetchi, M., Webber, F., Sanders, W.H., Seri, M., Ramasamy, H.V., Lyons, J., Courtney, T., Agbaria, A., Cukier, M., Gossett, J.M., Keidar, I.: An architecture for adaptive intrusion-tolerant applications. Softw., Pract. Exper. 36(11-12), 1331–1354 (2006)
19. Reynolds, J.C., Just, J.E., Lawson, E., Clough, L.A., Maglich, R., Levitt, K.N.: The design and implementation of an intrusion tolerant system. In: International Conference on Dependable Systems and Networks (DSN 2002), pp. 285–292. IEEE Computer Society (2002)
20. Sames, D., Matt, B., Niebuhr, B., Tally, G., Whitmore, B., Bakken, D.E.: Developing a heterogeneous intrusion tolerant corba system. In: DSN 2002: Proceedings of the 2002 International Conference on Dependable Systems and Networks, pp. 239–248. IEEE Computer Society, Washington, DC, USA (2002)
21. Shacham, H., Page, M., Pfaff, B., Goh, E.J., Modadugu, N., Boneh, D.: On the effectiveness of address-space randomization. In: Atluri, V., Pfitzmann, B., McDaniel, P.D. (eds.) Proceedings of the 11th ACM Conference on Computer and Communications Security, CCS 2004, pp. 298–307. ACM (2004)
22. Symantec: Symantec global internet security threat report – trends for 2008. Tech. Rep. Volume XIV, Symantec (2009)
23. Taylor, C., Alves-Foss, J.: Diversity as a computer defense mechanism: A panel. In: NSPW 2005: Proceedings of the 2005 Workshop on New Security Paradigms, pp. 11–14. ACM, New York (2005)
24. Lloyd's Emerging Risk Team: Digital risks: Views of a changing risk landscape. Tech. Rep. Volume XIV, Lloyd's (April 2009)

25. Totel, E., Majorczyk, F., Mé, L.: COTS Diversity Based Intrusion Detection and Application to Web Servers. In: Valdes, A., Zamboni, D. (eds.) RAID 2005. LNCS, vol. 3858, pp. 43–62. Springer, Heidelberg (2006)
26. Valdes, A., Almgren, M., Cheung, S., Deswarte, Y., Dutertre, B., Levy, J., Saïdi, H., Stavridou, V., Uribe, T.E.: Dependable intrusion tolerance: Technology demo. In: 3rd DARPA Information Survivability Conference and Exposition (DISCEX-III 2003), pp. 128–130. IEEE Computer Society (2003)
27. Veríssimo, P., Neves, N.F., Cachin, C., Poritz, J.A., Powell, D., Deswarte, Y., Stroud, R.J., Welch, I.: Intrusion-tolerant middleware: the road to automatic security. IEEE Security & Privacy 4(4), 54–62 (2006)
28. Wang, F., Jou, F., Gong, F., Sargor, C., Goseva-Popstojanova, K., Trivedi, K.: Sitar: A scalable intrusion-tolerant architecture for distributed services. In: Foundations of Intrusion Tolerant Systems. IEEE Computer Society, Los Alamitos (2003)
29. Weatherwax, E., Knight, J., Nguyen-Tuong, A.: A Model of Secretless Security in N-Variant Systems. In: Workshop on Compiler and Architectural Techniques for Application Reliability and Security (CATARS), In the 39th Annual IEEE/IFIP International Conference on Dependable Systems and Network, DSN 2009 (2009)
30. Whitehouse, O.: An analysis of address space layout randomization on windows vista. Tech. rep., Symantec (2007)

Author Index

GPSR Compliance

The European Union's (EU) General Product Safety Regulation (GPSR) is a set of rules that requires consumer products to be safe and our obligations to ensure this.

If you have any concerns about our products, you can contact us on ProductSafety@springernature.com

In case Publisher is established outside the EU, the EU authorized representative is:

Springer Nature Customer Service Center GmbH
Europaplatz 3
69115 Heidelberg, Germany

Batch number: 09490872

Printed by Printforce, the Netherlands